C000051196

Resistance in Western Europe

Resistance in Western Europe

Edited by
Bob Moore

Oxford • New York

First published in 2000 by
Berg
Editorial offices:
150 Cowley Road, Oxford OX4 1JJ, UK
838 Broadway, Third Floor, New York, NY 10003-4812, USA

© Bob Moore 2000

All rights reserved.
No part of this publication may be reproduced in any form
or by any means without the written permission of Berg.

Berg is the imprint of Oxford International Publishers Ltd.

Library of Congress Cataloging-in-Publication Data

A catalogue record for this book is available from the Library of Congress.

British Library Cataloguing-in-Publication Data

A catalogue record for this book is available from the British Library.

ISBN 1 85973 274 7 (Cloth)
ISBN 1 85973 279 8 (Paper)

Typeset by JS Typesetting, Wellingborough, Northants.
Printed and bound in Great Britain by Biddles Ltd
www.biddles.co.uk

Contents

Notes on Contributors

Gustavo Corni is Associate Professor of Contemporary History at the University of Trento and specialist on the social history of agriculture, and military and civil society in Germany during the two world wars. He was Humbolt Fellow in 1992, visting professor at the University of Vienna, 1995–6 and is author of *Hitler and the Peasants, the Agrarian Policy of National Socialism* (Oxford, 1990), *Storia della Germania, dall'unificazione alla riunificazione* (Milan, 1995), and with H.Gies, *Brot-Butter-Kanonen. Die Ernährungswirtschaft in Deutschland unter der Diktatur Hitlers*, (Berlin, 1997).

Dick van Galen Last is a graduate of the University of Amsterdam and is currently librarian and researcher at the Nederlands Instituut voor Oorlogsdocumentatie. He is the author, with Rolf Wolfswinkel, of *Anne Frank and After* (Amsterdam, 1996) and has written and reviewed extensively for Dutch academic journals and the national press.

Hans Kirchhoff is Professor of Modern History at the University of Copenhagen. His doctoral dissertation, *Augustoprøret 1943. Samarbejdspolitikkens fald. Forudsætninger og forløb. En studie i kollaboration og modstand*, 3 vols, was published in 1979. His later works include *Kamp eller tilpasning: Politikerne og modstanden, 1940–1945* (1987). He has also published books and articles about the German occupation, the Danish Holocaust and Danish foreign policy, 1939–40.

Pieter Lagrou is a researcher at the Institut d'Histoire du Temps Présent, Centre National de la Recherche Scientifique in Paris, working on the comparative history of World War Two and its consequences. He is the author of *The Legacy of Nazi Occupation. Patriotic Memory and National Recovery in Western Europe, 1945–1965* (Cambridge University Press, 1999).

Arnfinn Moland is a graduate in history for the University of Oslo and has been director of Norway's Resistance Museum since 1995. He is the co-author of *Hjemmefront* (*Resistance*), a volume in the series *Norge i Krig* (*Norway at War*) published in 1987, and also co-author (with Olav Riste) of *Strengt Hemmelig* (1997), a book on Norwegian Intelligence 1945–70. In addition, he has written and produced the TV series *Report from No.24*, shown on Norwegian television in 1994 and 1995.

Bob Moore is senior lecturer in modern history at the University of Sheffield. He has published extensively on the history of the Netherlands before and during the World War Two, and on the history of prisoners of war. Recent works include *Prisoners of War and their Captors in World War II* (1996), edited with Kent Fedorowich, and *Victims and Survivors. The Nazi Persecution of the Jews in the Netherlands 1940–1945* (1997).

Olivier Wieviorka is senior lecturer at the Ecole Normale Supérieure de Fontenay-Saint-Cloud. His recent publications include *Une certaine idée de la Résistance: Défense de la France, 1940–1949* (1995) *Nous entrerons dans la carrière. De la Résistance à l'exercise du pouvoir* (1994), and with Jean Pierre Azéma, *Vichy 1940–1944* (1997). He is currently research-ing the attitudes of the French political class during the occupation.

Louise Willmot is lecturer in modern history at the Manchester Metro-politan University. She has studied at the University of London and was awarded a DPhil from the University of Oxford for a thesis on the *Bund deutscher Mädel* in Nazi Germany. She has edited a new edition of *Clausewitz: On War* (Oxford: Wordsworth, 1997) and has also translated a variety of German academic texts.

Preface

There have been many books dealing with the history of resistance to Nazi occupation during World War Two, but they have generally concentrated on one country, one resistance movement, or on specific individuals. General syntheses of resistance in the English language have been rare, as have detailed accounts of the resistance in many European countries. Thus the idea behind this book was to bring together, in one collection, a series of country-specific studies on the nature, extent and historiography of resistance in the countries of Western Europe, each written by an acknowledged expert from within the country concerned. This, it is hoped, will act as an appropriate introduction to the subject and provide detailed information, ideas and an understanding of the historiography from inside each country, together with suggestions for further reading and research.

No book of this nature could be written without a great deal of co-operation. Seven authors from seven different countries could have been an editor's nightmare. However, it is a great pleasure to acknowledge their collective co-operation, good humour and punctuality in the face of the demands made upon them. Given the different languages involved, the success of this project rests in large part on the skills of those who translated the text into English. In some cases, this was admirably done by the contributors themselves, and in others, the responsibility fell to me as editor. However, I would like to record a personal debt of gratitude to Nicola Iannelli (Rome) and Maike Bohn (Oxford) whose help has been invaluable in translating and refining parts of the text for publication.

Greenwood Publishers have kindly allowed me to use short sections of my chapter 'Resistance' in Loyd E. Lee, (ed.) *World War II in Europe, Africa, and the Americas, with General Sources* (Westport CT, 1997) and Siedler Verlag (Berlin) have given permission to use an extended and updated version of Hans Kirchhoff's chapter on Denmark, which first appeared in *Europäischer Widerstand im Vergleich. Die Internationalen Konferenzen Amsterdam* (Berlin, 1985). I am also indebted to a number of academics who have contributed in some way to the completion of this volume, namely Henry Rousso (Institut D'Histoire du Temps Présent, Paris), Rod Kedward (University of Sussex), Patrick Salmon (University

Preface

of Newcastle), Philip Morgan (University of Hull) and Hans Blom (Nederlands Instituut voor Oorlogsdocumentatie, Amsterdam)

A final word of thanks should go to my publishers, Maike Bohn and especially Kathryn Earle, who was instrumental in persuading me to bring this collection together and has subsequently supported the project with charm and her customary good humour.

Bob Moore
Saddleworth

Introduction: Defining Resistance

Bob Moore

In the post-1945 culture of Western Europe, the term 'resistance' to Nazism and German occupation conjures up the image of an armed struggle against the enemy; of sabotage actions, assassinations, escape lines and secret agents risking their lives in pursuit of an ultimate Allied victory. This was the stuff of legends, heroes, a sprinkling of heroines and above all, of the action so beloved of novelists and film makers. Yet although it is important never to demean or undervalue the sacrifice of the many men and women who died or had their lives blighted in the cause of driving out the invader, it is equally important to realize that these high-profile activities and victims of Nazi terror were only a part of much larger story involving layers of non-cooperation, disobedience, and opposition to Nazism and the foreign invader. Thus at the outset, it is important to recognize that the nature of what has been interpreted as 'resistance' and the motivations of those involved are many and various and do not tolerate rigid categorization, either in relation to Germany itself or for any of the occupied countries.[1]

In the immediate aftermath of liberation in 1944–5, as the processes of national reconstruction began across Western Europe, there was a need to focus on the positive – on the elements within society that had not been drawn into collusion or collaboration with the occupying power. Although each country had its resistance organizations by the war's end, invariably encompassing many different political persuasions, the number of active participants was proportionally very small, and there was a tendency towards inflation – with all manner of people claiming to have been resisters in some way – or part of 'the resistance'.[2] This process of myth-making may have been necessary for national regeneration in the postwar world, but it had both positive and negative effects. On the positive side, it prompted some discussion about exactly what had constituted resistance. On the negative side, political reconstruction in every Western European state, while relying to some extent on the resistance myth, nonetheless ignored and marginalized many of those who had resisted. The most extreme manifestations of this trend occurred in relation to the various national communist parties and their members who had often been major elements in the resistance, but found themselves not only excluded but even demonized in the Cold War politics of the postwar era.[3]

In spite of all the published research on the topic, creating typologies of resistance has remained problematic. To begin with there are two separate issues. Firstly there is the question of what constitutes resistance? If it is accepted that the term has to go beyond the military (armed) and intelligence gathering aspects, then it becomes a question of where limits are set. Many have argued that any activity designed to thwart German plans, or perceived by the occupiers as working against their interests, could be included, but this trend has now been taken a stage further, both for occupied Europe and Nazi Germany itself, by examining the way in which entire societies reacted to a malevolent regime. This inevitably raises a subsidiary question. Against whom was the resistance directed? The answer may initially seem obvious, but there are all manner of complications. For example, in France where the collaborationist Vichy regime was often the focus for resistance activities, or in northern Italy after September 1943, where the remains of Mussolini's Fascist regime were just as much of a target as the occupying Germans.

This leaves the question of the forms that resistance took. The contributors to this book were left to define this for themselves, not least because the very definition of resistance is part of each country's national historiography on the subject, and is in some cases contested. There is no argument about including the armed resistance that emerged, to a greater or lesser extent, in all of the countries surveyed save the Channel Islands. Likewise all the activities associated with the Allied war effort; intelligence gathering, organizing escape networks for Allied air crew and sabotage operations. However, there were many other forms of civilian resistance, both organized and individual. The reconstruction of political organizations and the creation of a clandestine press to encourage unity, disseminate information and (ultimately) promote discussion of postwar reconstruction were apparent in most occupied countries. Evasion of the German forced labour draft undoubtedly provoked the largest response, with many hundreds of thousands of workers across Western Europe, both male and female, going 'underground' to avoid the authorities. However, these had not been the first people to go into hiding. Jews and others persecuted on racial grounds by the Nazis and threatened with 'resettlement in the East' had sought shelter almost from the beginning of the occupation, but especially after the deportations began in earnest in the summer of 1942.

Their collective plight led to a whole range of support activities including the provision of safe houses, money, false identity and ration cards. Helping those in hiding involved large numbers of men and women, and the complicity of many more. This may be clearly seen as resistance – thwarting German economic objectives, but what of those people who engaged in the provision, sale or purchase of black market goods? Certainly the Germans regarded this as criminal activity and against the interests of the occupier, yet for many people it became an imperative for families and individuals to stave off starvation towards the end of the war. It could be argued that this was merely self interest, albeit *in extremis*, but if the primary motive was profit rather than providing for one's essential needs should this change the way in which it is viewed? Buying and selling black market goods was widespread – as was theft when essential supplies became scarce, but should this be included within the definition? One can identify other, less vital, instances of avoidance or outright disobedience to German ordinances. In the Netherlands, for example, attempts to sequester bicycles in 1942 led to the widespread hiding or burying of good machines and the handing over of old frames, worn out wheels and tyres. Likewise, German attempts to have all the racing pigeons in the country killed and the feet sent in as evidence led to the owners removing one foot from each bird and then falsifying the returns.[4] Finally there are the individual acts that often went unnoticed (at least as forms of resistance) even by those against whom they were directed. What, for example, is one to make of gardeners' protests in growing flowers only of the national colour(s), or the old lady who spent her days sitting in a Parisian park and employing her walking stick to trip up German officers? Thus it can be seen that, while there were many obvious forms of the resistance activity, each author has also had to examine the 'grey areas' of behaviour in order to establish the definitions adopted in each national historiography.

If acts of resistance were many and various, so were the participants and their reasons for becoming involved. Resisters came from all classes, occupations and backgrounds, and from every urban and rural environment. When it comes to motivation, precise categorization even within individual countries has proved an almost impossible task, but some general areas can nonetheless be identified to act as a framework. Beginning with the early phases of the occupation, the first vestiges of resistance organization emerged primarily from each end of the political spectrum, from elements within the (defeated) armed forces and right-wing civilian circles, and from some individuals within the communist parties. The army officers from occupied countries saw their struggle as a nationalist crusade against a foreign (German) invader and they relied largely on informal contacts between friends and military colleagues to create their first networks. The same structures were evident inside Germany but with one crucial difference – namely that the military and right-wing resistance which emerged against Hitler and Nazism had to confront the fact that their activities were a treasonable betrayal of their own country.[5]

At the other end of the political spectrum, the communists were able to employ well-rehearsed tactics, many of which had been developed specifically to avoid the attentions of pre-war state agencies. Both the communists and other left-wing groups saw resistance primarily as an ideological struggle. In that respect, communist parties across Europe had been placed in a particularly invidious position by the Nazi–Soviet Pact of August 1939. Having operated a Popular Front policy of alliance with other left-wing and centrist groups to counter fascism and Nazism since the mid-1930s, they were then faced with *dictats* from Moscow that ordered them not to engage with the former enemy. Yet at the same time, the combined forces of the German occupation regime and indigenous police and security services were actively operating against them. Their salvation from this contradictory position came only with the German attack on the Soviet Union on 22 June 1941.

Other resistance organizations began in the universities; within the Christian Churches; and among members of outlawed political parties or professional groups. These could have an ideological, nationalist or moral basis, but many arose from opposition to one or more specific German measures that directly threatened the interests of the particular group. In all these cases, membership of such a group could act as the catalyst for an individual to become involved in some form of resistance activity. Yet there were many others, unaffiliated to any specific political, religious or professional group who were driven by a moral abhorrence to particular occupation policies, or to Nazism or things German in general. This would include German attempts to persecute, arrest and deport political and racial enemies, sequestration of property or indeed any act which was deemed to contravene the norms of the society in which they lived. Included here would be those people who sheltered Jews and evaders from forced labour schemes. Although they may initially have acted in isolation and have been unsupported, many were ultimately incorporated into specialist organizations. As the war progressed, so these organizations expanded to meet ever-increasing demands and were forced to recruit new members. Thus many people became involved primarily because they were prompted, either by friends, relatives, community or religious leaders, rather than because of their own initial commitment. The same might be said of those who evaded forced labour. As Kedward has so clearly shown in relation to France, while the act of becoming a *réfractaire* (evader) and going into hiding was resistance in one sense, there was no automatic progression from *réfractaire* to armed *maquisard*.[6] This represents only a glimpse of the myriad factors that prompted people to oppose the occupiers and collaborationist regimes. However, it would be wrong to assume that motivation was singular in each case, as even individuals could often cite a series of issues that had set them on the road to opposition and resistance. Combinations of religious-moral, ideological-moral, or ideological-pragmatic factors were common in most countries, but even these were by no means the only possibilities.

By the last year of the war, resistance – if broadly defined – was widespread in most occupied countries. The increasing numbers involved and the range and extent of activities were undoubtedly a function of the recognition that Germany was fast losing the war, and that for occupied Western Europe liberation was only a matter of time. However, it should not be thought that this increased participation was entirely without risk. In defeat, the German armies and functionaries imposed punitive directives and carried out their vengeance against civilian populations until the last moment. The penalties for defiance in the short term were still very much apparent.

To a large extent, early definitions of resistance were taken from the criteria used by former occupied states to recognize and honour those involved – criteria that often encompassed political agendas of the postwar era. However, as the foregoing summary suggests, categorization of resistance and resisters in this fashion served to exclude many people and many important elements, and only with the beginning of academic research on the subject did more sophisticated definitions begin to develop. The first attempts at a comparative approach emerged with two major international conferences devoted to the history of the resistance, which took place in 1958 and 1960. These set the agenda for subsequent research on the subject.[7] The first dealt with such themes as the psychological war, the role of the clandestine press, Jewish resistance, the *maquis* and guerrilla warfare, and the Allied relationship with the resistance. The second also concentrated on the resistance and Allies, as well as other aspects of national opposition to German rule. However, the implicitly comparative nature of the conference sessions tended to produce papers on the international and military importance of resistance, rather than its role in the internal history of individual countries. To some degree, this trend was continued in a further important conference volume. In *Resistance in Europe: 1939–1945*, Ralph White provided a comprehensive introduction, highlighting both the commonalities and diversities of the European resistance.[8] In so doing, he drew attention to the fact that, whatever the differences between the various forms of resistance, they were all directed towards the defeat of a common enemy. Moreover, he highlighted the fact that resistance in all countries could be not only active and tangible, but also internal and passive, and that it was likely to grow as the war proceeded, as German ideological and economic impositions increased, and as the possibility of liberation became stronger.

He drew four major conclusions from this comparative analysis. Firstly, that resistance to German rule served to create alliances of formerly antagonistic groups, for example between Catholics and communists. Secondly, resistance had differing long-term objectives: there was conservative resistance directed towards recreating the traditional order, and there was revolutionary resistance, which saw the defeat of Germany as the prelude to a transformation of government and society. Thirdly, there was the question of external links and where resistance movements looked for help. Some had contacts with the Western powers in London, some with the Soviets in Moscow and one or two looked to both sides for guidance and assistance. Finally, he noted that the scale and achievements of the resistance movements across Europe varied enormously and evaluating their contribution to liberation and postwar reconstruction would be a complex process.

This one publication demonstrated the direction scholarship was taking in the mid-1970s and also highlighted many of the problems involved in the study of resistance. In 1970, Henri Michel produced the first, and still perhaps the most comprehensive, attempt to synthesize all aspects of the European resistance in one comparative volume.[9] Starting with the nature of German occupation, he moved on to deal with exile resistance movements, the origins of clandestine organizations, their various types, the different forms of resistance and then finally an assessment of the achievements of the resistance throughout Europe. Inevitably, given the scope of the book, the treatment of each country was somewhat brief, but it remains an essential guide to the origins, conduct and achievements of the resistance. Moreover, it raised some further crucial questions that were to be taken up by other authors, most notably the place of resistance movements in the national historiographies of World War Two, the role of illegal publications and newspapers, and the vexed question of the resistance's 'contribution' to liberation and postwar reconstruction.

A more recent study by Jacques Semelin has looked in comparative terms at civilian non-violent resistance to Nazi rule in the occupied countries of Europe.[10] In summarizing the study of resistance, he identified three stages towards an understanding of resistance, which have also functioned as means of interpreting it. The first is the view of resistance purely in terms of its contribution to the Allied war effort, concentrating as it does on the forms that were of some direct assistance to military victory such as intelligence and sabotage. The second interpretation examines the political significance of internal resistance as a power embodying an alternative legitimacy to that of the occupiers and collaborators. In so doing, it not only charts the growing hostility of the civil population to the occupier but also sheds light on the role of internal resistance in reconstructing the legitimacy of postwar state structures. The third approach focuses more directly on the moral and spiritual aspects of resistance. Thus it concentrates primarily on the motivation of individuals and groups rather than on their activities. As Semelin points out, all of these approaches provide a limited perspective on the complex phenomenon called resistance.[11] However, he champions a fourth approach that looks not specifically at the resisters themselves, but at the psychological and social contexts from which they emerged.[12] Thus attention has been focused more on societies under occupation as a whole, comparing resisters with non-resisters and with collaborators. This trend has engendered comparative works on the nature of resistance and collaboration and further debates on the definitions of these two emotive terms.[13] One example of the changing perspectives on resistance can be seen in more recent work by Semelin himself. In the second edition of his book, he has marginally altered his definition of resistance from its original formulation, both altering his definition of what constitutes civil society, and also including the actions of state servants who used their positions inside the system to subvert the policies of the occupiers – something that he had previously discounted from civil resistance.[14]

While seasoned researchers are still adjusting their definitions of what constitutes resistance and continue to stress its complexities, it is nonetheless essential to have an outline structure to allow for comparative discussion of the subject. Perhaps the most comprehensive example emerged from a conference on resistance organized in the mid-1980s.[15] The product of five scholars with expertise on both Eastern and Western Europe, the schema had three major headings: the prehistory of resistance, the resistance itself, and the liberation and postwar era.[16] The prehistory of resistance encompassed the influence of fascist ideology, reactions to it in political and social circles, and the building of fascist regimes with extensive state repression. This perhaps has more relevance to the study of resistance inside Nazi Germany or Fascist Italy, but the framework provided for the study of resistance itself would be applicable to both Germany and all the occupied countries.[17]

Although the authors placed no particular importance on the ordering of the factors they outlined, it is nevertheless possible to arrange them into a loose series of categories. There is, first of all, the identification of all elements of both organized and non-organized resistance, the latter including individual acts, and the various facets of what have been termed passive resistance and social protest. From this follows the need to assess the organizational forms that emerged and the methods used, ranging from armed struggle at one extreme to minor acts of disobedience at the other. These two elements taken together provide the parameters for defining what could constitute resistance, but it is equally important to provide a periodization for the development of individual networks, movements and resistance in general which places their emergence and growth within the wider perspective of the changing war situation.

Turning to the organized resistance groups, one can begin by looking at their origins and membership, their objectives and programmes, their relative strengths and their size in relation to the population as whole. The attempts at alliance and unification of diverse groups prompted either from within the country or from outside, especially later in the war, are also crucial. There is an identifiable general trend towards greater cooperation in all the occupied countries, but this should not be allowed to disguise the many examples of continued non-cooperation and conflicts between organizations within each country that continued until the end of hostilities and beyond.

The question of numbers is also important to the analysis of resistance. How many people were actually involved – and at what levels? What proportion of the population did they represent, and how far do the participants mirror the social structure of the society from which they came in terms of gender, age, occupation and social class. In addition, there were the motivations of those who became involved; the role of religious belief and moral principles, the importance of religious congregations and secular or community organizations in initiating or mobilizing support, the impact of German rule and the degree of indigenous collaboration on the levels of participation and their extent.

All these factors are essentially about resistance as a purely internal phenomenon, but the international dimension cannot be ignored. Relationships between indigenous resistance networks and the agencies of the Allied powers were important for espionage, sabotage and escape lines, even if the military value and usefulness of the resistance generally was ultimately rather limited. However, consideration also has to be given to the links between the resistance inside a country and governments-in-exile and other émigré groups in London or elsewhere, and between resistance groups in different occupied countries. Finally there is the question of the role played by 'the resistance' in the plans and planning for the postwar reconstruction of each country, the realities of liberation, the achievements of the resistance and its importance in postwar politics, society, and culture over last fifty years.

In some respects, this survey represents a relatively traditional structure for the examination of resistance, coupling together Semelin's first three types, but only touching on the fourth, namely the need to look at the society as a whole in order to understand the subject. Moreover the relative importance of these headings will inevitably vary between case studies, thus making direct comparison difficult if not impossible. Nonetheless, it does provide an initial framework for encompassing the diversity of resisters and resistance activities inside Germany and in Nazi-occupied Western Europe.[18]

Historiography

For an essential bibliography on resistance in each of the Western European countries covered in this volume, one need look no further than the footnotes and historiographical sections of the chapters concerned. However, as this book is designed primarily to provide an introduction to the topic for English readers, the following is a short country-by-country discussion of resistance historiography, concentrating on what has appeared in the English language.

Perhaps not surprisingly, many English-language works on resistance see the topic primarily in terms of its contribution to the British and Allied war effort. Thus resistance as a part of the espionage and sabotage campaign against the Axis powers has been extensively analysed, notably in the works of M.R.D. Foot, whose wartime career and subsequent appointment as official historian for the British Special Operations Executive (SOE), gave him a great many insights into the relationships between the organizations like SOE, MI5 and MI6 working from London and the networks operating in occupied territory. In a monograph, he surveyed the various definitions of resistance used by other scholars and divided the subject matter into three functional categories: intelligence, escape and sabotage, where the latter heading is further subdivided into sabotage, attacks on troops and individuals, politics and insurrection.

Although acknowledging the more 'civilian' forms of resistance, such as passive and administrative resistance and the production of clandestine newspapers, he nevertheless concentrates on the military aspects of what was done, who was involved, and its relative importance to the Allied war effort.[19] This latter question has remained an important element in the debate on resistance. Authors such as Foot highlighted the heroic and the sometimes tragic history of the European resistance, but also placed it firmly within the military history of World War Two. For an analysis of the relationships between SOE and the European resistance movements, David Stafford's more-or-less chronological account highlights the problems and sometimes fraught relationships between the needs of the Allied war effort – as conveyed by SOE – and the objectives of national or regional resistance organizations.[20] He also makes mention of SOE's greatest failure, the so-called *Englandspiel* where agents sent to the Netherlands were captured by the German Sicherheitsdienst but whose attempt to alert their masters in London to their true fate were ignored – leading to the capture of forty-three agents, of whom thirty-six were executed.[21]

The study of resistance in most Western European countries, as well as inside Germany itself, has usually been divided into military and non-military, between communist, socialist, confessional, and right wing. The creation (or not) of single unified movements and the role of key individuals in this process has also remained a major debate, as has the definition of resistance and the difficulties of defining activities at the margins – in the grey areas between passivity and passive opposition – or of people and groups who were apparently collaborating and resisting at the same time. Other problems that seem common to more than one country include the dilemma of national communist parties after occupation but before the collapse of the Nazi–Soviet pact, and their later role in resistance activity; opposition (or lack of it) to the deportation of the Jews; the importance of resistance to the liberation of countries and its role in restoring national prestige in the postwar era after societies had been fatally divided between those who co-operated with the occupying power and those who were steadfast in their opposition. Finally, there has been an increasing interest in the role of women within resistance movements. Many of the central debates can be found in the key work by Margaret Rossiter,[22] but other authors have done much to further knowledge of this previously neglected area.

The historiography of resistance within occupied Western Europe has developed more-or-less separately in each of the countries concerned. This is in part due to the differences in the organization and nature of

German rule, even between neighbouring states. Most research has examined resistance as part of the domestic social and political history of the country under occupation. As such, attention has been directed to the origins, participants, structures, organizations, successes and failures of the resistance, and to its role in postwar reconstruction. Only a very few authors have been brave enough to try to make tentative comparisons between states. The fact that these historiographies are overwhelmingly national (and for the most part originally published in the language of the country concerned) provides the justification for taking each of the states in turn, to demonstrate both the development of these individual historiographies, and to highlight some of the parallel paths taken by scholars in looking at ostensibly similar problems.

The resistance movements in France have attracted more scholarly attention than in any other part of Europe. One reason for this is the importance of the resistance as a factor in restoring French national pride in the years after the war's end. However, this has also created problems and the need for historians to overcome the many myths that became associated with the 'heroic' view of French actions against the occupier. The first major history of the resistance as a whole, and still perhaps the most comprehensive and encyclopaedic, is the five-volume work by Noguères.[23] In spite of his participation as a regional chief of the movement 'Franc-Tireur' in Montpellier, the writing is both rigorous and scholarly, and has acted as the basic source for many other subsequent works. Divided until November 1942 into occupied and unoccupied (Vichy) zones, the history of the resistance has also tended to be divided along these lines. Frida Knight, who adopted a more-or-less chronological approach to the subject, wrote the first study in English.[24] More recently, Rod Kedward has contributed two major texts. The first, on resistance in Vichy France, clearly demonstrates the variety of movements and activities that existed and also the uncertainties of the participants, acting as they were against a *Pétainiste* French state. The second analyses the creation and development of the *maquis*, the resistance based in the countryside of the south, which began with men taking to the hills to avoid labour conscription and ended with some of them organizing a full-scale insurrection against the Germans in 1944.[25] John Sweets has also made a substantial contribution to the understanding of the motivations behind resistance in central and southern France and its structures.[26] As in every occupied country, there were many different resistance organizations established. One of the best accounts of an individual group is Martin Blumenson's careful reconstruction of the early Parisian network created around the staff at the Musée de l'Homme in 1940.[27] The role of the

French Communist Party (PCF) in the resistance, and its dilemmas in the months between the signing of the Nazi–Soviet Pact in August 1939 and the invasion of the USSR in June 1941 have been examined by a number of authors, most notably Kedward, Don Simmonds and, more recently, David Wingeate Pike.[28] A local study of the PCF resistance in the Haute-Vienne by Sarah Farmer is also instructive in showing that success was often based on identifying with local interests and defying or ignoring party orders.[29] Attempts have been made to uncover the role of women in the resistance, most notably in the monograph by Margaret Collins Weitz and by Paula Schwarz, who has looked specifically at female participation in PCF combat groups and shows that in the extreme conditions of underground warfare, women did trespass into 'male gender territory'.[30]

There have been innumerable texts on the relationships between the resistance movements and the Free French and allies in London. Apart from the works by M.R.D. Foot on SOE,[31] there is also the detailed study by Arthur Funk on the role of the resistance in the allied landings in Southern France in 1944.[32] Finally, at a more general analytical level, the problems of defining resistance in France have been addressed by Sweets, who notes that the traditional view of the French as a nation of resisters has come to be replaced by an image of them as a nation of colla-borators. He suggests that reconsideration of both these extremes should lead to a more tempered view of French behaviour under occupation.[33]

Perhaps more than any other Western European country, the resistance in Belgium has been considered as an internal matter. Moreover, its historians were slow to move into the field of contemporary history and it was not until the 1970s that scholars began to publish on aspects of World War Two. Given the high profile of the Royal question,[34] the punishment of collaborators and the continuance of the Flemish question, resistance did not command much attention. Archives remained closed and oral history untapped for many years. Perhaps as a result, little or nothing beyond a few memoirs has appeared in the English language and the interested reader has had to resort either to French or Flemish works for information.[35] Probably the most important and the most comprehensive devoted specifically to resistance is the volume by Herman van de Vijver and others in the general series on Belgium in World War Two.[36] The survey work by Henri Bernard is in French and somewhat older. It lacks the archival base of later works but benefits from the author's career both as an agent in the field and as a staff officer in London. His more recent work has concentrated specifically on the 'secret army' in Belgium, made up of diverse groups of soldiers and ex-servicemen, and on the (civilian) patriotic militias and armed partisans.[37] As with all other occupied European countries, the Communist Party in Belgium was placed in a compromised position by the Nazi–Soviet pact of August 1939. Their response to this dilemma and the internal debates on the various possible courses of action is carefully outlined by Rudi van Doorslaer.[38] Beyond this, one has to look at more general works. The most recent of these is by the highly respected Etienne Verhoeyen and deals with the whole period from the outbreak of war to the liberation.[39]

As with many other European states, scholars in the Netherlands have tended to place their country's resistance movement firmly and exclusively within the national historiography of World War Two. This has been to categorize all behaviour during the occupation as either *goed* (correct) or *fout* (incorrect). The major achievements of the Dutch resistance, the February strike of 1941 against the roundup of Jews in Amsterdam, the April–May 1943 strike against forced labour drafts and the stoppage of the railways to assist the allied landing at Arnhem in 1944, have all become central features of the literature.[40] A brief survey of the resistance can be found in a series of published lectures by Louis de Jong, the doyen of Dutch historians on World War Two.[41] This summarizes its main achievements by measuring them against the successes and failures of German policy. He argues that while the attempt to Nazify Dutch society failed, economic exploitation and the deportation of the Jews succeeded. Thus the record of the resistance was essentially mixed. On the one hand, contacts between the Dutch resistance and the British SOE were compromised by the network's penetration by the German security service, leading to the capture and death of many British agents. On the other hand, the resistance was more-or-less united into a single entity by the last year of the occupation and successfully hid several hundred thousand people underground. De Jong has published a limited number of papers in English, on anti-Nazi resistance and contacts with the Allies,[42] but other key works exist only in Dutch, for example the collection edited by Roegholt and Zwaan which surveys the main resistance elements in the Netherlands, including the military, left-wing and church based movements. Each chapter also charts the expansion of these groups, their activities, successes and failures.[43]

. An important critique of de Jong's writings has come from Blom, who argues against the use of a *goed/fout* structure to understand Dutch behaviour during the occupation. It is especially regrettable that no English version of this exists.[44] Scholarship in English remains scarce. For a brief summary, one can turn to the relevant chapters in the survey works on the occupation period by Werner Warmbrunn or Walter Maass and to the almost contemporary series of articles in the *Annals of the American*

Academy of Political and Social Sciences for May 1946.[45] On specific aspects of the debates on resistance, Michael Smith has examined the strange case of the short-lived but popular Nederlandse Unie, which the Germans perceived as an instrument to encourage collaboration, but its adherents saw it as a statement of continued patriotism and a means of protest against the occupation.[46]

As the first Western European country to be occupied by the Germans and the last to be liberated, the Norwegian resistance lasted longer than many of its European counterparts. The standard general texts in English remain those by Tore Gvelsvik and Gerd Gordon Stray, and these can be combined with the specific survey by Kjelstadli on the relationship between the Norwegian resistance and the allies.[47] A brief narrative introduction to the subject can also be found in the guide by Olav Riste and Berit Nökleby, which provides a chronological overview and discussion of the major issues.[48] An article by Paul Wehr examines the various aspects of (non-violent) civilian resistance to Nazi occupation.[49] More recent books on the subject have come from Magne Skodvin who stresses the broad-based civilian opposition to German rule and attempts at nazification. Certainly the lack of any popular support for the collaborationist indigenous Norwegian Nazi Party under Vidkun Quisling seems to have simplified some of the debates about Norwegian society under occupation, although question marks remain over the reaction to the deportation of the Jews and the 'economic collaboration' that was an integral feature of the German regime. Skodvin was an active participant in the resistance whose first-hand experiences combined with a detailed knowledge of the archival sources make this an essential text.[50] Other works cover aspects of the Norwegian resistance relationship with the Allies and the attempts to carry out sabotage actions.[51]

Danish resistance was complicated by the fact that Denmark was never formally at war with Germany but became a *de facto* participant in the common struggle alongside the Allies. For a comprehensive overview there is a three-volume work by Jørgen Hæstrup, which provides a detailed examination of the origins, development and structure of the Danish resistance.[52] Hæstrup has also commented specifically on its links to the Allied powers and this external element has been further examined by Hillingso who highlights the problems and conflicts between the movement in Denmark and the various allied agencies in London, including SOE and military intelligence.[53] The relationship was clouded by the allied mistrust of the Danes' will to fight and their inability to mount a sustained campaign. This can be read alongside the specialist studies by Jeremy Bennett on the British Broadcasting Corporation and its relationship with the Danish resistance and by Erik Lund on the clandestine press.[54] More recently, there has been a study which argues that the Danish resistance deliberately limited its use of violence and attempted to conduct its struggle against the Germans in a manner acceptable to Danish political culture.[55] However, the Danish resistance is perhaps most famous for having engineered the escape of its Jewish community to Sweden from under the noses of the German authorities. Key texts for this particular aspect can be found in the monograph by Leni Yahil, the edited collection by Leo Goldberger, which includes an extensive chapter by Hæstrup on the Danish Jews and the German Occupation, and the recent exchange of views by Gunnar Paulsson and Kirchhoff. Finally, there is an important work on Scandinavia during World War Two by Nissen, which contains important chapters by Grimnes and Trommer on the origins and development of resistance in both Denmark and Norway, and also contains a very useful critical bibliography written by the editor.[56]

When applied to the Italian context, resistance has a number of distinct aspects. Firstly there was the story of anti-fascist resistance to Mussolini and to fascism prior to the Italian surrender in September 1943, a struggle that continued against the Italian Social (Salò) Republic. Parallel to this was an increasing level of armed resistance to German occupation in the northern half of the country. The earliest comprehensive treatment of the subject came from Roberto Battaglia,[57] but the most detailed survey in English of the Italian resistance movement remains the monograph by Charles Delzell. He outlines the development of the armed resistance 1943–5, highlighting the various groups involved, their relationships with the Badoglio government and the Allied powers, and their role in the liberation of northern Italy from the Germans.[58] A more recent, but briefer, summary can be found in Dante Puzzo, which deals specifically with the partisan war in the northern half of the country. The nature of support given to the partisans against the Germans by Italian civilians has been the subject of much debate.[59] The orthodox line claims that the National Liberation Committee for North Italy had the support of the entire population. This view can be found in the extensive work on the Italian resistance by Guido Quazza, whereas a more revisionist approach, implying that German occupation produced more attentism and a form of civil war has its most recent expression in the book by Pavone.[60] The role of the resistance in the liberation of the north is also explored by David Ellwood, who highlights Allied worries about the partisans, and especially the communists, setting themselves up as alternative local or regional governments to those of Badoglio's regime.[61] At a more specialist level, Absalom has looked at the behaviour of peasants in the north of the country who assisted allied fugitives, such as prisoners-of-war, from the Germans. He points out that this type of resistance was separate from partisan activity and represented an entirely different response to the occupation. As long as all Italians were assumed to have supported the Allied/antifascist cause, then their singular behaviour was hidden, only to emerge when this particular myth was exploded.[62] As with most of the occupied European countries, the role of women in the resistance is now beginning to be analysed in more detail, and Jane Slaughter has provided the first comprehensive treatment of their participation in the Italian context.[63]

Although not directly comparable with the subject of this book, the resistance within Nazi Germany provides an obvious additional element for analysis and discussion. Moreover, the historiography of the subject in Germany has often provided new insights into questions of definition. Scholarship in this field has gone through a number of phases. The first focused on the moral resistance to Hitler and Nazism and concentrated on groups such as The White Rose led by Hans and Sophie Scholl.[64] This was followed by a closer examination of resistance by the élites, for example in the Kreisau Circle, and the military resistance that culminated in the July 1944 bomb plot.[65] In addition, there have been innumerable publications on the various espionage networks that provided information for the Allied powers, even from inside the German High Command itself. The most important study of the links between the German Resistance and the Allies both before and during the war is by Klemens von Klemperer who looks not just at the military and bureaucratic élites, but also at the German Churches and émigré groups.[66] There have also been works dedicated to the German Left, most notably Merson's study of the German Communist Party (KPD), but there are also a whole series of local studies which include material on left-wing anti-Nazi activity.[67] Both these 'schools' interpreted *widerstand* (resistance) in a fairly narrow sense, but from the 1970s onwards there was a growing trend towards the use of the term *resistenz* to categorizing behaviour patterns that, while not resistance, were also not in conformity with the wishes of the regime.[68] Interest in the subject has remained and has led to the appearance of a number of important monographs and edited collections as research has been extended into new areas of enquiry.[69]

Although Jewish resistance is often incorporated in the national histories of resistance, there is a case for seeing it as a separate entity. Certainly, there are a number of publications that deal with Jewish involvement in the partisan movements of the USSR and a substantial literature on Jewish resistance inside the ghettos and even in the extermination camps themselves. This research is beyond the scope of this study, but there are nevertheless some specialist studies on the Jewish communities in Western Europe and their responses to Nazi persecution. In many areas of Nazi-occupied Western Europe, Jewish resistance activity tended to parallel – or be incorporated with – other resistance organizations. In this respect, France has been reasonably well served, with Anny Latour's study of Jewish involvement in the resistance and the works of Lucien Lazare and Jacques Adler, which concentrate on responses to Nazi persecution.[70] An article by Claude Lévy has raised the issue of whether resistance by Jews was because they were Jews and whether there were particular forms of resistance directed towards specifically Jewish aims. Henry Weinberg has gone some way to answering part of this question by suggesting that Jewish communist resistance was more directed towards the communist agenda and took little direct action against anti-Semitic activities by the Germans or collaborators.[71] There is further work of note on the subject by Renee Poznanski, who shows that there were important divisions between French and foreign Jews, reflected mainly in the organizational divisions of the Jewish communist and Zionist resistance movements.[72] Literature on Jewish resistance in other Western European countries remains scarce. Exceptions are the Dutch publications of Ben Braber, who has combined archival material with oral testimony to survey the extent of Jewish involvement in the resistance.[73] For Belgium, there is the extensive study of the Holocaust in Belgium edited by Dan Michman and on Norway, the short summary by Oskar Mendelsohn.[74]

To facilitate the possibilities for comparison, the contributors were given a broad outline structure of issues to consider, adapted from the one discussed earlier in this chapter. Each author was asked to examine the main resistance movements and to give an indication of their size, scope and position within the society under occupation. They were also asked to highlight the changes which took place over time and the levels of co-operation and conflict which occurred between the various groups and the extent to which these were overcome in the creation of umbrella organisations. This was to be followed by discussion of the recent major debates engendered on resistance as a whole and the interpretations that have emerged within each national historiography. Some specific issues were also raised for consideration; for example the role of individual (unorganized) acts of resistance – their extent and importance; the role of women in the resistance and as resisters in their own right; and the role of Jewish resistance, both generally and to Nazi deportation and extermination policies. The contributors were also asked to reflect on the role and importance of resistance, both as a practical contribution to national liberation and in terms of its value to national reconstruction and the restoration of national honour in the postwar era. Finally, they were invited to comment on the new directions being taken by research on resistance, and conversely, where subjects were still being neglected. As each chapter is self contained, the ordering of the case studies has been decided by alphabetical order rather than any view of their relative importance or extent. However, in the first chapter dealing with Belgium, Pieter Lagrou raises a series of general issues that are also of relevance to the study and understanding of resistance in other countries. Inevitably, the structuring and organization of each chapter has been determined by the relevant national historiography and the views of the authors. Taken together, they form the first collection to provide a uniform framework for a discussion of resistance in Western Europe and a basis for comparative study.

Notes

1. Jacques Semelin, *Unarmed Against Hitler: Civilian Resistance in Europe, 1939–1943* (Westport CT: Praeger, 1993) p.25.
2. Sometimes referred to in France as resisters of the thirteenth hour – to differentiate them from the early resisters – of the first hour. H.R. Kedward and Nancy Wood (eds) *The Liberation of France: Image and Event* (Oxford: Berg, 1995) p.5.
3. For a detailed discussion of these issues see, Pieter Lagrou, *The Legacy of Nazi-Occupation in Western Europe: Patriotic Memory and National Recovery* (Cambridge: Cambridge University Press, 1999). A study of the Dutch communist resistance's transformation from contributors to the liberation to enemies of the state can be found in Joost van Lingen and Niek Sloof, *Van Verzetsstrijder tot Staatsgevaarlijk Burger* (Baarn: Anthos, 1987).
4. Bob Moore, 'The Netherlands' in: Jeremy Noakes (ed.) *The Civilian in War: The Home Front in Europe, Japan and the USA in World War II* (Exeter: Exeter University Press, 1992) pp.138–9.
5. See, for example, Dietrich Bonhoeffer, *Ethik* (Munich, 1949) pp.185f. cited in Ernst Wolf, 'Political and Moral Motives behind the Resistance', in: Hermann Graml, Hans Mommsen, Hans-Joachim

Reichhardt, Ernst Wolf, *The German Resistance to Hitler* (London: Batsford, 1970) p.230.

6. H.R. Kedward, *In Search of the Maquis: Rural Resistance in Southern France, 1942–1944* (Oxford: Oxford University Press, 1993) p.37.

7. *European Resistance Movements 1939–1945: First International Conference on the History of the Resistance Movements held at Liège–Bruxelles–Breendonk 14–17 September 1958* (London: Pergamon, 1960). *European Resistance Movements 1939–1945: Second International Conference on the History of the Resistance Movements, Milan 1960* (London: Pergamon, 1964).

8. Stephen Hawes and Ralph White, *Resistance in Europe: 1939–1945* (Harmondsworth: Penguin, 1976) pp.7–23.

9. Henri Michel, *The Shadow War: Resistance in Europe 1939–1945* (London: André Deutsch, 1972). In this context, Jørgen Hæstrup, *European Resistance Movements (1939–1945): A Complete History* (Westport CT: Praeger, 1981) should also be mentioned, but in spite of its title, this work deals only with organized resistance across occupied Europe and says little or nothing about other forms.

10. Semelin, *Unarmed Against Hitler.* There is now also a second updated edition with a new preface and introduction, *Sans armes face à Hitler: La résistance civile en Europe 1939–1945* (Paris: Éditions Payot et Rivages, 1998).

11. Semelin, *Unarmed against Hitler*, p.25.

12. Semelin, *Unarmed against Hitler*, p.26.

13. Werner Rings, *Life With the Enemy. Collaboration and Resistance in Hitler's Europe 1939–1945* (London: Wiedenfeld and Nicholson, 1982). See also, John Sweets, 'Hold that Pendulum! Redefining Fascism, Collaboration and Resistance in France', *French Historical Studies* XV/4 (1988) pp.731–58.

14. Semelin, *Sans armes face à Hitler*, p.viii.

15. Ger van Roon (ed.), *Europäischer Widerstand im Vergleich. Die Internationalen Konferenzen Amsterdam* (Berlin: Siedler Verlag, 1985).

16. W. Neugebauer, J. Jamojski, J. Gotovitch, M. Skodvin and T. Ferenc, 'Gesichtspunkte für eine vergleichende Untersuchung des Widerstandes: Schema und Erläuterung' in: van Roon, *Europäischer Widerstand,* pp.38–41.

17. W. Neugebauer J. Zamojski, J. Gotovitch, M. Skodvin and T. Ferenc, 'Gesichtspunkte' pp.38–9. The authors made it clear that their list of factors was not placed in order and some reordering has been attempted here.

18. For a more recent examination of scholarship on resistance in France, see H.R. Kedward, 'Resisting French Resistance', *Transactions of the Royal Historical Society*, Sixth Series IX (1999) pp.271–82.

19. M.R.D. Foot, Resistance: *An Analysis of European Resistance to Nazism* (London: Eyre Methuen, 1976). See also, M.R.D. Foot and J.M. Langley, *MI9: Escape and Evasion 1939–45* (London: The Bodley Head, 1979), M.R.D. Foot, *SOE in France* (London: HMSO, 1966) and M.R.D. Foot, *SOE: The Special Operations Executive 1940–1946* (London: BBC, 1984). Specific mention should also be made here of Alan Milward's provocative piece in Hawes and White, *Resistance*, pp.186–203, where he claims that resistance had little economic or strategic value for the Allied war effort.

20. David Stafford, *Britain and the European Resistance 1940–1945: A Survey of the Special Operations Executive, with Documents*, 2nd. edn (Toronto/Buffalo: University of Toronto Press, 1983 / London: Macmillan, 1983) David Stafford 'The Detonator Concept: British Strategy, SOE and European Resistance after the Fall of France' *Journal of Contemporary History* X/2 (1975) pp.185–217.

21. For a detailed examination of this issue, see Louis de Jong, *Het Koninkrijk der Nederlanden in de Tweede Wereldoorlog*, Vol. IX/2 (The Hague: Staatsuitgeverij, 1979) pp.936–1040. M.R.D. Foot, *Holland at War Against Hitler: Anglo–Dutch Relations 1940–1945* (London: Frank Cass, 1990). Nicholas Kelso, *Errors of Judgement: SOEs Disaster in the Netherlands, 1941–44* (London: Hale, 1944). E.H. Cookridge, 'Dutch Tragedy' in: E.H. Cookridge (ed.) *Inside SOE: The First Full Story of Special Operations Executive in Western Europe* (London: Tinking, 1966) pp.390–408. Leo Marks, *Between Silk and Cyanide: The Story of SOEs Code War* (London: Hammersmith, 1998). Nigel West '"Der Englandspiel": SOE in Holland, Belgium and Czechoslovakia. In: Nigel West, *Secret War: The Story of SOE. Britain's Wartime Sabotage Operation* (London: Hodder and Stoughton, 1992) pp.88–105.

22. Margaret Rossiter, *Women in the Resistance* (New York: Praeger, 1986).

23. Henri Noguères, (with Marcel Degliame-Fouche), *Histoire de la Résistance en France* 5 Vols. (Paris: Robert Laffont, 1967–1981)

24. Frida Knight, *The French Resistance 1940–1944* (London: Lawrence and Wishart, 1975).

25. H. Roderick Kedward, *Resistance in Vichy France: A Study of Ideas and Motivation in the Southern Zone 1940–1942* (Oxford: Oxford University Press, 1978). H. Roderick Kedward, *In Search of the*

Maquis: Rural Resistance in Southern France, 1942–1944 (Oxford: Oxford University Press, 1993).

26. John H. Sweets, *The Politics of Resistance in France (1940–1944): A History of the Mouvements Unis de la Résistance* (De Kalb IL: Northern Illinois University Press, 1976).

27. Martin Blumenson, *The Vildé Affair: Beginnings of the French Resistance* (Boston: Houghton Mifflin, 1977).

28. H. Roderick Kedward, 'Behind the Polemics: French Communists and Resistance 1939–1941' in Hawes and White, *Resistance in Europe*, pp.94–116. J.C. Don Simmonds, 'The French Communist Party and the Beginnings of Resistance' *European Studies Review* (1981) pp.517–42. David Wingeate Pike, 'Between the Junes. The French Communists from the Collapse of France to the Invasion of Russia' *Journal of Contemporary History* XXVIII/3 (1993) pp.465–85.

29. Sarah Farmer, 'The Communist Resistance in the Haute-Vienne' *French Historical Studies* XIV/1 (1985) pp.89–116.

30. Margaret Collins Weitz, *Sisters in the Resistance: How Women Fought to Free France, 1940–1945* (New York: John Wiley, 1995). Paula Schwarz, 'Partisanes and Gender Politics in Vichy France', *French Historical Studies* XVI/1 (1989) pp.126–51. See also, Claire Gorrara, 'Reviewing Gender and the Resistance: The Case of Lucie Aubrac' in: H.R. Kedward and Nancy Wood, *The Liberation of France: Image and Event* (Oxford: Berg, 1995)

31. See note 19 above.

32. Arthur Layton Funk, *Hidden Ally: The French Resistance, Special Operations and the Landings in Southern France* (Westport CT: Greenwood, 1992).

33. John Sweets, 'Hold that Pendulum! Redefining Fascism, Collaboration and Resistance in France', *French Historical Studies* XV/4 (1988) pp.731–58.

34. Essentially the postwar debate about the conduct of King Leopold III who chose to remain in Belgium after the German occupation. For more detailed analysis see, Emile Cammaerts, *The Prisoner at Laeken* (London: Cresset Press, 1941), and Roger Keyes, *Outrageous Fortune: The Tragedy of Leopold III of the Belgians 1901–41* (London: Secker and Warburg, 1984).

35. The exceptions are the memoir by Henri Bodson, 'Agent for the Resistance: A Belgian Saboteur in World War II', *Texas A&M Military History* XXXV (1994) and the narrative by Yvonne De Ridder, *The Quest for Freedom: Belgian Resistance in World War II* (Fithina Press,

1991), but this adopts an heroic rather than analytical view of the resistance.

36. Herman van der Vijver et al., *Het Verzet*, Vol.2 of *België in de Tweede Wereldoorlog* (Kapellen: DNB-Pelckmans, 1988).

37. Henri Bernard, *La Résistance 1940–1945* (Bruxelles: Renaissance du Livre, 1968). Henri Bernard et al., *L'armée secrète 1940–1945* (Paris-Gembloux: 1986). Henri Bernard, *Un maquis dans la ville. Historique du régiment des milices patriotiques de Schaerbeek* (Brussels: Renaissance du Livre, 1970).

38. Rudi van Doorslaer, *De Kommunistische Partij van België en het Sovjet-Duits Niet-aanvalspakt tussen Augustus 1939 en Juli 1941* (Brussels: 1975)

39. Etienne Verhoeyen, *La Belgique Occupée* (Bruxelles: De Boeck Université, 1994).

40. Louis de Jong and Joseph Stoppelman, *The Lion Rampant: The Story of Holland's Resistance to the Nazis* (New York: Querido, 1943). Werner Warmbrunn, *The Dutch under German Occupation, 1940–1945* (Stanford CA: Stanford University Press, 1963) David Mountfield, 'Netherlands' in: David Mountfield, *The Partisans. Secret Armies of World War II* (London: Hamlyn, 1979) pp.82–92.

41. Louis de Jong, *The Netherlands and Nazi Germany* (Cambridge MS: Harvard University Press, 1990).

42. Louis de Jong, 'Anti-Nazi resistance in the Netherlands' in: *European Resistance Movements 1939–1945: First International Conference* pp.137–49. Louis de Jong, 'Britain and Dutch Resistance 1940–1945' in J Améry et al., *Proceedings of a Conference on Britain and European Resistance 1939–1945 Organised by St. Anthony's College, Oxford, 10–16 December 1962* (Oxford, 1964). Louis de Jong, 'The Dutch Resistance Movements and the Allies, 1940–1945' *European Resistance Movements: Proceedings of the Second International Conference*, pp.340–65. See also Ed Groeneveld, 'The Resistance in the Netherlands', in: Van Roon, *Europäischer Widerstand*, pp.309–21.

43. Richter Roegholt and Jacob Zwaan (eds), *Het Verzet, 1940–1945* (Weesp: Fibula-Van Dishoeck, 1985)

44. A brief summary of Blom's main arguments can be found in Bob Moore, 'Occupation, Collaboration and Resistance: Som Recent Publications on the Netherlands during the Second World War' *European History Quarterly* XXVI/1 (1991), pp.109–18.

45. Walter Maass, *The Netherlands at War 1940–1945* (London: Abelard-Schuman, 1970). J.H. Boas, *Religious Resistance in Holland* (London: Allen & Unwin, 1945) Henry L. Mason, *Mass Demonstrations*

Against Foreign regimes: A Study of Five Crises (New Orleans, 1966) J. Bruins Slot, 'Resistance', H. Touw, 'The Resistance of the Netherlands' Churches' W. Noordhoek Hegt, 'The Resistance of the Medical Profession' *Annals of the American Academy of Political and Social Sciences* CCXLV (May 1946), pp.144–8, 149–61, 162–8. There have also been a number of resistance memoirs and autobiographies translated into English, namely, Gerard Dogger, *The Square Moon: The True Story of a Dutch Resistance Leader* (Lewes: Book Guild, 1985). Erik Hazelhoff, *Soldier of Orange: The Dutch Resistance to the Nazis – A Personal Story of Defeat and Triumph, Danger and Heroism* (London: Hodder and Stoughton, 1972). Herman Friedhoff, *Requiem for the Resistance: The Civilian Struggle against Nazism in Holland and Germany* (London: Bloomsbury, 1988).

46. Michael L. Smith, 'Neither resistance nor Collaboration: Historians and the Problem of the *Nederlandse Unie*', *History* LXXII (1987), pp.251–78.

47. Tore Gjelsvik, *Norwegian Resistance* (London: C. Hurst & Co., 1979). Gerd Gordon Stray, *The Norwegian Resistance during the German Occupation, 1940–1945* (Pittsburgh: University of Pittsburgh Press, 1978) S. Kjelstadli, 'The Resistance Movement in Norway and the Allies, 1940–1945', *European Resistance Movements: Proceedings of the Second International Conference*, pp.324–39. See also Gunnar Sønsteby, *Report from No.24* (New York, 1965) and the more general work on the occupation, Johs. Andenes, Olav Riste and Magne Skodvin, *Norway and the Second World War* (Oslo: Tanum, 1966).

48. Olav Riste and Berit Nøkleby, *The Resistance Movement* (Oslo: Tanum, 1986)

49. Paul Wehr, 'Nonviolent Resistance to Nazism: Norway 1940–1945' *Peace and Change* X/3–4 (1984) pp.77–95.

50. Magne Skodvin (ed.), *Norge i Krig*, 8 Vols. (Oslo: Aschehoug, 1984–88) Magne Skodvin, *Norsk Historie 1939–1945: Krig og Okkupasjon* (Oslo: Det Norske Samlaget, 1992).

51. David Howarth, *The Shetland Bus* (London: Thomas Nelson, 1974). Oluf Reed Olsen, *Two Eggs on My Plate: Famous True Story in Wartime Norway* (London: Arrow, 1966). Dan Kurzman, *Blood and Water: Sabotaging Hitler's Bomb* (New York, 1997).

52. Jørgen Hæstrup, *Secret Alliance: A Study of the Danish Resistance Movement 1940–1945*, 3 vols (Odense: Odense University Press, 1976–7).

53. Jørgen Hæstrup, 'Denmark's Connection with the Allied Powers during the Occupation' in: *European Resistance Movements:*

Proceedings of the Second International Conference, pp.282–97. K.G.H. Hillingso, 'The Danish Resistance Movement and its Relations with Great Britain', *Revue Internationale d'Histoire Militaire* LIII (1982) pp.105–12.

54. Jeremy Bennett, *British Broadcasting and the Danish Resistance Movement 1940–1945: A Study of Wartime Broadcasts of the BBC Danish Service* (Cambridge: Cambridge University Press, 1966); E. Lund, *A Girdle of Truth. The Underground News Service Information 1943–1945* (Copenhagen, 1970).

55. Bjørn Schreiber Pedersen and Adam Holm, 'Restraining Excesses: Resistance and Counter-Resistance in Nazi-Occupied Denmark, 1940–1945' *Terrorism and Political Violence* X/1 (1998) pp.60–89.

56. Leo Goldberger (ed.), *The Rescue of Danish Jews: Moral Courage under Stress* (New York/London: New York University Press, 1987); Leni Yahil, *The Rescue of Danish Jews: Test of a Democracy* (Philadelphia: Jewish Publication Society, 1969). See also Gunnar S. Paulsson, 'The "Bridge over the Øresund": The Historiography on the Expulsion of the Jews from nazi-Occupied Denmark' and Hans Kirchhoff, 'Denmark: A Light in the Darkness of the Holocaust? A Reply to Gunnar S. Paulsson' *Journal of Contemporary History* XXX (1995) pp.431–64, 465–79. Henrik S. Nissen, *Scandinavia during the Second World War* (Minneapolis: Minnesota University Press, 1983)

57. Roberto Battaglia, *The Story of the Italian Resistance* (London: Odhams, 1957).

58. Charles Delzell, Mussolini's Enemies. The Italian Anti-Fascist Resistance (Princeton NJ: Princeton University Press, 1961).

59. Dante A. Puzzo, *The Partisans and the War in Italy* (New York: Peter Lang, 1993).

60. Guido Quazza, *Resistenza e storia italiana* (Milan: Feltrinelli, 1976). C. Pavone, *Una guerra civile. Saggio storico sulla moralità nella Resistenza* (Turin: Bollati Boringhieri, 1991). For a recent discussion of the debate, see Richard J.B. Bosworth, *The Italian Dictatorship: Problems and Perspectives in the Interpretation of Mussolini and Fascism* (London: Arnold, 1998) pp.180–204.

61. David W. Ellwood, *Italy 1943–1945* (Leicester: Leicester University Press, 1985).

62. Roger Absalom, 'Hiding History: The Allies, the Resistance and the Others in Occupied Italy 1943–1945' *Historical Journal* XXXVIII (1995) pp.111–31.

63. Jane Slaughter, *Women and the Italian Resistance* (Denver CO: Arden, 1995).

64. Richard Hanser, *A Noble Treason: The Revolt of the Munich Students against Hitler* (New York: Putnam, 1979). Inge Scholl, *Students Against Tyranny: The Resistance of the White Rose: Munich 1942–43* (Middletown CT: Weslyan University Press, 1970, 1983). Annette E. Dumbach and Jud Newborn, *Shattering the German Night: The Story of the White Rose* (Boston/Toronto: Little, Brown, 1986). Hans and Inge Scholl, *At the Heart of the White Rose: Letters and Diaries of Hans and Sophie Scholl* (New York: Harper & Row, 1987).

65. Peter Hoffmann, *The History of the German Resistance 1933–1945* (London: MacDonald & Jane's, 1977). Peter Hoffmann, *The German Resistance to Hitler* (Cambridge MS: Harvard University Press, 1988). Hermann Graml, Hans Mommsen, Hans-Joachim Reichhardt, Ernst Wolf, *The German Resistance to Hitler* (London: Batsford, 1970). Hans Rothfels, *The German Opposition to Hitler* (Hinsdale IL: Regnery, 1948 / London: G. Wolf, 1970). F.L. Carsten, *The German Resistance to Hitler* (Berkeley: University of California Press, 1970).

66. Klemens von Klemperer, *German Resistance Against Hitler: The Search for Allies Abroad 1938–1945* (Oxford: Oxford University Press, 1992).

67. Allan Merson, *Communist Resistance in Nazi Germany* (London: Lawrence & Wishart, 1985). For examples of local studies, see K. Bludau, *Gestapo Geheim! Widerstand und Vervolgung in Duisburg 1933–1945* (Bonn: Neue Gesellschaft Verlag für Literatur und Zaitgeschehen, 1973). K. Klotzbach, *Gegen der Nationalsozialismus: Widerstand und Verfolgung in Dortmund, 1930–1945* (Hannover, 1969).

68. This began with a major research project by the Institute for Contemporary History in Munich and culminated in the publication of a six volume series, Martin Broszat et al, *Bayern in der NS-Zeit* (Munich, 1977–83). See also H. Siefken, 'What is Resistance' in: H. Siefken and H. Vieregg (eds) *Resistance to National Socialism: Arbeiter, Christen, Jugendliche, Eliten* (Nottingham: Nottingham U.P., 1993) Ian Kershaw, *The Nazi Dictatorship*, 3rd edition (London: Arnold, 1993) chapter 8, pp.150–79.

69. Detlev Peuckert, *Inside Nazi Germany: Conformity, Opposition and Racism in Everyday Life* (New Haven CT: Yale University Press, 1987). Francis R. Nicosia and Lawrence D. Stokes (eds) *Germans Against Nazism: Nonconformity, Opposition and Resistance in the Third Reich* (New York: Berg, 1990) David Clay Large (ed.) *Contending with Hitler: Varieties of German Resistance in the Third Reich*

(Cambridge: Cambridge University Press, 1991). Michael Balfour, *Withstanding Hitler in Germany, 1933–1945* (London/New York: Routledge, 1988). Michael Geyer and John W. Boyer, 'Resistance Against the Third Reich' *Journal of Modern History* LXIV (1992). Supplement. T.S. Hamerow, *On the Road to the Wolf's Lair: German Resistance to Hitler* (Cambridge MS: Harvard University Press, 1997).

70. Anny Latour, *The Jewish Resistance in France (1940–1944)* (New York: Holocaust Library, 1981). Jacques Adler, *The Jews of Paris and the Final Solution: Communal Response and Internal Conflicts, 1940–1944* (Oxford: Oxford University Press, 1985). Lucien Lazare, *Rescue as Resistance: How Jewish Organisations Fought the Holocaust in France* (New York: Columbia University Press, 1996).

71. Claude Lévy, 'La Resistance Juive en France. De L'Enjeu de Memoire a L'Histoire Critique' *Vingtième Siècle* XXII (1989) pp.117–28. Henry H. Weinberg, 'The Debate over the Jewish Communist Resistance in France' *Contemporary French Civilisation* XV/1 (1991) pp.1–17.

72. Renee Poznanski, 'La Resistance Juive en France' *Revue d'Histoire de la Deuxième Guerre Mondiale et des Conflits Contemporains* 35/137 (1985), pp.3–32. See also, Renee Poznanski, 'A Methodological Approach to the Study of Jewish Resistance in France' *Yad Vashem Studies* XVIII (1987) pp.1–39.

73. Ben Braber, *Passage naar de Vrijheid: Joods Verzet in Nederland 1940–1945* (Amsterdam: Balans, 1987). Ben Braber, *Zelfs als wij zullen verliezen: Joden in Verzet en Illegaliteit* (Amsterdam: Balans, 1990). Reflections on Jewish self-help can be found in Bob Moore, *Victims and Survivors: The Nazi Persecution of the Jews in the Netherlands 1940–1945* (London: Arnold, 1997) pp.168–70.

74. Dan Michman (ed.) *Belgium and the Holocaust: Jews, Belgians, Germans* (Jerusalem: Yad Vashem, 1998). Oskar Mendelsohn, *The Persecution of the Norwegian Jews in World War II* (Oslo: Hjemmefrontmuseum, 1991). For comparative purposes, see also Arnold Paucker, *Jewish Resistance in Nazi Germany: The Facts and the Problems* (Berlin: Gedenkstätte Deutscher Widerstand, 1991).

—2—

Belgium

Pieter Lagrou

Introduction

Before independence in 1830, Belgian territory had experienced a long history of foreign occupation, with a succession of Spanish, Austrian, French and Dutch governors and their armies.[1] The 'Belgian revolution' of 1830 had been the feat of an *alliance de fortune* of Catholics and Liberals against a Dutch, Protestant and authoritarian King. Yet, the constitutional monarchy of 1830 proved to be a remarkably durable construction. In the second half of the nineteenth century Belgium became a haven of stability, liberalism and industrial growth, especially when compared with the turbulent constitutional history of France prior to 1870, with the economic and political retardation in the Netherlands and with the authoritarian politics of its German neighbour. By the beginning of the twentieth century, Belgium was a self-conscious modern European nation, with one of the continent's strongest economies and at the command of a huge colony in Africa.

Yet at the same time, Belgium was also a very divided nation.[2] The conflict between the liberals and the Catholics, who had both founded the nation, dominated political life all through the nineteenth century. During the last quarter of the century, a strong labour movement emerged to give voice to the political demands of a growing working class. A third source of division was the language question. French had traditionally been the language of administration and high culture, but from the late nineteenth century onwards, Flemish activists asked for the legal equality of French with Dutch, the language of a large majority of the most populous northern part of the country. The three cleavages dividing Belgian society – in chronological order, religion, class and language – followed a complicated trajectory. The southern, Walloon part was historically French-speaking and the northern part, Flanders, Dutch speaking. The bourgeois élites and nobility in Flanders were however

French speaking and labour migration from the north to the south had imported a Dutch speaking working-class minority into the Walloon part. The capital, Brussels, was situated in Flanders, but was overwhelmingly French speaking. The Walloon region was the heartland of the nineteenth century industrialization, based on coal mining and steel. Industrialization had engendered secularization and a strong labour movement. Flanders had been much less affected by early industrialization, remaining more rural and more Catholic.

As a result, political boundaries were not absolute and every individual had multiple allegiances – religion, class and language – which would alter the alliances according to the issue of the day. Even though Belgium shared a common language with two of its neighbours, France and the Netherlands, its political geography was substantially different: possessing neither the primacy of the left/right cleavage of post-revolutionary France, nor the religious compartmentalization of the pluri-denominational Dutch. The Belgian compromise satisfied most parties and national allegiance was accordingly strong in pre-1914 Belgium.

August 1914 brutally introduced Belgium to the twentieth century.[3] In order to attack France through its weakest northern flank, the German armies violated Belgian neutrality. Despite fierce resistance, the Belgian troops were soon forced to retreat behind the Yser river, in a tiny north-western corner of the country, adjoining the French border. The government and the king, Albert I, established their headquarters in the French town of Le Havre, at a safe distance from the front lines. The German invasion had been accompanied by random violence against civilian populations and massive destruction. The ensuing occupation and the continental blockade strangled the Belgian economy and threatened to cause famine, and in 1917 the Germans deported over 120,000 Belgian workers to Germany. The reaction of Belgian society was one of patriotic solidarity against the enemy, both at home and abroad. At home, the leading economic élites organized food distribution and relief work and associated a wide range of organizations in this task. The government, which at the eve of the invasion had included the Labour Party for the first time in its history, continued the war from Le Havre. The king and that part of the army which had made a timely retreat, championed the national cause and reached unrivalled levels of popularity at the time of the armistice. German efforts to dismember Belgium by divisive policies were unsuccessful. These efforts had targeted primarily the Flemish nationalists, with promises of Flemish independence after a German victory and decreeing the administrative separation of Flanders and the Walloon part of Belgium in March 1917. Except for some support in the most radical quarters, national loyalty was strengthened, rather than weakened, by the war. The German generals faced national dissension at home long before they saw the first effects of their deliberately divisive policies in Belgium.

The Great War radicalized European society and politics, and Belgium was no exception to this process. King and government had anticipated this radicalization by granting the long-standing Labour Party demand for universal suffrage. This revolution of the electoral system transformed the political landscape. The parties of the leisured classes could no longer content themselves with a cosy delicate balance of their own interests, but had to conquer the masses and challenge the new radical parties. Even if the nation had been strengthened by the war, the new postwar challenges would destabilize it: reconstruction and economic crisis, political polarization and governmental instability. The alternation of Catholic and Liberal regimes gave way to changing multi-party coalitions including the Labour Party. The Catholic party itself lost its pre-war cohesion, with its electorate spread over all social classes. By the 1930s, the political landscape had become increasingly complex, and included a communist party and new fascist parties. Flemish nationalism had become more radical. A new influential movement had emerged after 1918, animated by war veterans who had discovered Flemish nationalism in the trenches in an army commanded by French speaking officers who had shown nothing but contempt for Flemish soldiers. The 'Front movement' initially pressed for Flemish language rights, democracy and pacifism, but a large wing soon moved away from this ideological platform and joined up with the authoritarianism and pro-German sentiments of the frustrated former collaborationists.[4] Some Belgian patriots had also been frustrated by the first convulsions of mass democracy and evolved in an authoritarian direction. This included the fascist Rex movement of Léon Degrelle, which was a radical offspring of the Catholic movement, but also more mainstream figures in the Catholic party and even socialists, such as chairman Henri De Man.[5] It certainly appealed to King Leopold III, who had succeeded his father in 1934 and who expressed his dissatisfaction with 'parliamentarism'.[6] On the eve of the Second World War, Belgian society was more democratic than it had been at the outbreak of World War One, but at the same time the apprenticeship with universal suffrage had been short and its results unconvincing in the eyes of many people. Political polarization had radicalized large groups of the electorate and both economically and politically, the atmosphere seemed insecure. Ideological experiments on the left and on the right with corporatism and a more authoritarian state had weakened the political consensus. Part of the Flemish movement was disgruntled with the slow progress of Flemish claims and increasingly turned its back on democracy.

Resisting Nazi Occupation

In 1936, when the threat of war became ever more present, Belgium returned to the policy of neutrality that had proved so disastrous in 1914.[7] On 10 May 1940, the German army did indeed invade Belgium, just as it had done only twenty-six years earlier.[8] August 1914 was on everybody's mind in May 1940, even those from the younger generation, the only ones who had not directly experienced it. Over 1.5 million Belgian citizens – about one fifth of the population – fled southwards, fearing a repetition of the atrocities of 1914.[9] So did the Belgian government, confident that the French and British armies would stop Hitler's advance and allow the Belgian army to continue the war at their side. King Leopold III made a different evaluation of the situation and decided on his own authority as commander-in-chief of the Belgian army, to surrender to the German invader after eighteen days of combat. Public opinion was at first grateful for this early surrender which had spared the army further useless bloodshed, and the complete collapse of France in June seemed further justification for this action. With Hitler's *Blitzkrieg*, a new era had started in the history of warfare, destroying all parallels with the immobilized war of the trenches. Having achieved the inconceivable – forcing the heroes of Verdun into a humiliating ceasefire in only six weeks – the Nazi army seemed invincible. In this light, the Nazi domination of the European continent seemed destined to last and any anticipation of their defeat entirely unrealistic. Moreover, the Nazi troops behaved in a disciplined way in 1940, unlike their forebears. The army had received instructions that war aims in the West were first of all pacification – that is, occupation and economic exploitation using as few German troops as possible – not the *Vernichtungskrieg* it had earlier initiated in Poland with the systematic brutalization of civilians and large-scale murder. The Belgian population was positively impressed and in the course of the summer of 1940 hundreds of thousands of refugees returned to the country.[10]

Meanwhile, the Belgian government fell prey to despair: the country it had chosen as a refuge had collapsed. Affected by the morose climate in which Pétain took power, the Belgian cabinet tried to return home, and even to resign – requests which were refused by Hitler and King Leopold respectively.[11] A message informing the British government that Belgium had pulled out of the war was intercepted by her ambassador in London and never delivered. It took several months before the main

Cabinet ministers could be convinced by their minister for the colonies that the Congo remained a major asset in their hands – an asset the British would soon confiscate if the government did not cross the Channel and ally itself with Britain. By the end of October, after a difficult journey, including imprisonment in Franco's Spain, Prime Minster Hubert Pierlot and Foreign Minister Paul-Henri Spaak arrived in London and finally set up a war Cabinet-in-exile. The government had virtually vanished for four months, having left the Belgian administration bereft of instructions and guidance to face the overwhelming practical problems created by invasion and defeat. It was repudiated by the King, ignored by Hitler, and remained unpopular in Belgium itself, where its exile was resented as desertion,

During the summer of 1940, the climate would have been ripe for the creation, with German blessing, of a new collaborationist regime. King Leopold aspired to play a role not unlike the one played in France by Marshal Pétain, as national saviour and leader of the national renaissance. He could thereby count on the support and collaboration of some first-rate pre-war politicians, the most prominent of whom was Henri De Man, president of the socialist party.[12] Yet, no German blessing came. There was no pre-existing plan in Hitler's mind for the political restructuring of the European continent after a total German victory.[13] Wild projections redrafting the map of Europe, incorporating the small nations of north western Europe into the *Reich* coexisted with the pragmatic attitude to postpone radical decisions – and the widespread resistance they were likely to provoke – until after the hostilities were over. While the war was on – the battle of Britain first, soon followed by the preparations for the attack on the Soviet Union – German troops were needed for other, more urgent tasks. Both attitudes were epitomized in the conflict between the army, which had the first responsibility of the occupation policy in Belgium (*Militärverwaltung*) and was directly interested in law and order at the smallest military cost, and the Nazi party, with its radical ideologues impatient to implement nazification and racial policies in the conquered territories.[14]

This policy limited the boundless political ambitions of Nazi Germany's most radical ideological allies in Belgium. The two main fascist parties, the Flemish VNV and the French-speaking Rex, nonetheless enjoyed a very privileged status.[15] While all other political parties were forbidden and dissolved, their belongings confiscated and their press silenced, Rex and VNV enjoyed protection, subsidies for their propaganda and appointments for their militants at all levels of the administration. They were brought in either to replace less cooperative civil servants, or as part of structural changes, such as the imposition of a new age limit for mayors and the wholesale replacement of older incumbents by younger men who espoused the New Order. Their expansion through youth organizations, cultural associations and paramilitary militias was encouraged. Even though these parties initially increased their membership, helped by the new climate created by Nazi victory and by sheer political opportunism, they soon reached their limit, and, when the occupation grew harsher, they were the first targets of popular resentment and hatred. Moreover, they grew frustrated by the prudence of the German authorities who refused to give them a leading role in the occupation and even pitted rival collaborationist formations against each other. The Nazi authorities also re-enacted a new version of the *Flamenpolitik* of World War One, deliberately discriminating between Flanders and the Walloon part of Belgium. The crudest discrimination was the early liberation of all Flemish POWs and the prolonged captivity of their Walloon counterparts. Even though the Flemish collaborators could argue that they had obtained greater German 'concessions' than the desperate collaboration drive of Léon Degrelle's *Rex*, they would increasingly become isolated from mainstream Flemish nationalism, which rejected their authoritarianism and betrayal of Flemish autonomy to German subservience.

With the legitimate government abroad, the King politically impotent and a 'prisoner of war', and Hitler abstaining from creating a new collaborationist government, the German military authorities appealed directly to the highest civil servants in the Belgian administration to manage day-to-day affairs. Faced with a political vacuum, these secretaries-general agreed to cooperate with the occupier to help the population and avoid chaos and also to avoid their replacement by sympathizers of the Nazi New Order.[16] They were forced to walk the thin line between obstruction and acquiescence in a slowly degenerating atmosphere of increasing German demands as the military situation worsened, with resignation as their only bargaining counter. The economic élites faced a similar dilemma: refusal to cooperate could lead to the dismantling of the economic infrastructure and the deportation of workers.[17] At the end of the war, both groups would claim that their strategy had retarded the implementation of Nazi policies and avoided worse. Some even went so far as to call their 'obstructive cooperation' a form of resistance against the enemy. This is not a definition that will be accepted here. A definition of 'resistance' in terms of its effects or functions – that is, did it counter the plans and policies of the enemy or did it at least constitute a 'nuisance factor'? – leaves much open to subjective appreciation and 'what if' suppositions. We will consider resistance from a more legalistic angle, namely activities against enemy aims, forbidden by the enemy and thus involving real risks for its perpetrators.[18]

For a proper understanding of the nature of the resistance against Nazi occupation in Belgium, it is essential to characterize the nature of this occupation. One of the main German aims in Western Europe was to avoid provoking large-scale resistance and this policy was to some extent successful.[19] In Poland, in the occupied regions of the Soviet Union, and in the Balkans, resistance was a matter of survival, since decimation of the local population was one of the main aims of the war on the Eastern front. The radicalism of the partisan war was provoked by the radical, murderous Nazi war. In some countries, such as France, or Italy after September 1943, the Nazi occupiers played on national divisions and accepted the services of local collaborationist regimes. In France, the Vichy regime was intent on taking an ideological revenge on the Front Populaire and even on the anticlerical Third Republic. In Italy, the occupiers used the radical fringe of the fascist regime in the puppet Salò Republic. In these cases, resistance against the foreign invader was inseparable from an internal civil war. However, the lack of a collaborationist regime in Belgium and the 'wait and see' attitude of the German occupier in Belgium, as in the Netherlands and Denmark, provoked a 'wait and see' attitude in large sections of Belgian society.

The nature of the occupation changed over time and it is this evolution that explains the evolution of resistance over time.[20] As the occupation radicalized, so did the resistance; as the occupier targeted new groups, so new groups entered into resistance action. Some correlation of proportionate response does provide a clue to understanding the evolution of 'resistance'. To moderate pressure, the occupied society answered with moderate protests. The sanctions on radical action were such that only two sorts of individuals or groups chose to endanger their lives: those whose lives were already directly threatened by the occupier and those inclined to radical action by tradition, temperament or political convictions. In the case of communists and prewar anti-fascists, both elements could very well coincide. A rough chronology can schematically distinguish three decisive moments in the entry of three different categories of individuals into active resistance: (a) the resurgence of Belgian patriotism and the milieus of veterans of World War One in 1940; (b) the unambiguous entry of the Communist Party into radical resistance after the invasion of the Soviet Union in June 1941, thus mobilizing a much larger anti-fascist constituency; (c) the broadening of resistance in late 1942 and early 1943, occasioned by the introduction of compulsory labour service and the turn of war at Stalingrad.

The patriots of the 'first hour'

The resilience of Belgian patriotism in the wake of the defeat of 1940 constitutes one of the particularities of Belgium in the European theatre. The echo of the Great War dominated these very early expressions of resistance, in the symbolism of the references, in the forms of action chosen and even, most spectacularly, in the very individuals who were at the forefront of these activities.

Military defeat had created a number of pressing problems. One was of isolated Allied soldiers who had gone into hiding or who had succeeded in escaping from captivity after having been captured on the battlefield.[21] MI9 had anticipated this problem by sending agents to the continent to make arrangements for new networks. Escape lines had been efficiently organized in occupied Belgium during World War I and executed heroines like Edith Cavell and Gabrielle Petit figured in the national memory as martyrs. British soldiers could count on the sympathy and assistance of the local population to offer shelter and food and, eventually, assistance to leave the country. One famous example involved four British soldiers, hidden for eight months in a village not far from Brussels.[22] Two of them were arrested at the demarcation line in France and taken into captivity, but the other two succeeded in returning to Britain. However, the operation cost the lives of seven of their helpers in Belgium after infiltration by agents of the German Abwehr. British servicemen had little to lose in an escape: if caught, they became prisoners of war, which would have been their fate anyway if they didn't try to escape. For their helpers, arrest meant death or a concentration camp. For the British army, the retrieval of experienced servicemen was priceless, not only because of the major psychological impact of their return, but also because the scarcity of trained pilots and technicians and the difficulty of replacing them made the return of downed air crew invaluable.

The organization of an escape line required sophisticated networks able to trace downed air crew as rapidly as possible, to screen the candidates to weed out German agents, to hide escapees and to provide them with civilian clothing and false identity papers for their journey through Belgium, France and Spain. Furthermore, it was essential to accompany them on their journey to avoid their being betrayed by their mother tongue, assuring them of safe hiding places on strategic points of the route, guides for crossing the Pyrenees and contacts in Spain to organize their evacuation to Britain. The logistics of such escape lines necessitated a high level of female participation and members were recruited from patriotic, pro-British milieus, especially amongst the aristocracy.[23] The most famous escape line was Comète, directed by a young woman, Andrée De Jongh.[24] Fiercely autonomous from both British and Belgian secret services, the network helped over 700 Allied servicemen to escape from Belgium through France and Spain, and involved the active participation of 2,000 volunteers. Over one-hundred-and-fifty, one-third of them women, paid for their activity with their lives. Other escape lines worked directly for the SOE, most notably the network of the Belgian agent Albert Guérisse in France, known under his codename Pat O'Leary.[25]

Intelligence networks had a similar profile. They orginated in the desire to 'do something' immediately after the defeat, a feeling that was strong in some military circles which had been so rapidly forced out of the war and for whom gathering military intelligence was the only way to contribute to the ongoing conflict.[26] They were strongly pro-British and often forged stronger links directly with the British Services than with their own government-in-exile. Patriotism was again their major motivation and references to World War One were ever present, when the Belgian network La Dame Blanche had been a major source of Allied intelligence from behind the German front line. Some of the founders of the networks were old British contacts or old 'rats' of the Great War, such as Walthère Dewè and Anatole Gobeaux.[27] Georges Leclercq, of the major Belgian network Luc, (later, for safety reasons, named Marc) had been a volunteer during the Great War and he named his organization after his son, who was killed by the Germans during the invasion and whose death he intended to revenge.[28] In the course of the war, forty-three intelligence networks were set up on Belgian territory, involving over eighteen thousand individuals.[29]

With the escape lines, intelligence was the resistance activity most appreciated by the British, as it provided information on German military movements and logistics on the ground. This facilitated the execution of air raids on transports, airfields, coastal defence constructions and other military targets, and ultimately the preparations for an Allied invasion. The Belgian government-in-exile was even more dependent on intelligence to keep abreast of what was going on at home, and its hunger for economic, social and political information was almost limitless.[30] It wanted assessments of public opinion, attitudes towards the king, the government itself and the occupation authorities. It also wanted details of collaborationist and other new social and political movements. The main technical problem for intelligence work was matching supply with demand and then finding ways to send information across the Channel safely. A further problem was whether to prioritize the British Services or the Belgian government-in-exile.

Until late in 1941, local intelligence networks had no direct radio contact with London. Reports, based on thousands of local individual observations were microfilmed and smuggled out of the country, through consular services in Vichy, Switzerland, Spain or Portugal. Few of them ever reached their destination. German counterespionage was continually infiltrating networks and inflicting great damage. The *Englandspiel* and its most sinister agent, Prosper De Zitter, rank as one of the greatest successes of counterespionage in the twentieth century. Even some networks set up by British agents, parachuted with radio equipment in occupied territory, were trapped. Until August 1941, the British Secret Intelligence Service (SIS) and the Sûreté d'État, which was set up by the Belgian government, worked independently, without any coordination and often in a climate of rivalry and mistrust. Only later did an agreement facilitate closer cooperation and the exchange of information on missions, agents and networks. Radio contact was established with the major networks through parachute drops of equipment and radio operators and reliable routes were established for the delivery of microfilmed reports – with a delay which took from six to twelve weeks – and these remained the main channel of communication until the end of the war. The British SIS expressed itself very satisfied with the quality of intelligence from Belgium, gathered by experienced agents. Likewise, the Belgian Prime Minister declared that by 1944, occupied Belgium was a 'glass house' for his government, thanks to detailed intelligence, amounting to tens of thousands of pages per week, but it had taken several years to reach this point.

A third expression of the patriotic military refusal to accept defeat – after escape lines and intelligence gathering – was the efforts to recreate an underground Belgian army. Originating among former career officers, these first groups had a decidedly conservative outlook which involved attempts to reconstitute a secret military hierarchy, register regiment listings of volunteer soldiers, eventually even gathering traditional military equipment for the recreation of a new regular army.[31] Their military ambition was limited: there was no question of engaging these troops in a combat with the occupying army; the entire organization was intended to prepare for the period after a liberation that could only come from abroad. Inconsiderate action before that date could only endanger the carefully built structure. With this went a reactionary political programme: the task of this new army would be to assure the maintenance of law and order after a German retreat. They professed an unswerving admiration of King Leopold, but contempt for 'parliamentarism' and the London government. They also espoused an authoritarian conception of the future postwar state and viewed communists and collaborationists as their main enemies. These initiatives were very comparable, at least in their early stages, with the development of the Dutch Ordedienst. From being a rather closed circle of active and reserve officers, the many groups that emerged during the summer of 1940 were ultimately merged into one formation, the Belgian Legion, early in 1941. During the course of that year, the organization purged itself of its most openly reactionary leaders, who had published a brochure pleading for a policy of neutrality and an authoritarian state. It also discovered the dangers of its very formal organizational structures when a wave of arrests removed its entire staff in one of the Belgian provinces.

In August 1942, its leader, Charles Claser, succeeded in crossing the Channel and reached London, where he was welcomed by the SOE. The SOE was created in July 1940, in the midst of the Battle of Britain, to carry the war back to the continent and mobilize local resources for widespread sabotage – in Winston Churchill's words, 'to set Europe ablaze'.[32] Successive SOE missions to occupied Belgium had produced few successes and SOE was accordingly relieved by Claser's offer of a ready made underground army willing to undertake carefully selected sabotage actions. The Belgian government was much less welcoming. Claser's allegiance to the king, his contempt for the government-in-exile and his political ambitions for restoring law and order after the liberation were at odds with the governments own plans. SOE did not consult with the Belgian government, who accordingly disavowed Claser through its own connections with the occupied country and broke off its contacts with SOE. The rivalry between SIS, with whom the government had good contacts, and SOE did not improve the situation. Unconvinced of its military effectiveness, SIS considered sabotage mostly as a perilous strategy, exposing precious intelligence networks to merciless repression. Only the arrest of the complete Belgian Legion leadership after it had been infiltrated by the Abwehr agent Prosper De Zitter, prompted a new start and a reconciliation between the Belgian government, SOE and the Belgian Legion.

At the end of 1942, the three parties agreed on mutual recognition, on condition that the military formations limited themselves to fighting the enemy and contributing to the liberation, after which their task would be over. Successive arrests in the course of 1943 weakened the organization and permanent links with the government-in-exile were established only at the beginning of 1944. At the government's insistence, the military formations adopted the name of 'Secret Army of Belgium', to underline that the organization would be dissolved after the liberation and a new regular army created, with a new hierarchy. The Secret Army also forswore all its ambitions for internal policing at the liberation. Of all the resistance formations, the Secret Army received the most financial aid and weapons' deliveries. Even though some specific sabotage actions were undertaken on orders from SOE, its activity only really started with the Allied landings in June 1944, when there was large scale sabotage of the railroad network. During the battles for liberation, which were relatively short because of the rapid German withdrawal, thousands of Secret Army volunteers assisted the Allied troops and 4,000 were killed.[33] After the war, it claimed a membership of more than 50,000, but this should be treated with caution, as most of them only joined at the very end of the occupation period.

Patriotic responses were not limited to these three highly organized forms of 'resistance'. Anti-German feelings found expression in many individual diffuse acts of sabotage, where German telephone cables were the main target.[34] The first reported acts of 'vandalism' date from June 1940 and, faced with an increase in these acts, the German authorities were obliged to publish severe warnings to the population in July.[35] In August, 30 hostages were taken after large-scale destruction in Zaventem, only to be released a little later. In spite of threats to reintern released prisoners of war, or extensions to the curfew, the German authorities tried not to antagonize the population or to publicise these sabotage actions, which they quite correctly interpreted as expressions of the 'widespread hatred of Germany, present as well in Flanders as in the Walloon part of Belgium'.[36] Between May 1940 and March 1941, the German authorities registered on average more than one act of sabotage per day, which was more a source of constant irritation than a genuine hindrance.[37] In the second half of 1941, after the Communist Party had become involved in resistance, this number would triple and the German reactions would escalate. The first death sentences on convicted saboteurs were handed down and carried out in August 1941. By the end of the year, the German authorities resorted to the execution of hostages at random when the perpetrators could not be arrested. As a result of the high price paid by innocent victims due to German retaliation, compared to the limited benefits for the Allied cause, the Belgian government did not encourage sabotage, which was another source of discord with SOE. Quite distinct from these early individual and uncoordinated acts were the well prepared and meticulously implemented sabotage actions by the Groupe G, a sabotage team headed by scientists and engineers of the University of Brussels.[38] This team inflicted substantial damage on the Belgian transportation network, particularly railroads and waterways, electricity supplies and telephone communications, especially in the last two years of the occupation. Actions were carefully planned, targets strategically chosen, and destruction limited to harm the German troops as much as possible while doing minimal damage to Belgian infrastructure.

Escape lines, intelligence, secret military formations and sabotage were four ways to circumvent the military impotence of the Belgian nation after the defeat and to make a modest contribution to the ongoing war against Germany. All four involved a limited group of people, working in the greatest secrecy, hidden not only from the German authorities, but also from the overwhelming majority of their fellow citizens. The most important expression of Belgian patriotism in the wake of the defeat and all through the occupation years was therefore the underground press.[39] Here again the Great War was the central reference point, when *La Libre Belgique* had been the internationally celebrated voice of the occupied country. It is no coincidence that major Dutch and French underground newspapers found inspiration for their titles from this illustrious Belgian, Great War publication. By October 1940, no less than eight different underground papers appeared in Belgium using the title of their glorious forebear. In addition, there was also some continuity of personnel. Camille Joset, editor of the second most important clandestine newspaper, *La voix des Belges*, was a hero of the resistance during the Great War, who by the end of the war could claim to have been condemned to death by two successive German occupation authorities.

The clandestine publications of 1940 were mostly home-produced, small-scale initiatives. Two thirds of the hundred or so different titles were stencilled and had between one and four pages. Less than a quarter had a circulation of more than two hundred copies and about half of them were produced by one individual or one family. The centre for these publications was Brussels, and the overwhelming majority was written in French. Rather than elaborate political programmes, their content consisted of traditional patriotism, with anti-German rather than anti-Nazi sentiments and a tendency to be pro-British rather than in favour of the government-in-exile. References to World War One, to King Albert, Cardinal Mercier and Adolphe Max (the heroic mayor of Brussels during the Great War) abounded. Originating mainly in bourgeois patriotic circles, the impact of these clandestine papers can hardly be overestimated. In a context of a censored press and massive amounts of German propaganda, they constituted a powerful counterweight and a demonstration of continuing independence of mind. Leaflets passed through many hands and, even if the production was originally an individual undertaking, the distribution of clandestine newspapers created networks of kindred spirits that would often constitute embryonic resistance organizations.

As the resistance against the occupation increased, the size of the underground press grew, both in the number of titles and in the circulation: 567 different titles and over 4,000 different issues are recorded for the entire occupation period, encompassing a whole range of political tendencies.[40] The Independence Front, whose actions will be detailed below, was one of the main publishers, with 167 different titles. It was also behind the most famous exploit of the occupation years: the 'fake' issue of *Soir*. *Soir* was the most popular newspaper authorized and controlled by the German authorities. On 9 November 1943, 50,000 copies with an identical title and layout, but with a sarcastic content ridiculing the collaboration newspaper, and including a press communiqué announcing a German surrender, was delivered to the usual news-stands in Brussels minutes before the arrival of the real *Soir*, to the joy and hilarity of thousands of readers. Clandestine publishing was nevertheless a perilous activity, mercilessly repressed by the Nazi authorities. Over 2,000 printers, writers and distributors were killed as a consequence of their actions, including 17 of the team of 22 behind the fake *Soir*. Through an extensive readership, who were very often also regular listeners to the BBC broadcasts, and spread even further by the word of mouth, the clandestine press was nonetheless the most effective form of subversion against a Nazi New Order that sought to control all spheres of public life.

The clearest expression of a widespread patriotic rejection of the German occupation in 1940 came on 11 November.[41] The commemoration of the Allied victory over Germany in 1918 had been an official holiday since 1922 and it had become a crucial date in the life of the nation. The German authorities predictably forebade all public demonstrations on 11 November, only allowing the Belgian population to honour their dead on the following Sunday, 15 November. As soon as the prohibition was published at the end of October, leaflets, graffiti, posters and intense vocal protest emerged, all demanding a public commemoration in spite of the German ban. On 11 November, gatherings were held in Antwerp, Liège, Charleroi, Mons and Verviers, followed by dozens of arrests, especially of war veterans and students carrying Union Jacks or RAF insignia. Yet the most impressive protest was staged in the capital. At the tomb of the unknown soldier and the British monument in Brussels, several thousands of protesters sang the national anthem, shouted slogans, including '*Vive l'Angleterre*' (Long live England) and even *Sales Boches* (Krauts stink), all this being rather ostensibly tolerated by the municipal police. A war veteran who addressed the crowd with a short speech was immediately arrested and the crowd dispersed by the German Feldgendarmerie.

What all these early manifestations of resistance had in common was their bourgeois patriotic origins and their reference to traditional symbols and forms of action (with the exception of sabotage). They were therefore mainly the achievements of isolated individuals or tight networks, rooted in specific social circles: career officers, war veterans, anglophile aristocracy, urban patriots. Even the 11 November demonstrations were urban, bourgeois phenomena and the occupier was eager to underline they did not involve workers leaving their factories or provincials joining up with the urbanites.[42] They all sprang from a spontaneous rejection of the occupation by groups and individuals who were not personally experiencing any special hardship. Indeed, the circles that were over-represented in this early stage were better protected from the scarcity of food and the massive unemployment that hit the lower classes during the first year of the occupation. Their actions were rooted in nationalist sentiment, albeit not always of the most democratic brand, or in a more enlightened attachment to the principles of the liberal state, which were being systematically trampled by the Germans. However, this rejection of authoritarian methods only became stronger when the methods of the occupier become more ruthless and bloody, and when it became linked with the anti-fascist resistance. Only then did forces from all quarters of society join together to form the basis for a mass movement.

Anti-fascists: Ideology and Persecution

Resistance in the early years of the occupation was never exclusively a bourgeois affair but certain types of action and certain modes of organization had their natural homes in these particular social circles. However, resistance based in other social classes, while it might have taken longer to emerge, nonetheless proved to be more influential and effective in the longer run.

Whereas patriots saw Germany as their enemy, anti-fascists identified fascism and more particularly its German version, Nazism, with its explicit racism and its cult of violence, as the enemy. Anti-fascism had been a crucial component of left-wing identity in the 1930s.[43] Belgium had hosted political refugees from Italy and Germany and solidarity with the Spanish Republicans during the Civil War had been a formative experience for a generation of young militants. Anti-fascism was not a marginal affair of a radical minority but mobilized many in the Parti Ouvrier Belge (POB – Party of Labour) too. With the international solidarity movement came a visceral rejection of Belgian fascist movements. The parades of Rex, Dinaso, VNV and their militias never came near to dominating the streets as their Italian and German counterparts had done and they certainly took more beatings from anti-fascist counter-demonstrations than they dispensed.[44] Yet, at the time of the German invasion, the anti-fascist movement itself was in deep crisis and its main protagonists paralysed.

Part of the crisis originated outside the country. All through the 1930s, the Communist Party had been ferociously engaged in the anti-fascist campaign.[45] It had the closest contacts with Italian, Spanish and German exiles and contributed the largest contingent to the 2,000 Belgian volunteers for the international brigades.[46] Its militants were at the forefront of anti-fascist demonstrations and the Party publicly criticized the Belgian policy of neutrality, the Anglo-French concessions to Hitler in Munich, and the recognition of the Franco government by the socialist Minister of Foreign Affairs, Paul-Henri Spaak, in March 1939. The Party and its militants were accordingly thunderstruck by the Nazi–Soviet non-aggression pact of 23 August 1939.[47] The psychological and organizational dependence of the Communist Party on the Soviet Union was such that a rupture with the homeland of scientific socialism was unthinkable. Guided by its Komintern instructor, the Party now improvised a new political line, replacing its radical anti-fascism by the slogan *Ni Londres, Ni Berlin* (neither London nor Berlin), with an emphasis on the condemnation of the imperialism of the capitalist countries. This sudden change disorientated many militants and isolated them, particularly from their erstwhile allies among the socialist. In contrast to France, the Party was not officially dissolved, nor were its militants arrested – which would have been difficult, given Belgium's status as a neutral country – but its newspapers were forbidden and the authorities compiled lists of militants to be arrested in the event of a German invasion. In this atmosphere, the Party gradually shifted its activities towards a semi-clandestine existence.

At the time of the invasion, a few hundred communist militants were arrested by the Belgian authorities and transferred to camps in the south of France – together with Belgian Nazi's and German nationals (mostly anti-fascists exiles or Jewish refugees). The invasion did not alter the Party's political line: it refused to choose sides in the conflict between Nazism and capitalist imperialism. The Party then tried to obtain official permission from the Germans to publish its party newspaper. This was refused, but it did publish a Flemish newspaper with permission, defending an ambiguous position of neutrality – all the more ambiguous as a foreign army occupied the country. Yet the constraints of occupation would soon stir different reactions at local level, where communist militants engaged in protests against food shortages and wage freezes, organizing house-wives' demonstrations and limited strikes, which partially paralysed the coal mines in the first months of 1941. At the same time the Party also developed a clandestine press, mostly for internal consumption. Even though the content was slightly more critical of the German occupier, the line of these clandestine papers did not fundamentally diverge from the official line of neutrality in a conflict that it pretended did not affect the Communist Party and its constituency.

The other part of the crisis of anti-fascism was entirely internal. The disarray of the communists following the Hitler–Stalin agreement did not benefit the POB. Having endured years of vitriolic condemnation by the communists for their supposed lack of anti-fascist zeal and participation in coalition governments after 1936, the POB was only too keen to denounce the duplicity and servility of the communists. However, the defeat of the Belgian army was rapidly followed by the collapse of the POB. As mentioned earlier, its president, Henri De Man, was the main initiator of a project for a 'Belgian Vichy', a new authoritarian regime around King Leopold. To clear the way for a new unitary political movement supportive of the new regime, De Man published a manifesto on 28 June 1940, dissolving the Labour Party and calling upon its members to join the new organization. De Man had mistakenly anticipated Hitler's intentions in relation to Belgium and his call destroyed his political career, but the consequences for the POB were equally disastrous. The Party was affiliated with the socialist trade union, which became the object of a New Order reorganization, through the creation of a new unitary corporatist Union in which all prewar unions were supposed to merge. Entirely controlled by the occupying power, it lost all legitimacy in less than a year, thereby drawing the participating unions into disrepute and creating a profound division between those who had refused to join the collaborationist venture and those who only repented at a later date.

It would take years for the socialists to free themselves from this morass and rebuild the Party and the union using a new generation of grassroots militants.[48] Ultimately this was an astounding success and, by the time of the liberation, the Party was able to re-emerge, but the result of the profound crisis of Belgian socialism during the occupation was that it concentrated all its efforts on its own regeneration rather than on the external enemy. Socialists also felt too threatened by the dynamism of the Communist Party after the summer of 1941 to ally with any of their organizations. At the same time they were well aware of their comparative weakness *vis-à-vis* the Catholic movement, whose immense institutional structures had been left untouched by the occupier and whose sense of self-preservation had protected it against the hazards of war and occupation and even created opportunities for proselytizing. By September 1941, a new clandestine Party of Labour organization had emerged that concentrated its efforts on preparations for postwar reconstruction, primarily through the pages of the Party's clandestine press.

On 22 June 1941, Hitler invaded the Soviet Union. This was accompanied by massive roundups of communist militants in all the occupied countries. German police authorities had made good use of the year of Nazi-Communist truce to observe the communist parties and blacklist their members.[49] In the Netherlands, where the Communist Party was only 25% of the size of the Belgian party, 500 militants and Party members were arrested, a quarter of the total membership. In France, where the Communist Party had been outlawed and persecuted since September 1939, many thousands of militants were arrested in June 1941. Comparatively, the damage to the Belgian Party apparatus was limited, with 300 arrests on a pre-war membership estimated at around 10,000. This was largely due to the refusal of the Belgian police to participate in the roundups. Still, the invasion and the arrests radically changed the situation for the Belgian Communist Party. Instead of standing aside in an ambiguous neutrality, the war had now become a matter of survival – survival of the Party apparatus in the face of Nazi persecution and survival of the Soviet Union, whose dire military situation had to be relieved through the opening of a 'third' internal front, while waiting on the opening of a genuine 'second' Western front. On instruction from the Komintern, the Party now designed a radically new strategy, involving on the one hand the organization of a broad national resistance coalition, the Independence Front, encompassing all social and political forces, and on the other hand a proper guerrilla force, the 'partisans'.

The organization, recruitment and the activities of the partisans evolved significantly during the course of the war.[50] The first generation of partisans were recruited from the inner circle of longstanding Party members, experienced and disciplined militants, whose loyalty to the Soviet Union was a major motivation in taking the high risks involved in clandestine warfare. In the mining region of the Borinage, the first partisan teams united veterans of the International Brigades with communist miners who had access to dynamite and were able to stage spectacular bombings of heavy industrial infrastructure. In Brussels the first teams were recruited in the intellectual milieu of engineers and scientists, all prewar anti-fascists and Party members, and whose main targets were German transportation and fuel supplies.

By the end of 1941, the strategy of avoiding human targets in sabotage actions was abandoned in response to heavy German repression. In December 1941 the Communist leader and Member of Parliament,

Georges Cordier, was tortured to death and in the following weeks seventeen communists were executed and several dozens sentenced to death or deported to Germany. The tone of the communist underground press became more extreme in the first months of 1942, focusing its feelings of hatred and revenge on the Belgian collaborationists who assisted the Germans in their effort and paraded their support for the Nazis in the streets. In April 1942, for example, it announced that all collaborators would 'perish as dogs'.[51] At the same time, the partisans began executing well-known informers who were blamed for the deaths of communist militants. Bombings also caused panic at gatherings of SS volunteers leaving for the Eastern Front. In the second half of 1942, the assassination of collaborationist personnel became an integral part of the partisan strategy, with sixty killings of symbolically chosen dignitaries of the Belgian New Order: mayors, collaborating police officers and officials of the labour offices who were starting to implement the labour draft for Germany. The campaign culminated in November 1942 with the assassination of three Rexist mayors, the most famous of whom was Jean Teughels of Charleroi. Members of collaboration movements started to feel threatened – which was precisely the intended effect of the killings – and pressured the German authorities to retaliate, thus provoking the German military commander to order the execution of 68 hostages, mostly arrested partisans and communist militants, in December 1942 and January 1943.

The escalation of German repression briefly provoked the partisans into a third phase, that of killing German military personnel. As an immediate reaction to the execution of the hostages, six German soldiers were killed at random, followed a little later by ten others. The German military commander retaliated by ordering the execution of another sixty-nine hostages and successive waves of arrests. In the first months of 1943 over 300 partisans and more than 500 party members were arrested, far more than in June 1941, inflicting severe damage on the partisan movement. In July 1943, the German authorities struck a further devastating blow with the roundup of the clandestine Party and partisan leadership. However, these partisan attacks on German soldiers remained an exception in Belgium. The occupier's retaliation had been catastrophic for the movement and the strategy was also unpopular, both with the public, for whom the costs largely outweighed the benefits, and with many Party militants, who objected to the assassination of regular German soldiers whose ideological commitment – unlike that of the Belgian collaborationists – was unknown.

After the disaster in first half of 1943, the partisans arrested or killed had to be replaced by new recruits from outside the heavily decimated ranks of Party members and longstanding militants. Some were workers forced underground to avoid the labour draft, drawn in because the movement could provide shelter, documents and, most of all, food stamps, to those in hiding. Others came from the patriotic organizations, frustrated by their inactivity and attracted by the spectacular and radical strategy of the partisans. By this time, the tide of war was seen to have turned and German troops were on the retreat on the Eastern and African fronts, thus creating an impatient atmosphere anticipating the German defeat. Collaborationist movements were blamed for all the hardships of the occupation and the unrelenting campaign against their buildings, meetings and leaders was increasingly popular. On 14 April 1943 a partisan commando killed Paul Colin, a leading collaborationist journalist and figurehead of the French-speaking cultural New Order. Partisan activity also spread out beyond the traditional communist strongholds. In the region around Leuven a group of young socialists engaged in a very violent campaign of sabotage and executions of local collaborationists, and in Limburg, miners joined forces with escaped Soviet POW's.[52] In the course of 1944, VNV, Rex and the Flemish SS no longer felt protected by their German masters and they engaged in retaliatory killings on their own initiative, killing several hundred people. Some of the murders were random violence by despairing Belgian Nazis, such as the massacres in the village of Meensel-Kiezegem and in Courcelles; others were deliberate political murders, such as the shooting of Alexandre Gallopin, governor of the Société Générale and probably the most influential individual in the occupied country, by the gang led by the Flemish Nazi, Verbelen, in February 1944. In the months between the Allied landing in June and the liberation in September, there was a devastating escalation of political murders on both sides. At the end of the war, the partisans claimed to have 'slaughtered' 1,100 'traitors'. They also boasted a membership of over 10,000, but an obvious distinction should be made between the partisans of the first two years (from the summer of 1941 to the summer of 1943), over one third of whom were killed, and the subsequent recruits who operated in a very different context.

The partisans were the most active organization engaged in what the German authorities called 'terrorism' and, in spite of their widespread recruitment in 1943 and 1944, they remained the closely controlled, armed branch of the Communist Party until the liberation. Yet the partisans were not the only group to execute collaborationists. The first political assassinations occurred in August and September 1941, when two leading members of Rex and two German soldiers were targeted by the Phalange Blanche, a tiny team of individuals from various backgrounds. Later in the war members of the Légion Belge, the Mouvement National Belge and the Groupe G would also engage in campaigns of political killings and the elimination of informers. One famous example was the murder of Léon Degrelle's brother by the Légion Belge in July 1944. Nevertheless, even if the Germans were sometimes prone to attribute the actions of others to the partisans on account of their virulent anti-communism, they were generally right to identify the partisans and the Communist Party as the most consistent source of violent action in occupied Belgium.

One group that engaged in the most radical and murderous actions requires a special mention, namely the Jewish communists. On the eve of the German invasion, the Belgian Jewish community was overwhelmingly a community of recent immigrants, living in Brussels and Antwerp.[53] Only 4,000 of the approximately 66,000 Jews living in Belgium in 1940 were Belgian nationals. The others had arrived in the 1920s, fleeing poverty and pogroms in Poland and the Soviet Union, or in the 1930s fleeing Nazi persecution in Germany and Austria. They formed a poverty-stricken urban proletariat, victims of anti-immigrant xenophobia as well as anti-Semitism, especially in Antwerp. Among them was an active minority of communists and militant anti-fascists, who had been strongly represented in the International Brigades. Their experiences of persecution and anti-fascist combat predestined them to become the vanguard of the partisan resistance and the first target of the occupier's repression. They constituted the majority of the three partisan battalions of the MOI (Main d'Oeuvre Immigrée), who performed many of the most dangerous tasks in 1942 and early 1943, incurring tremendous losses in the process. They also led the first concerted actions against the deportations of Jews.

The anti-Jewish policy of the occupation authorities remained relatively discreet until the end of May 1942. Jews were registered, geographically and economically isolated, and administered through a Jewish organization, the Association des Juifs en Belgique (AJB).[54] These preparatory steps towards mass murder were deliberately disguised as minor changes, in order not to awaken Jewish suspicion or protests by the Belgian public at large. This changed on 27 May 1942 when the Germans made wearing the Star of David compulsory for all Jews, thus making the antisemitic policy visible to all. Less than two months later, the first convoys of Jews left the Dossin barracks in Mechelen for Auschwitz, and in the following three months, two-thirds of the 24,000 or more Jews deported from Belgium were taken to Auschwitz. It would take the occupier two more years to apprehend, deport and kill a further 8,000 victims. The very speed of the operation had surprised very many Jews and the AJB, under direct German orders, had contributed to the deception by distributing 'employment cards' to all those summoned to Mechelen. This made immediate measures to stop the deportations imperative. On 25 July, a Polish-Jewish team of partisans set fire to the address files of the AJB – tragically destroying only duplicates. On 29 August, in the midst of the most extensive roundups, the same team shot the 'employment agent' of the Jewish Council dead on a Brussels' street corner. Violent action against the departures did nevertheless serve to alarm many Jews and about 30,000 survived the occupation in Belgium by going into hiding.

Broadening the basis

Patriots and anti-fascists, communists and victims of Nazi persecution all formed particular centres of active resistance against the occupation in the first half of the war. In the second half, the impetus to resist would extend into the population at large. This was dictated primarily by the changing military situation. The overpowering impression of the invincibility of Hitler's army during the summer of 1940 had already lost some of its force by the end of the year. The failure to defeat Britain had proved that resisting the Nazis was possible and that the war was not over. The stunning success of the invasion of the Soviet Union during the following summer did temporarily renew the myth of an army of *Übermenschen*, but by the end of the year it again became apparent that there was to be no total German victory in the foreseeable future. In the course of 1942, the German economy started to experience a labour shortage. Contrary to the regime's expectations, its soldiers could not return to their homes and factories and millions more had to be conscripted for the Eastern Front. Consequently, Nazi pressure to make the countries of occupied Western Europe contribute to the German war effort increased. This was disguised initially as an appeal to the populations of those countries to participate voluntarily in the struggle against a common enemy, Bolshevism. However, this appeal soon lost its effect as the occupation took on an increasingly grim character. This included the brutal mass deportations of Jews during the summer of 1942, the enforcement of labour conscription for war industries in the spring of the same year, followed by the start of large-scale deportations of workers to Germany during the autumn, and the increase in brutal repression of resistance activities by the end of the year.

Resistance was no longer just the preserve of a radical minority, and disobedience became a survival strategy for many sections of society. This applied most literally to the Jewish population, who collectively disappeared underground after the murderous raids of the summer of

1942. The Nazis had surprised a population that found it impossible to credit the realities of the persecution they faced or to believe the rumours of what awaited them in the east. Thus they were totally unprepared for a life in hiding. Disobedience required a radical break with their former lifestyles, and the ability to adapt quickly to finding protection, shelter, and food. The very brutal nature of the German raids served to hasten this process. A similar process occurred the following year with those called up for labour service. This extended disobedience to all social classes and to every part of the country. The Germans' initial success in drafting labour during the second half of 1942 was soon undermined, and they had to resort to increasingly drastic measures to levy the required quota, for example through the year-class actions implemented during the first half of 1943.

By the end of the summer of 1943 even these measures had lost their effectiveness. Whereas tens of thousands of workers had left every month in the first year of recruitment for forced labour in Germany, during the last year of the occupation, from the summer of 1943 to the liberation in September 1944, the occupier only managed to extract a few thousand departures out of Belgium each month.[55] Contrary to myth, the tens of thousands of workers who went into hiding did not enrol *en masse* in the partisan armies of the *maquis*. They did constitute a fertile ground for recruitment, but their greatest importance lay in the vast organization set up to ensure their survival underground. This involved the production of false identity papers, the complicity of employers, civil servants and local police, and the provision of money and food stamps to feed them, usually procured through theft, forgery or assaults on transports and post offices.

This created a new form of resistance. As François Marcot described it in a lucid essay on France, after the 'intentional' resistance of people predisposed towards resistance by their opinions, their character, and their traditions, emerged a 'functional' resistance of people drawn to resistance by what they could offer to a massive underground society.[56] This included farmers, clergymen, nuns, employers, police officers, municipal employees . . . in short anybody who, usually because of their professional occupation, could offer shelter, food or administrative help. This 'humanitarian resistance' was seldom the expression of a conscious political or ideological engagement. However, the coordination of this widespread goodwill and willingness to take risks required movements and organizations capable of mobilizing public opinion and bringing a wide spectrum of social and political forces into the resistance.

The Independence Front was the first and most influential movement to do so. The Front de l'Indépendance/Onafhankelijkheidsfront

(Independence Front) was the second part of the double strategy designed by the Communist Party in the summer of 1941 – radical action by the partisans on the one hand, broadening the base for resistance by building alliances with different social and political forces on the other.[57] The initiative benefited from the timing of its inception. Up to that point, the two main political forces had not engaged in any form of resistance activity. The Catholic Church, its political party and its affiliated organizations espoused a traditional conservatism and age-old sense of self-preservation, valuing the interests and long-term survival of the Catholic *patrimonium* higher than any immediate worldly cause. The socialists had also eschewed any activity, largely because of the crisis engendered by their chairman, Henri De Man. The trade unions of both groups had barely recovered from the fiasco caused by the official trade union established by the Germans, which had served to divide both their leaderships and memberships. In this context, the Communist Party was able to overcome the widespread traditional anti-bolshevism and become the catalyst for a new mass movement. Its experience with clandestine activity and subversion, its undeniable organizational talents, and the energy and total dedication of its militants formed the starting point for a plethora of organizations, underground newspapers, and assistance networks for people in hiding which attracted many non communists who would never have agreed to work with them in peace time. The Party tried to present the movement as politically neutral and open to all but at the same time it attempted to maintain firm control over the leadership. The terrible decimation of the Party ranks during the first half of 1943 made this last objective increasingly difficult to maintain and during the last year of the occupation the Independence Front developed into an energetic and diversified movement.

The initial leaders of the Front illustrate the Party's intentions. These were Albert Marteaux, a former socialist who joined the Communist Party; Fernand Demany, journalist for a major newspaper before the invasion, and André Bolland, a priest and former missionary to China. Leading socialists and Catholics were forbidden to join by their hierarchies, but many dissident figures and grassroots militants were attracted by the dynamism of the Front, as were many liberals. The Independence Front had the ambition to create organizations to mobilize the resistance against the occupier in all social circles: workers, farmers, police officers, judges, teachers, in the medical profession, the youth organizations . . . and it created a large number of underground publications to facilitate this. The achievements fell short of the claims made in its bellicose propaganda, but in some sectors the Front did succeed in mobilizing support. Appeals to the Belgian judiciary did reduce the cooperation of Belgian judges with German repressive policies. Another network mobilized public school teachers against the instructions of the New Order-controlled administration. The most successful actions were in humanitarian resistance. The Jewish Defence Committee (CDJ) provided shelter for Jews in hiding, saving the lives of, among others, 2,000 children. They were successfully hidden under false identities in various institutions, including some catholic schools and convents.[58] A subsidiary organization, 'Solidarity', provided shelter for militants on the run and assistance to families of deported or executed resisters.

The Independence Front was also very active in the fight against the labour draft. It aimed propaganda at the workers, organized some abortive strikes through its clandestine union cells and provided assistance to the *réfractaires*, the workers who went into hiding to escape deportation to Germany. When the numbers of *réfractaires* started to increase drastically at the end of the summer of 1943, the government-in-exile tried to organize the distribution of financial aid to them. Initially it did this by smuggling dollars into the country, which were then changed on the black market and distributed via the Independence Front. This rudimentary system soon proved insufficient to finance the tens of thousands of workers in hiding and the government appealed to a Belgian banker, Raymond Scheyven, to obtain budget advances from the major financial institutions inside the country to fund assistance to labour draft evaders. Any advances made were to be guaranteed by the government. Scheyven and his organization Socrates were remarkably successful, directly subsidizing more than 40,000 workers who refused to leave for Germany from April 1944 onwards.[59] Scheyven, however, refused to operate exclusively through the communist-tainted Independence Front and appealed to other resistance movements and prewar Catholic and socialist organizations to create alternative networks, thereby carefully reinforcing prewar power relations.

At the start of 1944, the Independence Front began preparations for the liberation. It created the 'Patriotic Militias', a volunteer force to assist the allied troops during the liberation, and local liberation committees that would organize popular insurrections, replace collaborationist mayors, and assume responsibility for local government in the transition period before postwar elections were held. These plans alarmed the government-in-exile, because they appeared to threaten the restoration of legal authority and properly elected or appointed officials. The Belgian ministers in London had consistently delayed recognition of the Independence Front, fearing its communist element. Positive reports by agents on its activities and its broad social and political composition resulted in official recognition in November 1943. Contacts were intensified in the course of 1944 and the government even persuaded the Independence Front to abandon its plans for a general insurrection and the creation of local liberation committees. In June 1944, Marcel Grégoire, a Catholic, arrived in London as a representative of the Independence Front to negotiate directly with the government-in-exile and, after the liberation, Fernand Demany joined the government as the representative of the Front.

Many other similar organizations emerged alongside the Independence Front. They usually originated with underground newspapers, such as *La Voix des Belges* of the Belgian National Movement and *Steeds Verenigd – Unis Toujours* of Witte Brigade – Fidelio, and later diversified into intelligence gathering, sabotage, occasional executions of collaborationists and informers, assistance to *réfractaires* and Jews in hiding.[60] An exhaustive list would demonstrate their social and political diversity and, moreover, underline that none of these spontaneous initiatives emanated from important prewar political parties, trade unions or Churches. Here, just four examples will have to suffice. The Belgian National Movement and Witte Brigade – Fidelio were rooted in liberal and Catholic patriotic circles, mainly in Brussels and Antwerp respectively. The former was mainly active as an underground press counting the Great War resistance leader, Camille Joset, as one of its leaders. Its ambitions ran parallel to those of the Independence Front, of building a large national alliance. Even though there was occasional cooperation, the political platforms of these organisations were widely divergent. In editorials, *La Voix des Belges* at times promoted a form of authoritarian conservatism, although this remained secondary to its anti-German and patriotic content.

Witte Brigade originated in liberal circles in Antwerp and was strongly rooted in the urban middle class, especially among civil servants and the police. The organization excelled in intelligence gathering and sabotage in the harbour, and also contributed to the rescue of Jews from deportation by offering shelter. Other organizations had a much less conventional outlook. The National Royalist Movement originated in a local Rex youth movement. It was fiercely anti-German, and also innately royalist and thus demonstrated its direct links to pre-war Catholic anti-democratic sentiment. The organization published an underground newspaper, gathered intelligence, engaged in sabotage, helped Allied pilots and Jews, and mobilized opposition to the labour draft.

The last example, the Liberation Army, originated in Christian-democratic circles in Liège which were opposed to the official collaborationist trade union. It was very active in dissuading workers from leaving for Germany, in sabotage and in intelligence work. This type of activity was unusual for Christian democrats as their Flemish leaders in particular had adopted a very compromising attitude during the occupation. As a result, the Liberation Army leadership created a short-lived, breakaway party, the Union Démocratique Belge, in 1945.

The extremely disparate nature of Belgian resistance organizations complicated their amalgamation under a national resistance council. Unlike in France, there was no need or incentive to gather all the elements of the resistance to create a political alternative to Vichy: the legitimate government was abroad and even the most radical scenarios foresaw its return alongside the Allied liberators. As in France and in the Netherlands, the initiative for a broader consultation between the different resistance movements came from London. In the expectation of an imminent invasion, the government-in-exile, as mistrustful of the authoritarian tendencies of the right-wing royalist military movements as of the revolutionary tendencies of the Independence Front and the partisans, wanted to impose some discipline and coordination between the major resistance organizations. A tentative 'coordination committee' was set up in May 1944, bringing together the Belgian Legion, the Belgian National Movement, the Groupe G and the Independence Front (including the partisans). In the end, this 'coordination committee' never really functioned as the whole of Belgium was liberated less than three months later.

Liberation and Legacy

The diversity of Belgian resistance organizations conditioned their later history. During the last year of the occupation, they crystallized into a mass movement that promoted disobedience and rejection of the occupation authorities. After the Normandy landings on 6 June 1944, this popular support became a tide of enthusiasm and, as the liberating armies approached, thousands of volunteers joined resistance movements whose existence they often only discovered at that time. This combination of organizational radicalism and mass-support was an explosive mix – all the more so since it was completely outside the control of the traditional forces and structures of the prewar Belgian political landscape. Moreover, it represented a potential threat to the plans, both of the Allies and of the returning government, which envisaged a return to prewar political structures.

The resistance movements saw the liberation as the culmination of their activities. They were no match for the Wehrmacht when acting alone and their role prior to the arrival of the Allied armies had been limited to undercover actions by small nuclei of specialists. However, working in concert with Allied military might they intended to play a crucial role as an auxiliary volunteer force. Part of this plan worked well: the resistance guided the Allied troops with precise information on the presence of German troops and prevented massive German destruction of Belgian infrastructure, such as bridges, railways, and most spectacularly, the port of Antwerp. Resistance groups also took prisoners, prevented the departure of a last deportation train, and arrested war criminals and collaborationists (albeit often as a means to save them from popular justice). However, there were also failures. For example, when units engaged in premature and ill-thought-through military actions and were massacred by well-armed and battle-hardened German soldiers. Perhaps fortuitously, the fighting did not last long – a matter of days for most of the country, as the German troops had decided to withdraw behind the Rhine and the great rivers in the Netherlands.

This *Blitz*-liberation was a source of frustration for the enthusiastic resistance fighters and most wanted to continue the war as a volunteer army alongside the Allies. The Belgian government opposed this, for fear that if they were given any degree of permanence they might transform themselves into mutually antagonistic communist and royalist political militias.[61] Instead, it wanted to rebuild a new Belgian army, with regular regiments into which the resistance battalions would be incorporated. However, in the short term, the presence of about 80,000 armed resistance fighters inside the country, gathered in camps, kept idle, and forced to live on a miserable stipend constituted a menace to public order. The government manifestly bungled in tackling this delicate problem. In France and in the Netherlands, the FFI and the Binnenlandse Strijdkrachten (NBS) constituted an outlet for resistant enthusiasm and a means of gradually demobilizing and controlling the fighters. The Belgian government refused such a solution, but at the same time it was incapable of offering an alternative. The new Belgian army had no infrastructure, no weapons and no clearly defined task in the Allied strategy. By February 1945, only 11,000 volunteers had been absorbed and sent to training camps in Northern Ireland – which was definitely in the opposite direction from the frontline. In comparison, the Dutch NBS had twice as many volunteers in the southern liberated part of the Netherlands alone and after the liberation of the whole of the country in May 1945, their numbers reached 120,000.

While the creation of a new army was slow and inefficient, the disarmament of the resistance was brutal and immediate. A first order to disarm and deliver all weapons to local police stations was issued on

2 October 1944, hardly a month after the liberation. The resistance movements refused to comply if the government refused to offer them the chance to continue fighting in the new Belgian army. On 13 November, the government then published a decree ordering immediate disarmament, with heavy fines and house searches for recalcitrant citizens. The decree was needlessly humiliating and resistance indignation culminated in a protest march on Brussels on 25 November. When protesters directed their anger towards the parliament building, the police opened fire, wounding forty-five. The British Prime Minster, Winston Churchill, would later claim in the House of Commons that British troops had prevented a communist *coup d'état*, but research has long since established there never was such a threat.[62] Churchill reacted to criticism against British support for conservative forces in Greece, Italy and Belgium, but Belgium manifestly did not belong to this group of countries on the verge of civil war. The resistance did ultimately disarm, reluctantly but spontaneously, but the episode left acrimonious memories on all sides.

'The Resistance' did not attempt to seize power in Belgium, because it was not and never had been, a political alternative to the government-in-exile. The hostility between the Secret Army and the Independence Front was much deeper than the hostility of any of them towards the government. Unlike the French National Resistance Council (CNR) the Belgian resistance did not conceive of itself as a counter-state with a coherent political programme. The occupation had undoubtedly been a profoundly disruptive experience, aggravated by the failure or disappearance of traditional organizations and political groups. Under the exceptional circumstances of foreign occupation, movements and milieus on the political margins with radical methods could emerge as effective agents of resistance. Yet at the liberation there was a return to the normality of mass politics and the population embraced the organizational conservatism of the prewar political forces once again.

The cleavage between the 'new' forces of the resistance and the 'old' forces of party politics was not destined to last. The resistance was almost by definition an ephemeral phenomenon, destined to disappear as soon as the occupation against which it resisted was over. It could only transform itself into a permanent political force in countries where the resistance came to embody claims for the transformation of society, such as in Yugoslavia, Albania, Greece or Italy. The rapid failure of the resistance party, the Union Démocratique Belge, bears witness to this, as does the rapid electoral decline of the Belgian Communist Party (albeit in the context of a growing Cold War). Within months after the war's end, the resistance as a movement had been consigned to history.

The legacy of the resistance in Belgium is inextricably linked to another legacy of the Nazi occupation with long lasting consequences: the so-called 'royal question'.[63] History had proven Leopold III wrong. Both his military calculation of a final German victory and his political calculation of the end of democracy and the beginning of a New Order in 1940 had been a disaster. The Allies considered him as a 'fascist' and opposed his return. Socialists, communists and a large majority of liberals considered his return to the throne unacceptable, all the more so because the King, discovered in an Austrian castle in April 1945 by American troops, was unrepentant and demanded an apology from the government rather than offering one. Yet, the King found support for this entirely unrealistic attitude in royalist quarters of the Catholic Party, who forced the Party to resign from the coalition government at the end of July 1945 in solidarity with King Leopold. The Party then embarked on a strategy of political polarization that could have been fatal for the unity of the country.[64]

An anti-Leopold coalition won the elections in February 1946 with the narrowest possible margin. The Catholic party campaigned as the party of the King and the government on the rebound profiled itself as the 'government of the resistance'. A secular, democratic and anti-fascist Belgium was thus opposed to a clerical Belgium, gathered around a compromised King and encompassing a profoundly Catholic Flemish movement that had sided with the enemy, adhered to fascism, and betrayed the Belgian nation. When the Cold War broke up the left-wing coalition in 1947, the Catholic Party returned to power in a coalition with the socialists and liberals. Still the Party continued to campaign for the return of the King, obtaining a referendum on the return of Leopold in 1949. The referendum showed a national majority in favour of the return, yet when split into regional results, the King had obtained massive support in Catholic Flanders but a marked majority opposed his return in Brussels and the Walloon part of the country. The Catholic Party subsequently obtained an absolute majority in the elections and it organized the return of Leopold under a homogeneously Catholic government. Predictably, the return provoked a general insurrection in large parts of the country and the King was finally forced to abdicate in favour of his son. The 'defeat' of the pro-Leopold faction, despite a mathematical political majority, created lasting rancour in Catholic public opinion. The Catholic Party lost its absolute majority at the next elections in 1954, and it had to undergo four more years of anti-clerical governance. The frustration was most acute in Flemish Catholic circles. They constituted an overwhelming majority in the most populous half of the country and yet they had not managed to impose their political will on the rest of the country and were relegated to the opposition for eight of the sixteen years between 1944 and 1958. This resentment alienated them gradually from the Belgian nation: only in a more independent nation would their demographic majority be translated into political power. It also alienated them from the national identity forged by the governing coalitions in the years 1945–7 and 1954–8: a strong identification with the resistance, anti-fascism and secularism. The Flemish wing of the Catholic Party gradually developed an alternative identification with Flemish collaboration, which, it claimed, had been the victim of unduly harsh punishment by the Belgian state and deserved amnesty, if not rehabilitation.

If this approach has been very rewarding politically for Flemish nationalism, historically it is a perversion. Political opponents have been pretending that the different reactions of different parts of the population are a cause of the current dismemberment of Belgium, yet the truth is precisely the opposite: the current dismemberment of Belgium has caused different discourses on this aspect of the Belgian past. History has become a political stratagem. This situation has hindered the emergence of a critical historiography on World War Two and the resistance for a long time. Academic study of the subject really began in 1971 with the publication of a study on *L'an 40* by Jules Gérard-Libois and José Gotovitch. The publication of this book more-or-less coincided with the creation of a Study and Documentation Centre on the history of the Second World War in Brussels. The creation of the Centre had been prompted by the trial and acquittal in Austria of Robert Verbelen, a notorious alleged Belgian war criminal. Comparable institutes had existed in the Netherlands and France since 1945. The Centre produced a periodical publishing crucial studies on the occupation period and the resistance and some first rate monographs, most prominently by José Gotovitch and Albert De Jonghe. During the 1980s and early 1990s, major monographs established a scientific consensus on crucial aspects of the history of World War Two in Belgium: on the Royal Question,[65] the occupation policy,[66] the genocide,[67] on the Communist Party,[68] on the collaboration.[69] Meanwhile, in 1965, the public broadcasting company had commissioned a series of documentaries on the war years, which finally appeared in the 1980s in the very influential weekly programme presented by Maurice de Wilde. This served to enhance public awareness of the war years and prompted further research.

In spite of these decisive advances in our knowledge on the war years, in spite of a growing consensus on the crucial aspects of the history of the occupation among professional historians, World War Two, resistance and collaboration remain favoured themes of Flemish and Walloon propagandists. It is the sad fate of many public debates in present-day Belgium, to be reduced to an artificial, often irrelevant and sometimes dangerous opposition between the two language groups.

Notes

1. For good introductions to the history of Belgium, see E. Kossman, *De Lage Landen 1780–1980.* (Amsterdam: Elsevier, 1986) and Hans Blom and Emile Lamberts, *History of the Low Countries*; (Oxford : Berghahn, 1999).
2. For an English language introduction, see Carl Strikwerda, *A House Divided: Catholics, Socialists, and Flemish Nationalists in Nineteenth-Century Belgium.* (Lanham MD: Rowman & Littlefield, 1997)
3. For Belgium during the First World War, see Sophie de Schaepdrijver *De Groote Oorlog – Het koninkrijk België tijdens de Eerste Wereldoorlog* (Antwerp: Atlas, 1997). A good introduction in English is Sophie De Schaepdrijver, 'Occupation, propaganda and the idea of Belgium' in: Aviel Roshwald and Richard Stites, *European Culture in the Great War. The Arts, Entertainment and Propaganda, 1914–1918* (Cambridge: Cambridge University Press, 1999) pp.267–94.
4. See Bruno De Wever, *De Greep naar de Macht. Vlaams-nationalisme en Nieuwe Orde. Het VNV 1933-1945* (Tielt: Lanno, 1994).
5. For REX, see Martin Conway, *Collaboration in Belgium: Leon Degrelle and the Rexist Movement, 1940–1944* (New Haven: Yale University Press, 1994). For the Socialist Party, see Gerd-Rainer Horn, *European Socialists Respond to Fascism: Ideology, Activism and Contingency in the 1930s* (Oxford: Oxford University Press, 1996).
6. Jan Velaers and Herman Van Goethem, *Leopold III. De Koning, het Land, de Oorlog* (Tielt: Lannoo, 1994), pp.67–99.
7. Ibid. pp.11–66 and 101–66.
8. On the *Blitzkrieg*, among countless contributions of military historiography, see two recent publications: Jean Vanwelkenhuyzen, *1940. Pleins feux sur un désastre.* (Brussels: Racine, 1995) and Brian Bond, *Britain, France, and Belgium, 1939–1940* (Oxford: Brassey's, 1990).
9. For a brilliant analysis of the Belgian society during the year 1940, see the pionneer-study of the scientific war historiography in Belgium:

Jules Gérard-Libois and José Gotovitch, *L'an 40. La Belgique occupée* (Brussels: CRISP, 1971).

10. For a general English language introduction, see Werner Warmbrunn, *The German Occupation of Belgium, 1940-1944. (American University Studies IX: History, Vol. 122)* (New York: Peter Lang, 1993).
11. See Jean Stengers, *Léopold III et le gouvernement. Les deux politiques belges de 1940.* (Paris/Gembloux: Duculot, 1980) and Velaers and Van Goethem, *Leopold III.*
12. See Gérard-Libois and Gotovitch, *L'an '40*, pp.200–32.
13. See Albert De Jonghe, *Hitler en het politieke lot van België* (Antwerp: De Nederlandsche Boekhandel, 1982).
14. See Albert De Jonghe, 'De strijd Himmler–Reeder om de benoeming van een HSSPF te Brussel (1942–1944)' *Bijdragen tot de Geschiedenis van de Tweede Wereldoorlog*, (1974–84) pp.3–8.
15. See Conway, *Collaboration in Belgium* and De Wever, *Greep naar de Macht.*
16. See Mark van den Wijgaert, *Tussen vijand en volk: het bestuur van de secretarissen-generaal tijdens de Duitse bezetting, 1940–1944* (Kapellen: DNB/Pelckmans, 1990) and Gérard-Libois and Gotovitch, *L'an '40*, pp.185–99.
17. See John Gillingham, *Belgian business in the Nazi New Order.* (Ghent: Jan Dhondt Foundation, 1977); Mark van de Wijgaert, *Nood breekt wet. Economische collaboratie of accomodatie. Het beleid van Alexandre Gallopin van de Société Générale tijdens de Duitse Bezetting* (Tielt: Lannoo, 1990) and for an analysis of the assessment of these attitudes after the war: Dirk Luyten, Danny Somers and Boudewijn Bardyn, *Burgers boven elke verdenking? Vervolging van economische collaboratie in België na de Tweede Wereldoorlog* (Brussels: Vubpress, 1996).
18. For an interesting reflection on resistance, see Semelin, Jacques, *Sans armes face à Hitler. La résistance civile en Europe, 1939–1943* (Paris: Editions Payot et Rivages, 1989).
19. See Pieter Lagrou, 'L'Europe Méditerranéenne dans une histoire comparative de la Résistance' in: Jean-Marie Guillon et Robert Mencherini (eds) *La Résistance et les Européens du Sud*, (Paris L'Harmattan, 1999) and José Gotovitch and Pieter Lagrou `La Résistance Française dans le paysage Européen' *Cahiers de l'Institut d'Histoire du Temps Présent* 37 (1997), pp.147–62.
20. For a chronicle of the war years, see the eleven volumes of *Jours de Guerre* (Brussels, 1990–8), based on a series of television documentaries for the Belgian French-language public broadcast. The nine

volumes based on the series of documentaries by the Belgian Dutch language public broadcasting company *België in de Tweede Wereldoorlog* are more thematic, especially volume 6, *Het Verzet* (Kapellen: De Nederlandsche Boekhandel, 1988), by Herman Van de Vijver, Rudi Van Doorslaer and Etienne Verhoeyen. An excellent synthesis is Etienne Verhoeyen, *België bezet. Een Synthese.* (Brussels: BRTN, 1993). It is interesting to observe that in Belgium and the Netherlands (De Jong's *Het Koninkrijk der Nederlanden in de Tweede Wereldoorlog*) major overviews of the war years were first produced for public television and later elaborated in printed form. This illustrates the general delay in academic scholarship on the war years. For a classic panorama of the Belgian resistance in the tradition of patriotic historiography see Henri Bernard, *La Résistance 1940–1945* (Brussels: La Renaissance du Livre, 1969). For a series of portraits, see H. Neuman, *Avant qu'il ne soit trop tard. Portraits de Résistants* (Gembloux: Duculot, 1985) and for a detailed regional study, see Fabrice Maerten, 'Du murmure au grondement. La résistance politique et idéologique dans la province de Hainaut pendant la Seconde Guerre Mondiale (mai 1940-septembre 1944)' *Analectes d'histoire du Hainaut*, vol. 7 (Mons, 1999).

21. See M.R.D.Foot, *MI 9: Escape and Evasion, 1939–1945* (London: Futura, 1980). A good overview for Belgium in Verhoeyen, *België Bezet*, pp.279–92.

22. Verhoeyen, *België Bezet*, p.280.

23. This is also the resistance activity that triggered most imagination in English language novelists. See, for example, Anita Shreve, *Resistance: a Novel* (Little Brown & Co, 1997) on a wounded American pilot in occupied Belgium.

24. See A. Neave, *Petit Cyclone* (Brussels: Novissima, 1954); Cécile Jouan, *Comète* (Brussels: Éditions du Beffroi Furnes, 1948) and Rémy (Gilbert Renault), *Réseau Comète* (Paris: Perrin, 1971).

25. See René Lesage, *La résistance en Artois occidental (juin 1940-mai 1944) Revue du Nord (hors série, 13, 1998)* pp.35–49.

26. See F. Strubbe, *Geheime Oorlog. De Inlichtings- en Actiediensten in België* (Tielt: Lannoo, 1992). See also Verhoeyen, *België Bezet*, pp.265–78.

27. See, for example, Henri Bernard, *Un géant de la Résistance. Walthère Dewé* (Brussels: La Renaissance du Livre, 1971).

28. Etienne Verhoeyen, 'Le Service de Renseignements Marc, 1942–1944' *Cahiers du Centre de Recherche et d'Etudes Historiques de la Seconde Guerre Mondiale* 14 (1991) pp.1–60 and 15 (1992) pp.117–60.

29. For a heroic account, see the narrative by Yvonne De Ridder, *The Quest for Freedom: Belgian Resistance in World War II* (Fithina Press, 1991).

30. For a detailed analysis, see Verhoeyen, *België Bezet*, pp.325–89.

31. See Van de Vijver, Van Doorslaer and Verhoeyen, *Het Verzet*, pp.65–75.

32. See Michael Foot, *SOE: an outline history of the Special Operations Executive, 1940-46* (London: Mandarin, 1980).

33. See the official history of the organisation edited by Henri Bernard, *L'Armée Secrète, 1940–1944*. (Paris/Gembloux: Duculot, 1986).

34. See, for example, Henri Bodson's account (edited by Richard Schmidt) *Agent for the Resistance: A Belgian Saboteur in World War II*. Texas A & M University Military History, 35. (Texas A & M UP, 1994).

35. Gérard-Libois and Gotovitch, *L'an 40*, pp.344–6 and 351–4.

36. Gérard-Libois and Gotovitch, *L'an 40*, p.353.

37. Verhoeyen, *België Bezet*, p.306.

38. See William Ugeux, *Le groupe G* (Sint-Stevens-Woluwe: Elsevier Sequoia, 1978); Verhoeyen, *België Bezet*, pp.307–11 and Van de Vijver, Van Doorslaer and Verhoeyen, *Het Verzet*, pp.85–7.

39. See Gérard-Libois and Gotovitch, *L'an 40*, pp.359–67. For an inventory, see J. Dujardin, J. Gotovitch and L. Rymenans, *Inventaire de la presse clandestine conservée en Belgique* (Brussels: Centre Nationale d'Histoire des Deux Guerres Mondiale, 1965).

40. Verhoeyen, *België Bezet,* p.295.

41. Gérard-Libois and Gotovitch, *L'an 40*, pp.367–76.

42. Gérard-Libois and Gotovitch, *L'an 40*, pp.373–74.

43. Horn, *European Socialists*.

44. For example, see the excellent memoirs by the partisan commander of the region of Leuven, Louis Van Brussel, *Partisanen in Vlaanderen. Met Aktieverslagen van korps 034-Leuven.* (Gent: Frans Masereel Fonds, 1971) and by Bert Van Hoorick, *In tegenstroom. Herinneringen 1919–1956* (Gent: Frans Masereel Fonds, 1982).

45. The Communist Party is the only political formation in Belgium to have benefited from a first-rate historical monograph for the war years: José Gotovitch, *Du Rouge au Tricolore. Les Communistes Belges de 1939 à 1944* (Brussels: Labor, 1992).

46. See Rudi Van Doorslaer, 'De Internationale Brigaden: de vrijwilligers uit België – een status questionis' *Belgisch Tijdschrift voor Nieuwste Geschiedenis*, 1–2 (1987) pp.159–64.

47. Rudi Van Doorslaer, *De Kommunistische Partij van België en het Sovjet-Duits niet-aanvalspakt* (Brussels: Frans Masereel, 1975) and Gotovitch, *Du Rouge au Tricolore*, pp.57–82.

48. See Nic Bal, *Mijn wankele wereld. Vier jaar in het socialistisch verzet* (Leuven: Kritak, 1984).
49. Gotovitch, *Du rouge au tricolore*, pp.135–47.
50. Gotovitch, *Du rouge au tricolore*, pp.155–93.
51. Gotovitch, *Du rouge au tricolore*, p.172.
52. See Verhoeyen, *België Bezet*, pp.415–36. Specifically on Limburg, see Jos Bouveroux, *Terreur in Oorlogstijd. Het Limburgse Drama* (Kapellen: De Nederlandsche Boekhandel, 1984).
53. See the excellent study by Rudi Van Doorslaer, *Enfants du Ghetto. Juifs révolutionnaires en Belgique (1925–1940)* (Brussels: Labor, 1997).
54. See Maxime Steinberg, *L'étoile et le fusil* 4 vols (Brussels: Vie Ouvrière, 1984–1986).
55. See Pierre Potargent, *Déportation. La mise au travail de la main d'oeuvre Belge dans le pays et à l'étranger durant l'occupation* (Brussels: Edimco, 1946).
56. François Marcot, 'La Résistance dans ses lieux et milieux: des relations d'interdépendance.' in *La Résistance et les Français. Nouvelles approches. Cahiers de l'Institut d'Histoire du Temps Présent,* 37 (1997), pp.129–46.
57. Gotovitch, *Du rouge au tricolore*, pp.195–287.
58. A number of these children have afterwards published memoirs, including some recently in English: Walter Buchignani, *Tell No One Who You Are* (Montreal/Quebec: Tundra Books, 1996) on Régine Miller, Suzanna Loebl, *At the Mercy of Strangers: Growing up on the Edge of the Holocaust* (Pacific CA: Pacifica Press Publishing, 1997); Beatrice Muchman, *Never to Be Forgotten: A Young Girl's Holocaust Memoir* (Ktav Publishing, 1997).
59. See, in addition to Gotovitch, *Du Rouge ou tricolore*, pp.230–6, Verhoeyen, *België Bezet,* pp.377–85.
60. See Van de Vijver, Van Doorslaer and Verhoeyen, *Het Verzet*, pp.88–96 and Jean Dujardin, 'Le Mouvement National Belge. Activités dans le domaine de Renseignement et de l'Action (1941– février 1944)' *Cahiers du Centre de Recherches et d'Etudes Historiques de la Seconde Guerre Mondiale* 15 (1992) pp.205–32.
61. See Pieter Lagrou,'US politics of stabilization in Liberated Europe. The view from the American Embassy in Brussels, 1944–46' *European History Quarterly* 25 (1995), pp.209–46 and Gotovitch, *Du rouge au tricolore*, pp.367–441.
62. See Geoffrey Warner, 'La crise politique belge de novembre 1944: un coup d'état manqué?' *Courrier Hebdomadaire du CRISP* 798 (1978).

63. For a good synthesis of the 'royal question', see Jules Gerard-Libois and José Gotovitch, *Leopold III de l'an 40 à l'effacement* (Brussels: Pol-His, 1991).

64. On the memory of the resistance and national identity, see Pieter Lagrou, Die Wiedererfindung der Nation im befreiten Westeuropa. Erinnerungspolitik in Frankreich, Belgien und den Niederlanden' *Transit. Europäische Revue* 15 (Autumn 1998), pp.12–28. Specifically on the national question, see Pieter Lagrou, 'Welk vaderland voor de vaderlandslievende verenigingen? Oorlogsslachtoffers en verzetsveteranen en de nationale kwestie, 1945–1960' *Bijdragen tot de Eigentijdse Geschiedenis* (Brussel) 3 (1997) pp.143–61. For a general overview of the legacy of the occupation in all its aspects, see Pieter Lagrou, *The Legacy of Nazi-occupation in Western Europe. Patriotic Memory and National Recovery* (Cambridge: Cambridge University Press, 1999).

65. Jean Stengers, *Léopold III et le gouvernement. Les deux politiques belges de 1940* (Paris/Gembloux: Duculot, 1980). Jan Velaers and Herman van Goethem, *Leopold III. De Koning, het Land, de Oorlog* (Tielt: Lannoo, 1994).

66. Albert de Jonghe, *Hitler en het politieke lot van België* (Antwerp: De Nederlandsche Boekhandel, 1982).

67. Maxime Steinberg, *L'Etoile et le Fusil* (3 vols) (Brussels: Vie Ouvrière, 1983–6).

68. José Gotovitch, *Du Rouge au Tricolore. Les Communistes Belges de 1939 à 1944* (Brussels: Labor, 1992).

69. Martin Conway, *Collaboration in Belgium. Leon Degrelle and the Rexist Movement, 1940–44* (New Haven : Yale University Press, 1994). Bruno de Wever, *De Greep naar de Macht. Vlaams Nationalisme en Niewe Orde. Het VNV 1933–1945* (Tielt: Lannoo, 1994).

—3—

The Channel Islands
Louise Willmot

Overview

On 30 June 1940, eight days after the fall of France, Guernsey was occupied by a small contingent of German troops. Jersey, Alderney and Sark surrendered within the next three days. The Channel Islands, which had been in the unbroken possession of the English Crown since 1066, fell without a shot being fired in their defence. Acting on advice that German control of the French coast would deprive the islands of their already limited strategic significance, and that British troops would be better employed in defence of the mainland, the War Cabinet in London had decided on 15 June to demilitarize the islands and to advise their governments to surrender in the event of invasion. Troops, military equipment and islanders of military age were evacuated during the following week and the islands were left defenceless against German bombing raids on 28 June, which killed forty-four people in their principal towns of St Helier and St Peter Port. When the invaders came, the island authorities had no option but to surrender. Subsequently they were left to deal with the occupying power without assistance from London.[1]

As the only British territories to fall into German hands during the Second World War, the Channel Islands have been studied as much for an indication of the fate that might have befallen an occupied Britain as for their own experiences of occupation and resistance. Yet they were far from being typical British communities in 1940. Lying in a shallow bay to the west of the Cherbourg peninsula, the islands are more than 60 miles away from the southern coast of England, but less than ten miles from the coast of France at their closest point. Their original link with the Duchy of Normandy had left other legacies: the law of the islands, modified by centuries of local precedent and custom, was in certain respects significantly different from that of the United Kingdom; French was still used for some official purposes and in rural districts a patois was widely spoken, although its use had been in decline for some time.

Legally the islands remained outside the United Kingdom. Acts of Parliament applied to them only by special provision, and in all matters save defence and foreign policy they enjoyed a large measure of self government. In 1940 Jersey was a self-contained bailiwick. The bailiwick of Guernsey included the outlying smaller islands, although Alderney and Sark also had a large measure of independence – in the case of Sark, in the form of a hereditary seigneurie that exercised quasi-feudal authority over its 600 inhabitants. Both main islands had long-established representative institutions – the Assembly of the States in Jersey and the States of Deliberation in Guernsey – presided over by a Bailiff appointed by the Crown. The management of their day-to-day affairs was undertaken in departments run by permanent civil servants under the supervision of members of the States.

These were societies in which traditions of hierarchy and deference not only remained strong but were incorporated into the structures of government. In both Jersey and Guernsey a significant proportion of representatives in the states were either parish rectors appointed by the Crown, or unpaid jurats who combined judicial with administrative and legislative functions and were elected for life by the ratepayers (Jersey) or by an electoral college (Guernsey).[2] Not even those deputies who were directly elected by the parishes had party affiliations. Indeed, political parties on the British model played no significant role in island life. The electoral system ensured a disproportionate influence for islanders with wealth and family connections: public life and the major offices were still dominated by a relatively small number of inter-connected families.[3]

Economically the islands were dependent on agriculture – potatoes and cattle in Jersey, vegetables and tomatoes in Guernsey, produced almost exclusively for the British market – and to a lesser extent on horticulture and the developing tourist industry. Before the outbreak of the World War Two they supported more than 90,000 inhabitants, almost all of whom lived in Jersey and Guernsey. In the days before the invasion, however, in conditions of confusion and some panic, nearly 30,000 of the civilian inhabitants took advantage of the offer of evacuation to the British mainland.[4] Though the vast majority of those who remained were island born, the population also included several thousand British-born residents drawn by the climate and the tax advantages, as well as several hundred seasonal workers – French, Irish, Spanish, Italian – working mainly in agriculture. All but about twenty members of the islands' small Jewish community had left, either on the outbreak of war or in the month before the occupation.

Conditions did not favour the early development of resistance. The mood in the first months of occupation was dominated not only by shock and fear of the Germans, but also by a sense of having been abandoned by Britain. The only significant acts of defiance took the form either of attempts to escape to England or of infrequent displays of frustration and resentment – occasionally in the form of fist fights, but more usually in verbal abuse of German soldiers. Not until almost nine months after the start of the occupation, in March 1941, did the first incidents of petty sabotage occur. Once begun, however, they became recurring features of the occupation. In the summer of 1941, and at intervals for the rest of the year, a minority of Channel Islanders took part in the 'V-for-Victory' signing campaign that swept occupied Western Europe in response to appeals broadcast by the BBC.

In much of Western Europe, the German invasion of the Soviet Union on 22 June 1941 had a galvanizing effect on resistance activity and organization as local communist parties became more fully involved. No such effect was perceptible on the Channel Islands: the tiny Jersey Communist Party had ceased to exist before the outbreak of war, and most of the handful of Communist sympathizers in the islands had been evacuated to England at the end of June 1940. Nevertheless, by the end of the year the first signs of a rudimentary organized resistance had appeared in Jersey. One group, linked with ex-army officers, engaged in spying and intelligence-gathering; the other, the Jersey Democratic Movement (JDM), was a left-leaning discussion group set up initially to plan for greater democracy in the island after the war.

Resistance activities continued to develop slowly in the first half of 1942. In May the first effective clandestine press, the Guernsey Underground News Service (GUNS), made its appearance. The year 1942, however, was notable primarily for an upsurge in unorganized disobedience, triggered in June by the German decision to confiscate wireless sets throughout the islands. The order to hand over sets was widely ignored. This mood of disaffection was intensified in September 1942 by the deportation of 2,000 British-born islanders to internment camps in Germany, an event that was greeted by the first significant demonstration of patriotic feeling in the islands.

Organized resistance remained extremely rare in 1942 despite the change of mood. At the end of the year, however, a small group of JDM members re-established the Jersey Communist Party (JCP) with the aim of taking direct action against the Germans. The most significant growth in organized resistance occurred during the following twelve months. It was in 1943 that the JDM and JCP began to produce a series of propaganda and news leaflets, and established a network of safe houses to provide food and shelter for a small number of escaped slave labourers.

By the end of 1943, the main forms of resistance in the islands were already established. At an organized level, the work of intelligence-gathering in the hope of smuggling material to the Allies, clandestine press and propaganda activity, and humanitarian aid were all under way, and unorganized resistance continued to involve petty sabotage and offers of food and clothing to Organisation Todt (OT) workers. Most islanders, however, remained quiescent. At least in part, this passivity was a response to the fact that German conduct continued to be more restrained than was the norm elsewhere in occupied Europe. In particular, there was no attempt to include the islands in the forced labour drafts that were driving hundreds of thousands of young men on the Continent into the underground resistance after 1943.

The last eighteen months of the occupation saw a significant increase in acts of petty sabotage, carried out mainly by adolescents and including, for the first time, the daubing of swastikas on the homes of alleged collaborators. After D-Day, resistance activities also encompassed a series of escapes from Jersey, as young men in particular sought to reach the French coast a few miles away and to join the advancing Allies. Throughout this period, the JCP continued to organize 'safe houses' for OT workers and to distribute propaganda material; in the last weeks of war, moreover, JCP members provided leaflets for disaffected members of the German garrison who were planning an armed uprising. These schemes, however, were curtailed by the peaceful end to the occupation in May 1945.

Phases of Resistance

As this brief outline of events indicates, the growth of resistance was slow and uneven. In analysing its development, it is tempting to adopt the schematic structure that has proved productive in the study of other countries of occupied Western Europe, and to deal with Channel Islands resistance as a series of consecutive or overlapping phases. According to this paradigm, the period between July 1940 and November 1941 can be interpreted as the phase of minor and spontaneous resistance, and the period between December 1941 and May 1943 as the phase of organizational development. Thereafter, however, the attempt to impose a chronological framework of analysis breaks down. Between early 1943 and May 1945 there were no new phases, but rather an increase – perceptible but far from dramatic – in the types of resistance that already existed. Arguably the islands were too small, and the prospects for resistance too limited, to make an interpretative framework of this kind either sustainable or appropriate.

In the case of the Channel Islands, therefore, it is more productive to highlight specific incidents and one key period as significant in the development of resistance activities. In particular, the decision to confiscate wireless sets in June 1942, followed in September by the deportation of British-born islanders to Germany, did much to change the attitude of the population and to make disobedience, at least in the form of listening to the BBC in family or extended groups, the norm rather than the exception. The most important period in the development of resistance fell between approximately November 1941 and May 1943. These months saw not only the confiscation of sets and the deportations but also the establishment and early operation of the various forms of organized resistance in the islands – the clandestine press work of GUNS and other groups, the spy network, and the propaganda and humanitarian activities of the JDM and JCP.

Those who engaged in active resistance were always 'very much a minority'[5] even at the end of the war. The most common attitude throughout the German occupation was one of 'passive antagonism'[6] or grumbling conformity:[7] islanders loathed the German presence, but felt that there was little they could do to oppose it. Among the factors persuading them not to engage in active resistance was geography. The Channel Islands are small, densely populated and flat. They offer no mountains in which partisans might take shelter, making sustained armed resistance of the kind that occurred in Eastern Europe, and in France in the later stages of the war, an impossibility. Even escape was difficult and dangerous. Moreover, the lack of native industries ensured that there were few obvious targets for saboteurs – 'no railways to blow up, no factories to sabotage'.[8]

Potential resisters were also intimidated by the sheer scale of the German presence. By May 1943 there were more than 30,000 German troops – one German soldier to every two islanders, and on Guernsey rather more than that – accommodated in hotels and private homes across the islands. Their presence undoubtedly did much to 'stifle' islanders' ability and willingness to resist.[9] Moreover, islanders were conscious that the Germans were behaving relatively well. The German military government in the islands, established as Feldkommandantur 515, part of the Département de la Manche, contained relatively few fanatical Nazis; police matters were the responsibility of the military police, the Feldgendarmerie and Geheime Feldpolizei, rather than the Gestapo.[10] For both pragmatic and propaganda reasons, the military government not only kept the island administrations and courts in place but also, as a safety valve, permitted limited expressions of national identity such as prayers for the Royal Family during church services. Relief at this apparent moderation extended to the conduct of ordinary soldiers, which was widely recognized as correct and sometimes even friendly.[11] After the war, German soldiers recalled the islands as the only place in occupied Europe where they were able to walk the streets without fear. Yet the inhabitants were constantly aware that German restraint depended on the continued absence of all resistance. Reprisals – though they were mild compared to those imposed elsewhere in Europe, usually taking the form of extended curfews and forcing local men to perform guard duties – were enforced after escapes and acts of sabotage. Islanders engaging in minor acts of defiance were imprisoned and sometimes beaten, and individuals caught in more serious resistance faced possible deportation to the continent, where some died.[12] The threat of the iron fist not only deterred most people from taking action, but also made a substantial number hostile to any resistance to the occupying power.[13] Fear of betrayal by neighbours or colleagues added to islanders' sense of insecurity and reinforced their reluctance to step out of line.[14]

Not least, avoidance of resistance was encouraged, and even demanded, by the island governments. Immediately before the occupation, the traditional executive structures of the islands had been streamlined and new Cabinets, the Superior Council in Jersey and the Controlling Committee in Guernsey, established. Their Bailiffs were advised by London to remain at their posts and to 'administer the government of the island to the best of [their] abilities in the interests of the inhabitants'.[15] Led in Jersey by the Bailiff and President of the Superior Council, Alexander Coutanche, and in Guernsey by the Attorney General, Ambrose Sherwill, and his successor as President of the Controlling Committee, John Leale, the island authorities strove to establish cordial relations with the German military government. Their aim was to act as a buffer between the occupying power and the civilian population, and to establish a 'model' occupation.[16] This conduct, it was hoped, would persuade the Germans to rule with restraint and to allow the island governments, as Sherwill noted after the war, to 'run their occupation for them'.[17] For their part, islanders would have to obey German orders to the letter and refrain from all resistance.

The dilemma facing the island governments cannot be doubted, and is now recognized by many of those who were once their sternest critics.[18] It is not the task of this paper to examine the rights and wrongs of their conduct or whether it amounted to collaboration. Nevertheless, by choosing to work closely with the military government, the Controlling Committee and the Superior Council severely restricted their ability to oppose any aspect of German rule. Such protests as they did make were rare and strictly limited – for example, they refused to carry out building work of a purely military character, and objected to efforts to force unemployed islanders to work for the Germans. On the other hand, the authorities failed to object to the confiscation of wireless sets in June 1942, although the order violated the Hague Convention. The island bureaucracies also obeyed German requests to compile a register of Jewish inhabitants, which was used to implement discriminatory measures against them, and there were no official protests against the deportation of British-born islanders to internment in Germany in September 1942.[19]

In the same spirit, the island governments roundly condemned those who engaged in resistance. From the outset, island as well as German courts were used to try those who defied the occupiers. Escapers from Guernsey were criticized by the Controlling Committee and warnings were issued that any future attempt would bring reprisals and thus be 'a crime against the local community'.[20] Incidents of sabotage were condemned by the authorities in Jersey as 'senseless acts' that would bring only damage to 'innocent members' of the community.[21] Participants in the 'V-for Victory' campaign of 1941 were attacked in both islands for their 'foolish actions' and in Guernsey a £25 reward was offered by the Bailiff, Victor Carey, for information leading to their arrest.[22] Moreover, the islands' police forces were used to investigate minor incidents of defiance and to assist in tracking down escaped slave labourers of the Organisation Todt.

The factors that limited the extent of resistance activity also did much to shape its form and, in particular, to ensure that no armed movement ever developed. Among islanders, the only plans for an armed uprising were hatched by small groups of teenage boys eager to contribute to the liberation of the islands. A number served prison sentences for stealing German equipment and weapons, and one, James Houillebeq, died in Neuengamme concentration camp in 1945. The overwhelming majority of islanders, however, rejected these notions as suicidal. Their sentiments were shared by many of those who did resist, such as Norman Le Brocq:[23] 'You couldn't take to the mountains in Jersey with arms in hand. First we've got no mountains and second we had no arms.' Opposition to the Germans therefore took other, less dramatic, forms.

Organized resistance groups operated in the fields of intelligence gathering, clandestine press activity, the distribution of anti-German propaganda and the provision of aid to escaped Organisation Todt workers.

The earliest – and the smallest – worked in Jersey to gather military intelligence. Led by the island's ARP Controller, William Crawford-Morrison, and the States Surveyor, L'Amy, the group consisted of a handful of men, mostly army veterans, who spied on military installations under cover of their official positions or as employees of the Germans. Plans of the fortifications, complete with map references, were smuggled off the island in February 1943 when Crawford-Morrison and his wife were among those deported to internment in Germany. Eventually the plans reached the British intelligence services after a number of internees were repatriated to England on grounds of ill health. The network intensified its operations after D-Day on the assumption that the islands might be liberated by force; further details of military installations were brought to the Allies by a party of escapers in February 1945. The moderate successes of this group owed much to the military background of the participants, which gave them the skills to interpret their material, and to the fact that their official positions enabled them to travel freely in the island – in Crawford-Morrison's case by car at a time when most vehicles had been confiscated – and to observe military installations without arousing suspicion.[24] Although the network was tiny, it was not completely isolated: there were important contacts not only with parties of escapers but also with the Medical Officer of Health, the Irishman Noel McKinstry, who was linked with further resistance groups in Jersey. Like other tiny intelligence-gathering groups on the islands, the network operated without assistance from British intelligence.

Just as the work of intelligence gathering was undertaken most effectively by army veterans, so the most successful clandestine press work, this time on Guernsey, was organized by employees of the local newspaper. Several underground news services operated in the islands during the occupation, some of which lasted for only a few issues whereas others developed rudimentary distribution networks. By far the longest-lived was the Guernsey Underground News Service (GUNS), run by employees of the Star newspaper as a reaction against strict German censorship and, subsequently, the confiscation of wireless sets. A bulletin appeared every day from May 1942 to February 1944 in the form of a 700-word digest of BBC news. Though no more than five individuals were responsible for the work of typing and copying the bulletin, the network by which it was distributed throughout the Channel Islands – for example by shopkeepers or by tradesmen who delivered it under cover of their daily rounds – was much larger. According to one of its creators, Frank Falla, GUNS 'directly affected at least 300 people daily and probably many more'.[25] The press was destroyed in February 1944 after a raid on the home of the linotype operator Charles Machon. Two of the leaders of GUNS, Machon and Joseph Gillingham, died in German prisons.

The most active and effective organized resistance on the islands, in Jersey, was inspired by two small, interlinked groups: the Jersey Democratic Movement and the Jersey Communist Party. The JDM, formed late in 1941 by the Communists Les Huelin and Norman Le Brocq, was initially little more than a discussion group of Labour Party and Communist supporters who hoped to make Jersey 'a much more democratic island'[26] after the war was won. In effect, members were concerned more with the archaic political system and the alleged collaboration and corruption of the island authorities than with an occupation they felt powerless to resist. By 1945 the JDM, which began with a dozen members, had developed into an embryonic political force with perhaps 'a couple of hundred members'[27] scattered in every parish in the island. Its ideas strongly influenced a number who subsequently escaped from the island,[28] and it carried its demands for reform into the postwar period.

At the end of 1942, a small but significant element within the JDM had become dissatisfied with this 'endless tramping over what was going to happen'[29] and formed the JCP. In particular, the deportation of British-born islanders and the manifest ill treatment of OT workers persuaded Huelin and Le Brocq to engage in more active resistance. Although it never had more than a handful of members – seven at its inception and only twenty at the end of the war – the JCP remained at the heart of organized resistance in the island until the Liberation. Initially it concentrated on propaganda work. Leaflets were produced and distributed in print runs of approximately 300 for the Communist Party, the JDM and the banned Transport and General Workers Union. These concentrated mainly on news but, in the case of the JDM, included 'atrocity' stories of corruption and collaboration on the part of the island governments. Versions in Spanish, French and Russian were smuggled into OT camps throughout the island by Spanish medical orderlies and delousing teams set up to combat outbreaks of typhus. In 1945, moreover, Le Brocq made contact with disaffected members of the garrison and produced leaflets in German inciting the troops to rise in revolt against Nazism.[30]

In 1943 the JCP also established an aid network to provide food and shelter to escaped Organisation Todt workers. Between 1941 and 1944 some 16,000 of these workers were brought to the islands in order to build fortifications against Allied invasion. They included Western Europeans and Spanish Republicans, but the largest contingent – almost half, and by far the worst treated – came from the occupied eastern territories, particularly the Ukraine. Islanders could not avoid an awareness of their condition: parties of wretchedly dressed and half-starved OT workers were a common sight. Several thousand of them were starved or beaten to death, mainly in the camp on Alderney but also in Guernsey and Jersey. A small number, dozens rather than hundreds, managed to escape their captors and to seek refuge in the islands.

Escapers could not survive for long without shelter and a regular supply of food. In Jersey they were helped by a network of 'safe houses', the homes and farms of sympathetic islanders, and supplied with food and clothing collected by the JCP 'from people whom we knew to be solidly patriotic and trustworthy'.[31] After 1943 there were never fewer than seven OT workers at liberty in the island, and as many as twenty by the end of the war. These escapers were hidden with local families and were moved to new safe houses when their safety and that of their protectors was under threat. Although the JCP was the focus of the group, its successful operation depended on individuals unconnected with the Party: on the Spanish-speaker Bob Le Sueur, who contacted sympathizers and arranged for the transfer of escapers; on Noel McKinstry, the Medical Officer of Health, who transported escapers across the island by ambulance and provided medical care; and on several officials who provided them with the identity cards, photographs and ration cards essential to their survival in the long term. The motives of those who took part were varied: political sympathy with Spanish Republicans and Soviet prisoners in some cases, ties of nationality and language in others, a personal response to family tragedy in at least one. For all those involved, offering shelter to OT workers was a courageous act of resistance that could have tragic consequences. Louisa Gould, who hid a Russian prisoner at her home in St Ouen, perished in Ravensbrück in 1945, and both her sister and brother served terms of imprisonment.

In 1965 the Soviet government gave official recognition to twenty people who had sheltered escaped Russian slave labourers. In fact, the testimonies of members and surviving escapers reveal that the network was considerably larger than this. For each resister honoured, there were several more who provided refuge for shorter periods, or money and food to the aid network, or who, as neighbours, offered escapers their support and friendship. Furthermore, the safety of the participants, especially in the town of St Helier, depended on the willingness of others not to 'give the game away'.[32]

Whilst the courage of these islanders, like those involved in GUNS and the spy network, is beyond question, it remains the case that organized resistance played a smaller role in the Channel Islands than in the rest of occupied Western Europe. The attitude adopted by the British government is partly responsible for that. Having discounted the islands as strategically insignificant and rejected all proposals to retake them by force of arms, the War Cabinet saw no point in encouraging resistance activities that appeared futile and probably suicidal. None of the eight commando raids against the islands was launched with the intention of making contact with resistance groups, although a few islanders offered assistance during these raids and were punished with deportation; MI9 offered no assistance to island escapers; SOE made no attempt to provide resisters with money or equipment, and never sent agents to the islands with the aim of coordinating their activities. The islands were even deliberately excluded from BBC broadcasts aimed at encouraging resistance among the occupied peoples of Western Europe. Island resisters, when they acted, did so alone.

Moreover, they acted within a hierarchical society with little tradition of protest against authority and few organizations capable of coordinating it. The Churches, although playing an important role in island life, did not protest against the treatment of Jews or slave labourers. The only clerics known to have been involved in resistance activities acted solely as individuals: Canon Cohu, of St Saviour's in Jersey, who was arrested with some of his parishioners for evading the wireless ban and spreading the news to his parishioners, and who died in Spergau concentration camp in September 1944;[33] and the Catholic priest Father Rey, who constructed and distributed crystal sets. Otherwise, the most that can be said is that religious conviction may have played a part in motivating some islanders to resist. Several Methodist lay preachers, for example, were among the founder members of the JDM in 1941. The foremost example of Christian resistance, however, is that of Marie Ozanne, a member of the Salvation Army, who continued to preach after the suppression of the Army in Guernsey in January 1941, and who protested to the German authorities about the ill treatment of OT workers the following year. Ozanne died in February 1943 from injuries sustained after her arrest.[34]

Even more important, there was little tradition of political debate and protest in the islands. As we have seen, these were rural societies in which disproportionate influence – in the composition of the States as well as appointments to high office – had traditionally been wielded by a wealthy and socially restricted elite of interconnected families. Politics, in general, was the politics of the parish pump; the British political parties either did not exist at all in the islands, or were supported by a small number of enthusiasts with little influence on island life. Trade union organization was limited. Those traditions of deference and depoliticization that had long shaped island life now did much to encourage a stoical acceptance of occupation. The institutional basis for effective organized resistance was largely absent.

All these factors ensured that most acts of resistance would be passive and unorganized. The majority of islanders adapted, however reluctantly, to the occupation. If they showed their feelings in public, it was in ways that were safe – by pointedly ignoring the Germans, or by walking out of cinemas during the showing of the compulsory German newsreels. More frequently than adults, teenagers engaged in mockery, jeering the newsreels or undermining the order to salute uniformed German officers by saluting the postman and the milkman as well.[35] On a few occasions, however, islanders were able to demonstrate their loyalties on a much larger scale. In September 1942, 2,000 British born islanders were deported to Germany on the order of Hitler, partly in retaliation for the internment by Britain of 500 German men in Iran, and partly in an attempt to drive a wedge between native and British-born islanders. Their departure was marked by farewell parties in Guernsey, by collections of food and clothing and, on Jersey, by a gathering of large crowds on the quayside in St Helier to bid farewell to the deportees and to sing patriotic songs. Apart from some scuffles between a few young islanders and German soldiers, the event has lived in the memory of most observers for its dignity and restraint.

Other displays of patriotic feeling occurred during the funerals of British servicemen in the islands. In June 1943, for example, thousands of people attended the burial of RAF aircrew who had been shot down over Jersey. The most impressive display of popular feeling, however, came in Guernsey on 17 November 1943, at the funeral of 21 British sailors whose bodies had been washed ashore after the sinking of HMS Charybdis and HMS Limbourne in the Channel on the night of 22/23 October. Shops were closed throughout the island for the ceremony, which included a funeral oration given by the commander of the occupation garrison, Graf von Schmettow. More than 4,000 islanders – approximately 20 per cent of the population – attended the funeral and laid 900 wreaths.[36] These demonstrations of loyalty were an example of passive patriotism and not active resistance: they were legal and, apart from an occasional scuffle, entirely peaceful. Nevertheless, the German authorities were sufficiently alarmed at the intensity of feeling shown at the demonstrations to take precautions aimed at preventing further incidents.

Opportunities such as these were rare. Most spontaneous opposition to the occupiers consisted of illegal acts, undertaken by lone individuals or isolated groups in the fear of detection and punishment. Though some formed part of a consistent pattern of anti-German conduct, many were acts of daring or bravado that were rarely or never repeated. Escape, either to the south coast of England or, after D-Day, to France, was an example of the second type, although the strong currents and rocky outcrops surrounding the islands, as well as the distance to be travelled, made it a difficult and dangerous choice even for experienced sailors. Of Guernsey's seventy-eight escapers, well over half left in the first two days of the occupation, frequently in family groups that included significant numbers of women. They were strongly condemned by the Controlling Committee. In September 1940, the military government responded to another escape by introducing restrictions on access to the sea, which were subsequently tightened further: most boats were confiscated and others concentrated in designated harbours; engine capacities were limited and petrol supplies strictly rationed; beaches were patrolled and heavily mined; boats were forbidden to put to sea when visibility was poor. These measures, later accompanied by a threat to deport men of military age, had the desired effect. Only five more boats escaped from Guernsey before the Liberation, although one of these, in January 1945, carried intelligence collected by the French Consul, Lambert.[37]

Escape from Jersey to England was more difficult still, not only because of the greater distance to be travelled but also because boats had to run the gauntlet of German defences on the other islands. Only three boats reached England before June 1944, although although at least one of these escapes, by Denis Vibert, required remarkable endurance and daring. After D-Day, however, the proximity of the French coast ten miles away made escape appear a reasonable risk despite the dangers of mines and German patrols. Most of Jersey's eighty would-be escapers were young men who had reached military age under the occupation and were eager to link up with the Allies – as one recounted later, 'to join the forces, really to have a go at the Germans'.[38] Several escape attempts ended with the capture and some with the death of the participants, especially after the Germans issued orders that escapers in difficulties should be shot or left to drown rather than be rescued. Although escape was an act of unorganized resistance, in Jersey some planning was required to obtain a boat and move it into place, to obtain scarce supplies of rationed petrol, to find a suitable site and helpers to launch the boat. In accounts of these escapes, a few names appear repeatedly: the elderly boat-builder William Gladden, who also sheltered Organisation Todt workers; the farmer 'Bill' Bertram and his family, who helped several parties of escapers from their farms near Fauvic; and Noel McKinstry, who provided the petrol for more than one attempt.

For islanders lacking boats and seafaring skills, escape was hardly a possibility. For several months, the only spontaneous resistance to occupation took the form of outbursts of frustration and resentment. A small number of islanders simply lost their tempers with German soldiers and insulted them, an offence for which they were sentenced to short periods of imprisonment by island as well as German courts. The cases of Guernseywomen like Ruby Langlois and Winifred Green became part of island folklore. Though minor, such cases were taken sufficiently seriously by the Germans for some offenders to be categorized as 'politically unreliable' or 'previously received mild punishment' and earmarked for deportation to Germany along with Jews and army veterans in February 1943.[39] In a few cases, offenders were sent to continental prisons, and at least one – the lawyer Leonce Ogier – did not return. Even more rarely, island men attacked German soldiers with their fists and were punished either with beatings or with sentences of up to two years' imprisonment.[40]

After March 1941, these minor acts of defiance were accompanied by petty sabotage – telephone cables were cut, signposts defaced, German vehicles damaged, and, increasingly, uniforms and equipment stolen.[41] The military government responded to more serious incidents by extending the nightly curfew, and on very rare occasions by taking hostages. Nevertheless, the attacks continued throughout the occupation and increased significantly during the last months of the war, when they were extended to include the daubing of German depots and the homes and shops of alleged collaborators with swastikas. These activities were never coordinated and, as the Germans suspected, were frequently the work of adolescents. Their perpetrators, too, recognized them for what they were – 'pinpricks' that annoyed the Germans and boosted the morale of those involved without inflicting serious damage on the occupying power. As a leading participant has acknowledged, they were carried out in a mood of 'half patriotism and half devilment'. For teenage boys especially, petty sabotage was 'how you got your kicks. These days they'd call you hooligans.'[42]

Only once during the war did minor actions of this kind take on the aspect of a concerted campaign. Following the BBC broadcasts by 'Colonel Britton' (Douglas Ritchie) in July 1941 calling on European peoples to display the V-sign as a symbol of their will to defeat the Germans, V-signs were chalked or painted on doors, walls and gateposts across the islands; they were made into badges and Christmas cards; they were cut into paper shapes and scattered along streets.[43] The Germans took the campaign seriously enough to have the island police forces question schoolchildren, and to imprison small numbers of islanders for 'insulting the German army' or 'engaging in an anti-German demonstration'.[44] As elsewhere in Europe, the campaign had lost its momentum by the end of the year. It was always the work of a small minority, criticized not only by the island authorities but by some ordinary islanders as 'a few people acting foolishly'.[45]

The most widespread refusal to comply with the orders of the occupying power was provoked by the German decision, in June 1942, to confiscate wireless sets throughout the islands in order to prevent inhabitants from listening to the BBC. The policy was bitterly resented and widely flouted. Families hid sets in attics, under the stairs, in garden sheds, or walled up behind chimneys; young islanders broke into stores and stole back confiscated sets; after D-Day, and especially after electricity was cut off early in 1945, the manufacturing of 'crystal sets' became something of a cottage industry.[46] It seems probable that the majority of islanders, even if they did not keep a set themselves, had access to the news through friends and neighbours. The effect on morale, which should not be underestimated, was summarized by Frank Falla:[47] 'To have heard the BBC news inspired us with a feeling of knowing the truth, and gave us heart to carry on.'

After the war, islanders who referred to the withholding of sets did so almost casually and without interpreting it as an act of resistance. Many of their tales of narrow escapes from German searches – with sets thrown into the washing up, or hidden in beds or under tea-cosies – were related almost as a joke. This tendency to underplay the dangers is understandable, particularly as some German soldiers allowed islanders to listen on their sets. At one stage, arrests for withholding wirelesses were so common that offenders had their three-month sentences deferred because the prisons were full. Nevertheless, evasion of the ban deserves to be regarded as a form of passive resistance. Keeping a wireless set was never without an element of risk: German searches were random and could be extremely thorough. For those islanders who chose to listen in larger groups, moved sets around the islands, or passed on the BBC news by word of mouth or on scraps of paper, the dangers were considerably greater and the punishments more severe. Several islanders never returned from imprisonment on the continent for these offences, yet their 'crimes' were little worse than those of thousands of others who went unpunished.[48] Evading capture, one participant has noted, was largely a matter of luck.[49]

No examination of unorganized resistance would be complete without brief analysis of its humanitarian aspect. The obvious ill-treatment of OT workers in the islands, combined with the orders of the military government that they were not to be given food, turned minor acts of charity into a form of resistance. In some cases, the attitude of islanders towards OT workers could be ambivalent and even hostile. Their wretched appearance could arouse fear and disgust as well as pity, especially when they stole food from islanders who were themselves going hungry. Some escapers were betrayed to the authorities by people to whom they had turned for help. Much more frequently, however, the accounts of islanders and surviving OT workers reveal gestures of kindness – small gifts of food and clothing, occasional offers of a night's shelter – often made by local housewives to men whose condition they recognized as desperate. Many of these were chance encounters, although on a number of occasions island families stuck up brief friendships with individual OT workers and offered them food until they were moved to another location.[50]

Some Jewish lives were also saved by the actions of individual islanders. Discrimination against the Jews who remained in the Channel Islands began in October 1940 with an order that defined 'Jewishness' and required Jews to register with the authorities. In Jersey twelve people registered under the order, eight of whom had Gentile spouses and were not practising the Jewish religion; another five, including three foreign-born Jewish women, registered in Guernsey and Sark. The order was followed by eight others, which cumulatively destroyed the basis of Jewish economic and social life. The island authorities offered little resistance to these measures. Only one official, the Guernsey Jurat Sir Abraham Lainé, refused his assent to the first order when it came before the courts. In both islands, the register of Jews, subsequently to be used as the basis for further measures of discrimination and deportation, was compiled by local officials. Later orders were registered and implemented without opposition, except for the refusal of Alexander Coutanche and his Attorney-General, Duret Aubin, to accept the eighth order of June 1942 requiring Jews in Jersey to wear the yellow star. The Germans did not insist upon it.

Jews on the register thereafter had little opportunity to resist their fate. In April 1942 three foreign-born Jewish women were deported to their deaths from Guernsey, despite appeals for clemency from employers in two cases and privately, in one case, from John Leale. In February 1943, several British Jews were deported to internment camps in Germany along with army veterans and political undesirables, where they survived the war largely, it appears, because of their British nationality. The best chance of survival – and for foreign-born Jews, the only chance was to avoid registering as Jewish, an act that was itself a form of resistance. Three British Jews, two of them half sisters married to island men, survived the occupation by living as gentiles, undetected by the Germans and undenounced by their neighbours. Another three, foreign-born, Jewish women were hidden by non-Jewish islanders who thereby put their own lives at risk: by Albert Bedane, who also sheltered OT workers and offered help to escapers; by Dorothea Weber, an island woman married to an Austrian soldier; and by a middle-aged couple in St Helier. All survived the war.[51]

Liberation and Reconstruction

Resistance played no part in the liberation of the Channel Islands. Allied military strategists rejected proposals for invasion on the grounds that the strategic advantages were minimal and the likely costs in terms of lives and property too great; instead, the garrison would be forced to submit by the defeat of German armies on the European mainland. The unconditional surrender of the German garrison was accepted by a task force on HMS Bulldog and HMS Beagle in the morning of 9 May 1945. This peaceful end to the occupation, welcome though it was, intensified the inclination of islanders as well as outsiders to overlook the activities of resistance groups: no islanders were involved in fighting to liberate their communities, and not even the military intelligence gathered by the Crawford-Morrison group was used.

Nor did resistance groups play a significant part in the reconstruction of the islands after the war. True, the JDM led calls for the democratization of the islands in the immediate postwar period and for an inquiry into wartime collaboration and corruption. There was, the Commander of the Liberation Force, reported, 'growing discontent with the previous some-what archaic and undemocratic form of government on the islands'.[52] By the end of the decade, moreover, reforms had been introduced in both Jersey and Guernsey to remove voting rights from unelected members, to reduce the influence of indirect election and election for life, and to increase the number of directly elected deputies in the States. Yet it would be incorrect to attribute these changes specifically to the influence of the JDM and its supporters. Amendments had already been suggested by influential London-based islanders during the war, and were finally proposed by the States themselves with the proviso that the 'institutions, laws and customs are held very dear by the great majority of the people'.[53] In effect the reforms confirmed, in modernized form, the old system of government in the islands and the influence of their traditional élites.

Furthermore, the brief British government inquiry into allegations of collaboration in the islands largely upheld the stand taken by the authorities. Reporting its findings to the House of Commons on 20 August 1945, the Home Secretary, James Chuter-Ede, acknowledged that mistakes had been made but emphasized how vital it had been to retain the island governments in place; in general, he concluded, islanders had 'every reason to be proud of themselves'.[54] The subsequent honours list included knighthoods for the Bailiffs and honours for other leading members of the wartime administrations. Critics of the island governments complained, with some justification, of a whitewash. Certainly the British government had opted to stifle debate, probably fearful of reviving islanders' resentment at their treatment in June 1940 and unwilling to draw attention, at a time of national celebration, to behaviour which appeared uncomfortably close to collaboration. Vindication of the island authorities went hand in hand with failure to acknowledge the achievements of resistance. Apart from the British Empire Medal awarded to 'Bill' Bertram, resisters were – and have remained - conspicuous by their absence from the honours list.

The islands, too, have been slow to recognize the achievements and sufferings of the resistance. The reluctance of their governments needs little explanation. Not only had resisters engaged in conduct that the authorities had attacked as futile and even damaging, but they had also led the calls for radical changes in the islands' system of government and for investigations into alleged wartime collaboration. Moreover, some of them were communists and thus, in the Cold War, particularly suspect. Yet the first historians of the occupation, writing in 1955, also noted an apparent indifference among ordinary islanders.[55] More recently and controversially, the historian and journalist Madeleine Bunting has argued that a tacit agreement was reached to forget the bitterness of the recent past and to establish a sanitized version of the occupation for the particular benefit of the tourist industry. Acknowledging resisters, she claims, would only have drawn unwelcome attention to the passivity of the great majority.[56] The point can be taken too far – after all, some prominent resisters were elected to the Jersey States after the war, including, astonishingly, the Communist Norman Le Brocq – but it is certainly the case that no 'resistance myth' was ever created to assist in the reconstruction of island pride and identity after the humiliation of defeat. Nor was one deemed necessary. Instead, the honour of the islands was seen to lie in the stoicism with which they had withstood the hardships of occupation and in the courage of those 10,000 islanders – a strikingly high proportion – who had contributed to the liberation of Europe as members of the British armed forces. It is only in recent years that there has been a major revival of interest in the achievements of the islands' resistance, stimulated above all by the fiftieth anniversary celebrations of the Liberation in 1995. In Jersey, in particular, memorials have been unveiled to honour those who lost their lives following their deportation for political offences and acts of humanitarian resistance. There has also been considerable press coverage of the fate of individual resisters.[57]

Much of the literature reflects a similar hesitancy. Islanders have published numerous accounts of life under occupation, particularly in the immediate postwar years and as part of the fiftieth anniversary celebrations. Most of these concentrate on the material hardships of occupation and the resourcefulness of the population in overcoming them and are emphatically not stories of resistance, although they do reveal the widespread evasion of the wireless ban and depict, almost in passing, many acts of kindness to slave labourers. Few of those involved in resistance activities have published their stories.[58]

Historians, too, have produced general accounts of the occupation that deal primarily with the everyday life of the islanders and the conduct of their governments. The official history of the occupation by Charles Cruikshank, commissioned by the States of Jersey and Guernsey and published in 1975, devotes remarkably little attention to resistance and is critical of most of those who engaged in it for 'failing to see the harm it could do to their fellow islanders'. Refusing to engage in futile resistance is described as 'good sense'.[59] By contrast, the early history by Alan Wood and Mary Seaton Wood, and the recent accounts by King and Bunting, are sympathetic to those who took 'the dangerous and lonely decision'[60] to resist. In the last two cases, however, the dominant theme is not resistance but the extent of collaboration. This, too, is the approach taken by a recent French work, the revealingly titled *Vichy sur Manche*.[61] Not surprisingly, the topic retains the power to arouse passionate resentment in the islands. In the rest of Britain, the controversy surrounding Bunting's book reveals two distinct if somewhat contradictory impulses: on the one hand, an implied moral condemnation of islanders for collaborating too much and not resisting enough, and, on the other, a desire to debunk myths of the superiority of the British national character by using the experience of the Channel Islands to argue that there would have been little resistance in the rest of Britain, either.[62]

None of this encourages an objective assessment of island resistance, which has never been the subject of academic study in its own right. It may even lead to an underestimation of its extent. Thus, resistance historians have emphasized the failure to produce a resistance 'movement' akin to those which existed on the continent, and they have been embarrassed by the alleged lack of resistance heroes to rank alongside those of

France or Greece.[63] The dismissive summary of an unnamed German officer – that islanders were 'obsequious peasants'[64] – has been the unspoken reproach informing many of these assessments. Such judgements fail to do justice either to the conditions the islanders faced, or to the resistance they did offer.

Nevertheless, the aim should be to move beyond what has become a sterile debate. The temptation to make direct comparisons between the wartime experiences of the Channel Islands and the fate that would have befallen an occupied Britain should be resisted. The geographical isolation of the islands, their unique political and social traditions, the fact that they were not a defeated 'country' but part of an undefeated nation in whose armed forces many islanders were fighting – all were factors which made their experience unique. Opportunities for productive research lie elsewhere. There is room, for example, for investigation of the relations between native and foreign-born islanders during the occupation and of the role played by resisters who were not island born. The part played by women also merits further study, taking as its starting point their political, social and economic position in island life. Although it is clear that women were hardly involved at all in petty sabotage but were responsible for many acts of charity towards OT workers, their place in organized resistance networks is still obscure. Here they remain shadowy figures, participating as the wives, fiancées or blood relatives of the male protagonists but rarely portrayed as being involved in their own right.

From a wider perspective, the Channel Islands provide the historian with an opportunity to study the possibilities and limitations of resistance in small and well-ordered communities that were cut off from outside help. Thanks in no small part to the interviews with islanders carried out by Madeleine Bunting, a tentative working model of the ways in which resistance actually took place can be established. These were societies, as we have seen, in which the majority of inhabitants did not resist and were encouraged by their governments to cooperate with the occupying power. A minority, despite their fear of the Germans and even of betrayal by fellow islanders, were involved in active resistance at an unorganized level, sometimes on a regular basis but more often in the form of occasional or single acts of defiance. Incidents of petty sabotage tended to be the work of adolescents or young adults who were attracted to gestures of patriotic daring and lacked the family or financial responsibilities that might otherwise have acted as a brake on their conduct. Much broader sections of the community, on the other hand, gave illegal offers of assistance to slave labourers and took part in legal demonstrations of patriotism and loyalty. Nonetheless, evasion of the ban on wireless sets was the only form of disobedience to be undertaken on a massive scale, and perhaps involved over half of the population. Only a small minority of islanders, hundreds rather than thousands of people out of a wartime population of 60,000, engaged in organized resistance. Their networks – to gather intelligence, to disseminate news and propaganda, to shelter slave labourers – operated as self-contained groups and not as an organized resistance movement. Yet there were tenuous and informal links between them. These were forged by a small number of people with contacts across the islands: for example, by Noel McKinstry, who was in touch with the intelligence network, with the JCP and its efforts to organize aid to OT workers, and with escapers; by Norman Le Brocq and Les Huelin, who were responsible for much of the propaganda work of the JDM and JCP, as well as organizing the aid network for slave labourers and establishing contacts with disaffected German soldiers; and by men like Albert Bedane and the boat-builder William Gladden, who were known to would-be escapers, to slave labourers, and to the resistance groups as likely sources of help. Individuals like these, acting from a variety of motives and frequently making use of particular skills and occupations, played an irreplaceable role in giving resistance to the German occupation such coherence as it possessed.

Notes

1. For the invasion and the events leading up to it, see M. Bunting, *The Model Occupation: the Channel Islands Under German Rule*, (London: HarperCollins, 1995) pp.11–40; C. Cruikshank, *The German Occupation of the Channel Islands. The Official History of the Occupation Years*, (Guernsey: the Guernsey Press Co.Ltd., by arrangement with the trustees of the Imperial War Museum, 1975) pp.12–79; P. King, *The Channel Islands War 1940–1945*, (London: Robert Hale Ltd, 1991) pp.1–10; A. Wood and M. Seaton Wood, *Islands In Danger London*: (London: New English Library Four Square edition (first published 1955), 1965) pp.21–67. This paper deals with resistance on the main islands of Jersey and Guernsey, home to all but a few hundred of the islands' wartime population, and not with Alderney, Herm, Sark and the tiny islands. I am grateful to Debbie Marston, a former student

at Manchester Metropolitan University who studied the Channel Islands for her final-year dissertation, for helpful comments and references.

2. Rectors were clergymen appointed by the Crown to serve the parishes of the islands. Jurats were appointed from a relatively narrow social circle and could not by tradition be publicans, brewers, or Roman Catholics. Cruikshank, *German Occupation*, p.3.

3. Cruikshank, *German Occupation*, pp.2–3. On the constitutional and political structure of the islands see also King, *Channel Islands War*, pp.52–4; R.C.F. Maugham, *Jersey Under the Jackboot*, (London: W.H. Allen, 1946) pp.71–4.

4. On the evacuation see Bunting, *Model Occupation*, pp.21–30; King, *Channel Islands War*, pp.3–4; Cruikshank, *German Occupation*, pp.39–52. Almost half of Guernsey's population departed (17,000 out of 41,000) compared to only 6,500 of the 50,000 residents of Jersey. On Sark, 129 of the population of more than 600 left. On Alderney, only 18 of the 1,400 residents remained. The discrepancy between Jersey and Guernsey was due largely to the fact that in Jersey, leading public figures made impassioned appeals for the inhabitants to remain.

5. IWM Documents: Misc. 2826. Interview with Norman Le Brocq, p.17.

6. IWM Documents: Misc. 2826. Interview with Norman Le Brocq, p.8; IWM Sound Archive: Le Brocq; IWM Documents: Misc. 2826: Interview with Tony Faramus.

7. This attitude was described by one resident, Arthur Kent, as follows: 'One went about one's work, to the best of one's ability as though the Germans were not there at all.' IWM Documents: Misc. 2826: Interview with Arthur Kent.

8. IWM Sound Archive: Michael Ginns. See also IWM Sound Archive: Peter Crill; Leslie Sinel; IWM Documents: Misc. 2826: Tony Faramus.

9. IWM Sound Archive: Peter Crill.

10. On the structure of the occupation administration, see Wood and Seaton Wood, *Islands in Danger*, pp.94–5; Bunting, *Model Occupation*, pp.328–9; Cruikshank, *German Occupation*, pp.103–7; King, *Channel Islands War*, pp.40–1.

11. Comments about the good behaviour of the German troops appear with striking frequency in islanders' memories of the occupation. IWM Sound Archive: Peter Crill; Michael Ginns; Norman Le Brocq; IWM Documents: A. Laine, 'German Occupation of Guernsey 1940–1945', p.18; IWM Documents: Misc 2826: Vernon Le Maistre; PRO

HO 144/22176: A.F. Butterworth, Boots the Chemist, Report of Business during German Occupation to the end of 1944, Guernsey, 7 May 1945; R. Mollett, *Jersey Under the Swastika*, (London: Hyperion Press, 1945) p.48; John Lewis, *A Doctor's Occupation*, (Guernsey: Guernsey Press Co. Ltd., 1982) p.42. Even some resisters had friendly relations with individual German soldiers: see for example Bunting, *Model Occupation*, pp.53, 140.

12. For instances of German punishments for petty infringements see Jersey Archives: Bailiff's Files: W50/33: Feldkommandantur to Bailiff, 23 October 1941; Island Archive Service, Guernsey: FK 1–11: Inselkommandantur to B.d.b.K. Feldkommandantur 515, 18 March 1941. For details of islanders deported for political offences and who died on the continent see Jersey Archives: Joe Miere collection L/C/24/A/5; also see *Jersey Evening Post*, 28 April 1995, p.13.

13. The German authorities noted that local people in Guernsey were hostile to petty sabotage: IAS, Guernsey: FK 1–11: Feldkommandantur 515, Schumacher to Bezirkschef A Abt Ic Kommandostab, St Germain, 30 April 1941; Nebenstelle Guernsey der FK 515 to Inselkommandantur Guernsey, 9 May 1941. Escapers from Guernsey in August 1943 were convinced that '50% of the islanders will be horrified and angry at their own escape because it may entail reprisals': PRO ADM 223/288: MI 19 (RPS)/1742, 23 August 1943: Report Channel Islands Guernsey. See also IWM Documents: R.E.H. Fletcher, 'Diary of the Occupation Years', pp.98,122; Bunting, *Model Occupation*, p.206.

14. On betrayals see Wood and Seaton Wood, *Islands in Danger*, esp. p.191 on the resistance of postal workers who deliberately 'lost' over 400 letters of denunciation.

15. King, *Channel Islands War*, p.52.

16. Speech delivered by Ambrose Sherwill at the first occupation meeting of the Guernsey States, quoted in Bunting, *Model Occupation*, p.77.

17. Quoted in Bunting, *Model Occupation*, p.74.

18. See for example the comments of two resisters: IWM Sound Archive: Norman Le Brocq; IWM Sound Archive: Bob Le Sueur.

19. On the conduct of the island governments see Bunting, *Model Occupation*, pp.89–96, drawing attention to the more cooperative attitude of the Controlling Council in Guernsey; see also more Cruikshank, *German Occupation*, p.157; King, *Channel Islands War*, p.57.

20. Bunting, *Model Occupation*, pp.193–4.

21. King, *Channel Islands War*, pp.57–8.
22. Jersey Archives: Bailiff's Files: B/A/W50/21: Bailiff's Warning, 21 May 1941. The President of the Public Instruction Committee at the States Offices also sent a letter to head teachers instructing them to explain the Bailiff's Warning to their pupils and referred to 'stupid and wicked acts of sabotage'. See also Bunting, *Model Occupation*, p.206.
23. IWM Documents: Misc 2826: Interview with Norman Le Brocq, p.17.
24. On the Crawford-Morrison – L'Amy network see Wood and Seaton Wood, *Islands in Danger*, pp.164–5; King, *Channel Islands War*, pp.85–6; Bunting, *Model Occupation*, pp.203, 210.
25. F. Falla, *The Silent War*, (London: Leslie Frewin, 1967) p.127. For the story of GUNS see Falla, Silent War, pp.127–65; Bunting, Model Occupation, p.212; King, Channel Islands War, pp.90–1; on the arrest of Machon, see IAS, Guernsey: FK 4-7: Feldgendarmerie 515 Nebenstelle Guernsey, 11 March 1944.
26. IWM Sound Archive: Le Brocq.
27. Ibid.
28. PRO WO 199/2091 B: MI 19 (RPS)/2438, 2 October 1944: Report on five Jerseymen who left for France in September 1944; PRO ADM 223/687: MI 19 (RPS)/2510, 27 November 1944: Report Jersey. Siege Conditions.
29. Société Jersiaise, GO Box 10/33: Transcript of talk given by Norman Le Brocq talk to the Channel Islands Occupation Society, 4 April 1998, p.2.
30. For further details of this work see Société Jersiaise, GO Box 10/33: Le Brocq; IWM Sound Archives: Le Brocq; IWM Documents: Misc 2826: Le Brocq; Bunting, *Model Occupation*, pp.213–14. An example of the JDM leaflet can be found in PRO HO 144/22237: MI19 (RPS)/ 2510: Statement issued by the JDM and brought over by escapers, 14 October 1944. Examples of the leaflets distributed among German soldiers can be found in Maugham, *Jersey Under the Jackboot*, pp.139–43.
31. Société Jersiaise, GO Box 10/33: Le Brocq, p.2.
32. See the account by one participant: F. Le Sueur, *Shadow of the Swastika. Could It All Happen Again?* (Guernsey: Guernsey Press Co. Ltd, 1990) p.53.
33. For the story of Canon Cohu see PRO WO311/105: FO SW, 27 March 1946 to A.H. Kent of the Treasury Solicitor's Office and attached correspondence; also Bunting, *Model Occupation*, pp.209–10; Wood and Seaton Wood, *Islands in Danger*, pp.192–3.

34. On Marie Ozanne see Richard Heaume, 'Marie Ozanne', *Channel Islands Occupation Review* No. 23, pp.79–82.

35. For examples of these types of behaviour, see IWM Documents: Misc 8286: Dixie Landick; IWM Documents: Fletcher, 'Diary of the Occupation Years'; Société Jersiaise: GO Box 10: Diary of Mrs Dorothy Monckton, 29 July 1940; IWM Sound Archive: Maurice Green.

36. For reports of such gatherings see IWM Sound Archive: Joe Miere; IWM Sound Archive: Bob Le Sueur; Maugham, *Jersey Under the Jackboot*, p.48; Bunting, *Model Occupation*, pp.197–8; Canon E.L. Frossard, 'The German Occupation of Guernsey', *La Société Guernsiaise. Report and Transactions*, vol. XVIII, part IV, (1969) pp.383–404; J. Wallbridge, 'The Sinking of HMS Charybdis and HMS Limbourne', *Channel Islands Occupation Review*, (1976) pp.43–8.

37. D. Krekeler, 'Escapes from Guernsey during the Occupation' (1978), *Channel Islands Occupation Review*, pp.6–19. On German measures see King, *Channel Islands War*, p.99; Bunting, *Model Occupation*, pp.201–03.

38. IWM Sound: Peter Crill. On Jersey's escape attempts see R. Mayne, 'People Who Escaped from Jersey during the Occupation', *Channel Islands Occupation Review*, (1975) pp.22–4; Maugham, *Jersey Under the Jackboot*, pp.66–7; Bunting, *Model Occupation*, pp.201–3; Wood and Seaton Wood, *Islands in Danger*, pp.237,266; King, *Channel Islands War*, pp.97–101.

39. IAS, Guernsey: FK 12-14: Transportliste 25 February 1942. On sentences for such offences generally, see Wood and Seaton Wood, *Islands in Danger*, p.145; King, *Channel Islands War*, p.92; Bunting, *Model Occupation*, pp.198–9.

40. King, *Channel Islands War*, p.92; Bunting, *Model Occupation*, p.193; IWM Sound Archive: Joe Miere.

41. Evidence of such incidents can be found in Jersey Archive: Bailiff's Files: W50/20: Feldkommandantur 515, letter to Bailiff, 17 May 1941; W50/21: Feldkommandantur, letter to Bailiff, 20 May 1941; similar letters covering 1941, 1942 and 1944 in W50/25; W50/39; W50;58; W50/64; W50/133; IAS Guernsey: FK 1-11: Nebenstelle Guernsey, Feldgendarmerie to Feldkommandantur 515, 26 July 1941; similar letters in November 1941.

42. IWM Documents: Misc 8626: Interview with Joe Miere. See also IWM Sound Archive: Joe Miere; IWM Documents: Misc 8626: Tony Faramus; Stella Perkins.

43. Jersey Archive: Bailiff's Files: W50/24: Feldkommandantur 515 to Bailiff, 9 June 1941; 27 July1941; 28 July 1941; for punishments and further outbreaks see W50/33: Feldkommandantur 515 to Bailiff 23 October 1941; 27 December 1941; 6 January 1942; W50/39: Feldkommandantur 515 to A.J.Brackenbury, Olympia amusement arcade, 23 November 1941; IWM Sound Archive: Maurice Green.

44. See for example Bunting, *Model Occupation*, pp.205–6.

45. IWM Documents: Fletcher, 'Diary of the Occupation Years'.

46. IWM Sound Archive: Peter Crill; Société Jersiaise: GO Box 10: Anne Perchaud, 'Childhood memories', (1995) p.10; Société Jersiaise: GO Box 10: Mrs E. Huchet to Mrs Dean 1945; J. Bouchere, 'A Boy At War', *Channel Islands Occupation Review*, (1979) pp.27–9; D. Pickard Higgs, *Life in Guernsey Under the Nazis 1940–1945*, (Guernsey: Toucan Press, 1987) p.43; M.J. Le Page, *A Boy Messenger's War: Memories of Guernsey and Herm 1938–1945*, (Guernsey: Arden Publications, 1995) p.57; M.M. Mahy, *There Is an Occupation*, (Guernsey: Guernsey Press Co Ltd, 1992) pp.72, 78, among many more.

47. Falla, *Silent War*, p.125.

48. Here see Wood and Seaton Wood, *Islands in Danger*, pp.194–6; IWM Sound Archive: Arthur Kent.

49. Société Jersiaise: A.A.Chardine, reminiscences taped by his daughter (1995).

50. For such incidents see IWM Sound Archives: Maurice Green; Joe Miere; Société Jersiaise: talk given by Norman Le Brocq; Société Jersiaise: GO Box 10: Mrs Emma Huchet of St Lawrence to Mrs Dean, 12 June 1945; N. Le Ruez, *Jersey Occupation Diary*: (St Helier: Seaflower Books, 1994) p.115; IWM Documents: Laine, pp.50–1, 60; Bunting, *Model Occupation*, pp.216–17; King, *Channel Islands War*, p.100; Lewis, *A Doctor's Occupation*, pp.87 149,158. For one German orders against feeding OT workers, see Jersey Archive: Bailiff's Files W50/65: Feldkommandantur 515 to Bailiff, 21 September 1942. For the testimony of surviving OT workers see letters to the *Jersey Evening Post*, 18 May 1945, 9 March 1995.

51. For the fate of the Jews in the islands see F. Cohen, 'The Jews in the Islands of Jersey, Guernsey and Sark during the German Occupation 1940–1945', *Journal of Holocaust Education* VI (1997), pp.27–81.

52. Bunting, *Model Occupation*, p.264.

53. Cruikshank, *German Occupation*, p.322.

54. Bunting, *Model Occupation*, p.306.

55. Wood and Seaton Wood, *Islands in Danger*, p.302.

56. M. Bunting, 'Secret Heroes', *Guardian Weekend*, 14 January 1995, p.18.

57. *Jersey Evening Post*, 28 April 1995, p.13; see also collection of newspaper items in Société Jersiaise GO Box 2.

58. For islanders' recollections of the occupation, see bibliography below. Works by resisters include Falla, *Silent War*; Le Sueur, *Shadow of the Swastika*; and Lewis, *A Doctor's Occupation*.

59. Cruikshank, *German Occupation*, p.152,157.

60. The heading used by Peter King, *Channel Islands War*, p.82.

61. J.-Y. Ruaux, *Vichy sur Manche*, (Ouest-France, 1994).

62. For a collection of these reviews see Société Jersiaise, GO Box 14/1. See also David Cesarani in *The Guardian*, 3 November 1998. But for a very different counterfactual interpretation of what would have happened if Britain had been occupied, see A. Roberts, 'Hitler's England: What if Germany had invaded Britain in 1940?' in N. Ferguson (ed.) *Virtual History: Alternatives and Counterfactuals*, (London and Basingstoke: Picador, 1997) pp.281–318.

63. See the comments by Norman Longmate, quoted in King, *Channel Islands War*, p.83, and by M.R.D.Foot in *Model Occupation*, p.326.

64. First quoted by the Director of Public Prosecutions, Theobald Mathew, in relation to Guernsey, in his report on 'The Conduct of the Population and the Administration of the Channel Islands during the German Occupation', 9 July 1945: PRO HO 45/22399.

Denmark
Hans Kirchhoff

Background Determinants: The Socio-economic and Political Factors

There was no tradition of active resistance in neutral and pacifist Denmark, which had not waged war since its conflict with Prussia and Austria in 1864. Not only were its people deficient in weapons and experience in illegal activities but the country did not provide the geographical and physical preconditions for guerrilla war. The majority of the population of 3.8 million was essentially homogeneous and highly socially integrated.[1] The welfare policy of the Social Democrat–Radical Liberal coalition (from 1929) had had a class-levelling effect, reducing alienation and creating a national consensus behind parliamentary democracy and democratic political parties. At the outbreak of war the economic crisis was receding and unemployment falling. Class cooperation was now broadly accepted by the mainstream reformist labour movement, insulated against proletarianization by extensive social legislation. The crisis had brought about a temporary breakthrough for the Communists and the Danish Nazis, but both parties remained small and their influence on the masses marginal. In the elections of 1939, the Danish Nazi Party polled 1.8 per cent of the vote and the Danish Communist Party 2.4 per cent. The crisis caused strong contrasts between town and country. In the country it gave rise to an agrarian reaction that, at its height, included more than half of all farmers. The movement manifested some fascist features and in 1940 it entered into a functional alliance with the Danish Nazis. It was already then on the decline, and ultimately most of its followers were reabsorbed by traditional organizations and parties. Ethnic and religious minorities had extensive freedom and constituted no political problem. (The nazified German minority in Northern Schleswig was a threat only if it was supported by Germany.) The kinds of social and political tensions that could be exploited by resistance movements in, say, Eastern Europe, the Balkans or France, existed in Denmark only to a minor degree.

The policy of German-oriented neutrality, practised throughout the 1930s,[2] was likewise of essential importance in nourishing a political culture alien to the use of armed resistance. With its concomitant weak defence policy, the policy of neutrality and adaptation effectively determined Denmark's decision not to fight on 9 April 1940, and it continued to condition the norms of foreign policy, carried out, as it was, by the same politicians and the same administrative officials who had advocated neutrality before the war. This 'real world' doctrine of Denmark's total dependence on Germany (not least in the area of foreign trade) and of adaptation as the only feasible policy for a small power in a world of conflict, was also deeply rooted in the general population and was bound to create a political climate inimical to resistance. The only possible survival strategy for the nation was a fight for minds and culture like the one the population in North Schleswig had carried out under Prussian rule from 1864 to 1920 – not an armed fight. The national government, which was responsible for the collaboration (*collaboration d'état*), thus had the backing of democratic parties, the King, the administration, the Church and the media, industry, the trade unions and the employers' organizations plus more than 90 per cent of the electorate – a loyalty it was able to maintain right up to August 1943.

The German Occupation Regime

The peaceful occupation of Denmark on 9 April 1940 was decisive for the structure and growth of resistance organization during the first years.[3] The Government capitulated after a few hours' fight, having been promised that Germany would respect the 'territorial integrity' and 'political independence' of the country. It meant a promise not to move the 'bleeding' frontier of 1920 northwards to annex North Schleswig and to allow the continued functioning of democratic institutions, including the party system, the police and the military. For the Wehrmacht, a peaceful occupation was important to ensure the smooth completion of Operation Weserübung. But the arrangement also proved to be so advantageous to the Germans for military, economic and propaganda reasons in the long run that it was maintained until August 1943.

Operation Weserübung was a marginal German operation that involved the deployment of only a small force. Thereafter, indirect rule saved German combat troops, who could therefore be more efficiently employed elsewhere. Until the middle of 1943, this made it possible to secure the safety of the German occupation with just two reserve divisions and a German civil administration consisting of no more than 215 men. At the same time, the peaceful occupation could preserve the propaganda picture of Denmark as a model protectorate in Hitler's *Neuropa* for the benefit of neutral and friendly public opinion. Finally, the economic factors also became more and more important. From 1941 Denmark supplied agricultural products to the German economy. For example, meat and butter, which constituted 10 per cent of the annual consumption of 'Greater Germany', as well as fish (18 per cent) and sugar (11 per cent). The export of industrial products was of less importance, with the possible exception of cement. The danger that more heavy-handed interventions might raise trouble and start strikes, and in this way destroy the Danish *Lieferfreudigkeit*, (willingness to supply) was one of the most important arguments throughout the occupation for not changing the status quo.

At the same time, the fiction of Denmark's unbroken sovereignty and neutrality meant that throughout the occupation, the country would be under orders of the pragmatists in the Auswärtiges Amt (German Foreign Office), who were was also interested in maintaining the peaceful occupation and in keeping out the Wehrmacht and the Party for institutional reasons. Of course these arguments in favour of the maintenance of the peaceful occupation could still be set aside if the internal or external pressure became severe enough. However, until 1943, the advantages compensated for the security risks which the Wehrmacht had to take in allowing the Danes to administer the occupation themselves. In August 1943 the Government resigned and the political collaboration came to an end. Yet even after this, the Danish administration continued, both centrally and locally. The old lines of communication to the Auswärtiges Amt remained open and contributed to continuing German moderation.

The Reichsbevollmächtigter (Reich Plenipotentiary) and the Befehlshaber der deutschen Truppen in Dänemark (Commander of German Troops in Denmark) were given equal standing in the occupation apparatus, but supreme political responsibility rested with the Reichsbevollmächtigter, and it was he who negotiated on day-to-day problems with the Danish Government. Because of Denmark's low military strategic priority and lack of organized resistance the Wehrmacht was cautious and relatively tolerant during the first years. From a security point of view the military was opposed to Nazi experiments which might lead to a revolt, and therefore it constituted a stabilizing element in the occupation. Not until the defence of 'Fortress Europe' was extended to Denmark in the winter of 1942 to 1943 and organized sabotage had started did the

Befehlshaber abandon his velvet glove policy and adopt a more severe occupation regime.

We have only vague indications of the Nazis' ultimate intentions in Denmark. According to remarks made by Hitler it appears that the country was to be turned into a German province, but that Danes being 'Aryans' and 'Teutons' were meant to have a privileged status as part of the Grossgermanische Reich, the core, and the racial centre of power, in a Europe dominated by the Nazis.[4] The integrating factor was supposed to be the SS, but until the establishment of the police regime in the autumn of 1943, it was of only marginal importance. The SS was primarily interested in the recruitment of Danes for the Waffen-SS, and even the appointment of Werner Best, the SS General and Gestapo-lawyer, to the post of Reichsbevollmächtigter in November 1942 did not lead to any change in the balance of power. This was largely because Himmler supported Best's policy of collaboration until it broke down in August 1943. There is evidence that during the military victories in 1940, Party circles in Germany worked towards bringing the Danish Nazis to power but that the attempt was stopped when Operation Barbarossa was brought up for discussion in Berlin. At any rate, we can state that in the tension between the more shortsighted military and economic aims and the more long-term ideological and dogmatic Party line, the pragmatists always won.

The result was that during most of the war Denmark had a less repressive rule than the other occupied Northern and Western European countries. During the war the Danish food rations could thus be kept at a higher level than in Germany, and public health was never seriously compromised. No direct plundering was ever carried out and in terms of national income, the costs of occupation amounted to 22 per cent per annum whereas in Norway they were 67 per cent and in Belgium 52 per cent. Forced labour was never introduced and as for the judiciary, it remained in Danish hands even when litigation was directed against the Wehrmacht. Thus such cases were investigated by the Danish police and tried in Danish courts. Only after three-and-a-half years of occupation did the Gestapo move into Denmark equipped with executive powers. This heralded the first execution, which came in August 1943, the first mass deportations to German concentration camps in October 1943, and the attempted implementation of the 'Final Solution' in the same month.

The turning point came on 29 August 1943, when the Befehlshaber declared a state of emergency to crush a rebellion against collaboration and the Danish Government resigned. The collapse of the collaboration policy did not formally change the position of the Auswärtiges Amt, but in reality the general militarization of the occupation during the last eighteen months of the war and the establishment of an independent German Police power under a Höherer SS- und Polizeiführer in the autumn of 1943 undermined the power of the Reichsbevollmächtigter and diplomacy was replaced by police terror and military reprisals. It was in the light of this increasing radicalization of the German occupation policy that the resistance movement reached its fullest extent in 1944–5.

The Phases of Resistance

The Danish resistance movement went through a number of overlapping phases,[5] which in their general structure correspond to developments in the rest of northern and western Europe. (a) An initial phase of *passive and symbolic resistance* until the summer of 1941 where opposition was directed mainly against indigenous Nazism. (b) From the summer of 1941, a *first organizational phase,* which was prompted by the ban on the Communist Party and where the emphasis was mainly on civil resistance (propaganda and the illegal press). (c) From the summer and autumn of 1942, but overlapping the organizational phase, a *first phase of combat.* Sabotage began sporadically, but accelerated in extent and effectiveness from the spring of 1943 when SOE became involved. This phase lasted until August 1943, when the breakdown of state collaboration marked the turning point for the resistance. (d) From the autumn of 1943 until the winter of 1944 there was a *second and more vigorous organizational phase.* Resistance groups were centralized under the Freedom Council; communication and sabotage activities were expanded and made more effective. The most significant structural innovation, however, was the formation of the underground army and its linkage to the command structure of SHAEF. (e) From the spring of 1944 and lasting until the end of the occupation, there was a *second phase of increased combat,* with sabotage against railways, ships and the munitions industry, and an extension of the resistance, forming a mass basis for the chain reaction of national strikes during the summer. (f) Towards the end of the war – from the autumn of 1944 – a *final phase characterized by an increased build-up of the national front* comprising the resistance movement, the politicians and the professional army, and at the same time an increased concern with the problems of peace and postwar adjustments. In the military sector there was a sharper focus on defensive tasks in anticipation of an armed conflict on Danish soil, a precaution rendered superfluous by the peaceful surrender of the German army on 5 May 1945.

Hans Kirchhoff

The Social and Political Structure of the Resistance

In the 1950s and 1960s the view that resistance had grown from below in a spontaneous way and that it encompassed a large and representative section of the Danish population went largely unchallenged. This view, which can be traced back ideologically and emotionally to the national slogans during the war, has been contradicted by a new generation of historians in the 1970s. Various regional investigations in particular show clearly that resistance was an urban phenomenon and that it was initiated from above and centrally both in the initial phase, when it had to be built up from scratch, and later, when disrupted contacts had to be re-established. Moreover, the organizational unit was not the single individual, but social communities such as clubs, associations and parties.[6] There was, of course, an element of chance in recruitment, but it took place within organizational, primarily political, frameworks. This, of course, is particularly true of the Communist Party (DKP), which dominated the early resistance until the autumn of 1943. It is also true of the large nationally based organizations such as Frit Danmark (Free Denmark), Ringen (The Circle) and Dansk Samling (Danish Unification), all of which were built up around a central leadership in Copenhagen. The same can be said for the establishment of officer groups from the professional army in the autumn of 1943. Likewise, SOE was a powerful source of initiative and integration, both in the establishment of sabotage groups and reception committees (from the spring of 1943), and later in setting up radio communications as well as in forming and expanding the underground army from the winter of 1943–4.

From the winter of 1943–44, the Danish resistance movement presents a picture of strong centralization that is unique among the resistance movements in Europe. At the top stood the Freedom Council and its subcommittees as the leadership of both the civilian and the military resistance, a structure in which there was little room for the distinction between networks, movements and parties so familiar to histories of the French resistance. The leadership even extended its authority to the free Danes abroad, who nonetheless never constituted a political counterweight to the home front. There were right-wing groups that looked sceptically at the strong communist influence in the Freedom Council and who backed it only late. Moreover contacts between Copenhagen and the resistance organizations in Jutland could be rather tenuous. Only the Copenhagen officer groups of the professional army and some Social Democratic Party groups remained totally outside the organization on the orders of the politicians, so that they could act as a counterweight to the Freedom Council.

As to social structure, the majority of resisters came primarily from the extreme wings of politics where loyalty to parliamentary democracy was weakest. On the right, the basis of recruitment was provided by the small nationalist, Christian and anti-parliamentarian Dansk Samling[7] as well as by parts of the Conservative People's Party Youth Section, which had flirted with totalitarian ideas in the 1930s. For them, as for many conservative nationalists in general, the policy of neutrality – and the concomitant fiasco of the defence policy of 9 April 1940 – became the great challenge to national honour and it was the desire to defend the Fatherland which led them into illegal activity. Their gradual absorption often occurred through paramilitary orienteering clubs, which had flourished during the nationalist wave in 1940 and that prepared the way for some kind of later resistance without any clear goals being set. On the left were the communists and members of various anti-fascist groups, many of whom had already been engaged in semilegal or illegal activities in connection with the provision of help to German emigrants or to Republican Spain. For many, the anti-fascist front of the 1930s became a preparation for later illegal work and the acquaintances made at this time became important contacts in the first resistance groups, when the resisters were isolated and faced with a hostile public. Thus the majority of the early resisters were either opponents of or at least strongly critical of the political system. Their attack on collaboration was thereby also an attack on its guarantors, the party politicians and the political establishment.

1940–1941: Passive and Symbolic Resistance

The problem for the nation in the first year of occupation was not the choice for or against collaboration but a question of defence against the fascist and conservative reaction, which had attacked parliamentary democracy on the back of the great German military victories in the West.[8] This was the period of passive resistance when the population joined hands round *folkestyret* (national symbols and values), the Royal Family, Danish culture and history, thereby demonstrating a direct rejection of totalitarian ideals and an indirect dissociation from the Germans and the occupation. This national revival became a mass movement. It was supported and encouraged by the political parties and coupled with the national coalition in Parliament. Politically and culturally it meant a forceful step to the right and socially and economically it resulted in deep cuts into the social democratic welfare state. The working class, which was already suffering with high unemployment as a result of changes in production, was especially hard hit with the prohibition of strikes, a fall in wages, and a fall in standards of living – whereas agriculture and large sections of manufacturing industry profited. The sharpened class struggle, which saw the key party of collaboration, the Social Democratic Party,[9] losing ground, created a platform from where the Communists could attack the policies of collaboration after June 1941.

This national revival has many features in common with the first reactions against the occupation, for example in the Netherlands, France and the Protectorate of Bohemia-Moravia. The movement contained dispositions for both collaboration and resistance, adjustment and protest. In Denmark it was institutionalized as part of the national support behind the policy of collaboration. It therefore became a target for the illegal press, when it brought the general attack into action in 1943.

June 1941–Autumn 1942: The First Organizational Phase

Danish neutrality and the policy of collaboration experienced a series of great defeats during 1941 as the Germans stepped up their demands. The internment of Communist officials took place and their party was liquidated and then banned. The government was forced to declare in favour of the German war against Russia and the despatch of a free corps to the Eastern Front was sanctioned. Finally, in November, Denmark was forced to accede to the anti-Comintern pact. This action provoked the first major demonstrations against collaboration in Copenhagen initiated by students, but the communists failed to carry the protest to the factories. Similarly the attempts to mobilize popular protest for the second anniversary of the occupation on 9 April 1942 were in vain. Not until late in the autumn of 1942 did the factories begin to become involved, when the economic depression was somewhat stabilized and the wartime conditions had begun to change. The unrest coincided with more adverse public opinion when Berlin enforced a change of government because it was worried about the strength of anti-German feeling in the population and dissatisfied with the *attentisme* of the politicians. This resulted in the appointment of Erik Scavenius, the Foreign Minister, as Prime Minister in November 1942. He was more willing to adapt the country to German demands, and the party-political element in the government was marginalized. The change intensified national agitation against collaboration and started to undermine loyalty to the government and Parliament. Ten months later, this discontent exploded in the August rising of 1943.

Individuals and small isolated groups had published pamphlets from the summer of 1940 against collaboration, but it was the banning of the DKP in June 1941 that initiated the first organizational phase of the resistance.[10] The Communists had suffered badly as a result of the Nazi–Soviet non-aggression pact and the Finnish-Russian Winter War. (As a rough estimate the DKP membership was 4,000 in 1940, of this about half in Copenhagen.) Though the leadership had prepared for illegality, the prohibition of the DKP and the internment of its leaders (carried out with great alacrity by the Danish authorities) destroyed large sections of its organization. An intensive reorganization was begun and by October the Central Committee could bring out the first issue of the Party paper called *Land og Folk*. This became the first and largest circulation illegal newspaper of the occupation with an estimated 120,000 copies of each issue in the last year of occupation. During the early years, the DKP completely dominated the illegal press and out of a total of forty-seven clandestine papers in August 1942, forty were either Communist or Communist inspired. However, the tone of these papers was nationalist and the class war clearly subordinate to the strategy of the national front. In April 1942 the alliance with the middle classes was extended through a non-Party newspaper organization called *Frit Danmark*, which cut across party lines.[11] This came about through negotiations with the former leader of the Conservative party, Christmas Møller, who had been forced out of politics by the Germans. Shortly after Møller fled to London in September 1942 he had urgently requested the home front to carry on sabotage in a broadcast over the BBC. This had already been started by the Communists in Copenhagen and the big provincial towns in the summer. The old fighters from the Spanish civil war formed the core of what later developed into BOPA, the biggest sabotage organization of the occupation. The sabotage material was primitive and the means limited, but the results were good enough to provoke the Wehrmacht and the Danish Government to take counter measures. Sabotage was thus developing fast when SOE consolidated its position in Denmark in the spring of 1943.

External Relations

Throughout the war the Danish resistance movement was oriented towards the West, either directly via radio and aircraft or indirectly via neutral Sweden. How important this latter country was for illegal foreign communication, as a haven for refugees, and later (from 1944) as a supplier of weapons, can hardly be overrated. (The DKP had a sporadic contact with Moscow via wireless transmitter or via the Swedish Communist

Party, but Soviet influence does not seem to have extended beyond general instructions.)

All through the war, England was the closest and most important ally of the resistance. From April 1940 about 5,000 Danish seamen, the strongest pro-British supporters in the first long and dark period, sailed under the British flag.[12] In September 1940 the Danish Council was founded in London as an umbrella organization for the Free Danish Movement, with Christmas Møller as president from 1942.[13] The Council consisted of exiled Danes and naturalized Britons, for the most part journalists and wealthy businessmen, all of whom worked energetically to support the British war effort and to restore Denmark's reputation. However, the Council never created an important political power base that can be compared with the allied governments in exile, and it was never given the status of a national committee. The Allied governments in exile – especially the Norwegian one – were opposed to giving Denmark such a status, and the British Foreign Office (FO) hesitated for fear of creating a precedent in the relationship with the Free French. The FO tried to bolster the Council's weak position, initially so that it could function as an alternative if the government in Copenhagen collapsed, and from 1942 as a counterweight to the influence coming from the Free Danish Movement in the US. This organization was led by Henrik Kauffmann, the Danish Ambassador to Washington.[14] On 9 April 1940 he refused to accept orders from Copenhagen that conflicted with his conscience as a patriot, and in 1941 he signed an agreement with the American government on the establishment of bases in Greenland. In the following years, the ambitious Kauffmann became the undisputed leader of the Danish diplomats, who, as independent chiefs of mission, disengaged themselves from the Foreign Ministry in Copenhagen. The rivalry between Kauffmann and Christmas Møller symbolized the contrast between a more tolerant attitude to Danish collaboration, represented by Kauffmann and Washington, and a more critical attitude, represented by Møller and London. In a wider perspective, London looked upon this as a question of who would be the dominant political force in Denmark after the war – a matter which was settled to the advantage of those in Great Britain during 1944. Conflicts within the Free Danish Movement contributed to the fact that it never had any appreciable influence on political developments at home.

When the normal diplomatic relations between Denmark and England broke down in April 1940, SOE was the only direct connection between the two countries.[15] Danish intelligence was in a very favourable position and regular reporting to London began at the end of 1941. Although

SOE was not an essential element in the instigation of illegal activity, it was an important factor in structuring the resistance movement. In addition, it made an important political contribution to the breakdown of state collaboration in 1943. Because SOE did not have to take account of a Danish government in exile, the organization had a strong position vis-à-vis the early non-communist resistance, and it exerted a constant influence through its de facto monopoly on the delivery of material and weapons. In the winter of 1943–44, its directives on the buildup of the underground army put a stop to the polycentric tendency of the different organizations establishing their own 'private' armies. And through its directives in June 1944 and February 1945 it directly stipulated the functions and tasks of the resistance.

The Danish section of SOE was founded in October 1940 and established contact via Stockholm with the intelligence officers of the Danish General Staff, who had already cooperated with the Secret Intelligence Service (SIS) before the war. In December 1941, the first two agents were dropped into Denmark, but limited resources combined with misadventures and the efficiency of the Abwehr and the Danish police crippled SOE throughout 1942. For long periods, the Danish intelligence officers were SOE's only contacts, and they opposed sabotage that could damage the intelligence net and overthrow the Government.[16] Like other representatives of the secret army concept in occupied Europe, the intelligence officers wanted to keep the cadres of the army intact in preparation for a final battle in tandem with a British invasion and/or a German collapse. Moreover, of equal weight in their calculations was the fear that the Danish Nazis might bring off a coup in 1940 or 1941; or that a communist coup might occur in the events of a German collapse. The intelligence officers' desire to avoid sabotage and disorder in Denmark was supported by the leading authorities in London in 1942; by the SIS whose need for intelligence from occupied Northern and Western Europe was a high priority; by the Chiefs of Staff who gave Denmark a low priority from a strategic point of view – in the directives from the Chiefs of Staff to the SOE during this period Denmark is not mentioned at all; and by the FO, which had supreme authority in respect to matters pertaining to Denmark. The FO wanted collaboration, particularly economic collaboration, reduced, but not in a way that could provoke open revolt, as this might endanger constitutional continuity and block cooperation on foreign and defence policy in a western union after the war. In this way the FO prevented SOE as well as Christmas Møller and the militant Danish section of the BBC from demanding more military effort on the home front, and any attempt to make the Danish Council a government-in-exile was opposed.

Not until the Spring of 1943, when propaganda, in the form of the Political Warfare Executive (PWE) demanded a tougher line towards Denmark, was it possible for SOE to escalate its activities and to start on the first droppings of weapons and material.

Autumn 1942–August 1943: The First Phase of Combat

The main point in the resistance movement's 1942–3 programme was to demand that the government and Parliament reduce or abandon collaboration and the *de facto* support of the Nazi war effort, and instead join the Allied front as the only honourable way of achieving Denmark's national liberation. Among the right-wing resistance, the motives were a cluster of anti-German, pro-British, Christian and humanist ideals; on the left wing humanist, anti-fascist and socialist attitudes prevailed. The Communists clearly employed a two-pronged tactic. While avoiding revolutionary overtones, they coupled the national liberation struggle with the struggle for economic and social liberation, and they attacked the dominant Social Democrats as class traitors and collaborators with German fascism. The broad popular basis for the policy of collaboration made it extremely difficult to agitate for a programme of active resistance, which would unleash the misfortunes of war on the population. The desire for 'Norwegian conditions' was thus a two-edged sword, and it was wielded with great caution. It was only in the winter of 1943 that the illegal press ventured to openly agitate for sabotage and no demand was ever made for the resignation of the government.

The most important tools for influencing public opinion in favour of the resistance were the BBC and the illegal press. Unlike in Norway and the Netherlands, radio sets were never confiscated in Denmark. The BBC broadcasts were extremely popular, and listening to the Danish voice from London became essential and the climax of the day in many homes.[17] Contrary to the BBC's perceptions, and much historiography after the war, the broadcasts were often strongly coloured and propagandist and they became an important factor in the destruction of the authority of the collaborating government. With the population's access to the BBC (and to a lesser degree also to Swedish radio and newspapers) the main task of the illegal press became reporting domestic news – and influencing public opinion.[18] The political slogans were plain and clear and one sided. There is little or nothing of the sophisticated dialogue and literary quality that could sometimes be found in the French illegal newspapers. The illegal press developed enormously, both in scope and technique, with about fifty new newspapers during the first eight months of 1943, with about half of them in the non-communist camp. Spurred by the German defeats at El Alamein, Stalingrad, Tunisia and Kursk, the thoroughly pro-British public opinion increased its pressure on the collaboration. Between March and August 1943, SOE dropped seventeen agents and less than one hundred containers (compared with about fifty agents and about 4,860 containers during the whole war). The agents were attached to the existing communist apparatus and new groups were activated. At the same time plastic explosives made sabotage safer for the perpetrators and permitted greater, tactically coordinated actions. This development can be seen in statistics for recorded sabotage actions from January to August 1943, the actions carried out with explosives are in parentheses: 24 (4), 38 (8), 68 (24), 80 (24), 80 (27), 47 (16), 94 (62), 94 (62) and 213 (124).[19] In its last stage, sabotage had a clearly political objective: namely to destroy the *collaboration d'état*. As early as September 1942 non-communist resistance had rejected Christmas Møller's request for sabotage, but a secret 'Gallup poll' in the summer of 1943 showed that 50 to 70 per cent of the population now unconditionally accepted sabotage as a weapon. External events in Italy in July (the landing on Sicily and the fall of Mussolini) were the first to create the atmosphere of a crisis that, coinciding with the sabotage offensive and the increasing unrest in the factories, brought about tremendous anti-collaborationist feeling in public opinion, which escalated into the so-called 'August Rising'.

The rising began in the large provincial towns towards the end of August 1943 in the form of mass demonstrations and strikes, where the workers, in alliance with the middle classes and resistance groups, went into the streets to demand the end of collaboration.[20] The DKP became the great organizer of the rising, but without any master plan of action. The movement began in an improvised and uncoordinated way and was neither directed from Copenhagen – which was not in the centre of things – nor from London, where the Danes in the BBC whipped up public discontent but had no direct influence in the field. Moreover, the diplomats in the Foreign Office and the Chiefs of Staff never liked the idea of a *levée en masse*. In the provincial centres of Esbjerg, Odense, Aalborg and Aarhus the demonstrations developed into bloody clashes with German soldiers. People were killed and there were hundreds of wounded. The government and the political parties, the workers' and the employers' organizations tried to crush the strikes, but in vain. The Wehrmacht, which had had responsibility for defence against an invasion since the autumn of 1942 and who looked upon the disturbances as a forewarning of an Allied invasion, now intervened and declared a military state of emergency on 29 August. At the same time the rump of the Danish army was disarmed and disbanded as being a threat to internal security. That was the end of political collaboration. The government resigned and the King and Parliament stopped functioning constitutionally.

Autumn 1943–May 1945: the Second Organizational Phase

A state of war in the sense of international law never existed between Denmark and Germany. The Secretaries General of the different ministries continued administrative and economic collaboration and also made political decisions in secret consultation with the leading politicians. What decided the nature of the occupation was, above all, the growing priority of Denmark in German military strategy, first as part of the defence bastion against an invasion, later as part of *das Heimatgebiet*. In September 1943, the Gestapo was established in Denmark and began the Nazi police-terror of the last years of occupation.[21] About 6,000 Danes were deported to German concentrations camps, of whom about 10 per cent died. About 200 others were executed and more than 100 murdered by the SD's terror squads.

August 1943 is remembered as the turning point in the history of resistance in a political and psychological sense as well as in an organizational sense. In the political and psychological sense, the rupture meant that wide sections of the population now accepted the resistance and the Allies now felt that Denmark had become a comrade-in-arms in the common struggle. From the organizational point of view, the events of August led to a coordination and centralization of the resistance which until then – except for the Communists – could hardly be called a movement. In September, the resistance forces were united through the establishment of the Danish Freedom Council, whose principal components were the four biggest resistance groups, the Communists, Dansk Samling, Frit Danmark and Ringen, which had so far worked semi-legally in the dissemination of news, but now went underground. During the winter of 1944, the Freedom Council was recognized by all resistance groups as leading the fight against the Germans and during the middle of 1944 it won the status of the *de facto* clandestine government, whose orders were followed by the population. The Council was also recognized in London and Washington and it re-established connections with the Soviet Union through a special mission in the summer of 1944.

With the breakdown of state collaboration in August 1943, the main objective of the resistance movement's programme was an accomplished fact, and all efforts could now be directed towards the struggle against the occupation forces. An indication of this to the outside world was the diplomatic effort to be recognized as an ally in 1944. This was supported by London, but ran into objections from the Russians, who played on the antagonisms between the Freedom Council and the politicians, and who had no desire to give absolution for the country's anti-Soviet sins of 1941. From the autumn of 1943, concerns were increasingly directed towards postwar problems. In October 1943, the Freedom Council proclaimed its postwar programme: 'When Denmark is free again.' This was both an attempt to raise postwar concerns and to allay fears among politicians and middle class groups that the Council was planning to seize power in the event of a German collapse. The programme made clear that the resistance movement was steadfastly committed to the reintroduction of parliamentary democracy immediately after the end of the war, the repeal of all the special laws enacted during the occupation, and a settling of accounts politically and juridically with all those who had defaulted. There was broad agreement, too, within the resistance movement, that Denmark should join the United Nations as an international peace and security organization, and that Danish neutrality should be protected by a strong defence force, capable of genuinely defending national security.

As regards the resistance organization, it developed strongly both in quality as well as in quantity from 1943 to 1945. Thus communication was improved and extended, for example with a regular service across the Sound to Sweden for the movement of couriers, weapons and refugees.[22] Before August 1943, it had been almost impossible to leave the country without visa, now it became routine, albeit still illegal. An important factor in this development was the rescue of the Danish Jews from the Germans' Holocaust. This involved around 7,000 people who, during October 1943, were successfully transported across the Sound in 600 to 700 crossings, mainly in fishing boats. The action brought new people into the resistance work: naval officers, undergraduates, journalists and those with money, and important organizational expertise was acquired, both at sea and ashore. At the end of the war almost 20,000 refugees were living in Sweden. Stockholm was the central office for intelligence work in Denmark, for the illegal communication of news and it also became the central contact point for the foreign affairs of the Freedom Council. The illegal press also developed enormously between 1943 and 1945 with a total of 254 recorded newspapers which distributed about 11 million copies in 1944 and an estimated 10 million copies in the first five months of 1945.

The most rapid growth and most conspicuous structural innovation within the Resistance was the development of the underground army during and after the winter of 1943–44.[23] From 1942 onwards, the

Communists had started to set up military groups, followed by other organizations from the autumn of 1943. This tendency to set up private armies was picked up by the Freedom Council and in December it was reinforced by a directive from SOE, which demanded the formation of an underground army before March 1944 in preparation for the invasion. Via the underground army, the resistance was bound up directly with western Allied strategy for the first time, but was still in a secondary position, as part of the large-scale diversion, called 'Bodyguard', which was designed to cloak the main Operation Overlord. SOE lost its independent position with regards to the Danish resistance movement and was placed under COSSAC (Chief of Staff, Supreme Allied Commander). Denmark was now divided into six regions, each of them with its own regional command and its own independent wireless-transmitter connection to London, so that SHAEF could take over direct command in case of fighting.

A characteristic feature of the development of the Danish resistance movement from 1943 to 1945 was the final integration of the professional army into the resistance forces.[24] After disarmament in August 1943 and a short internment, the army command decided to submit to the Freedom Council and to place the officers' military experience at the amateurs' disposal. In this way a split between military and civilians was avoided. In the course of 1944, many officers were distributed to the regions as instructors and leaders, and the army chief was appointed the commander-in-chief of the resistance forces in action. It was done under British pressure and after opposition from the Freedom Council. For the supreme command still felt loyalty to the politicians and suspected the resistance movement of political ambitions. Similarly, the politicians wanted the officer corps preserved as a force within the system if the Communists – as feared – carried out a coup d'état after a German collapse. Therefore the supreme command set up their own groups outside the control of the Freedom Council – and favoured them with weapons. A corresponding picture appears in relation to the police after they were dissolved by the Germans in September 1944 and integrated into the resistance. This double loyality of the supreme command – or more precisely its double dealing – explains a number of conflicts that affected the resistance movement internally in the final stage of the war.

Spring 1944–May 1945: The Second Phase of Combat

For want of a proper partisan war in Denmark, sabotage became the most prominent military activity of the resistance. In August 1943, sabotage had attained its immediate political end, namely the end of collaboration. Its tempo then slowed down, and in the winter of 1943–4 London tried to stop sabotage actions altogether so that they would not delay the building of the underground army. When the ban on sabotage was revoked in the spring of 1944, a new offensive was begun with a highly developed and effective apparatus. Sabotage actions could now be carried out as proper partisan attacks on the large, closely guarded, armament factories. Just as in the summer of 1943, the sabotage actions were one of a number of factors that prompted the big strike in Copenhagen in June–July 1944. The demonstrations, and the clash with the German military and the police cost hundreds of dead and wounded and ended with the Germans making a number of concessions. The Copenhagen strike became the signal for a wave of protest strikes against the German terror actions all over the country in July, August, and September 1944. The strikes created an unprecedented breadth of national solidarity behind the resistance and formed the turning point of the Freedom Council as a political factor.

Sabotage policy was directed by the Freedom Council, but only controlled in the Copenhagen area where the largest sabotage organizations, the Communist BOPA[25] and the Holger Danske of Dansk Samling, were operating. Of the estimated 2,680 major industrial sabotage actions which took place during the occupation, about 800 took place in Copenhagen. Railway sabotage was directed against the German transport of divisions from Denmark and Norway through Jutland to the Eastern and Western fronts. About 1,800 actions in all with a total of about 8,400 explosions were effected during the war, with 90 per cent in the years 1944 or 1945. Sabotage was carried out by a small professional elite. Only around a few hundred saboteurs were operating at any given time and the total involved by the end of the war probably amounted to no more than 1,000 or 2,000.

While the great military importance of sabotage was a fact beyond dispute during and after the war, the revisionist tendency of the 1970s has spread uncertainty about this. A military-historical examination of the railway sabotage in Jutland has shown that it had no effect on the German troop movements to the front.[26] The wrong trains were sabotaged and the coordination between the individual groups was too bad to obtain the accumulating effect of delays which was necessary to impede the very quick and effective repairwork. The attempt to wear railway *materiel* down was correspondingly ineffective. Industrial sabotage has been examined by a team of historians in the Danish Liberty Museum, but it is doubtful whether the question of its effectiveness can be answered clearly.[27] In any case the Danish contribution to the German war economy

was of small importance – with the possible exception of cement production and the shipyards. Moreover, Denmark's most important contribution
to German warfare, the agricultural exports, were never touched. Definitive conclusions will have to wait for further examination, especially of
German sources, but will no doubt show that the importance of Danish
sabotage is to be found primarily on the psychological and political levels.

Winter and Spring 1944–45: Waiting for the Liberation

The last six months of the occupation were characterized by negotiations
between the politicians and the Freedom Council, culminating in the
forming of a government of liberation with a half-and-half allocation of
ministerial offices. The politicians supported the resistance movement
with government funds from the middle of 1944, were in charge of
weapons bought from the Swedish government, and took part in the endeavours to get Denmark recognized as an ally.

However, the politicians never accepted the wartime programme of
the resistance.[28] On the contrary they opposed it openly, for example
during the national strikes in the summer of 1944, and secretly they
continued a principal strategy of the collaboration which was to keep
Denmark away from the war, albeit now on the Allied side. Their support
for the resistance, for example through the professional army, was thus
dictated by a wish for control, and the final identification with the
resistance was a manifestation of a sober recognition of the prevailing
balance of power in the country. To the last, collaboration was thus an
important element in shaping the dynamics and the character of the
resistance.

From a military point of view, the plans to secure Danish infrastructure
(such as harbours, power stations etc.) in the event of a German *Endkampf*
(last-ditch stand) on Danish soil were stepped-up in the final phase of
the conflict. At the same time, the buildup of the underground army
continued with the greatest increase in numbers during the last months,
from about 25,000 men in February to 50,000 men in April 1945. At any
given time, the structure was determined primarily by British arms
deliveries, which did not reach a level that really mattered until the autumn
of 1944. Many men carried no weapons at all. Others were members on
paper and their training was modest. The British never reckoned on using
the underground army or the 5,000-strong force of volunteers in Sweden
called 'Danforce', equipped with Swedish weapons, for direct action
against the German troops but only for support and guard duties if a
German collapse took place.[29] On the whole it was the objective of the

British to avoid fighting in Denmark, primarily because they looked upon the liberation as a question of maintaining order and reestablishing the lawful authorities, and they were afraid that the guerrilla war would radicalize public opinion and prepare the way for the Communists. Therefore the FO and the SHAEF supported the reconciliation between legal and the illegal forces in the final stage of the war and they secretly supported the weakest side, the politicians, as a counterweight to the Freedom Council and the DKP.

None of the inter-Allied conferences designated which of the Allied forces would liberate Denmark. The resistance was linked to Western-Allied strategy and expected to be liberated from the West. This, therefore, created a feeling of insecurity and unrest when it became clear in the course of the winter that the question would only be solved militarily.[30] After the events in Belgium and in Greece, many non-communist groups, and especially the politicians, feared that a Russian liberation would form the basis for a revolutionary situation. Not until 2 May 1945 was the situation clarified when the British armoured offensive towards Lübeck closed the bottleneck to Jutland. On 5 May, the German troops capitulated without fighting. Thus the underground army never became engaged in an armed conflict, and the resistance in Denmark never developed to the point of instigating a general rising.

In connection with the discussion about the problems of transition from occupation to liberty it is important to point out that the Danish resistance never had any revolutionary potential. The formation of the underground army had been determined by the political structure of the resistance. The recruiting base had been primarily Ringen, and unlike the old organizations it had not sprung from the milieu hostile to the political system. Its members and supporters, academic and professional men with a certain leaning towards the Social Democratic Party, were all strongly in favour of parliamentary democracy. When the Communists and the Dansk Samling, for instance, tried to rally the Freedom Council behind a modest economic and social postwar programme in April 1945, the initiative was stopped by the 'non-political' elements within the movement such as Ringen, who feared a popular-front style conspiracy. Except for demands for a purge, this put an end to the efforts to keep the resistance movement together as a postwar political force.

So there was no revolutionary situation that the Red Army might have taken advantage of, even if it had arrived in Denmark first in May 1945. The question, however, is whether the Soviet Union had any plans for Denmark in 1945 at all. The speculations have been extensive. They were especially inspired by the Soviet Union's liberation of Bornholm, on the

9 May, and the occupation of the island until April 1946.[31] Subsequently they have been strongly marked by the fear of the Russians during the Cold War. As mentioned above, the Soviet Union had established diplomatic relations with the Freedom Council in the summer of 1944.[32] This came about through the Council's position as representative of 'Fighting Denmark', and also represented a rejection of the Western Allies' attempt to have all Denmark, including all the old politicians, recognized as an Allied nation. With access to the Freedom Council, the Russians acquired a platform in Danish domestic policy and at the same time drove a wedge between the political system and the resistance movement. Thus, during the winter of 1944–5, the Danes were informed that the country was a Soviet sphere of interest and that a pro-Soviet Denmark was expected after the war. Soviet pressure was put on the Danes through Thomas Døssing, the envoy of the Freedom Council to Moscow, and this gave a decisive advantage to the resistance movement in the power game with the politicians. This resulted in a more powerful position for the Freedom Council in the liberation government than the politicians had wanted. The Soviet signals caused great anxiety in the non-Communist part of the resistance movement and with the politicians. The anxiety was shared by London, which secretly tried to oppose the Russians and restrict Døssing's influence in Moscow. The newly opened Soviet archives seem to certify that this fear was unfounded.[33] The Russians, like any other Great Power, naturally tried to maximize their influence in Denmark, especially given the country's strategic position as the plug of the Baltic. Therefore they would also have willingly taken part in the liberation of Denmark – but only after an invitation from the Freedom Council in the form of a military agreement. Such an agreement was never brought about. Nonetheless, the liberation of Bornholm was seen as a territorial gain which could give the Soviet Union a voice in the discussion about the international development of Denmark after the war. In order to secure its interests here, Moscow thought in terms of a democratic bloc consisting of the resistance movement and the 'progressive' section of the politicians. But nothing came from these speculations either, and in reality the Russians did not want to challenge the Western Allies in Denmark and *de facto* they accepted the country as a British sphere of interest.

The Importance of the Resistance Movement and its Historical Role

For many years after the war, the military importance of the resistance was very much overrated. A sceptical view, which could be found in the

Allied staffs and among the professional officers and which regarded the resistance as ineffective, demanding considerable resources, uncontrollable and the cause of reprisals, was never voiced. Historians themselves were also parties to this overestimation.[34] In the light of well-intentioned, but non-committal praise from London and for lack of countervailing evidence in the Allied and German archives, the importance of the resistance was estimated in quantity (the number of sabotage activities, the number of telegrams containing intelligence material for London, the number of illegal papers etc.) without bringing it into a tactical or strategic context. However, from the 1970s onwards, a re-evaluation has set in that has served to tone down the military importance of the resistance.[35] The role of sabotage has already been discussed above. The importance of military intelligence needs to be seen in relation to our knowledge about ULTRA and the criticisms that can be found in the British archives. The underground army never got into combat. Neither the latter nor the saboteurs managed to tie up any German forces in Denmark that were not already stationed there, and the occupying troops were in any case of poor quality and not frontline units. Whether SHAEF believed that the underground army had fulfilled its role as a diversion for invasion in France is unknown. The importance of the underground army was first and foremost psychological and political. It made it possible for the many volunteers to take part in illegal work, a possibility the elitist and exclusive nature of the resistance had not been able to offer otherwise, and it was democratized by it.

The strong focus on the military importance of the resistance is comprehensible, as it is natural to want to see a positive outcome from an effort that claimed so many victims. But in reality, the way the problem presents itself is very narrow. For, as mentioned above, the military importance of the resistance cannot be regarded as being independent of the psychological, moral and political dimension. The sabotage actions are a clear example of this. Time and again they provoked diplomatic crises that then exposed the 'true' face of the occupying power and led to increasing anti-German and anti-collaboration feelings. To this must be added the moral and psychological effects on the resistance forces internally. In these forces, the military fight became the engine that could keep the men going and recharge them for the long-awaited D-day. Finally, for the neutral and allied foreign countries, the military fight became the strongest visible proof of there being another Denmark than the official one, one which did not accept collaboration and thus demonstrated German failings, even in the *Modelprotectorate*. Later on, the military fight became the admission fee for Denmark to the Allied camp. The propagandistic and political functions are obvious here.

Historians are unanimous in accepting the great importance of the illegal press in the years 1942 and 1943, when it was instrumental in changing opinion away from collaboration and in preparing the rising in August 1943.[36] By virtue of its monopoly of the 'real', news it became a media factor that both the government and the Germans had to take into account, much to their annoyance. However, the illegal papers also had an even more direct influence as joint-instigators of the big mass-demonstrations of the occupation. Again one thinks here of the August rising in 1943 and the national strikes in 1944. It is essential to stress the important moral and psychological function of the demonstrations. At critical times they gave the organized resistance a popular breadth and support that made the ordinary Dane a fellow-combatant and gave him and her a place in history. The absolute success of the national strikes shows that the 'people's war', especially as characterized by the communists, was justified over and above the Western Allies' and SOE's more limited and professionalized conception of resistance.

In short, it can be concluded that the historical role of the resistance movement became psychological, moral and political rather than military. Its psychological role was to make the population conscious of the slippery road of collaboration at the same time as showing the people a way out of their inability to take direct action. In so doing it gave back to the nation its self-respect after the disgrace of 9 April 1940 and the subsequent humiliations of the collaboration. The moral significance of the resistance became the following: it had contributed to the national liberation and the downfall of Nazism – whether in large or more modest terms. In so doing, it had preserved both internally and externally the attitudes of solidarity, which became central in the post-war era. And finally the important political role of the resistance was, against the odds and right from the beginning, to have taken up the fight against the policy of collaboration and neutrality. At the risk of life and the welfare of its members it had brought the nation from the Axis to the Allies.

Post-war Influence

Whereas a great deal of thorough research has been carried out on the history of Denmark during the years of the occupation, the same cannot be said of the periods immediately preceding and following it. Here there are still many unanswered questions. In particular there are questions about the extent to which various post-war developments can be reasonably traced mainly to fundamental societal changes already occurring in the 1930s, which can be attributed to the experience of the war years in general, and which may be more specifically connected to the role and results of the resistance movement? So far, any answers to these questions must be tentative and largely impressionistic.

Firstly there is the question of a distinct continuity from the 1930s to the postwar-period.[37] This hypothesis is related mainly to domestic developments and its inherent thrust is to diminish the postwar importance of the resistance movement. The arguments in its favour come from the fact that Danish society, including the economy and the ruling elite, came out of the war years virtually intact. In 1945 there had been no under-nourishment. There had been no significant loss of life among the younger generation. Education was not disrupted. Productive industrial plant was worn, but had not deteriorated decisively and by 1946 per capita production was already back to prewar levels. It is true that throughout 1945 there was social unrest that can be attributed to a kind of war radicalism and what has been termed 'the revolution of rising expectations', but this entailed no shift in the balance of relative class strengths as the war economy continued and employees were still on the defensive. After the disruption of 1943–5 the political system was re-established, and the purge of political and economic collaborators was never more than superficial, despite the demands of the resistance movement, and it was never strong enough to change society as happened, for example, in Eastern Europe.

When we turn our attention more specifically to the role and results of the resistance movement, we run headlong into an apparently decisive fact: the resistance movement never succeeded in uniting around a post-war economic and social programme, and as a consequence it failed to maintain itself as a united political force. On the contrary, the movement liquidated itself in the course of the autumn of 1945, ground to pieces between the pressures of internal fragmentation and the counter-offensive of the established political party machines. Thus in Denmark the resistance movement created no specific party formation or pressure group to exert influence on the postwar political life of the country. Resistance leaders with political ambitions were absorbed into the established parties.

In the summer of 1945, the Communist Party began negotiations with the Social Democrats on an amalgamation of the two worker parties.[38] None of the leaders believed seriously in the possibilities of a fusion, but they were forced to the negotiating table by the mood in the factories and their own agitation during the occupation. In fact the united front strategy broke down in August. Having embarked on a parliamentary and reformist course, the Communists cut themselves off from any radical political exploitation of vigorous protest movements among the masses. New elections to parliament took place in October 1945 after the liberation government of party politicians and members of the Freedom Council had resigned. The Communists won 18 seats and 12.6 per cent of the vote at the expense of the Social Democrats, but their gain proved short-lived. Dansk Samling made an insignificant gain from 2.2 per cent to 3.1 per cent of the vote and won only four seats out of 149 for the whole Parliament. The attempt of the resistance organizations to make the election into a Day of Judgement against the policy of collaboration failed, and the resistance movement itself henceforward ceased to exist as an extra-parliamentary factor in the political system. The electors wanted to forget and wanted normalization as quickly as possible. The winner of the election and the new government party was the farmers' party (the liberal Venstre), which had had the least contact with the illegal struggle.

Claims for the importance of the resistance as a distinct social group are rather dubious. Its members never reached any particular prominence in public life by virtue of their connection to the movement. Those who were active in political parties acted in their individual capacities, and none ever rose to the top echelon of the leadership. Much the same can be said for those who went into the military, to which many of the middle level leaders of the resistance movement were drawn by their war experiences. None of them ever reached the higher ranks.

As soon as we move beyond the sphere of immediate and directly observable effects, it becomes much more difficult to assess the influence of the resistance movement on political and social developments – and especially so in relation to long term effects on politics and culture in general. The extent to which the war and the resistance had an emanci-pating effect on the working class or the position of women and young people (cf. the discussion in the USA and Great Britain) has not been examined at all. This also applies to the more general effects on the relationship between the state and the citizen, and between authority and obedience and protest. However, it is possible that the lowering of the voting age to 23 in the constitutional revision of 1953 can be seen as belated thanks for the resistance in its form as a young people's revolt.

The influence of the resistance on postwar changes in Danish foreign and defence policy after 1949 is also unclear. In the winter of 1944, the Freedom Council presented its foreign policy programme, and it was accepted by the politicians as part of the general settlement on the libera-tion government. This stipulated that Denmark was to relinquish its isolationist and militarily weak neutrality policy, which had proved a failure on 9 April 1940, and instead join the coming international peace organization, the United Nations, with whatever obligations this entailed, military and otherwise. This was later followed up by an additional demand to establish a national militia, a demand that emanated directly from the experience with the underground army and which was realized in 1947. This, however, did not prevent the Danish policy of 'bridge-building' between East and West after 1945 becoming, in reality, a return to the policy of neutrality before the war. Not until the worsening of international relations in 1948 and 1949 was the situation changed.[39] At first it resulted in Danish, Swedish and Norwegian negotiations about a Nordic defence union, which was looked upon as the ideal solution to the perceived threat, because it would maintain Scandinavia as an area of low tension between the USA and the Soviet Union. When these negotiations broke down because of the Norwegians' opposition to an isolated Nordic neutrality, the government decided to join NATO in April 1949. This was done with some hesitation as opinion was divided, especially within the large Social Democratic Party. The question remains as to how important a part the experience of occupation played in the transition from neutrality to alliance. Important features in this are the trauma of the occupation on 9 April 1940, which took place without a fight and gave rise to the slogan 'Never more a 9 April', the humiliations of the collaboration, the breach with neutralism in August 1943 which marked a victory of the resistance movement, the will of the resistance movement to fight and its belief in the need and effectiveness of military power, and finally the movement's international orientation and solidarity. However, the continuity from the resistance to the western alliance in 1949 should not be overrated given the radically changed international situation inaugurated by the Cold War. Moreover, even in the NATO-alliance, Denmark maintained important elements of the tradition of neutrality in its low profile attitude and non-provocative line towards the Soviet Union.

However, it is impossible to detect a direct line from the resistance to the endeavours to create a European federation after the war. The European visions that are evident in the resistance movements elsewhere in Western Europe cannot be found in the Danish illegal press. The principal part of the resistance was oriented towards the other Nordic and Atlantic countries, and for many years the recollections of the Nazi *Neuropa* plans were a complication for the advocates of closer cooperation with the Continent. Thus veterans from both the nationalist right wing and from the communist and radical left wing formed one of the centres of opposition against Denmark joining the European Economic Community in 1972.

Historiography and Annotated Bibliography

The central theme in the history of Denmark during World War Two has been the nation's fight for existence against Germany, the conqueror. This theme has left its mark on the view of the occupation and the national consensus. In the postwar era it has created the big myth of a whole nation's resistance against the German barbarism, a fight against the superior force that was won by the Danes thanks to their heroism, their sense of humour, their ingenuity and their democratic culture. This myth is found in all occupied countries, but it holds a particular dynamism in Denmark by virtue of the second theme of the occupation, namely the conflict between the collaborationist regime and the resistance or, expressed in other terms, the difference between the political establishment and the non-parliamentary and anonymous strategy of resistance.[40] In this way the myth is also supposed to mask the national disgrace that the whole Danish bureaucracy and almost the whole population supported collaboration with Germany for the longest period of time (and thus directly or indirectly Hitler's war). With the breakthrough of resistance thinking in 1943 and its final victory in 1945, an extensive harmonization between the frontlines took place. This applied to the individual Dane and also to the old politicians so that they adapted themselves to the euphoria of peace or were carried away by its anti-collaborating atmosphere. The politicians who were to secure the survival of the political system after the German capitulation consciously tried to identify with the resistance and emphasized their 'legal' resistance as the basis of, and supplement to, the illegal resistance, while at the same time minimizing their fight against the pioneer resisters in 1941–3. With the political defeat of the resistance movement in the autumn of 1945, there were no obstacles to the inception of criticisms of its aims and actions, for example, its anti-democratic and irresponsible tendencies, a criticism that accelerated at the end of the 1940s on account of the worsening Cold War and the discrimination against the Communists and the left-wing intellectuals. Jørgen Hæstrup's central works on the history of the resistance movement, his thesis *Contact with England* (1956) and later *Secret Alliance* (1959), must be regarded as a response to this 'against-the-resistance movement'. Hæstrup's studies have been republished in English with the title *Secret Alliance. A Study of the Danish Resistance Movement 1940–45*. Their main focus is the top level of the resistance organization in 1941–3 as seen from the SOE point of view, and in 1943–5 as seen from the point of view of the Freedom Council. They were written from the perspective of the national consensus view espoused by the occupation generation, emphasizing the common objectives, and the military value of the resistance and giving prominence to the fortunate compromise between the Freedom Council and the politicians in 1945.

Taking their starting point in Hæstrup's works, and often criticizing the consensus view, a number of Danish and foreign historians published their theses and analytical works in the 1970s. Three tendencies specific-ally characterize their works: They were written by a new generation of historians who were too young to have played an active part during the occupation. They worked with more comprehensive contemporary material, especially after the opening of the state archives at home and abroad for research purposes. They worked in a period of thaw of the old conflicts of opinion, nationally as well as internationally, and often they were influenced by new theoretical approaches or revisionistic currents within their subject. Examples of this are the West German historian Rüdiger Eckert's *Die politische Struktur der dänischen Widerstands-bewegung. Eine Untersuchung über die Bedeutung der illegalen Presse und einiger repräsentativer Vertreter der Widerstandsgruppen* (Hamburg 1969), which encompasses the political ideas of the big organizations, especially their thoughts on the postwar era, and discloses the politicians' infiltration into the illegal press during the last stage of the occupation. Aage Trommer's critical examination of railway sabotage in Jutland, mentioned earlier, *Jernbanesabotagen i Danmark under den anden verdenskrig* (Railway Sabotage in Denmark during the Second World War), and his pioneer work about the 'grass roots' in the resistance organization in the region of South Jutland, *Modstandsarbejde i nærbillede. Det illegale arbejde i Syd- og Sønderjylland under den tyske besættelse af Danmark 1940–45* (Close-up on Resistance Work. The Illegal Work in South- and Southern Jutland during the German Occupation of Denmark 1940–45), which took issue with the 'theory of spontaneity' put forward by the generation of occupation and its picture of the resistance as an all-national war; *Hjälp till Danmark. Militära och poli-tiska förbindelser 1943–45* (Assistance to Denmark, Military and Political Relations 1943–45, Stockholm 1973) by the Swedish historian Ulf Torell, a book that included a survey of Social Democratic politicians' efforts to get assistance from the Swedish government in the event of a Communist take-over and an analysis of the Danish Brigade in Sweden as a white guard for the politicians in a German collapse. Ib Damgaard Petersen's study *Modeliten* (*The Counter Elite*) which is an examination of the social structure of the resistance movement and, based on the biographies of the 900 resisters who were killed, supports the pattern of the recruitment published by Trommer. This author's own thesis, *Augustoprøret 1943.*

Samarbejdspolitikkens fald. Forudsætninger og forløb. En studie i kollaboration og modstand I–III (The August Rising, 1943. The Downfall of the Policy of Cooperation. A Study of Collaboration and Resistance), analyses German–Danish relations from the autumn of 1942 to the autumn of 1943 concentrating on an examination of the strikes and the resistance in the summer of 1943 that led to the resignation of the Scavenius government, and includes a critical analysis of the consensus theory which had maintained that the politicians sought and wanted an end to the policy of collaboration. One should also mention Palle Roslyng-Jensen's *Værnenes politik – politikernes værn. Studier i dansk militærpolitik under besættelsen 1940–45* (The Politics of the Armed Service. The Service of the Politicians. Studies in Danish Military Politics during the occupation 1940–45), which includes an examination of the triangular relationship between the politicians, the professional army and the resistance 1943–45. It presents the first documented analysis of the double-dealing of the supreme command as regards the resistance. Anders Bjørnvad: *Hjemmehæren. Hovedtræk af det illegale arbejde på Sjælland og Lolland-Falster 1940–45* (The Home Army. An outline of the illegal work in Seeland and Lolland-Falster from 1940 to 1945), examines the resistance organizations in the islands (except Copenhagen) and confirms the main conclusions about the development of the resistance drawn by Trommer. The occupation generation pointed out the great importance of Danish intelligence for the British war effort and Hans Chr. Bjerg: *Ligaen. Den danske militære efterretningstjeneste 1940–45* (The League. The Danish Military Intelligence Service 1940–45) has been written in this tradition. The research presents important material from the war archives of the intelligence service, but has not been able to use the archives of SIS and SOE in London and therefore cannot answer the central question of how important the intelligence was to London.

The relations between England and Denmark have been illustrated in Jeremy Bennett's *British Broadcasting and the Danish Resistance Movement 1940–45* which is written completely from the BBC perspective; and Susan Seymor: *Anglo-Danish Relations and Germany 1933–45*, which is based on material from the Foreign Office, but unfortunately is rather brief when it comes to the war period itself. Erik Thostrup Jacobsen: *Foden i døren. Danmark mellem Sovjetunionen og England 1944–45* (The Foot in the Door. Denmark between the Soviet Union and Great Britain 1944–1945), is based on a closer analysis of the British diplomatic documents. With access to the newly opened Soviet archives, Bent Jensen has provided a brief survey of Soviet policy towards Denmark in, *Den lange befrielse. Bornholm besat og befriet 1945–6* (The Long Liberation. Bornholm occupied and liberated 1945–46). Danish–American relations centred round the Danish ambassador to Washington, Henrik Kauffmann and the negotiation of the Greenland treaty in 1941 has been dealt with by Finn Løkkegaard: *Det danske gesandtskab i Washington 1940–42* (The Danish Embassy in Washington, 1940–42) and by Bo Lidegaard: *I kongens navn. Henrik Kauffmann i dansk diplomati 1919–58* (In the Name of the King. Henrik Kauffmann in the Danish diplomatic Service 1919–1958). All the Danish works (except Trommer's second title and that of Thostrup Jacobsen) have a summary in either English or German.

As far as the main features of the illegal struggle, its organization and conditions are concerned, the works of Hæstrup are still second to none. Nevertheless, a third generation of occupation historians have made useful supplements. The illegal press has recently been examined from a communications-theory perspective by the American historian Nathaniel Hong: *Sparks of Resistance: The Illegal Press in German-occupied Denmark, April 1940 - August 1943* (Odense 1996). Esben Kjeldbæk has made a study of the BOPA, the organization for sabotage that was responsible for the majority of the actions in the Copenhagen area. He describes the everyday life of the saboteurs based on a large number of interviews: *Sabotageorganisationen BOPA 1942–1945* (BOPA, the Organization of Sabotage, 1942–1945). Henrik Lundbak has published a study of the Christian national 'Danish Unification' movement: *Fra provokation til modstandskamp. Dansk Samling 1941–1945* (From Provocation to Resistance. The Danish Unification, 1941–1945), and finally there are two studies of the illegal communications with Sweden, *De illegale Sverigesruter 1943–45. Studier i den maritime modstandshistorie* (The Illegal Routes to Sweden, 1943–1945. Studies in the History of the Naval Resistance) by Henrik Dethlefsen and Rasmus Kreth and Michael Mogensen: *Flugten til Sverige. Aktionen imod de danske jøder oktober 1943* (The Flight into Sweden. The Action against the Danish Jews, October 1943), the latter based on a large amount of material from the Swedish archives. The best English-language work that places the resistance movement in the general context of occupation is edited by Henrik S.Nissen, *Scandinavia during the Second World War*.

During the 1980s and 1990s, the study of the resistance movement has lost much of its tempo – in spite of the fact that the public continues to take a vivid interest in the resistance. There are several reasons. The general research interest has moved to the post-war era and in a small country like Denmark, having a limited number of university posts and limited grants, such a change rapidly becomes evident. The generation of resisters will soon be gone and thus a driving force in research will be gone too. This also means that research carried out on the basis of interviews will be more difficult to conduct and produce fewer results. Thus an essential element for much-needed studies of grassroots resistance will be lost. Finally, it looks as if the third generation of occupation historians will turn away from areas that they regard as thoroughly explored and concentrate their attention on other themes of the war years, for example, collaboration, the occupying power, the refugees in Sweden and the political and social groupings that were outside the national community. This does not mean that all research has stopped. Several works are in progress. A study of the role and significance of the SOE in Denmark, based on the newly released SOE archives in London is currently being undertaken, and there is new research into the national, non-communist groups in the resistance – a hitherto neglected field – and into the strategy of the Danish Communist Party during the transitional period in 1944–5. Finally a three-volume edition containing documents to illustrate the history of the resistance 1940–3/4 is being prepared.

The five years of occupation are some of the most closely explored fields in the history of Denmark, smiled upon by the public's enormous interest and support through large funds. Considering that this 'golden' period will never return, it is unrealistic to suggest large-scale or ambitious research projects for the future. Although the surface landscape of the resistance has been uncovered, there remain gaps in research into local and regional history, and research into the individual organizations and groups which may serve to answer questions about recruitment and motives. We also lack studies of individual groups and biographies of the main leaders that might show their way into the resistance. We have no history of the women in the resistance and no research into the latter's emancipatory effect on the sexes and the generations. Also missing is any attempt to provide a more systematic integration of the resistance into the story of everyday life of the war, or into its role in influencing political and public opinion. Apart from gaining many new insights, this might also serve to demystify some elements of the illegal struggle. Finally we lack research into the decline and fall of the resistance movement in 1945. This also goes for the latter's importance to the political and spiritual culture in the postwar era, about which we can still only speculate.

Notes

1. Henrik S. Nissen, *Danmarks historie*, vol. 7 (1914–1945) ed. Søren Mørch (Copenhagen: Gyldendal, 1988).
2. Viggo Sjøqvist, *Danmarks udenrigspolitik 1933–1940*, (Copenhagen, 1966).
3. Hans Kirchhoff, 'Die dänische Staatskollaboration' in Werner Röhr (ed.) *Okkupation und Kollaboration, 1938–1945* (Berlin, 1994).
4. Hening Poulsen, *Besættelsesmagten og de danske nazister* (Copenhagen, 1970).
5. Jørgen Hæstrup, *Secret Alliance*, vols.I–III, (Odense: Odense University Press, 1976–7).
6. Aage Trommer, *Modstandsarbejde i nærbillede* (Odense: Odense University Press, 1973).
7. Henrik Lundbak, *Fra provokation til modstandskamp*, (Copenhagen: Frihedsmuseets Venner Forlegs Fonds, 1995).
8. Henrik S.Nissen and Henning Poulsen, *På dansk friheds grund*, (Copenhagen, 1963).
9. Hans Kirchhoff, 'Vor eksistenkamp er identisk med nationens kamp – Om Socialdemokratiets overlevelsesstrategi under besættelsen' in: *Årbog for Arbejderbevægelsens historie* (1994).
10. Hans Kirchhoff, *Augustoprøret*, vol.1, p.223 (Copenhagen: n.p., 1979).
11. Hans Snitker, *Det illegale Frit Danmark*, (Odense: Odense Universitetsforlag, 1977).
12. Christian Tortzen, *Krigssejlerne*, (Valby: Pantheon, 1995).
13. Erik Thostrup Jacobsen (ed.), *Gør jer pligt – gør jer værk. John Christmas Møllers dagbøger, 1941–1945*, (Copenhagen: Selskabet for Udgivelse of Kilder til Dansk Historie, 1995).
14. Bo Lidegaard, *I kongens navn. Henrik Kauffmann i dansk diplomati, 1919–1958* (Copenhagen: Sweden, 1996).
15. Knud J.V.Jespersen, *Det lange tilløb, 1940–1943* (Odense: n.p., 1998).
16. Hans Christian Bjerg, *Ligaen*, (Copenhagen: n.p., 1985).
17. Jeremy Bennett, *British Broadcasting and the Danish Resistance Movement, 1940–1945*, (Cambridge: Cambridge University Press, 1966).
18. Nathaniel Hong, *Spark of Resistance*, (Odense: Odense University Press, 1996).
19. Kirchhoff, *Augustoprøret*, vol.1, p.173.
20. Kirchhoff, *Augustoprøret*, vol.2, *passim*.

21. Bjørn Rosengreen, *Dr.Werner Bestog tysk besættelsespolitik i Danmark, 1943–1945* (Odense: Odense Universitetsforlag, 1982).
22. Henrik Dethlefsen, *De illegale Sverigesruter, 1943–1945*, (Odense: Odense Universitetsforlag, 1993).
23. Jørgen Hæstrup, *Secret Alliance*, vols. II and III.
24. Palle Roslyng-Jensen, *Værnenes politik – politikernes værn*, (Copenhagen: Udgiverselkabet for Danmarks Nyeste Historie, 1980).
25. Esben Kjeldbæk, *Sabotageorganisationen BOPA, 1942–1945*, (Copenhagen: n.p., 1997).
26. Aage Trommer, *Jernbanesabotagen i Danmark under den anden verdenskrig*, (Odense: Odense Universitetsforlag, 1971).
27. Jesper Vang Hansen, Esben Kjeldbæk and Bjarne Maurer, *Industrisabotagen under besættelsen*, (Copenhagen: n.p., 1984).
28. Hans Kirchhoff, *Kamp eller tilpasning*, (Copenhagen: Gyldendal, 1987), p.156.
29. Ulf Troell, *Hjälp till Danmark. Militära och politiska förbindelser, 1943–1945*, (Stockholm, 1973).
30. Kirchhoff, *Kamp eller tilpasning*, p.166.
31. Bent Jensen, *Den lange befrielse*, (Odense: Odense Universitetsforlag, 1996).
32. Erik Thostrup Jacobsen, *Foden i døren – danmark mellem Sovjetunionen og England, 1944–1945*, (Odense: n.p., 1984).
33. Jensen, *Den lange befrielse*.
34. Jørgen Hæstrup, *Europe Ablaze* (Odense: Odense University Press, 1978).
35. Kirchhoff, *Kamp eller tilpasning*, p.187.
36. Hong, *Sparks*. Kirchhoff, *Augustoprøret*, vol.II.
37. See, Henrik Dethlefsen and Henrik Lundbak (eds), *Fra mellemkrigstid til efterkrigstid* (Copenhagen: Museum Tusculanen, 1998).
38. Mogens Nielsen, *Socialdemokratiet og enheden i arbejderbevægelsen, 1943–1945* (Copenhagen: Københavns Universitet Institut for Samtidshistorie, 1978).
39. Poul Villaume, *Allieret med forbehold* (Copenhagen: Eirene, 1994).
40. Claus Bryld and Anette Warring, *Besættelsestiden som kollektiv erindring*, (Frederiksburg: Roskilde Universitatsforlag, 1998). Hans Kirchhoff, 'Den store myte om det danske folk i kamp' in: Dethlefsen and Lundbak (eds) *Fra mellemkrigstid*, p.397.

—5—

France
Olivier Wieviorka

'Whatever happens, the flame of French resistance must not die and will not die.' This was Charles de Gaulle's assertion in his famous appeal of 18 June 1940. It should be made clear at the outset, however, that during the dark years of the war this flame was always flickering. By 31 December 1994, 260,919 CVR resistance veteran's cards had been issued[1] – which illustrates profoundly the marginal nature of the resistance in France. Compared with some other European countries such as Greece, Albania, or Yugoslavia, the resistance should therefore never be mistaken for a mass movement. Moreover, the clandestine forces rarely represented a genuine military threat to the occupying forces, and without the support of the Allied armies they would not have been capable of liberating the country in 1944. Yet the effect of the resistance cannot be measured only by its military significance. Its moral value notwithstanding, it was undoubtedly effective in protecting the civilian population, facilitating the development of a clandestine state, and in preparing for the peaceful devolution of power between the Vichy régime and General de Gaulle's provisional government: these factors reveal the versatile nature of a movement that cannot be reduced simply to its warrior element.

Origins

Having been at war with Germany since 3 September 1939, metropolitan France was finally attacked by the armed forces of the Third Reich on 10 May 1940. Within five days, German armour had penetrated French defences between Namur and Sedan and on 19 May Guderian's panzer divisions had reached the Channel near Abbeville. A sizeable proportion of the French army was surrounded and, although some managed to escape with the British from Dunkirk, many others fell into captivity. As the remaining forces attempted to stem the German advance southwards, opinion inside France polarized between those who advocated capitulation and those who favoured a negotiated armistice. The former would stop the conflict but would leave the political leadership to continue the struggle from the empire in North Africa, whereas the latter offered the prospect of a negotiated peace that might limit the powers of the conquerors.[2] In the event, it was the champions of the negotiated settlement, led by Marshal Philippe Pétain, and backed by the Military High Command, who won the political battle. The French delegation met Hitler and other Nazi leaders in the forest of Compiègne and in the same railway carriage that had been used for the armistice of 1918. They were presented with an 'immutable' armistice of twenty-four articles that they had no choice but to sign on 22 June 1940. Hostilities ceased three days later.[3] Only a small number of dissidents refused to follow the path favoured by the Marshal but instead chose exile in belligerent Britain. Led by the relatively unknown Brigadier-General Charles de Gaulle, these Free Frenchmen were recognized by Churchill as part of the Allied cause in the hope that they would attract more high profile defectors and might persuade the French imperial territories to continue the fight. Neither of these aspirations were fulfilled but De Gaulle and his colleagues nonetheless became the focus for external French resistance to Nazi occupation.

The terms of the armistice were severe. German forces were to occupy three-fifths of France, encompassing the northern half of the country and the Atlantic seaboard, and parts of the Pas-de-Calais and the area round Lille were to be administered by the German commander in Brussels. Germany annexed Alsace and Lorraine and French soldiers from these areas were enlisted in the Wehrmacht. A further zone adjacent to the new border was designated as reserved for ultimate German colonization, although none of these latter provisions were included in the armistice terms. In effect most of the country's industrial wealth and the majority of its population were placed under direct German control. In addition, the French army was limited to 100,000 men but 1.8 million French servicemen were interned and taken to Germany as hostages. Occupation costs were demanded at the astronomic level of 20 million Reichsmarks per day, putting into question the long-term viability of the French economy.[4] In theory, the sovereignty of the French state remained intact across the whole of France, but civil servants and administrators in the occupied territories were 'invited' to conform to regulations set out by the German military authorities.

The French resistance appeared during troubled times. The 'brutality of the defeat' (Marc Bloch) deeply traumatized the nation. The structural framework of the country collapsed.[5] Discredited by its own incompetence, the Third Republic abdicated, and virtually the entire political class handed over full powers to Marshal Pétain on 10 July 1940. With Paris occupied, Pétain's French government needed a temporary base. The spa town of Vichy was chosen as it had an abundance of empty hotels, but primarily because of its proximity to Pierre Laval's house at Chateldon and Pétain's refusal to stay in either Lyon or Marseilles. Rejecting parliamentary structures, the regime was committed to a 'national revolution', which encompassed a return to traditional nationalist values of rural life, church, home and family, and corporatism in industry. Incapable of devising an alternative to the Vichy régime, political parties and trade unions remained silent despite their links with the previous government. The army had been crushed by the Wehrmacht in a mere six weeks and could not claim to be a useful resource. When the traditional structures were removed, the ensuing atomization of French society meant a withdrawal into the private sphere.[6] Thus Jean Cassou observed: 'Everyone has gone home.' Faced with severe material problems − unemployment and rationing, not to mention the 1.8 million prisoners transferred from France across the Rhine − the population was disinclined to become involved, particularly because it could not imagine any realistic means to oppose an all-powerful Reich. Furthermore, the presence of the Vichy régime encouraged a wait-and-see policy. The French surrendered to the victor of Verdun as much to defend national interest as to protect themselves.[7] Ultimately, General de Gaulle was only known by a handful of people, and getting to England posed practical problems for the recruitment of Free French Forces.

Overwhelmed by these circumstances, the resistance began, above all, as a form of individual revolt. The apathy of the great organizations (political parties, the army, the Churches, the unions) forced individuals to act alone and to set the parameters of their fight. Some actions certainly reflected spontaneous exasperation or rebellion − for example, on 17 June 1940 Madame Lemaire, daughter of President Doumer, assassinated a German non-commissioned officer at Cosne-sur-Loire, and on 19 June a farm worker, Etienne Achavanne, severed a few communication cables. But following these crude acts more refined forms of opposition soon emerged, which reflected the conceptual variety of the struggle. Initially, some of the early resisters greatly feared the moral consequences of the defeat. Concerned that public opinion would give in to the siren voices of collaboration, either through weakness or personal interest, it sought first of all to protect society from this danger. This group therefore aimed to carry out its fight by civilian means and mostly made use of the clandestine press. '*France, prends garde de perdre ton âme*' ('France be careful not to lose your soul') was the title of the first *Cahier* published clandestinely by Témoignage Chrétien (Christian witness), a Lyons group that assembled a few patriotic Catholics around Father Chaillet.[8] The young students who launched the journal *Défense de la France* with Philippe Viannay in mid-1941 were following the same logic and their first editorial asserted that 'the struggle has left the military terrain'. If France 'recovers its spiritual power, the source of all power, then the barbarians will be crushed'.[9] Meanwhile, other pioneers of resistance concentrated on a different approach. Noting the resistance of Great Britain, they based the struggle on a military rather than a spiritual level and sought to support the British war effort by repatriating soldiers left behind on the continent, and above all by supplying information about the German army. In 1940, Paul Joly, an industrialist, set up an escape network (Caviar) which helped repatriate British soldiers via Spain. In December of the same year Gilbert Roulier (alias Rémy) transmitted the first mail through the network, which, under the name of Confrérie-Notre-Dame, was to become one of the largest Gaullist information networks.[10] Whatever their level of improvization, the resistance organizations thus initially opted for either a civilian strategy or a military approach, although the two occasionally overlapped.

The course selected shaped the form of organization adopted by this early resistance. It is helpful to take up the distinction made by Claude Bourdet, a leader of Combat, between networks and movements.

An organization set up as a precise military operation, essentially for information, secondarily for sabotage, frequently also for the escape of prisoners of war and particularly of pilots brought down in enemy territory, the network 'is in close contact with an organ of the headquarters of the forces for which it is working.[11] The primary purpose of the movement, on the other hand, was 'to raise awareness and to organize the people as broadly as possible. Of course there are also specific objectives' (such as information and sabotage). But 'above all *it is in relation to the people* that it undertakes these tasks, it is *this* which is its objective and its chief concern'.[12]

The distinction between civilian and military action, relevant for the definition of 'networks' and 'movements' is also useful in defining the various organizations that emerged in France from 1940 onwards. Some groups deliberately concentrated on a civilian strategy, following the example of Libération-nord or Défense de la France (DF), whereas others chose military action, such as Ceux de la Libération (CDLL) or Ceux de la Résistance (CDLR). Some tried at times to combine the two elements. Thus Combat, founded in the southern zone by Captain Henri Frenay, combined information and commando units in ROP (recruitment, organization, propaganda). These decisions were not made without debates and confrontations. At the heart of the Organisation Civile et Militaire (OCM), Colonel Touny (who favoured an apolitical military strategy) thus opposed the approach of Maxime Blocq-Mascart (who favoured propaganda).[13]

Geographical factors, on the other hand, made little difference to the choice of strategy. In both occupied and Vichy zones, 'civilian' (Défense de la France, Libération in the North, Franc-Tireur, Témoignage Chrétien in the South) and military-style movements (CDLL, CDLR in the occupied zone, Organisation Métropolitaine de l'Armée in the South) coexisted with mixed forms of organization such as the OCM or Libération-sud.

Networks and movements had a variety of ways of carrying out their specific objectives. Groups pursuing a civilian strategy concentrated on psychological warfare and distributed leaflets or clandestine newspapers. In a France ruled by censorship, repression and poverty – and particularly because of the lack of printing ink and paper – this form of action was extremely problematic. To succeed the groups generally turned to professional printers who, despite the surveillance imposed on them, agreed to work for the resistance. For example Henri Chevalier, a Lyons printer, made himself available to Franc-Tireur. A very few movements, in contrast, set up their own systems – notably Défense de la France. But whichever solution was chosen, the initial results were modest. *Le Franc-Tireur* printed 6,000 copies of its first issue and in 1942 *Défense de la France* distributed no more than 10,000–30,000 copies. Early resisters, often prompted by BBC broadcasts, also turned to the streets to demonstrate their rejection of the occupier or the French state. On 11 November 1940 students and school pupils marched along the Champs-Elysées to commemorate the national holiday and on 18 March 1942, 600 people protested in Lyons against the visit of the Berlin Philharmonic. Military actions, on the other hand, employed very different methods. Until 1942 organized sabotage remained relatively rare – even though a commando group of three men did manage to blow up the electricity station at Pessac in 1941. Although the escape of prisoners and pilots and the supply of information met with better luck, the movement of men or information to Great Britain depended on complicated logistics. Passages by sea or land (via Spain) remained dangerous and uncertain, even if the Comète network managed to take some eight hundred men across the Pyrenean frontier. Radio links with Great Britain, however, were hindered by the lack of equipment (Gaullist networks in France had no more than twelve sets at the end of 1941), by the poor miniaturization of transmitters, and by the effective German pursuit of the so-called 'pianists' (radio operators), 75 per cent of whom were eliminated in 1941 and 1942. In overall terms, therefore, the poor resources available to the resistance limited its potential for action.

The linkage between indigenous resistance organizations and the Free French and Allied military commands in London was, however, an increasingly important element in the equation. Some of the earliest contacts were between Rémy's Confrérie-Notre-Dame and Section F of the British Special Operations Executive (SOE). It took some time for these relationships to develop, but between 1942 and 1944, various branches of SOE (and there were at least six dealing directly with France) funded and armed countless local resistance groups. In exchange for the money and weapons, these groups carried out sabotage operations, such as the famous attack on the Peugeot factory at Montbéliard, provided intelligence material and escape routes for Allied airman, and were later enlisted to help with preparations for the invasion of Normandy. The British Secret Intelligence Service (SIS/MI6) operated its own networks and agents in France, as did the Free French intelligence service, the Bureau Central de Renseignements et d'Action. Competition rather than cooperation between the various agencies did create problems, and there were reservations in London about funding or arming groups with overtly communist sympathies, but the symbiotic relationship between London and forces 'on the ground' was of great importance in the development of resistance activities inside France.

Until 1942 however, the Gaullists in London and the various British secret services allocated only modest sums of money to the resistance organizations inside France, and they had to depend on the generosity of their own circles in order to survive. Such support was severely limited, for although Défense de la France received 100,000 francs in 1941 through the generous patronage of Marcel Lebon, Henry Frenay had no more than 14,000 francs in mid-December 1940 to launch Combat. The resistance was therefore always forced to be very resourceful to make up for its lack of weapons, paper or money. But these material shortages do not explain everything. The 'repertory of protest' – the 'total means of resistance activity'[14] – also depended on the culture of protest among the resisters. Thus where this culture was weak, resistance activity was likely to be limited.

Although linked to an anti-fascist or patriotic struggle in postwar historiography and memory, resistance activity was also subject to other parameters. Obviously, the resisters expected to fight Germany and/or the Vichy régime and organizations therefore mobilized certain images that enabled activists to identify Nazism or Pétainism as enemy elements.

Family traditions, memories of the Great War, even regional memories (the people of the north had not forgotten the occupation of the First World War), encouraged a traditional Germanophobia that provided a safe point of reference from 1940 onwards, as did reference to the ideals of 1789. Similarly, the horror of Nazism, whether it was made public by press reports or direct accounts from refugees taking shelter in France, destroyed any illusions the supposed restraint of German troops or the reported benefits of collaboration might have created. Although the greater part of public opinion ultimately shared these anti-German feelings, it did not necessarily manifest itself in membership of the resistance. It was other parameters that effectively created commitment, above all the feeling that it could be useful. Yet the means employed by the resistance between 1940 and 1942 in many ways seemed ineffective to the population. A large proportion of French citizens could not imagine how they could help activities in networks where professionalism seemed to exclude all amateur support. People also considered the propaganda undertaken by the movements as superfluous, and were scarcely able to believe that the outcome of the war could be affected by secretly distributed leaflets. As a result, the groups and individuals who did commit themselves were those who agreed with the actual terms of the proposed struggle.[15]

This relationship depended partly on the individual's position within society. Thus peasants felt little incentive to fight in the resistance as they were aware of their status in French society: they were cherished by the Vichy régime, which showered praises on their virtues, and were relatively protected from hunger and cold.[16] Urban workers, on the other hand, who were increasingly victims of rationing, exploited in their factories which were working for Germany, and threatened by the Service du Travail Obligatoire (forced labour service) imposed in February 1943, found it easier to join a movement that combined patriotic combat and class struggle. This was not only illustrated by the great miners' strike that began in the Nord-Pas-de-Calais (27 May–10 June 1941) but was also confirmed by statistics.[17] In Ille-et-Vilaine, for example, farm workers represented some 52 per cent of the working population but only 7 per cent of active resisters. For factory workers, on the other hand, the proportions were reversed (9.5 per cent against 13.5 per cent).[18] Cultural factors also came into play. Sensitive to the prestige of the written word and doubtful of its military value, students willingly joined the 'civilian' movements. Soldiers, on the other hand, who assumed that the war would be won by weapons, preferred to join the networks, sometimes mistaking propaganda for childishness. Christian Democrats were in many cases also quick to join the resistance, as for example in the case of Georges

Bidault, François de Menthon or Pierre-Henri Teitgen. Well informed through their press of the misdeeds of Nazism, confident as Catholics in the power of the Word and linking their resistance activity to the primitive religion of the catacombs (where a minority of the persecuted did their best to preach the Good Word), they had no difficulty in disobeying the hierarchy of Pétainism, which they had rejected even before the war for its reactionary attitudes.[19] In other words, differing levels of commitment corresponded to social and cultural differences. But this heterogeneity also explains the difficulties in drawing up the terms of conflict. Although the networks could prove their value as time passed despite their material difficulties, the 'civilian' movements had difficulty in breaking away from a form of action that confined itself to moral exhortation without true influence. Apart from condemning collaboration and the black market unreservedly, they did not succeed in giving the population a real lead, a factor that limited their scope for recruitment. However, the developments after 1942 had an immediate and substantial impact on the forms of action suggested.

Maturity

The progress of the war modified the context in which resistance developed, and brought about deep splits. In international terms, Operation Barbarossa (22 June 1941) swept away all equivocation. Trapped by a Russo-German pact of which it had approved, the French Communist Party (PCF) had until then followed a line that was ambiguous, to say the least. Immediately hostile to Vichy, in which it had recognized an old enemy, it had tried to achieve a legal status in the occupied zone. The Party unsuccessfully petitioned the German authorities for the right to publish *L'Humanité* and invited its members to come out of the shadows where the interdict of the Daladier government had placed them since 26 September 1939. Meanwhile, Hitler's pressure in the Balkans incited Stalin to harden his tone and precipitated the PCF's enlistment in the resistance, which many militants, either cut off from the Party's leadership, or as wholehearted patriots, had joined as soon as 1940 (in particular Georges Guingouin and Charles Tillon). In the summer of 1941 the Party enlisted in the resistance, with results that were varied to say the least.[20] On the one hand, the support of determined and experienced activists did strengthen the resistance. With professional knowledge in organizing propaganda and demonstrations, expertise in sabotage, and familiarity with armed struggle (a legacy of involvement in the International Brigades), the Communists could draw on a wide repertoire that extended the range of clandestine activity. On the other hand, their practices (in particular the execution of German soldiers) and their obedience to the Comintern did stir up opposition, which was to endure among most other elements of the internal resistance.

At home, the Allied landings in North Africa on 8 November 1942, followed by the German invasion of the free zone (11 November), and the scuttling of the Fleet (27 November), discredited the Vichy government and highlighted its impotence. Stubbornly rejecting collaboration, public opinion had found it easy to credit Philippe Pétain with sympathy for resistance, and thought that he would protect the nation against the demands of the occupying force. Some resistance movements with right-wing leanings shared this belief and also adhered to some of the Vichy values – corporatism, clericalism and even anti-Semitism. 'We are passionately attached to the work of Marshal Pétain' proclaimed Frenay in November 1940. 'We subscribe to all the great reforms that have been undertaken.' But, he specified, 'the necessary National Revolution will not take place as long as Germany is in a position to impose her wishes'[21] – a logic shared by the founder of Défense de la France, Philippe Viannay. By firmly embracing collaboration, the French state had raised doubts but it was the invasion of the free zone that repudiated the pseudo-sovereignty of Vichy and thus provided the *coup de grâce* for this fable. Paradoxically, this event simplified choices. By destroying the myth of a supposed connivance between London and Vichy, it clarified the position of the movements on the right and discredited the patriotic wait-and-see policy of those French people who were relying on Vichy to resist German demands. Asserting the emptiness of their dreams, a section of the patriotic right, which at one time had supported the French state turned back to dissent. Military officers who had hoped to prepare for *la Revanche* – revenge – in the shadow of Vichy, by concealing arms and equipment, for example, founded the Organisation Métropolitaine de l'Armée in the winter of 1942, the future Organisation de Résistance de l'Armée (ORA). Some senior civil servants also vanished underground or went to Algeria, following the example of Maurice Couve de Murville who arrived there in March 1943.

These developments reinforced the legitimacy of 'the rebel' General de Gaulle, who led the struggle with Churchill's support and some elements of the Empire, but with few resources.[22] Although his speeches made him a widely known figure – 70 per cent of French people listened to the BBC[23] – his 1940 predictions appeared bold, even insane; yet the progress of the war confirmed De Gaulle's assumptions of 18 June 1940. The armistice that had been doomed from the start soon showed its deleterious effects; the war confirmed de Gaulle's forecast by spreading across the whole world. Beyond the accuracy of his prophecy, by 1942 de Gaulle had become the sole alternative to the reign of slavery. Far from preparing the *Revanche*, the Vichy state showed up the frailty of the hopes of some patriots as it plunged further into collaboration. Furthermore, those who defected to North Africa lost credibility by refusing to condemn Philippe Pétain. By maintaining Vichy rule in North Africa even after its liberation General Giraud similarly discredited himself and in 1943 had to bow out to his rival de Gaulle. London and then Algiers became the rallying points for all resisters.

Changes in circumstances affected the very core of the interior resistance, first of all by changing its objectives. By hunting down Jews, communists and freemasons, the Reich and the Vichy régime had multiplied the categories of the persecuted. Moreover, the move to total war, announced by Joseph Goebbels in 1943, resulted in growing demands from the occupying Germans. Henceforward, within the framework of the STO, they gave notice of their intention to exile thousands of workers across the Rhine. By directly threatening millions of families, this measure (February 1943) created a shockwave in public opinion and revealed the scale of the tribute demanded by the Nazi *Moloch*.[24] This situation forced the resistance to act, and transformed it into the natural protector of the nation. The movements wished, in effect, to protect the civilians, even to transform them into combatants. Turning out hundreds of thousands of false papers (Défense de la France, for example, manufactured 12,500 false rubber stamps), they also attempted to incorporate these *réfractaires* into *maquis* groups. True, and contrary to pious myth, not all *réfractaires* joined the *maquis*, although the proportion of those who rallied to the cause varied between *départments* (6 per cent in the Aude, 30 per cent in Isère). Similarly, numbers of members fluctuated. Owing to shortages of weapons and food, several *maquis* groups could not take in all the available volunteers. In the autumn of 1943 it is estimated that between 15,000 and 20,000 young men signed up in organizations, which defined themselves either as refuges or as combat bases.[25] From that time, and despite the inability of the resistance to absorb the thousands of men who turned to it, the STO provided a concrete focus, vital and popular in the eyes of public opinion. Moreover it allowed the movements to progress beyond the vague moral protests and exhortations against collaboration to which they had previously restricted themselves.

Similarly, the rumoured imminence of Allied landings strengthened the resistance's military role in mainland France. At a senior level, movements and networks were encouraged to intensify their sabotage operations and news gathering, and the rescue of downed Allied aircrew. They responded. The escape networks altered their priorities and achieved greater efficiency. In eight operations in Brittany between 18 January and 21 July 1944, the Shelburne network evacuated 143 people. Six hundred helpers in the Basses Pyrénées provided passage across the Spanish frontier.[26] News items for London grew in number and quality. In March 1943 a member of OCM, Duchez, obtained the plan of coastal defences planned for Calvados, an essential document for the landings to come. Philippon, in Brest, and Stosskopf, in Lorient, detailed the movements of the German fleet. In 1944, Colonel Passy's Gaullist information services received 1,000 telegrams every day, and nearly 2,000 plans each week.[27] Acts of sabotage proliferated. In October 1942 the Franc-Tireur groups paralysed the Francolor chemical factory, near Roanne. On 13 November 1943, Aimé Requet blew up the Wehrmacht artillery testing range at Grenoble. On 26 April 1944 a DF group run by Yves Hall dynamited the Jupiter factories in Brest, and 400,000 litres of fuel designated for German submarines went up in smoke. And as a result of resistance activity, railway traffic dropped by 37 per cent in April 1944. Further down the system, movements and networks prepared for the coming landings. The leadership developed a series of plans for the resistance to carry out on the mainland: the *plan-Vert* to interrupt railway and river traffic, the *plan-Bleu* to paralyse the electricity network, the *plan-Tortue* to slow down German military convoys. The movements also created a 'secret army', which, by taking in previously registered volunteers, could play its part in the Battle of France when the day came.[28]

Charles de Gaulle finally urged the resistance to consider the nation's political future. Set up by Jean Moulin in July 1942, the Comité général des Experts – soon renamed the Comité Général d'Etudes (CGE) – developed a theoretical approach to deal with the material, institutional and economic problems that would face liberated France. Above all, a plethora of organizations waited for the administrative handover of the nation. Apart from the CGE, charged with selecting future leaders, prefects of the liberation were named by the Commission des Désignations, a commission that also organized the departmental liberation committees that were to replace the Conseils Généraux ahead of elections. Invited to take office within these circles, resisters in the interior were thus closely linked with France's political renewal.[29]

The missions delegated to the internal resistance thus tended to expand. Originally limited to one or two missions, the resistance organizations became multipurpose groupings broadly shaped by the pattern of the war and by the new problems that faced them. Those in the Ceux de la

Résistance initially refused to become involved in the procedures of political nomination, as, according to their leaders, this would be liable to encourage 'certain ambitions among those who took it up'. Pressed by London, the movement yielded and created a civilian branch, which covered false papers, communications and propaganda.[30] Défense de la France, on the other hand, had eschewed all military activity, but pushed by a rank and file impatient to break out and anxious to take a military part in liberating the country, Philippe Viannay set up two *maquis* groups, in Seine-et-Oise and in Bourgogne-Franche-Comté. These developments, although a proof of maturity, nonetheless had paradoxical effects since they helped simultaneously to unite and to divide the resistance.

Military and political logic encouraged unification of the clandestine forces. Unity representing strength, the sharing of men and resources was essential. Integrated into the calculations of the Allied planning staff, the resistance had to coordinate its activity and even agree to submit to instructions from British or American commanders. General de Gaulle's political frailty, finally, forced the secret formations to close ranks. As is well known, Roosevelt saw the General as an incipient dictator. In order to gain Allied recognition and win the battle of legitimacy, it was essential for De Gaulle to unite the resistance forces so as to present a common front in the eyes of the world. Unification now became a pressing necessity but it could not be achieved without posing formidable difficulties.

The unification of the clandestine formations ran into obstacles both internally and externally. In France, the resistance remained riven by divisions, which even the common objectives of routing the occupier and defeating the Vichy régime found hard to erode. First of all, trivial squabbles pitted groups against each other. In order to win favours from London, movements and networks sought to present themselves in a favourable light even at the cost of discrediting their fellow resisters. Taking advantage of the close links between Free France and Colonel Rémy, the OCM asserted that it represented the largest organization in the occupied zone, a wishful untruth designed to win overall command of the resistance in the north.[31] Similarly, Libération-sud and Combat, via their leaders Emmanuel d'Astier de la Vigerie and Henri Frenay, engaged in a minor war to win Gaullist blessing.[32] However, more serious confrontations spread through the resistance, primarily over the place and the role claimed by communists in the struggle. A section of the resisters, recalling the Russo-German pact, suspected the PCF of not having broken its umbilical link with Moscow and, under cover of patriotism, of undertaking a private war to place themselves in power at the liberation. Methods adopted by the red units were challenged in other respects. On 22 August 1941 'Colonel Fabien' executed a German soldier at Barbès-Rochechouart metro station, setting off a bloody cycle of attacks and repression, with the Germans shooting dozens of hostages in reprisal. Although other elements within the resistance did not reject this procedure in principle, they did question its effectiveness, considering the cost to be too great.[33] Designed to prove the vitality of the communist resistance at a time when the Red Army was in retreat on the Eastern front, these acts gave the communists a martyr's crown but also fed a debate that was to continue until the Liberation. Should immediate action be undertaken, as the Party insisted? Or should fighting be delayed until D-Day, as proposed in particular by the ORA and some movements that were accused by their rivals of wait-and-see tactics? In the event, this dilemma was never settled; groups decided their approach according to the context and the principles that they adopted. The strategy followed by the communists also fed suspicions. Launching a Front national de lutte pour l'indépendance de la France (FN) in May 1941, the PCF claimed to be bringing together all patriots who wished to struggle against the enemy, independent of political labels. Asserting a veneer of ecumenism, this formula was more prosaically aimed at extending the hegemony of the PCF over the resistance as a whole, by bringing all clandestine forces under its wing.[34] The attempt was short lived, despite help from various individuals (for example the Christian-Democrat Georges Bidault and the radical Justin Godart), because the other movements refused to support this arrangement.

In fact, the resisters did not intend to restrict their activity to the military liberation of the country. They denounced the impotence of a Third Republic that was incapable of preparing for the war and then winning it; they observed the desertion of the traditional élites – who were in truth scarce in their ranks; and they aspired to economic and social renewal. The movements considered themselves qualified, through foresight and courage, to take the fate of the nation in hand. These claims aroused animosity among the politicians who did not intend to be stripped of their role at the liberation. As Léon Blum wrote to General de Gaulle on 15 March 1943 'The denial pure and simple of political parties is equivalent to the denial of democracy . . . The resistance organisations which have sprung from French soil will not in any circumstances be able to replace them.'[35]

But the movements' political ambitions were also at variance with the Gaullist line. Concerned to achieve national unity, the latter could not encourage the dreams fostered by the resistance in France on pain of alienating the crucial support of the political parties. Conversely, the groups refused to sign a blank paper in his favour. Setting their relationship with de Gaulle on the plane of an equal partnership, they recognized the head of Free France as a symbol, but rejected any hierarchical subordination. Internal quarrels, communist loyalties, conflicts with the parties, and disagreements with the General himself – the obstacles to unification were manifold. Yet thanks to the work of Jean Moulin, the resistance managed to overcome all of these and unite its forces.

Close to progressive radicalism before the war, Jean Moulin[36] – a *Préfet* dismissed by Vichy – reached London in October 1941. Having set out to show General de Gaulle the progress of the resistance in the southern zone, Moulin returned to France on 2 January 1942, parachuted in with a threefold mission: to unite the southern movements, to rally them to Free France, and to encourage each organization to make a clear distinction between political and military matters. After long discussions, exacerbated by tensions caused by the harsh conditions of life in hiding, Moulin finally got his way. Apart from recognizing the authority of Free France, the three main southern organizations agreed to turn over their military members to an Armée Secrète (secret army) and put their activities under the authority of a coordinating committee, presided over by Jean Moulin but with three managers in control – Frenay, d'Astier and Jean-Pierre Lévy (2 October 1942). In January 1943 a second step was achieved: the three movements joined together to form the core of the Mouvements unis de la Résistance (MUR), although each group retained its own press outlet. Some seeds of conflict undoubtedly remained. The command of the Armée Secrète, initially granted to General Delestraint, was claimed by Frenay who, in addition, saw the separation between political and military elements as foolish. Moreover, the founder of Combat wished to retain his autonomy and only agreed to a conditional submission to Gaullist power. Similarly, the political parties, with the socialists at their head, considered themselves cheated, with the coordinating committee excluding them *de facto* from clandestine activity. They therefore suggested the creation of a clandestine 'parliament' of the Resistance, bringing together movements and parties, a formula which Moulin and de Gaulle finally accepted in February 1943.

In the north however, unification had barely moved forward; but the prospect of an Allied landing placed such importance on the occupied zone that General de Gaulle expedited its reorganization. Despatched as part of the Brumaire–Arquebuse mission (January–March 1943), Pierre Brossolette and Colonel Passy pursued three objectives: to separate, within the movements, information from civilian and military activity; to estimate the forces available for D-Day; and to select the future administrators of liberated France. The movements did, in fact, isolate information activity, which was thenceforward entrusted to independent networks, with autonomous posts taking over the radio transmission of information gathered. By limiting the risks, this division of labour lowered losses, with the rate of radio operators intercepted falling to under 25 per cent (against 75 per cent in 1941). Similarly, the north was now divided into six military regions, this division of territory being designed to encourage coordination of efforts. But in defiance of directives from De Gaulle, Pierre Brossolette set up a coordinating committee for the northern zone on 26 March 1943. Apart from perpetuating the division of France into two zones, which London wished to eliminate, this initiative proved dangerous in that it gave too much weight to the communists. Faced with a *fait accompli*, Moulin confirmed the creation of the Committee but founded the parallel Conseil National de la Résistance (CNR), consisting of representatives of political parties, unions and resistance movements on 27 May 1943. Since this authority had only consultative powers, the London delegate sought to create a coordinating committee covering the two zones, but his arrest on 21 June 1943 prevented its formation.[37]

After these vicissitudes, the resistance did achieve internal unity. The combination of General de Gaulle's symbolic position, Jean Moulin's political intelligence and the goodwill of the France-based movements explain a miracle that stands out against the fratricidal squabbles that ravaged other European lands, for example in Yugoslavia. In distributing weapons and money, London was undoubtedly strongly placed to make its voice heard: in January 1943 Libération-sud, Franc-Tireur and Combat received 1,500,000, 600,000 and 2,500,000 francs respectively.[38] In any case, this unification helped the resistance. In military terms, it enabled it to coordinate its efforts and to integrate with the Allied forces. From the political viewpoint, the CNR considerably strengthened the legitimacy of General de Gaulle, by revealing the wide range of forms of support available to him. Bringing together the ensemble of unions (CGT, CFTC) and parties (PCF, SFIO, radical-socialists, Alliance démocratique, Fédération républicaine) in concert with the main movements (MUR, OCM, CDLL, CDLR, FN), enabled de Gaulle to supplant General Giraud in 1943. The Conseil National (CNR) also cemented a political consensus that took shape in its famous programme (15 March 1944). Demanding the re-establishment of the great republican freedoms and the introduction of a social security system, and pleading for nationalization of 'the major monopolised means of production', the programme outlined a body of reforms on which all the political tendencies represented could agree.[39]

Despite this positive outcome, the unification of the resistance drew a modest veil over a number of disagreements. Resistance strategy was not firmly established, the communists pleaded for a widespread popular insurrection while soldiers and right-wing movements preferred to base the national uprising on the progress of the Allied troops. The question of command also remained open, although the formation of the Forces françaises de l'Intérieur (FFI) in February 1944 seemed to provide a definite answer. Commanded by General Koenig, the FFI depended at the local level on departmental and regional leaders, most of whom came from interior resistance ranks. In practice, however, this arrangement barely functioned. Dominated after Moulin's death by the communists, the 'action commission' of the CNR (the COMAC) claimed the management of operation for itself, which was unacceptable in London. Similarly the FFI hierarchies frequently clashed with the regional military delegates (DMR) sent by London. Entrusted originally with helping the resistance without directing it, the DMRs, in practice, frequently acted like local emperors, using the means at their disposal (such as weapons, money, connections) to claim command of the forces.[40] Finally, the unification included some perverse political effects. By accepting parties that some movements had sworn to eliminate, the CNR destroyed the hopes of the internal resistance by depriving it of its political monopoly inside France. Some clandestine groups that were aware of this danger reacted by joining together. Founded in January 1944, the Mouvement de Libération Nationale (MLN) consisted of Défense de la France, Résistance et Lorraine as well as MUR. This federation explicitly intended to become a political party at the Liberation, a hope that the vitality of its press and the strength of its forces appeared to justify.

Liberation and After

On the eve of the Allied landings in June 1944, the resistance was therefore a rapidly expanding force; but in numerical terms it remained a minority element within the nation as a whole. However, it could count on some 300,000 active members while the FFI counted 500,000 combatants[41] and its numbers were rising. From the fifty members initially included in Défense de la France in 1941, in 1944 the movement could count on 3,000 members. The OCM probably counted some 10,000 members, and the networks perhaps represented 150,000 agents, not including occasional activists.[42] Although representing a minority, the resistance was nonetheless more than a minor force, even if its composition did not accurately reflect that of French society. Peasants (10 per cent) were underrepresented, whereas workers and the ill-defined group that made up the middle classes were overrepresented. In Franc-Tireur, office employees or middle management made up 38 per cent of the total membership.[43] Similarly, younger members were noticeably more numerous than older age-groups, for example, 60 per cent of Défense de la France militants were under thirty. Despite these uneven features, the resistance remained a classless phenomenon, with all social elements being present in its ranks, albeit in unequal proportions.

Women were also reputedly underrepresented in the ranks of the resistance, although this perception depends to some degree on the criteria used to define involvement or membership. Nonetheless, it has been argued that those who did become involved 'rendered indispensable services to their country'.[44] There are some very well-known stories of women who were parachuted into occupied France as agents or wireless operators for SOE,[45] but recent research has concentrated on women inside France and has shown that they engaged in nearly every form of resistance activity, albeit not in large numbers and not necessarily with the full blessing of military and *maquisard* units. They were reputedly more adaptable to clandestine life than their male colleagues and could also carry out some tasks that were impossible for males - such as acting as couriers when all men seen on the streets were likely to be arrested as *réfractaires*. A few took up arms or became saboteurs – activities that were entirely at odds with their traditional role within society.[46] The majority of the others were engaged in more recognized female roles, for example organizing the sheltering and provisioning of resisters. As archival research and oral histories have uncovered more about the nature of female participation in the resistance, the debates have shifted to asking whether this participation had an emancipating effect on the women involved, either at the time, or more importantly in the postwar era. Analyses to date have not produced a definitive answer to either question, and the scope of enquiry has widened to include women with other experiences of war and occupation, for example the many wives of prisoners-of-war.[47]

One question asked subsequently of women resisters in France was the existence of role models for their behaviour. For the most part, the answers refer to fathers and stepfathers who fought in the First World War. However, this search for the antecedents has raised general questions about resistance traditions within France. There are general references to the activities of the revolutionaries of 1789, and in Roussillon to the Cathar heretics of the thirteenth century. These parallels have to be treated with caution, but the forms of resistance and the strategies adopted in certain localities may have owed something to local particularities and traditions. In making this claim, however, it should be remembered that it may be more important to ask 'what the maquis contributed to regional consciousness rather than vice versa'.[48]

Strengthening its cohesion in the latter stages of the occupation, the resistance also gained in effectiveness. Apart from information supplied to the Allies and acts of sabotage carried out, its clandestine press developed into a powerful force. In January 1944 *Défense de la France* was producing 450,000 copies and the print-run of *Franc-Tireur, Combat* or *Libération-sud* each varied between 125,000 and 160,000 copies.[49] The resistance did not hesitate to display its strength. On 11 November 1943 the *maquisards* of Colonel Romans-Petit marched in impeccable ranks past the war memorial in Oyonnax. The communist militants preferred to loot shops that traded with the occupying forces in order to distribute groceries to the people – a successful exercise carried out in Paris in the rue de Buci and then the rue Daguerre in 1943. Finally, the resistance attempted to protect civilians who were threatened by the occupiers. It mobilized its powers to sabotage the STO by issuing false papers, taking in those who refused the work, and even destroying government files – an operation set up by Léo Hamon in the Ministry of Labour in February 1944. However it is also true that the struggle against racial persecution was not a priority. Restricted by a republican model that ignored communities and saw only individuals, most resistance organizations failed to recognize the tragic fate hanging over the Jews and refused to identify precise categories of victim.

This should not imply that help for the persecuted Jews in France did not exist. Indeed, there were examples both of help from non-Jews and of Jewish self help. The rescue of Jews is often treated as separate from resistance, yet it was directed towards confounding one of the Germans' central ideological aims, the deportation of all Jews from western Europe to the death camps in the East. Rescue could be the action of a single family or individual, or be part of a wider initiative. Moreover, it could be prompted by a wide range of factors, both secular and religious. Some Roman Catholic clergymen created whole networks. For example, Father Chaillet who founded Témoignage Chrétien, which sheltered Jews and helped them to cross the border into neutral Switzerland.[50] Catholic clergymen and priests in other parts of the country were also involved and, in some cases, outspoken, but they remained a minority and received no backing from the Vatican. Also prominent were pastors from Protestant communities, perhaps the most famous being André Trocmé and his congregation of Le Chambon, which sheltered Jewish children. Given the secrecy attached to this work, its often individual character and the fact that many rescues were ultimately unsuccessful make any quantification impossible, yet there is no doubt that it should be included in any assessment of resistance.

There were also examples of Jewish involvement in the resistance. Some Jews on the run from deportation joined with *réfractaires* in the countryside and some ultimately became *maquisards*. Others came via prewar Jewish political or welfare organizations, many of which were merged to form the Union des Juifs pour la Résistance et l'Entre'aide (UJRE) in April 1943. There was also an appreciable number of Jews who had come to France as political refugees in the 1930s and who had joined the Communist Party's foreign workers section, the Main d'Oeuvre Immigrée (MOI). Both organizations carried out a wide range of resistance activities and even gave rise to special units. One of the most famous, the Manouchian group, numbered twelve Jews among its twenty-three members and reputedly carried out 459 military actions before their capture in November 1943.[51] Aside from this direct involvement, Jewish resistance was also about self help. Many prewar Jewish children's welfare organizations, most notably the Oeuvre de Secours aux Enfants (OSE), Organisation pour la Reconstruction et le Travail (ORT) and Éclaireurs Israélites de France became involved in the rescue activities as a natural extension of their original work. Estimates suggest they may have saved between 7,500 and 9,000 children from deportation.[52] In general, it seems that Jewish resistance developed in parallel with, or even in advance of, non-Jewish resistance, but was hampered by the German assault on Jewry in France taking place before other Nazi ideological and economic demands rendered popular opinion more sympathetic to opponents of both the occupiers and the Vichy regime.

These protean forms of action endowed the resistance with genuine prestige in the eyes of the public. Rejecting the Vichy régime and detesting the occupier whose mask of correctness had long since disappeared, the population developed a 'delaying tactic of complicit solidarity'.[53] Without joining the resistance, people proved their sympathy for it, even occasionally supporting its activity by providing supplies or by closing their eyes to suspect comings and goings. However, such connivance should not be overemphasized. Faced with their deteriorating standard of living, the French wished above all to survive, and material concerns determined their priorities. Awaited with impatience, the liberation was equally dreaded – and this ambivalence fed fears. To the fear of bombardment was added the dread of seeing France turned into a battlefield once more. In this respect, acts of violence and the presence of the *maquis* were not always appreciated as they were seen as synonymous with risk for a nation that, with reason, feared German reprisals. Vichy propaganda played on these fears, and one Philippe Henriot, much heard on Radio-Paris, found it easy to represent resisters as a criminal mob.

The combination of these facts helped to define the true role played by the resistance at the liberation. From the military point of view, this role appeared, at the very least, unequal in its effects. True, the plans drawn up by Allied headquarters were generally carried out, and in some cases the FFI helped to liberate whole regions. In Brittany, the concentration of volunteers forced the Wehrmacht to abandon the interior to concentrate on the coastline. Colonel Guingouin's troops controlled the Limousin region; and in Issoudun the resisters achieved the surrender of the Elster column, 20,000 men strong, although in general the unequal ratio of forces as well as the lack of heavy armaments limited the effectiveness of the FFI. A few episodes will illustrate this impotence. The Vercors *maquis*, strengthened by élite troops, surrendered within three days (21–23 July 1944), a disaster underlined by the Germans' bloody reprisals against more than 600 victims, and the Wehrmacht scattered the 6,000 men gathered at Le Mont-Mouchet in the Auvergne during June 1944. Estimated by Eisenhower as a contribution of 15 divisions, the work of the resistance cannot therefore be overestimated. Although it did facilitate the Allied advance, undertook valuable *coups* here and there, and sometimes protected important strategic facilities (such as the port of Marseilles), it could not liberate the country on its own.[54]

The setback of the national insurrection confirmed this position. Accepted by the resistance as a whole, the uprising of the population combined military objectives (to speed the departure of the occupier) with political aims (to associate the French people with their liberation). Agreement on principles, however, only thinly disguised disagreement over methods. In unleashing an insurrection that they hoped to contain, the communists intended to create a favourable power relationship and to deprive De Gaulle of the fruits of victory. This imperative incited them to unleash operations without waiting for the Allied arrival. Fearing German reprisals and the political destabilization associated with the explosion of these modern Communes, De Gaulle and the movements in return rejected any premature action. The insurrection was brief and not supposed to develop except in accord with the Allied advance, but the wait-and-see attitude of the population made this impossible. Out of 212 prefectures or sub-prefectures, only five liberated themselves and 85 per cent passively awaited the German departure.[55] And although Paris provided the dazzling example of a city in revolt, holding its own for a brief week against the enemy forces, the capital nonetheless remained an untypical model.[56] The people's fear, the speed of the Allied advance, the lack of arms, the refusal to become a mass formation manipulated by the communists – all are features that explain a passivity that the fierce will to live, more than to fight, no doubt reinforced.

From the political point of view, the role of the resistance turned out to be crucial. The Vichy rule in effect dissolved itself and the authorities instituted by the provisional government of the French republic (GPRF), created on 3 June 1944, took power unopposed. Mayors and the prefects of the former government resigned and were immediately replaced by men designated during the dark days of the occupation. This success – crowned by the absence of civil war – was twofold. It revealed the effectiveness of propaganda that, in addition to its capacity to denounce the French state, had successfully established the resistance as a legitimate power. The authorities set in place were, in fact, never challenged by the local people – even though they had not been legitimized by universal suffrage. This velvet revolution also illustrated the organizational talents of the resistance, because the counteradministration designated in the shadows immediately took up the reins. True, a few incidents here and there tarnished the image. The wounded commissioner of the Republic designated for Toulouse, Jean Cassou, could not take up his post but Pierre Bertaux immediately replaced him. Similarly, the CDLL in the Calvados, deprived of its leader at the end of 1943, was reconstructed with much difficulty in the spring of 1944. It never really played any active part. Overall, however, republican legality followed on from the Pétainist rule without a break. Well served by a talent for words, the political genius of General de Gaulle provides most of the explanation for this peaceful devolution of power. We should not, however, underestimate the decisive role played by a resistance, which, inside France itself, popularized his instructions and broadly contributed to the installation of his élites. Although the military balance sheet invites interpretation, the political operation can scarcely be questioned. France escaped both communist dictatorship and a bloody or insidious civil war as in Greece or Belgium. Thus even General de Gaulle's talent should not overshadow the major role played by the resistance.

The resistance moreover payed a high price for its involvement. Thirty thousand French people were shot during the dark years; 60,000 resisters were deported to Nazi prisons; 20,000 FFI were lost in action. Listed by organization, the figures suggest the scale of the losses. For example, Franc-Tireur lost a third of its activists. Out of 3,000 militants, DF counted eighty-seven shot, forty dead in action, 322 deported.[57] The addition of those missing or imprisoned means that a quarter of its activists were victims of repression in one form or another. The Nazi and Vichy police forces followed different policies. Although Gaullist propaganda was seen as a danger, the services of Nazi repression reserved their hardest blows for the communists, the networks, the *maquisards* and the FFI. The last three of these categories represented a genuine military danger, which inspired Field Marshal Keitel to order captured 'snipers' to be shot immediately. The Vichy police forces used classic but largely ineffective methods such as searches and cordons in their struggle against clandestine forces, but depended above all on informers. Infiltration of agents or the turning of resisters – out of fear or profit – delivered the hardest blows to clandestine formations. For example, Multon's treason led to the arrest of Jean Moulin at Caluire. For 60,000 or 80,000 francs per informer, Emile Marongin betrayed forty-eight members of DF. A radio operator, Marty, set up the arrest of Estienne d'Orves. Turned by the Abwehr, André Grandclément, a leader of the OCM, betrayed his organization in the south-west in a spirit of anticommunism. Followed sometimes by execution, mostly by deportation, the arrest was often accompanied by the worst tortures inflicted by monsters of whom Klaus Barbie, the scourge of Jean Moulin, was the archetype and the old troopers of the Milice the symbol. From this the courage shown by the resisters can be judged, first of all in enlisting and sometimes in defying torture and its incalculable sufferings.

Inheritance

Firmly determined to achieve the occupiers' departure, the resisters also intended to transform politics at the liberation. But the balance sheet here shows a remarkable contrast.[58] First, the resistance failed to create a new party. Faithful to the nation rallying to the cause, Charles de Gaulle in effect refused to found a body carrying his colours, thus depriving the resistance of a prime trump card. The MLN, for its part, divided between those favouring unity of action with the PCF and a majority that gravitated towards the socialist movement.[59] The split that occurred in January 1945 between the two approaches broke the unitary dream sustained throughout the hidden years. A small party, the Union démocratique et socialiste de la Résistance (UDSR), was to emerge from these ashes, but its constituency would remain limited despite the fame of its leaders, in particular René Pleven and François Mitterrand. Although the Mouvement Républicain Populaire (MRP) also wore the colours of the resistance because of the importance of its founders (such as P.H. Teitgen and F. de Menthon), its Christian Democrat orientation alienated the support of the clandestine workers who remained faithful to republican secularism. Incapable of creating new formations, the resistance also showed itself unable to renovate old ones. Faced with its electoral hopes blighted in May 1945, the SFIO, having initially been ready to cooperate with the resisters, now renewed its links with the isolationist *Guesdiste* tendency so as not to disorientate its traditional supporters.[60] At the same time, the French Communist Party, glorified by the sacrifice of its martyrs, remained faithful to its Stalinist orientation. Representing a minority within the nation, the resistance programme failed to embody a true political alternative – either because its proposals were too vague (moralization of political life, moving beyond traditional divides), or because they were fundamentally accepted by a political class ready to support nationalizations, social security and equal access to education. The political legacy of the resistance therefore appeared limited – with one reservation. By popularizing themes that were hitherto taboo, on the right at least – particularly nationalizations – and by picking out an élite of patriotic and modernizing senior civil servants (Pierre Lafaucheux at Renault; François Bloch-Lainé at the head of the Treasury, and so forth), the resistance undoubtedly helped to establish and then perpetuate the economic and social consensus that was to confer its originality on *les Trente glorieuses* (the glorious postwar thirty years). In contrast to Germany, the state played an active role in planning and the nationalization of business while limiting social inequalities through the transfer of resources operated by the social security system. On the left as on the right, governments would not question this unassailable elite until the early 1980s.

Incapable of revitalizing political life, the resistance was also shortlived in national memory. Although for a long period it provided an important reference, it played a minor role in defining national identity. This was mainly the fault of the combatants. Too few in number to set up mass organizations – in contrast with the survivors of the Great War – they had lived through situations that were too diverse to create a feeling of cohesion. Although millions of Frenchmen had suffered in the trenches in 1914–18, the experiences of the *maquisard*, of the newssheet distributor and of the saboteur turned out to be too varied to inspire shared memories. The veterans' societies therefore tended to jog along quietly, barely visible in public life. Further, political squabbles helped to orchestrate memory, forestalling adherence to common references. During the Algerian war its opponents denounced the use of torture in the name of humanism and defended the right of nations to decide their own fate (Claude Bourdet), whereas others rejected the cheap selloff of French territory (Georges

Bidault). In latching on to the heroic deeds of the dark years, the Gaullists (reducing the resistance to the work of the General), like the communists (who presented it as the struggle of a people united behind the Party), operated an extremist simplification with little chance of mobilising the masses. The 1970s, however, marked a turning point. The death of General de Gaulle and the fading of the PCF, undermined by the Prague Spring and the 'revelations' of Solzhenitsyn, favoured dissident voices that had hitherto found difficulty in making themselves heard. Through the mediation of its great leaders (Henri Frenay in 1973, Claude Bourdet in 1975), the internal resistance proclaimed its participation and declared its detachment from the double handicap of Gaullism and communism. Some unorthodox figures in the Party also reappeared, such as Charles Tillon, whose memoirs were published in 1977. These elements restored the complexity of the resisters' involvements, but fragmented the field of memory by preventing the development of unequivocal points of reference. A sign of this atomization is that no single site of memory embodies the spirit of the Resistance.[61] The Crypt of the Deported in the Ile de la Cité merges together political and racial victims; and Mont Valérien presents itself as a Gaullist fortress. Often installed on the initiative of local societies without the support of public bodies, the innumerable commemorative plaques that proliferate in towns and villages emphasize this fragmentation of memory.

Weighed down by these factors, historians initially chose to remain silent. At the end of the war and up to the 1960s the dominant tone of historiography, apart from a brief period of quiet (1952–7) was one of heroism, which glorified clandestine action and the merits of General de Gaulle. For obvious reasons, the Gaullist cult reached a peak between 1958 and 1964; some historians, around Henri Michel, rejected this approach. But although they focussed on the activities, the organization or the ideas of the resistance, they neglected the sociology, the relationship with the people and the political conflicts. The following decades, however, brought new research.[62] The conflicts between London and mainland France, the strategy of the French communists, the sociological composition of the movements and the links that they formed with their environment, thenceforward formed the core of historical enquiries. True, the history of the networks, the sociology of the resistance, and the relationship with the people, still remain poorly understood. But beyond the passionate quarrels, the resistance is, in the best meaning of the term, in the process of historicization. This page of history, sometimes tragic, often cruel but indicative of French ambivalence, deserves our efforts to penetrate its mystery far beyond merely paying homage to its heroes.

There is no current overall history of the resistance. For an outline, see Jean-Pierre Azéma, *Munich to the Liberation 1938–1944*, Jean-Pierre Azéma and François Bédarida (eds) *La France des années noires*, and Henri Noguères et al., *Histoire de la Résistance*. On the crucial role of Jean Moulin, see Daniel Cordier, *Jean Moulin, La République des catacombes*, and the summary by Daniel Cordier and Robert Laffont, *Jean Moulin, l'inconnu du Panthéon*, the first volume of which includes a preface of 303 pages outlining the factors that set London in opposition to the indigenous Resistance inside France. In this context, see also Pierre Laborie's book, *L'Opinion française sous Vichy*.[63] Resisters' memoirs offer valuable insights, notably Claude Bourdet, *L'Aventure incertaine*, Henri Frenay, *The Night Will End*, Philippe Viannay, *Du bon usage de la France*.[64] On the initiative of Institut Historique du Temps Présent, five conferences were held during the 1990s on 'la Résistance et les Français', and the proceedings have subsequently been published. Laurent Douzou et al. (eds), *Villes, centres et logiques de décision*, Jean-Marie Guillon and Pierre Laborie (eds), *Mémoire et histoire: la Résistance*, François Marcot (ed.), *Lutte armée et maquis*, Jacqueline Sainclivier and Christian Bougeard (eds), *Enjeux stratégiques et environnement social*, and Jean-Marie Guillon and Robert Mencherini, *La Résistance et les Européens du Sud*.[65]

For a thematic approach to the study of resistance, see Rod Kedward, *In Search of the Maquis. Rural Resistance in Southern France 1942–1944;* Henri Michel, *Les courants de pensée de la résistance*, and Antoine Prost (ed.), *La Résistance, une histoire sociale*.[66] On individual regions, there is the work by Rod Kedward, *Resistance in Vichy France*, and more specifically, Jacqueline Sainclivier, *La Résistance en Ille-et-Vilaine*, and François Marcot, *La Résistance dans le Jura*. In addition, there is the excellent but unpublished thesis by Jean-Marie Guillon, *La Résistance dans le Var*.[67] There are also a number of important studies on individual movements and networks, most notably Alya Aglan, *Mémoires résistantes. Histoire du réseau Jade-Fitzroy, 1940–1944*, Renée Bédarida, *Témoignage chrétien. Les armes de l'esprit*, Laurent Douzou, *La désobéissance. Histoire du mouvement Libération-sud*, Dominique Veillon, *'Le Franc-tireur', un journal clandestin*, Alya Aglan, *La Résistance sacrifiée. Histoire du mouvement Libération -nord* and Olivier Wieviorka, *Une certaine idée de la Résistance, Défense de la France, 1940–1949*.[68]

There are several studies on the political parties during the occupation, on the Communist Party, Jean-Pierre Azéma, Antoine Prost, Jean-Pierre Rioux (eds) *Le PCF des années sombres*, Philippe Buton, *Les lendemains qui déchantent, le Parti communiste français à la libération*, and Stéphane

Courtois, *Le PCF dans la guerre*. On the socialists, there is Marc Sadoun, *Les socialistes sous l'occupation. Résistance et collaboration.*[69] On the liberation and after, see Philippe Buton and Jean-Marie Guillon, *Les pouvoirs en France à la Libération*, Charles-Louis Foulon, *Le pouvoir en province à la Libération*, and Olivier Wieviorka, *Nous entrerons dans la carrière. De la Résistance à l'exercise du pouvoir*, Finally, on memory, Serge Barcellini and Annette Wieviorka, *Passant, souviens-toi. Les lieux du souvenir de la Seconde guerre mondiale en France*, and Henry Rousso, *Le Syndrome de Vichy.*[70]

Notes

1. Participation in the resistance entitled people to certain rights (for example pensions) that depended on the recognition of the status of *combattant volontaire de la Résistance* (CVR). The card was handed out by a fairly strict commission therefore the figures given here are cautious. See Serge Barcellini, 'La Résistance française à travers le prisme de la carte CVR' in Laurent Douzou et al. (eds) *La Résistance et_les Français: villes, centres et logiques de décisions*, colloque IHTP-CNRS, (Paris: ENS Cachan, 1995).
2. Jean-Pierre Azéma, *From Munich to the Liberation, 1938–1944* (Cambridge: Cambridge University Press/Maison des Sciences de l'Homme, 1984) pp.40–1.
3. Philippe Burrin, *Living with Defeat. France under the German Occupation 1940–1944* (London: Arnold, 1996) p.11.
4. Burrin, *Living with Defeat*, pp.77–8. Azéma, *Munich*, pp.45–6.
5. Jean-Pierre Azéma, *1940, l'année terrible*, (Paris: Seuil, 1990).
6. Olivier Wievorka, 'A la recherche de l'engagement', *Vingtième siècle, revue d'histoire,* No. 60, October–December 1998.
7. Pierre Laborie, *L'Opinion française sous Vichy*, (Paris: Seuil, 1990).
8. 'Cahier' No. 1, *Le Témoignage chrétien*, March 1941.
9. Indomitus (Philippe Viannay), 'Une seule France', *Défense de la France* no. 1, 15 August 1941.
10. Dominique Veillon, 'les réseaux de résistance' in François Bédarida and Jean-Pierre Azéma, *La France des années noires*, vol. 1, p.385 et seq. (Paris: Seuil, 1993).
11. Claude Bourdet, *L'Aventure incertaine*, (Paris: Stock, 1975), pp.95–6.

12. Ibid.

13. Arthur Calmette, *L'OCM*, (Paris: PUF, 1961), chapter III.

14. These phrases are taken from Charles Tilly, *La France conteste*, (Paris: Fayard, 1986), p.542, p.15.

15. Olivier Wieviorka, *Une certaine idée de la Résistance. Défense de la France 1940–1949*, (Paris: Seuil, 1995), p.143 ff.

16. François Marcot, 'Les paysans et la Résistance: problèmes d'une approche sociologique' in Jacqueline Sainclivier et Christian Bougeard (n.d.), *La Résistance et les Français. Enjeux stratégiques et environnement social*, (Rennes: Presses Universitaires de Rennes, 1995), p.245 et seq.

17. Etienne Dejonghe, 'Les problèmes sociaux dans les entreprises houillères du Nord et du Pas-de-Calais durant la seconde guerre mondiale', *Revue d'histoire moderne et contemporaine*, January-March 1971.

18. Jacqueline Sainclivier, *La Résistance en Ille-et-Vilaine, 1940–1944*, (Rennes: Presses universitares de Rennes, 1993), p.79 et seq.

19. René Rémond, 'De la Résistance spirituelle à la lutte armée' in Xavier de Montclos et al., *Eglises et chrétiens dans la Seconde guerre mondiale.* (Lyon: Presses universitaires de Lyon, 1982), p.411 et seq. See also Renée Bédarida, *Témoignage chrétien. Les armes de l'Esprit*, (Paris: Editions ouvrières, 1977), p.109 et seq.

20. Jean-Pierre Azéma and Jean-Pierre Rioux (n.d.), *Le Parti communiste des années sombres, 1938–1941*, (Paris: Seuil, 1986).

21. This manifesto was rediscovered by Daniel Cordier, *Jean Moulin. L'Inconnu du Panthéon*, (Paris: Jean-Claude Lattès, 1989), p.25 et seq.

22. Jean-Louis Crémieux-Brilhac, *La France libre. De l'appel du 18 juin à la Libération*, (Paris: Gallimard, 1996), particularly chapters 2, 3 and 5.

23. Jean-Louis Crémieux-Brilhac, 'La France libre et la radio', *Mélange de l'Ecole Française de Rome*, vol. 1, 1996, p.73.

24. Harry Roderick Kedward, 'STO et maquis' in J.P. Azéma and P. Bédarida, *La France des année noires* vol.2, op. Cit., p.271.

25. Ibid, p.281 and p.292.

26. Dominique Veillon, 'les réseaux de résistance', pp.390–1.

27. Dominique Veillon, 'les réseaux de résistance', pp.390–1.

28. Henri Michel, *Histoire de la Résistance*, (Paris: PUF, 1984), pp.107–9.

29. Diane de Bellescize, *Les Neuf sages de la Résistance, Le CGE dans la clandestinité*, (Paris: Plon, 1979). René Hostache, *Le Conseil*

national de la Résistance, les institutions de la clandestinité, (Paris: PUF, 1958).

30. Marie Granet, *Ceux de la Résistance*, (Paris: PUF, 1960). See in particular the Manifesto of this movement, p.271.

31. Olivier Wieviorka, *Une certaine idée*, p.217 et seq.

32. Laurent Douzou, *La Désobéissance. Histoire du mouvement Libération-sud*, (Paris: Odile Jacob, 1995), p.354 et seq.

33. Which he spelled out in his speech of 23 October 1941.

34. Philippe Buton, *Les lendemains qui déchantent. Le Parti communiste français à la Libération*, (Paris: Presses de Sciences-Po, 1993), p.20 et seq.

35. Léon Blum, letter of 15 March 1943, quoted in Daniel Mayer, *Les socialistes dans la Résistance*, (Paris: PUF, 1968), p.212.

36. On the man and his work, Daniel Cordier, see *Jean Moulin*.

37. On these discussions, see Daniel Cordier, *Jean Moulin*, Guillaume Piketty, *Pierre Brossolette, un héros de la Résistance*, Piketty in Douzou et al. (eds) *La Résistance et les Français*, pp.309–20, Odile Jacob, Olivier Wieviorka, *Une certaine idée*, p.212 et seq. and vol III of the Mémoires du colonel Passy, *Missions secrètes en France*, (Paris: Plon, 1951).

38. 'Relevé de comptes de Rex/Jean Moulin/ pour janvier–mai 1943, juin 1943', Archives nationales, FIA 3721; 'Budget octobre et novembre 1943, source Bingen', Archives nationales, 72 AJ234.

39. The text is reproduced and analysed by Claire Andrieu, *Le Programme commun de la résistance. Des idées dans la guerre*, (Paris: Editions de l'Erudit, 1984).

40. Philippe Buton, 'La France atomisée' in Jean-Pierre Azéma and François Bédarida, *La Frances des années noires*, p.382 et seq.

41. Ibid, pp.384–5.

42. Figures given respectively by Olivier Wieviorka, *Une certaine idée*, p.164, Jean-Pierre Azéma, *De Munich à la Libération*, (Paris: Seuil, 1979), p.251, Dominique Veillon, 'les réseaux de résistance', p.411.

43. Dominique Veillon, *Le Franc-Tireur. Un journal clandestin, un mouvement de résistance*, (Paris: Flammarion, 1977), pp.247 et seq.

44. Margaret Collins Weitz, *Sisters in the Resistance* (New York: John Wiley, 1995) p.287.

45. M.R.D.Foot, *SOE. The Special Operations Executive, 1940–1946* (London: Pimlico, 1999) pp.75–7.

46. Weitz, *Sisters in the Resistance*, p.291.

47. Weitz, *Sisters in the Resistance*, pp.301–7. Paula L.Schwarz, 'Partisanes and Gender Politics in Vichy France' *French Historical Studies*

XVI/1 (1989). Karen Adler, 'No Words to Say It? Women and the Expectation of Liberation' and Hanna Diamond, 'Women's Aspirations, 1943–47: An Oral Enquiry in Toulouse' both in: H.R. Kedward and Nancy Wood, *The Liberation of France. Image and Event* (Oxford: Berg, 1995) pp.77–90 and 91–102. Sarah Fishman, *We Will Wait: Wives of French Prisoners of War 1940–1945* (New Haven CT: Yale University Press, 1991).

48. Kedward, *In Search of the Maquis*, p.151.

49. Philippe Buton, 'La France atomisée', p.377–8.

50. Barnett Singer, 'France and its Jews in World War II' *Contemporary French Civilisations*, II/1 (1977) p.10.

51. Jacques Adler, *The Jews of Paris and the Final Solution. Communal Response and Internal Conflicts, 1940–1944* (Oxford: Oxford University Press, 1985) pp.210–17. Kedward, *In Search of the Maquis*, p.118.

52. See Hillel J. Kieval, 'Legality and Resistance in Vichy France: The Rescue of Jewish Children' *Proceedings of the American Philosophical Society* CXXIV/5 (1980) pp.339–66. Note also his critiques of earlier works on Jewish resistance, Anny Latour, *La Résistance juive en France* (Paris: 1970) and Jacques Ravine, *La Résistance organisée des Juifs en France* (Paris: 1973). More recently, see, Renée Poznanski, *Être juif en France pendant la Seconde Guerre mondiale* (Paris: Hachette, 1994).

53. Pierre Laborie, *L'Opinion française sous Vichy,* p.311.

54. For the military evaluation, see Henri Michel, *Histoire de la Résistance*, pp.109 et seq. and Jean-Pierre Azéma, *De Munich*, pp.326 et seq.

55. Cf Philippe Buton, *Les lendemains qui déchantant,* pp.102 et seq.

56. The ambivalent nature of the Paris example are analysed in the collected volume, *Paris 1944. Les enjeux de la libération*, Albin Michel, 1994.

57. The overall total is given in Jean-Pierre Rioux, *La France de la Quatrième République*, Seuil, 1980 p.31; the figures for Franc-Tireur are taken from Dominique Veillon, 'les réseaux de résistance', p.394, those for DF from Olivier Wieviorka, *Une certaine idée*, p.332 et seq.

58. Olivier Wieviorka, *Nous entrerons dans la carrière. De la Résistance à l'exercice du pouvoir*, Seuil, 1994.

59. Alexander Werth, *France 1940–1955* (London: Hale, 1956) p.243.

60. Steven J. Kramer, 'La stratégie socialiste à la Libération', *Revue d'Histoire de la Deuxième Guerre Mondiale*, no. 98, p.77 et seq.

61. Serge Barcellini and Annette Wieviorka, *Passant, souviens-toi! Les ieux du souvenir de la Seconde guerre mondiale en France*, (Paris: Plon, 1995).

62. Jean-Marie Guillon, 'La Résistance, cinquante ans et deux mille titres après' in Jean-Marie Guillon and Pierre Laborie, *Mémoire et Histoire: la Résistance*, (Toulouse, n.p., 1995), p.27 et seq.

63. Jean-Pierre Azéma, *De Munich à la Libération 1938–1944* (Paris: Seuil, 1979) published in English as *Munich to the Liberation 1938–1944* (Cambridge: Cambridge University Press, 1984) Jean–Pierre Azéma and François Bédarida (eds), *La France des années noires*, 2 Vols. (Paris: Seuil, 1993). Henri Noguères et al., *Histoire de la Résistance*, 5 Vols. (Paris: 1967–81). Daniel Cordier and Robert Laffont, *Jean Moulin, l'inconnu du Panthéon*, 3 Vols. (Paris: J.C. Lattès, 1989–93) Pierre Laborie's book, *L'Opinion française sous Vichy* (Paris: Seuil, 1990) Daniel Cordier, *Jean Moulin. La République des catacombes* (Paris, 1999)

64. Claude Bourdet, *L'Aventure incertaine* (Paris: Éditions du Félin, 1997). Henri Frenay, *La Nuit Finira* (Paris: Livre de Poche, 1974) published in English as *The Night Will End* (London: Abelard-Schuman, 1976). Philippe Viannay, *Du bon usage de la France* (Paris: Ramsey, 1988).

65. Laurent Douzou et al. (eds), *Villes, centres et logiques de décision* (Paris: ENS Cachan, 1995) Jean-Marie Guillon and Pierre Laborie (eds), *Mémoire et Histoire: la Résistance* (Toulouse: n.p., 1995). François Marcot (ed.), *Lutte armée et maquis* (Besançon: Annales littéraires de l'université de Franche-Comté, 1996). Jacqueline Sainclivier and Christian Bougeard (eds), *Enjeux stratégiques et environnement social* (Rennes: Presses universitaires de Rennes, 1995). Jean-Marie Guillon and Robert Mencherini, *La Résistance et les Européens du Sud* (Paris: L'Harmattan, 1999).

66. Rod Kedward, *In search of the maquis. Rural resistance in Southern France 1942–1944* (Oxford: Oxford University Press, 1993). Henri Michel, *Les courants de pensée de la résistance* (Paris: PUF, 1962). Antoine Prost (ed.), *La Résistance, une histoire sociale* (Paris: Éditions de l'Atelier, 1995).

67. Rod Kedward, *Naissance de la Résistance dans la France de Vichy* (Paris: Champvallon, 1989) originally published in English as *Resistance in Vichy France* (Oxford: Oxford University Press, 1978). Jacqueline Sainclivier, *La Résistance en Ille–et–Vilaine* (Rennes: Presses Universitaires de Rennes, 1993). François Marcot, *La Résist-*

ance dans le Jura (Besançon: Cêtre, 1985) Jean-Marie Guillon, *La Résistance dans le Var* (unpublished MS).

68. Alya Aglan, *Mémoires résistantes. Histoire du réseau Jade-Fitzroy, 1940–1944* (Paris: Cerf, 1994). Alya Aglan, *La Résistance sacrifiée. Histoire du mouvement Libération-nord* (Paris, 1999). Renée Bédarida, *Témoignage chrétien. Les armes de l'esprit* (Paris: Éditions Ouvrières, 1977). Laurent Douzou, *La désobéissance. Histoire du mouvement Libération-sud* (Paris: Odile Jacob, 1995) Dominique Veillon, *'Le Franc-tireur', un journal clandestin, un journal clandestin, un mouvement de résistance, 1940–44* (Paris: Flammarion, 1977). Olivier Wieviorka, *Une certaine idée de la Résistance, Défense de la France, 1940–1949* (Paris: Seuil, 1995).

69. Jean-Pierre Azéma, Antoine Prost, Jean-Pierre Rioux (eds), *Le PCF des années sombres* (Paris: Seuil, 1986). Philippe Buton, *Les lendemains qui déchantent, le Parti communiste français à la libération* (Paris: Presses de Sciences-Po, 1993). Stéphane Courtois, *Le PCF dans la guerre* (Paris: Ramsay, 1980). Marc Sadoun, *Les socialistes sous l'occupation. Résistance et collaboration* (Paris: Presses de Sciences-Po, 1982).

70. Philippe Buton and Jean-Marie Guillon, *Les pouvoirs en France à la Libération* (Paris: Belin, 1994). Charles-Louis Foulon, *Le pouvoir en province à la Libération* (Paris: Presses de Sciences-Po, 1975). Olivier Wieviorka, *Nous entrerons dans la carrière. De la Résistance à l'exercice du pouvoir* (Paris: Seuil, 1994). Serge Barcellini and Annette Wieviorka, *Passant, souviens-toi. Les lieux du souvenir de la Seconde guerre mondiale en France* (Paris: Plon, 1995) and Henry Rousso, *Le Syndrome de Vichy*, 2nd.edition (Paris: Seuil, 1990), published in English as *The Vichy Syndrome: History and Memory in France since 1944* (Cambridge MA: Harvard University Press, 1991).

—6—

Italy
Gustavo Corni

From the Crisis of the Fascist Regime to the Resistance

The decision, taken by Mussolini and the King in June 1940, to wage war alongside Hitler's Germany, had aroused little consensus amongst the general Italian population. There was rather a fear of losing both those advantages achieved in social and economic fields and the international prestige that Italy had attained during the fifteen years of Fascist rule. Some feared Great Britain's strength and, although accepting the war as a 'lesser evil', hoped for a quick German victory since it was felt that unless Italy declared her position, she might suffer disastrous consequences.[1]

What tepid enthusiasm there was for the war quickly disappeared and the combination of a series of strategic errors and an evident lack of military preparation led to major defeats. The defeat suffered in Greece was one of the most significant and was particularly felt because the regime's propaganda had consistently proclaimed that it would be a 'walk over'. In January and February 1943, the annihilation of the military expedition in Russia, with tens of thousands of dead and missing, increased the distance between the regime and the population. Further-more, there was serious material and psychological damage caused by Allied bombing, which any anti-aircraft defence seemed powerless to prevent. In 1942 and 1943 the military crisis was accompanied by an increasing economic and social crisis where salaries and wages collapsed below prewar levels, the food supply situation became critical and the black market flourished. It has been calculated that consumption in 1944 was barely half what it had been in 1938.[2]

The traditional leadership elite, and notably the heads of the armed forces, attempted to bypass the crisis by means of a political manoeuvre that aimed to save the status quo whilst using Mussolini as the sole scapegoat. In July 1943 these manoeuvres were endorsed by a section of the Fascist party headed by Galeazzo Ciano, Foreign Secretary and son-in-law of Mussolini, together with Dino Grandi, the former Italian ambassador in London. Mussolini's resignation, imposed by King Victor Emmanuel III on 25 July following a vote of no confidence in the Fascist Grand Council, seemed to mark the end of an era. The Fascist regime faded away without a struggle, and in an atmosphere of general relief because it was hoped that this event signified the end of the war. During the following weeks, the so-called 'forty-five days', Marshal Badoglio, the new head of government, secretly attempted to conclude an armistice with the Allies and thus bring a tired and disillusioned country out of the conflict. However, at the same time, no measures were taken to counteract any possible attempt by German troops to take over control of the country, and widespread hopes that the conflict would end immediately were soon shattered by Badoglio's public declaration that the war must continue alongside the country's ally, Hitler.

Any hopes for a political change were also disappointed and in this phase a series of parties seeking to put forward proposals for a democratic revival were born, or rather reborn. However, this rebirth of the political parties, composed of a insubstantial minority of intellectuals and members of the bourgeoisie, was greeted by Badoglio's government with a policy of severe repression as was the renewal of industrial conflict in the factories.[3] The links between the first post-fascist parties and the birth of the Resistance are very slight. Only the Italian Communist Party (PCI) had survived the fascist regime's oppression and could count on an apparatus of Party officials and members, (about 15,000 throughout the whole of Italy), and moreover had some modest support from the masses of workers and students, mostly in the north.[4]

The general expectations of a painless withdrawal from the war were then destroyed by the unexpected announcement that an armistice had been signed with the Allies on 8 September. The German command had been well prepared for this eventuality and had carried out a perfectly timed occupation of key installations and had also destroyed the power of the Italian armed forces, whereas the latter were taken completely by surprise. Deprived of any command, the army dissolved and about 600,000 officers and men were captured by German troops.[5] Although isolated, there were some heroic instances of armed resistance prompted more by an upsurge of pride than by any clear strategic plan. Between 9 and 18 September all of central-northern Italy was occupied by the Germans. After the flight of the king, Badoglio and the government to the south, which had already been liberated by the Allies, the country was left without either guidance or an apparent future.[6] The 8 September can therefore truly be considered as the beginning of the resistance.

At this moment of inglorious defeat, a certain number of officers, non-commissioned officers and men, together with some civilians, having retrieved some of the many abandoned weapons, decided to 'take to the hills' and organize an armed resistance against the occupying Germans. Initially only a very small number of people were involved and for a variety of reasons: hatred for the occupier and ex-ally: a still somewhat vague desire to change the political course of the country; but also as a means of self-defence and to avoid the deportation and imprisonment which had been the fate of the 600,000 captured members of the Italian armed forces.[7] These first groups were concentrated in the peripheral and almost impenetrable areas of the Alps but also in the Apennines (Liguria, Emilia and the Abruzzi). These were, in reality, just 'bands' of men, lacking any form of coordination between them. The first mention of the existence of these 'bandits', as they were officially called in the Wehrmacht's bulletins, can be found in that of 22 September for the Friuli region, significantly so, given the importance of the example provided by the neighbouring Yugoslavian partisan movement.[8] It can be assumed that most members of these first partisan groups had not made a specifically political choice in joining but rather one of an ethical or patriotic nature. Hence, the historian Spriano writes: 'The chance for a total renewal, almost a catharsis, through the torque of political rigour and a programmed socialist content are substantially present at the beginning of the Resistance, in some ways more so at the beginning than during the course of its existence.'[9]

Independently of these first armed partisan groups, 8 September triggered off a new political dynamic. In Rome the following day, representatives of the principal and mostly newly founded anti-fascist parties created a Committee for National Liberation (CLN) from which a network of regional and urban CLNs developed. The first president of the CLN was the elderly reformist socialist, Ivanoe Bonomi, and the Committee issued a proclamation for the liberation of the country from the German invader: 'so that Italy might reclaim her role among the community of free nations'.[10] However, the question of the future constitutional structure remained open, since in this phase CLN links with the monarchy were still strong.

At this stage, the armed resistance and the political battles were not coordinated and whilst the former was uncertain and very weak, the latter were still an abstract concept. It is sufficient to consider the case of Turin, a city rich with traditions of working-class and industrial conflicts. The anti-fascist parties, led by the PCI, produced proclamations inciting the factory workers to insurrection and the destruction of the factories, but without apparently being aware of the fact that such a programme would find little support. Contrasting strategies were also evident between the communists in Rome and those in the northern regions, so that the former favoured a strategy that aimed for a socialist revolution, whereas, in the north, under the leadership of Luigi Longo, there was a greater awareness of the necessity of an alliance with the Catholics and the moderates and of attributing priority to the liberation of the nation.[11]

This initial stage of armed resistance was characterized by one exceptional event: the 'four days of Naples'. The city, reduced to famine levels, rebelled against the rigid policies being enforced by the occupying Germans who were rounding up thousands of men to work behind the lines. On 27 September, the insurrection broke out in a manner that was both totally spontaneous and lacking in organization. In fact there were numerous individual insurrections, often limited to single neighbourhoods, involving large numbers of young men, mostly of working-class origin. The German troops reacted with great brutality but were nonetheless obliged to abandon the city hurriedly. The uprising cost the lives of sixty-six civilians, eleven of whom were women, and hundreds of wounded. Although the military significance of this event was modest it was nonetheless significant because it originated in a city of the south where political passivity was traditional.[12]

Political parties and the Resistance

The front line thus divided the country in two. In the south, the old ruling classes continued to support the monarchy in order to maintain the status quo once the war was over, but there were various exponents of anti-fascism, notably the elderly philosopher Benedetto Croce, who felt that the errors committed in the past deprived the monarchy of the right to continue governing the country. This kind of criticism was reinforced by the uncertainty with which both the King Victor Emmanuel III and his Prime Minister Badoglio continued to move. On 13 October 1943, it was decided to declare war on Germany but only after the king had issued a proclamation over the radio on 24 September which, while never once mentioning the word 'fascism', was nevertheless a feeble attempt at self defence. The decision was reinforced by the pressure applied on Badoglio's government by the Allies. Making common cause against the Germans allowed Italy to be considered by the Allies as a 'co-belligerent'. Under pressure from the moderate anti-fascists, the king finally decided to hand over command to his son, Umberto, on 16 March 1944 and thus avoid controversy whilst at the same time maintaining the hereditary rights of the House of Savoy to continue governing the country.

In the South the presence of the Allies was directly felt although the preparations for the landing in the North West Europe, the 'second front', meant that the Italian front assumed secondary importance. This may explain the sluggishness with which the advance northwards was made by the Allied troops, supported by French, Polish and Commonwealth contingents and, later, around 10,000 Italian soldiers who made up the so-called Italian Liberation Corps.[13] This pace was in noticeable contrast to the expectations of the first partisan divisions who had imagined that the peninsula would be liberated in a matter of months.

On the chequered board of the Italian situation, it was the British government that dictated the political line to be taken. Prime Minister Churchill clearly expressed his contempt for the Italians, whom he considered as unreliable. His own strategy found this moment appropriate to redefine Italy's role as a regional power in the Mediterranean and British policy concerning the resistance was consequently influenced by such prejudices. British experts favoured a reinstatement of the monarchy at the conclusion of the war whereas the Americans preferred a democratic renewal within the nation that would allow more scope for the anti-fascist parties. Although this idea was opposed by Churchill, on 21 September 1943, Roosevelt nonetheless expressed the opinion that, once the war was over, the Italian people should be allowed the right to choose their own form of government. The conference of foreign ministers, which took place in Moscow on 2 November, limited itself to a compromise which expressed the desire that: 'the Italian government (should) become more democratic, with the inclusion of representatives from those sectors of the population which had consistently opposed Fascism'.[14] However, the American position remained weak since, on both a political and a military level, matters in Italy had been 'assigned' to Great Britain.[15] What united the two Allied nations was a common desire to avoid any strengthening of the Italian Communist Party at all costs. Consequently this implied that, since the communist element was very strong within the resistance movement, little attention should be paid to the armed groups in the occupied territories. In the late autumn of 1944 these concerns were highlighted when civil war broke out in Greece between the communist partisans and the monarchists who were supported by the British. In January 1945, Harold Macmillan, responsible for British politics in Italy, wrote: 'The lesson of Greece is that nothing matters except 'disarmament' [of the partisans].'[16] It was also felt that on a military level a partisan 'army' would be unable to aid the advance of the Anglo-American troops in any significant way. Therefore, preference was given to the formation of small groups of saboteurs led by Allied experts.

These various elements meant that the relationship between the Allies and the resistance was characterized by reciprocal incomprehension and fundamental distrust. The Allies were accused of a reluctance to acknowledge both the partisans and their political organizations, the Committee for National Liberation (CLN) and the CLN-Alta Italia (CLNAI),[17] but also of distributing arms and aid with extreme parsimony and moreover of favouring the non-communist partisan groups. This was only partially true since the SOE and OSS 'missions', which were parachuted behind enemy lines, enjoyed considerable autonomy in determining the destination of aid for specific objectives or areas, without reference to the political 'colour' of the individual partisan groups. For their part, the Allies feared an excessively left-wing emphasis and distrusted the increasing military activity of the partisan groups. According to Edgardo Sogno, a partisan leader of conservative ideas: 'the organizers and the leaders of political bands appeared to be agitators who hindered the serious work of the armed forces with problems and activities which had no real immediate justification.'[18]

The considerable importance of the Allies' political and military actions was not the sole factor conditioning analogous activities within the resistance. From the very beginning, the constitutional problem was something that concerned the coalition of anti-fascist parties. The question remained of whether it was necessary to establish some form of collaboration with the monarchy which – as already noted – had Allied support, or rather to increase the potential of the CLN network that had been established in the months following the armistice. Supporters of the 'CLN government' both then and subsequently, were primarily socialists and 'actionists'. The Action Party (Partito D'Azione – Pd'A), founded after 25 July 1943, comprised intellectuals, students and members of the professional classes. It was a political party that drew heavily on the ideas and values of the anti-fascist exile movement Justitia e Liberta (Justice and Freedom) which had been founded in the 1920s, espousing radical-democratic and anti-clerical ideas and hostility to the monarchy.[19] It also contained some of the more important figures of the resistance, including Ferruccio Parri who became Prime Minister at the end of the war. Pavone has claimed that the 'actionists' considered themselves as the representatives of 'absolute anti-fascism' and consequently were little disposed to any form of compromise.[20] Apart from its disparate attitudes towards economic questions, which ranged from radical socialism to the support of large-scale industrial interests, it was this 'absolutism' which prevented the Pd'A from surviving for any significant period after the end of the war. The positions held by the Catholic world on institutional problems were far less clear,[21] largely because the Christian Democrat party (led by Alcide De Gaspari), aimed to conquer an extensive and cross-class section of Italian society. Within the PCI, which maintained the principal role in the resistance movement, there was initially a tendency to consider the CLN as a fully matured structure for political democracy. It was to be the leader of the party, Palmiro Togliatti, who would provide strategic guidelines in the Spring of 1944 on his return from a long period of exile in Moscow. Togliatti, in the so-called 'Salerno reversal', (Salerno being at this time the seat of the government in the south), considered the constitutional problem to be of secondary importance, something to be confronted at the end of the war. In the meantime, priority must be given to procuring the largest possible consensus amongst the popular and the anti-fascist forces, with an aim to liberating the country and eliminating all traces of Fascism. Although this priority remained evident, Togliatti made no bones about his main strategic objective, which was the introduction of a so-called 'progressive democracy' by the genuinely popular forces of the communists, socialists and the Catholics.

At the time and subsequently, this 'Salerno reversal' was criticized by many, in particular by the 'actionists' and the socialists, but also from within the Communist Party itself.[22] It was felt that this form of compromise would automatically weaken the 'revolutionary' potential of the Resistance movement. However, postwar debates will be discussed at a later stage and it is here sufficient to underline the fact that the change imposed by Togliatti on Communist policies was not merely an abstract idea – it was already practice in occupied Italy where the leading communists (Luigi Longo, Pietro Secchia and Pietro Amendola) favoured political and military agreements with the other parties while ignoring any ideological differences. In point of fact, although they managed to avoid any overt divisions, the principal parties within the CLN held differing, if not divergent, positions on central questions, such as the constitutional problem or political and social reform etc. The desire to avoid ruptures and to maintain unity in order to achieve the common objective of defeating Nazi-fascism, felt particularly strongly by the PCI, ultimately condemned the CLN to inaction on the political front.

In the January of 1944 the Milan CLN, by this stage renamed 'CLN Alta Italia' (CLN Northern Italy), was designated by the Roman branch as the 'special, or exceptional, government of the north'. In the first document published by the CLNAI, it declared itself in favour of a 'clear and effective democracy . . . In the government of the future . . . workers, peasants, artisans and all the working classes will play a decisive role'. The distance thus created between the CLN in Rome and the CLNAI also served to increase that existing between the political parties in the two halves of the country. Those in the south were primarily involved in ideological debates and projects for the future whereas those in the north were overwhelmingly influenced by the armed resistance of the partisans.

The Motivations and the Structure of the Partisan Groups

It is not easy to establish the precise numbers of those involved in the partisan 'bands' during the winter of 1943–4, although Parri estimates that they did not exceed 9,000 armed men. During the winter months, it is clear that these bands worked in a totally uncoordinated manner and caused few real problems[23] either for the German troops or for those of the Italian Social Republic (RSI). This Republic had been expressly promoted by Hitler at the end of September 1943 to allow his friend Mussolini an appearance of power.[24] In this initial phase of occupation, the German military command was more troubled by the organized groups of communists in the cities than by the bands of partisans in the mountains.[25]

With the coming of Spring, the intensification of German activity exposed the partisans' inability to fight effectively in the open. Thus the directives of the PCI in Milan, issued on 28 January 1944 had little foundation in reality when they called for a mass uprising and the organization of provisional civil administrations in the areas to be liberated. Nonetheless, hopes that the improving weather would permit a new Allied offensive to break through the front line brought in a considerable number of new recruits. It can be estimated that by April 1944 there were around 12,000–13,000 fighting men supported by an equal number of auxiliaries, of whom a large proportion were women. About half the partisans fought within the communist 'Garibaldi' brigades. Alongside these, but of slightly less importance, were the 'Justice and Freedom' brigades organized by the Actionist Party. The so-called 'autonomous' brigades, which claimed to be apolitical, were also of some importance, while the Catholic partisans (The Green Flames), the socialists and the monarchists had a more modest presence.[26]

The Garibaldi brigades were directed by an extremely strong centralized power system with a 'political commissar' who worked alongside the military commander according to a traditional soviet model. The political commissar's role was multifarious and included providing a form of political education for the many partisans who were largely uninformed in this field. However, it must be recognized that, overall, the political indoctrination provided by the Garibaldi brigades was not rigidly communist, but had a rather wide-ranging democratic style that encompassed all the various political orientations of the day. The political commissar also played the role of friend and provider of psychological support, or, as Pavone has recently written, as a sort of 'lay chaplain'.[27] Furthermore, it was his job to maintain relations with the civilian population and iron out any disagreements.

In some of the Catholic groups, such as the 'Osoppo' brigades that were active in the north-east, there were some priests who acted as military chaplains. In the majority of the partisan bands there was an attempt to permit discussion and the operation of internal democracy. The same did not always hold true for the 'autonomous' bands, which were frequently led by ex-officers and were rigidly disciplined. However, the pressing everyday realities of the partisan struggle often meant that the application of forms of democracy 'from below' were of necessity put aside. Spontaneity and organization were intimately linked in the partisan bands and applied according to specific local conditions or personal dynamics. Charismatic leaders, commanding total loyalty, would frequently emerge from the groups. The role of women was important but they were often allocated secondary or subordinate positions and frequently acted only as couriers.[28] Thus although they enjoyed a considerable degree of equality, very rarely were they entrusted with positions of real responsibility.

What were the motivations behind the partisan struggle? It is impossible to claim that the majority of partisans were inspired by political motives, just as it is unrealistic to imagine that after twenty years of fascist government, the nation became spontaneously anti-fascist following the downfall of Mussolini. Other factors also clearly played an important role, primarily the disorientation of the army after 8 September, and the desire of its officers and men to avoid the conscription implemented by the Social Republic. For many, the desire for adventure played a part while others were moved by the determination to defend their own 'little corner of the country'. When considering the beginnings of the partisan struggle, it is opportune to cite the analysis made by the partisan Eugenio Artom:' We are what we are; a complex group of individuals: in part disinterested and sincere and in part political opportunists; in part disoriented soldiers fearful of deportation to Germany and in part motivated by a desire for adventure and loot.'[29]

However, the tendency to politicize the partisan groups gradually prevailed. This meant that the collaboration between groups of different political leanings was often far less than perfect. The clashes were particularly bitter between the 'Garibaldi' brigades and the 'autonomous' groups who were largely anti-Communist.[30] The most extreme example of this was the massacre of several dozen members of the autonomous

Osoppo brigades by a group of 'Garibaldi' partisans at Porzûs in eastern Friuli on 7 February 1945. This execution was inspired by the discord between these two political schools of thought within the resistance and highlighted by the tendency of the 'Garibaldi' groups in Friuli to collaborate with the Yugoslavian partisans with a view to becoming part of the Yugoslavian communist state at the end of the war.[31]

Based on an in-depth analysis of the motives expressed by partisans in both contemporary documents and subsequent memoirs, Pavone has recently hypothesized three kinds of war fought simultaneously: a class war that hoped to introduce socialism into the economy and that harked back to the workers' battles of the post World War One period; a war of liberation fought against the hated German invader; and a civil war which saw Italians fighting their countrymen, partisans against '*repubblichini*' (as those adhering to the RSI were called). These three elements often co-existed, although one would frequently tend to predominate[32] and there is evidence that partisans would often express a greater hatred for those Italians enrolled in the RSI army than for the Germans themselves. This undoubtedly worked against the attempts made to avoid intensifying the civil war because of the obvious necessity for national reconciliation at the war's conclusion.

Both the RSI and the Catholic Church did not hesitate to issue appeals for reconciliation. The most famous came from the philosopher Giovanni Gentile, one of the few intellectuals not to have abandoned Mussolini. Attention was drawn to the dangers of this kind of appeal by Concetto Marchese, another intellectual and classical scholar but also a communist:

'It is better that the war should continue if it is destiny that it should be fought. To sheathe the sword only because the hand is tired and the damage is great, can only encourage the assassin. The sword must not be laid aside, but broken.'[33]

This controversy helps explain why a group of communist partisans assassinated Gentile on 15 April 1944, which in turn created conflict and polemics within the partisan world, which have not been resolved to this day.[34]

These three strands of class, civil and patriotic war, which frequently had undefined and overlapping lines of demarcation, often gave the war an extremely violent aspect. The most recent literature on the subject readily recognizes the substantial differences between the violence of the Nazi-fascists, which was often directed against helpless civilians, and that of the partisans, which was overwhelmingly defensive or reactive. Pavone again writes: 'the decision to kill . . . was a consequence of the fundamental necessity of opposing the violence of others.'[35]

In addition to the partisan bands that fought in the hills and the mountains there were other groups of armed partisans formed to fight within an urban context. These were the so-called Gruppi d'Azione Patriottica, (GAP or patriotic action groups), modelled on the French Francs-Tireurs et Partisanes, and set up by the PCI in the major conurbations. These were small groups who worked in typical terrorist formations and were mostly made up of young people, ideologically motivated and who voluntarily embraced a life of clandestinity under constant threat. They were totally committed to the cause, fearless and convinced that history is determined by heroic individuals. The GAP's activities created a conflict of opinions within the anti-fascist parties who generally opposed urban terrorism on the grounds that it endangered the lives of innocent civilians. Pope Pius XII, in a speech made on 25 December 1943, condemned the terrorist activities of the GAP, which were particularly active in Rome. The task assigned to the GAP was to 'make life impossible for the occupying forces' whilst attempting to provoke a head-on conflict in order to eliminate all traces of the 'wait-and-see' attitude prevalent among the anti-fascists. To that end, they carried out a series of sensational attacks that began on 18 December 1943 with the assassination of Aldo Resega, 'Federal' head of the Fascist Party in Milan. However, the most famous of these was the assault against German troops in the Via Rasella in Rome, carried out on 23 March 1944, which drew a terrible reprisal involving the shooting of 335 hostages in the Fosse Ardeatine.[36]

Relations with the Civilian Population and the Question of 'Waiting'

The problem posed by the violence used against civilians who did not participate directly in the resistance begs the more general question of the relationship between the civilian population and the partisans, but it is again necessary to evaluate specific situations and to avoid sweeping statements that have little foundation in reality. There was a considerable portion of the partisan movement and of political elements within the local CLNs that, while agreeing with the need to arm and organize themselves, nevertheless rejected the idea of attacking the enemy and consequently provoking reprisals on account of their relative weakness. This attitude was known as *attendismo* or *wait-and-see'* The reasons behind this were varied: the need to economize on energies and conserve the few weapons available for the final push forwards; the expectation that the war would soon be won by the Allies: but also a form of diffidence towards the constant activity of the 'Garibaldi' and 'Justice and Freedom' brigades who were the most pronounced enemies of *attendismo*. Secchia, one of the leading communists, had already criticized this attitude in November 1943 claiming that it was necessary to act immediately and with determination in order both to engender the widest possible participation amongst the population and also to lay down the foundations for the renewal of Italy's international status at the conclusion of the war.[37]

There was, however, a fundamental logic behind this *attendismo*. The civilian population showed little enthusiasm for the partisan movement, especially in rural areas. The peasants and their families were politically apathetic in general, although there were some notable exceptions. In both Tuscany and Emilia, the partisans could count on the widespread support of the rural populace, and particular significance can be attributed to the general strike proclaimed in the countryside of the provinces of Bologna and Ferrara in June 1944, where anti-fascist slogans were the order of the day.[38] Elsewhere, however, it was demonstrably more difficult to involve the rural population in the movement. It was always a risk to have partisan bands in the area since the population was exposed to the dangers of round-ups and the violence and destruction which these might entail and in any case, many partisans were either the friends or the relatives of those living in these areas. The divergences between partisan and rural inhabitant were also due to the fundamental lack of interest shown by the anti-fascist parties in the problems afflicting the countryside. Rural apathy towards wholehearted support for the resistance as such, did not conflict with the widespread tendency of the peasant population to assist errant Italian soldiers and, above all, Allied prisoners of war who had escaped from abandoned camps after 8 September 1943. Several thousand prisoners found shelter on the farms of central-northern Italy, often for considerable periods of time, and cases of betrayal or the handing over of such men to either the Germans or the RSI were exceptionally rare.[39] During 1944, the gulf between the peasants and the partisans was consistently reduced, above all due to the looting and hoarding that both the German and Fascist Republican (*repubblichini*) troops carried out in the countryside. The passive resistance to hoarding and the active supplying of food to the partisans thus became the main agencies fostering mutual understanding between the rural population and the partisans, although this was never fully completed. As far as the Veneto area was concerned, which was both rural and Catholic, it has been claimed: 'Rather than on the grounds of a common recognition of the goals of the struggle, the alliance between the peasant and the partisan [grew] out of compelling common interest; of a shared economic situation which was equally compelling; and a common identification of the enemy.'[40]

However, Renzo De Felice sees the situation in a different light, since he maintains that, above all in the conclusive phase of the war, the weariness and indifference of the rural population was actually accentuated by the necessity of providing for a continuously growing number of partisans.[41]

The Catholic world was noticeably characterized by *attendismo*, and this was encouraged by the wary and prudent attitudes assumed by the ecclesiastical hierarchy. Thus while there were some, such as the Bishop of Cremona who declared that 'the Italian clergy cannot oppose the will of the majority of the Italian people which is against fascism', by contrast, others preached the independence of a Church that condemned all violence, from whatever viewpoint.[42] The fear that the communists might predominate was such that some members of the clergy openly supported the (Fascist) Italian Social Republic (RSI). This caution was largely shared by the clergy in those rural and mountain parishes where their main aim was to support the local communities and hope for a speedy end to the conflict. However, there were also many parish priests and members of the clergy who were either actively participant in the resistance or at least tacitly supported it. It is no coincidence that in the areas where the Catholic tradition was most deeply established, such as the provinces of Varese, Brescia and Bergamo, as well as a large part of the Veneto area, the partisan movement was notably weaker than in the surrounding areas.[43] It was only in the spring and summer of 1944 that Enrico Mattei, a Christian Democrat leader, began to found autonomous Christian Democrat resistance groups. Nonetheless, it must be added that there was undoubtedly an exaggeration in the estimate of 65–80,000 Christian Democrat partisans that was in circulation after the war.

Rome provides a particularly noteworthy case of *attendismo*. A tight network of clandestine partisans had been organized in the capital and had the support of a considerable proportion of the population, which put up a stubborn form of passive resistance against the occupying forces. There were many higher civil servants and bureaucrats involved, who simultaneously maintained an attitude of caution and ambiguity, and there were certainly cases of double agents, such as those who both aided the partisans with arms and information and at the same time took part in the repression of the resistance movement so as not to antagonize the Germans. Thanks to shrewd Vatican mediation it was possible to avoid a popular uprising to liberate the city. With a certain degree of bitterness, Bocca has written that: 'The Resistance in Rome was a compact mass of "waiting", with sporadic outbursts of armed conflict.'[44] Thus, on 4 June 1944, the Allied troops entered the city as liberators, whilst the Germans had withdrawn unhindered. However, the manner in which the capital was liberated represented a political defeat for the forces of democracy.

The Resistance and the Working Class

As has already been seen, the anti-fascist parties and the partisan movement encountered great difficulties in breaking down the traditional political passivity of the rural population. There were, however, greater opportunities for the creation of a closer form of symbiosis with the working classes who were concentrated in the conurbations of the so-called 'industrial triangle' of Lombardy, Piedmont and Liguria. Since the end of the nineteenth century, left-wing parties had established solid foundations within the working classes here but twenty years of fascist repression, together with the severe living conditions during the war had led to the breaking down of the common links between the two elements. Nonetheless, the great strike movements of March 1943, which had provided an early indication of the increasing divergence of outlook and ideas between the Fascist regime and the civilian population, had also shown the extent to which the working classes of the north were potentially disposed towards an anti-fascist political mobilization.

After the German occupation and the foundation of the (Fascist) Italian Social Republic, the reborn anti-fascist parties, with the Communists to the fore, belatedly realized the potential contained within the working classes. The industrialists' politics created further obstacles as they attempted to tread the line between the Germans and the resistance, whilst avoiding offence to either party. Thus they were prepared to have their factories used for war production, on condition that the Germans supplied the raw materials, fuel and means of transport. The majority of the industrialists, together with some of the Germans and especially those representing Albert Speer's Armaments Ministry had an interest in maintaining some level of normal productive output although other agencies of the occupying forces favoured the gradual dismantling of Italian industry and the mass deportation of the workers to the Reich.[45] The industrial workers were, however, fully aware of this latter possibility.

Consequently, it is reasonable to assume that the so-called 'socialist' proclamations of the RSI had little effect upon the behaviour of the working classes. At the Congress of Verona, held in November 1943, the RSI launched a plan for the principal industrial sectors to become 'gradually more socialist' while vague promises were held out to the workers. However, it is more likely that it was the extremely difficult prevailing conditions that influenced working-class behaviour and attitudes, since real wages were diminishing, housing was chronically short after the damages caused to thousands of homes by bombing, and food, fuel and other essential necessities were scarce. It should also be remembered that there was a consistent, although admittedly not very significant presence of the Communist Party within the factories, whereas other political parties were virtually unrepresented. Thus, for example, at the beginning of 1944 out of the 5,000 workers of the Innocenti factory in Milan, six were members of the PCI. In the Caproni factory in Brescia there were forty paid-up communists out of a work-force of 4,000 whilst at the Pirelli factory there were fewer than 200 out of a work-force of 10,000 (a third of whom were women). In Genova, at the Ansaldo Meccanica works, there were only fifty communists out of 4,000 workers and fifty-six out of the 6,000 strong workforce of the Fiat Lingotto factory in Turin.[46] However, even amongst those workers who declared little political interest, there was a strong emotional identification with the USSR, considered as the 'homeland of socialism' and as the bulwark against the expansion of Nazism.

In the light of the March 1943 strikes, the leaders of the PCI realized that there was still the problem of combining the more immediate demands of the workers with the more general and political ideals contained within the struggle against the Germans and the Fascists. This was only partially resolved, as is shown by recent studies that have managed to shake off the mystique of the resistance, which was so widespread in the first postwar decades. It is possible to identify two cycles of industrial class conflicts between the autumn of 1943 and the spring of 1944.[47] Their development was determined by specific local circumstances and by the kind of reaction that the strikes provoked from both the German authorities and the industrialists themselves. The first cycle of strikes was initiated in mid-November by the Fiat works of Turin, over the non-payment of wages. The strike rapidly spread and became more radical, so that the strikers put forward a package of concrete wage and normative demands. In the following days, the strike was taken up in Milan and Genova and in the face of this solid industrial-class front, both the industrialists and the Germans attempted a form of dialogue that bypassed the local and ineffectual RSI authorities. Nonetheless, force was also employed alongside these negotiations so that there were hundreds of arrests and deportations to Germany. The CLN belatedly appreciated the potential of these strikes and the PCI's factory committees did attempt to influence them by including explicit references to the fight for an anti-fascist liberation in the material requests made to the authorities. 'However, those who have carefully studied these strike cycles have ultimately arrived at the conclusion that the working class was barely receptive to a political influence that was actively anti-fascist and remained strongly anchored to the problems of economic demands.'[48]

Nonetheless, in addition to the concession of a wage increase and the improvement in supplies of food and fuel, it is undeniably true that the PCI was strengthened by these November strikes. It was bolstered to the extent that its members became aware of the inherent possibilities of strike action and also managed to consolidate communist influence amongst the workers. An official German document of the following February illustrated how the strike had become gradually more politically orientated and foresaw that the working class would soon take increasing advantage of this kind of 'highly valuable instrument of power'.

Fortified by these experiences, the PCI began to prepare for a general strike in January that would naturally be linked to the insurrection which, as previously noted, its leaders felt was imminent. This new cycle of conflict began on 1 March 1944, again in Turin and Milan, and rapidly escalated. The characteristics of this brief, eight-day cycle of strikes, can be seen as indicating a greater geographical extension of the movement, since industrial cities in both the Veneto and Emilia regions were involved, together with much greater level of participation which was itself much more politically orientated. The numbers involved in the strike, which was widely reported in the international press,[49] have been calculated as ranging from 500,000 to one million in the whole of northern Italy. The wide discrepancies in numbers underlines the difficulty of evaluating an industrial conflict that was spread across a wide area and had specific local characteristics. The impact of this particular strike cannot be overestimated in that it finally expressed economic demands alongside political slogans demanding the expulsion of the occupying forces and an end to the war.[50]

However, despite such massive levels of participation, the results were decidedly disappointing. The economic demands were only partially met and the long-awaited insurrection did not materialize. Involvement in the strike was particularly disappointing in the factories of Genova but this could possibly be explained by the fact that, in the preceding months, the city had been wearied by a series of minor social conflicts. Nonetheless, at the end of this second cycle of strikes it can be seen that the PCI had managed to consolidate further its position on the shop-floors, establishing the foundations for a political hegemony which would last for many decades. As far as the anti-fascist struggle was concerned, when faced with strong German repression, the vast expenditure of organizational resources and strength again gave disappointing results. There was one direct result, however, as both the industrialists and the occupying power were forced to acknowledge the dangers implicit in the potential political mobilization of the industrial classes of the north. In the following months these social battles died down, except for one brief outbreak in Milan in November of the same year. In the meantime, the CLNAI concentrated all its resources on the armed partisan movement that underwent its most active phase in the summer of 1944.

The Summer 1944 Partisan Offensive and the 'Free Zones'

During the spring and summer of 1944, the partisan groups were numerically strengthened thanks to the arrival of thousands of deserters from both the conscription laws of the RSI and the work gangs destined for deportation to Germany. According to one of the RSI's own estimates 82,000 men had joined the partisans by mid-June alone: 25,000 from Piedmont, 16,000 from the Venezia-Giulia area, 14,200 from Liguria and 17,000 from Emilia-Tuscany.[51] This vast numerical increase obviously created considerable problems of integration since those partisans who had suffered the terrible conditions of the preceding winter were often naturally suspicious of new arrivals who were only partly conscious of the ideological and political implications of their situation. The maintenance of ever larger groups also created important logistical problems. Nonetheless, the partisan groups became more self-assured, to such an extent that it became possible to engage in significant manoeuvres against both German and Fascist *repubblichini* troops. The latter now rarely left their barracks except when involved, in a secondary role, in round-ups led by the Germans.

In the Emilia region, it is possible to cite various examples of the numerical and qualitative growth of partisan activity. In the month of June 1944, the partisans reported the killing of 519 German soldiers and 336 *repubblichini,* the derailment of two trains, the interruption of sixteen railway lines, twenty armed attacks on military barracks and road blocks and thirty-seven sabotage attacks against electricity, telephone and telegraph cables. The following month 831 Germans and 737 *repubblichini* were killed, nearly 1,000 wounded, five trains derailed, fifty-five sabotage attacks carried out on railway lines and forty-eight on electricity, telephone and telegraph cables.[52]

The German military authorities were compelled to acknowledge the growing danger presented by the partisan movement, particularly since the battlefront was gradually receding northwards. The strategic significance of the partisan activity thus became abundantly evident, even to the Allied command. The liberation of Rome, on 4 June 1944, did not have the effect desired by the Allied generals because German forces continued in their tenacious defence and the Allied advance proceeded slowly, despite the promises of the inter-allied commander, General Alexander, to break through to the Po valley by August. Moreover, the offensive was further weakened by the discord between the British and American commands.

The problems of security for German lines of communication and transport became acute as the Allies advanced northwards, particularly in the Ligurian and Tuscan-Emilian Apennine areas and it became essential to introduce a decidedly more drastic policy of anti-partisan repression than had previously been necessary. On 17 June, Marshal Kesselring issued an ordinance that acknowledged the growing danger from partisan bands and ordered the strongest reprisals against civilians who were in the least way suspect of aiding and abetting them, regardless of the consequences. Thus he provided official sanction for the most murderous proceedings and guaranteed the immunity of their perpetrators.[53] Extremely violent roundups were thus initiated, which had very little to do with the effective presence of partisans in the area. One infamous example of this is the bloodstained march of an SS battalion, led by Major Walter Reder, through the Tuscan-Emilian Apennine area from the middle of August until 1 October. This included the massacres of S. Anna di Stazzema with 560 victims, Valle with 107 victims, S. Terenzio with 53 victims, Frigido with 108 victims and finally Marzabotto where 770 civilians, mostly women, children and the elderly, were murdered.[54]

While the final stages of the Allied offensive were considered imminent, the intensification of clashes between the partisan groups and German troops posed problems of a political nature. The leaders of the CLN and the CLNAI were forced to consider the question of an effective coordination of the various groups' activities on the battlefield and to this end it was decided that General Raffaele Cadorna should be nominated as military advisor in June 1944. However, he demanded the role of effective military commander of all the partisan formations and this role, supported by the Allies as a means of controlling the partisans, became the focus point for a political confrontation. A compromise was only reached the following November when Cadorna was nominated as commander but was flanked by two vice-commanders, (Longo and Parri), who represented the two strongest anti-fascist political parties. Despite this, effective coordination between the groups did not really exist, either on a regional level or between groups of different political leanings. The individual groups jealously defended their own autonomy and their links with the surrounding areas and only with great reluctance would they accept orders from a general governing body.

The union of all the partisan groups was given the title 'Corpo Volontari della Libertà' (CVL – Voluntary Liberty Corps). Despite its fragmentation, the leadership issued orders for a general offensive that, together with the Allied advance, would finally break through the enemy front line. This offensive, where collaboration was poorly organized both with the Allies and between the various partisan groups themselves, saw the development of 'Free Zones', or rather, as they have somewhat controversially been known, 'Partisan Republics'. They were a complex phenomenon, with specific regional characteristics, but they nevertheless permit an evaluation of the great progress made by the resistance in its organizational capacities and long-range strategies, but also of its limitations in the political and administrative spheres.[55]

The chronology and characteristics of these zones varied enormously. In June 1944, 'Free Zones' were established at Montefiorino, in the Apennine area around Modena,[56] and in the eastern part of Friuli. In mid-July there was a 'Free Zone' in Carnia, an area that embraces forty-two mountain communities, and beginning in September the two Piedmont Zones of Val d'Ossola and Alto Monferrato were established. These two were possibly the most important because they included both hillsides and plains, which were quite densely populated.[57] There were other 'Free Zones' but these were geographically smaller and lasted considerably less time. Between the beginning of August, at Montefiorino, and the first days of December, at Monferrato and Torreglia in Liguria, all the 'Free Zones' were liquidated by the Germans and the Fascist *repubblichini* in open battles, which saw the deployment of several thousand men and a vast range of weapons and transport, all recalled from the front for this purpose. There were also severe losses of life.

All the 'Free Zones', by differing means and methods, attempted to initiate a form of self-administration by the populace and created popular councils, which included all the political parties of the CLN. In some cases these councils were elected by civilians, including women, but they did not always find themselves in complete agreement with the partisans. For example, in the 'Republic' of Montefiorino, the local population was unwilling to take on the running of the popular council and the partisan leaders were therefore obliged to assume this responsibility. As the leading scholar of the 'Free Zones' has noted: 'The objective of the transition from military control to a political organization was only partially fulfilled.'[58] This was primarily due to the differing attitudes to be found between the radical communist partisans and the conservative (and Catholic) mentality of the rural and mountain population.

The situation in the Val d'Ossola, with a population of about 80,000 is possibly the best example of the way in which an intelligent and capable group of leaders could look beyond immediate everyday and military problems. Although it was only partially fulfilled, it is possible to identify a wide-ranging political project; the wholesale replacement of administrative and judicial personnel, the organization of a system for gathering food supplies and the provision of guaranteed prices for the peasants that would be twice or three times those imposed by the Fascist RSI. Elsewhere and with varying methods, there were attempts to eliminate the inequity of the existing fiscal system and to introduce progressive taxation. In the Monferrato area agricultural rents were frozen as a means of meeting the peasants' demands. It must be admitted that many of the economic measures enacted were fundamentally demagogic and aimed to gain the approval of a generally diffident population. Ultimately, it proved impossible to carry out all the promised measures and consequently a considerable degree of disillusionment set in.

The 'Free Zones' underlined the extreme fragility of Mussolini's puppet state and highlighted the potential contained in the partisans' form of democracy. The military situation and the enormous logistical difficulties determined the duration of these Zones, so that none lasted more than three months. From a military viewpoint, they can be considered as an error, since they confined thousands of partisans to specific and often marginal areas where open battles would necessarily be waged against superior forces, risking the destruction of some of the most aggressive and effective partisan formations. Luckily this was avoided, but only by the ability with which the partisans were able to utilize their thorough knowledge of the terrain. It is opportune to recall the judgement made by Giorgio Agosti, one of the leading members of the Pd'A in Piedmont, who noted that the 'Free Zones' noticeably damaged the relationship between the partisans and the civilian population because of the onus placed upon the latter of supporting thousands of armed men and being exposed to particularly violent reprisals.[59]

The defeat of the 'Free Zones' is one of the reasons why, in the autumn of 1944, the partisan movement suffered yet another moment of crisis when faced with the prospect of a second winter in the mountains, and the military front again ground to a halt.

From the Alexander Proclamation to Insurrection

On 13 November 1944, the Allies broadcast a proclamation signed by General Alexander, commander of the inter-allied forces in Italy. This declared that the Allied offensive was over and gave instructions to the partisan formations to disband in view of the coming winter and to return to their homes and await further instructions. This was a profound psychological blow to the resistance movement since it underlined the Allies' lack of faith in the partisans, whilst ignoring the objective difficulties of those who had been outlawed for the past one or two years to return home without being captured. Together with the dramatic round-ups of the autumn which had swept aside the 'Free Zones', and the failure of the coordinated offensive of the Allies and the partisans, the Alexander proclamation increased the crisis existing within the partisan movement that winter.[60]

Longo clearly expressed the CNLAI's response to the proclamation in a reply given on 2 December: ' The battle continues and must continue. We must ensure that in the coming weeks and months, there will neither be a reduction nor a weakening of the partisan fight but rather an intensification and an expansion of its groups.'[61] It is not possible to establish clearly the effects of the proclamation or the dimensions of the crisis it encouraged, nor is it possible to determine whether the many people who abandoned the partisans during the winter months did so out of fatigue or rather from the desire to economize on energies with a view to the spring offensive. Some scholars have held that the so-called *pianurizzazione,* the return of many partisans to their home towns, should be considered as a strategic success because it led to the saving of thousands of lives.

However, the Allied command quickly realized that they had committed a serious error and on 22 November, General Wilson, commander for the entire Mediterranean area, stressed that the partisan formations would continue to receive supplies as before. In fact, two months later, new strategic directives were issued that included the partisan formations in the plans for a new and final offensive. Ultimately, on 7 December, the so-called 'Protocols of Rome' were signed between the CLNAI leaders and General Wilson himself. These represent an important political acknowledgement of the CLNAI as it was thereby recognized as the political partner of the Allies in the final offensive and, as a result, obtained substantial financial support. Undoubtedly, the signing of the 'protocols' did not eliminate those reciprocal misunderstandings, which had been a permanent feature in the relationship between the Allies and the Resistance. The former had always intended to control the partisans whilst leaving the future political and constitutional structure undefined. Nonetheless, a basis for a triumphant revival of partisan activity in the spring of 1945 had been created.[62]

The final phases of the partisan war have not yet been studied in depth[63] and therefore it is still difficult to evaluate the validity of either the claims of a profound crisis in the winter of 1944/45 or of the theory that maintains that the nucleus of the Resistance remained intact and ready for the final insurrection. According to one German estimate, during the winter months, the total number of 'bandits' decreased to about 50,000. In March 1945, when the German Reich was suffering defeat on all fronts, the Allied offensive began again in Italy. By this time, the partisan formations comprised about 80,000 fighting men, a figure that rose to around 100,000 by the next month and to 250,000–300,000 by the end of April. Industrial conflict in the factories regained strength and, above all in the Emilia area, peasant demands were vigorously expressed once again. Even politics began to move again and missives were sent by both the Allies and the government in the south in an attempt of persuade the CLNAI to adopt an attitude of *attendismo*, arguing that an insurrection, which would undoubtedly cost numerous innocent lives, would in any case be useless given that the war would inevitably be concluded in the near future. Despite this, on 10 April 1945, the Milan PCI issued directives for the preparation of an uprising that would highlight the fight conducted by the masses and establish the right of the Italian people to decide their own future. Because the stakes were so high, CLNAI adopted this communist policy as if it were its own because to impede a general uprising would signify the undermining of the partisan movement at both a political and a moral level. The destiny of the nation would be played out around this insurrection. Even the Nazi-Fascists attempted by various ways and means, including secret negotiations, to impede this insurrection and organize a less traumatic transition from war to peace.

There was no lack of debate in the spring, even within the CLN itself, and the imminent end of the conflict obliged a clarification of the various ideological positions involved. The 'actionists' were in favour of a CLN government even in the part of Italy that was already liberated, thus making a decisive break with the past. On the other hand, Christian Democrats and liberals argued that the CLN no longer had any reason to exist once the war was over. The communist position was more nebulous as there was a divergence between the group of leaders in the north who favoured change (Longo and Secchia), and the more cautious Togliatti. Nonetheless, while the insurrection was imminent, it was at least possible to maintain an appearance of unified action.

The CLNAI's orders foresaw concentrated attacks by the partisans supported by members of the GAP organizations within the cities. The industrial workers were ordered to defend factories and the urban infrastructure and to impede any sabotage attempts. The case of Genova is emblematic as the partisans responded to German attempts to mine the harbour with a widespread and effective tactic of mine clearance. The proposed goal was the liberation of all the principal cities before the arrival of the Allies, and the installation of self-governing bodies that would assure public order and the functioning of essential services.

On 10 April, partisan groups launched an offensive on the Ligurian and Emilian fronts. On 18 April, a general strike broke out in Turin and the following day the GAP liberated Bologna. In nearly all the cities of the Emilia area the liberation was accompanied by hard-fought battles with German troops but the partisans nevertheless managed to salvage nearly all the important infrastructures. The insurrection broke out in Genova on 23 April, in Milan the following day, and in Turin during the night of the 25/26 April. In Genova, the German commander General Meinhold, finding himself surrounded by the partisans, was forced to surrender. The uprising in Milan was less dramatic and the following day, the CLNAI established the first tribunals to deal with the purging of the area, and set up commissions for the management of industry by the workers themselves, which would limit the profits to be made by industrialists. In all these instances, the Allied troops entered the cities only after they had been liberated.

On 30 April, an Italian partisan insurrection broke out in Trieste, but was immediately forced to relinquish control to the Yugoslavian partisans, thereby creating one of the most difficult problems of the postwar period. Mussolini had been shot by the partisans two days earlier in a small village on Lake Como and on 2 May the Germans still remaining in the country surrendered. The general uprising was carried out according to plan, city by city, and was greeted with joy and relief by a population exhausted by a long and brutal conflict. It was followed by numerous acts of violence, many of which were purely vindictive, despite orders to the contrary issued by the CLNAI. Such acts of violence continued for the following two or three years, particularly on the plains of Emilia. As will be seen below, right-wing propaganda claimed that the partisans killed at least 300,000 persons during the month of April, but official government figures issued in 1952 estimated that 'only' 1,732 Italians were killed by their fellow countrymen in those days of joy and liberation.

Thus the war of liberation came to an end at a cost to the partisans of 44,720 men fallen in combat and 9,980 killed in reprisals, to which must be added 21,000 wounded, mutilated or incapacitated. The casualty figures for the Italian Social Republic are not known just as it is not possible to estimate the number of German soldiers who were killed in conflicts with the partisans.[64]

The 'Myths' of the Republic

The resistance quickly changed from being a historical fact to becoming a political myth, particularly because a considerable number of political parties and a large proportion of pubic opinion held that the democratic republic, founded on 2 June 1946, was the 'child' of the resistance. It became surrounded by a sort of rituality (the celebration of 25 April as a public holiday), which became yearly more rhetorical and had ever less impact upon subsequent generations.[65]

The imposing political and ideological component in the history of resistance has made any objective historical analysis extremely complex, despite the works of many scholars. The first to study the phenomenon were the Historical Institutes of the Resistance, which grew up all over the country from the 1950s onwards. Today there are still more than sixty of these, coordinated by the National Institute in Milan, and they produce a large number of publications, magazines and monographs and have access to important historical archives. Although the work of this network of research centres is highly commendable,[66] it has nonetheless been profoundly influenced by the fact that many of its founders and members were ex-partisans themselves.[67] The 'spirit of the CLN', which inspired the Institutes' research for many years, has to some extent favoured the perpetuation of various forms of censorship. However, for some time now, the Institutes have managed to break free from the tradition of resistance rhetoric.

One of the fundamental myths of the resistance was that which claimed that it had been a spontaneously popular movement. More in-depth studies have in fact revealed that the resistance movement was limited to a minority who found only partial support from the population. Although it is relatively easy to count those who can be considered as partisans if one looks at the official postwar figures, it is much more difficult to evaluate the extent of the support that they may have received from the civilian population, because this varied according to location and over time. One of the decisive factors that may have determined this support was the degree of severity with which the German and Fascist *repubblichini* troops carried out their anti-partisan repression. However, some importance must also be given to the roundups and other actions carried out against the civil population by the occupiers, which offended against what E.P. Thompson has called the moral economy. In Italy, as elsewhere, left-wing historiography has depicted the working class as possessing an inflexible class-consciousness and as being consistently willing to carry out a class war, and consequently the involvement of the working class in the resistance has generally been interpreted in these terms. However, further studies, undertaken from the 1970s onwards have shown that the workers were motivated primarily by economic and material necessity and that their relationship with the PCI was not entirely straightforward.[68]

Alongside the myth of the resistance as a spontaneous uprising of the entire population that saw the need to redeem Italy from the shame of twenty years of Fascist regime, various other interpretations, which then became myths in their own right, have been formulated. Particular consideration should be given to the myth of the 'betrayed resistance'.[69] This was advanced by historians of the 'actionist' and extreme left-wing schools of thought, and originated with the supposition that a potentially revolutionary situation existed in Italy during the years 1943–5. It is hypothesized that the conciliatory policies of the PCI, beginning with the famous 'Salerno reversal', nullified this potential and sacrificed it in the name of a compromise with the moderate Catholics. This interpretation was revived in the 1960s and 1970s by the students' movement that frequently claimed to consider itself as a 'second resistance'. As can be seen from the preceding pages, the theory of a 'betrayed resistance' is not credible since it takes no account of the Allied presence, which would certainly never have tolerated a development of this nature. Neither does this theory acknowledge the huge variety and lack of unity within the same partisan movement nor does it take into consideration the fact that the supporters of the resistance represented only a minority of the Italian population. The south, where there was effectively no resistance movement, was deaf to all programmes for a radical political renewal.[70] It is sufficient to consider the figures emerging from the constitutional referendum of June 1946, which was held to decide between the monarchy and the Republic. In the south, support for the Republic was only 32.6 per cent, whereas in the country as a whole, those in favour numbered just over 54 per cent.

It is however true that the myth of the 'betrayed Resistance' illustrates various elements of a change that would play a significant role in the post-war period but, nonetheless, confuses reality with the hopes (or illusions) of a particular élite. The elements that are part of a 'civil war' category can be seen as a sort of counter-myth to the idea of a 'war for national liberation'. This would imply that during these years many Italians fought on opposite sides against each other, each side being inspired by honest ideals and worthy values. By placing both sides on the same level, this theory effectively nullifies the superior moral worth of the resistance and cancels out the concept of 'collaborationists'. This idea is also intimately linked to the theory that many partisans acted from purely personal motives and were guilty of private acts of revenge even after the end of the war. This 'civil war' theory, although present in the works of some of the first scholars concerned with the resistance, has mainly been the prerogative of right-wing historians.[71] It is only in this last decade that the works of Claudio Pavone[72] have broken the taboo surrounding it and have introduced into discussions concerning the resistance the possibility that there might also have been an element of 'civil war'.[73] His authoritative arguments have consequently influenced the historiography of the resistance and have brought new and varied elements into the discussion.

The radical political changes that have taken place in Italy since the beginning of the 1990s have encouraged the bypassing of the more rigid, ideological models.[74] Until now, despite their notable differences, those political parties which were originally components of the CLN, considered themselves as all part of a so-called 'constitutional umbrella', which excluded the neo-fascist party (Movimento Sociale Italiano). However, since 1993–4 the sudden change in the old political structure has brought the extreme right (by this stage included in a new party named Alleanza Nazionale), within a political discourse that has officially recognized the historical significance of the resistance as a fundamental element in the founding of the democratic republic. On the other hand, the traditional left-wing rhetoric of the resistance movement appears now to permit a more frank and less ideologically conditioned perspective.[75] In this way the foundations have been created [76] for a more balanced and less rigid analysis of the complex phenomenon of the resistance, whilst subtracting nothing from its significance for Italian society since 1945. In the future it will be possible to critically re-evaluate the resistance as an element of unity and self-identification for the Italian people.[77]

Notes

1. S. Colarizi, *L'opinione degli italiani sotto il regime 1929–1943*,(Rome: Laterza, 1991), and Lepre, A., *Le illusioni, la paura e la rabbia* (Naples: ESI, 1989).

2. G. Bertolo, et al., *Operai e contadini nella crisi italiana 1943-1944* (Milan: Feltrinelli, 1974) p.18.

3. Milan was one of the major centres of the rebirth of political activity. See L. Ganapini, *Una città, la guerra. Milano 1939-1951* (Milan: F. Angeli, 1988) pp.50ff.

4. P. Spriano, *Storia del Partito Comunista Italiano,* Vol.IV, (Turin: Einaudi, 1975) p.311.

5. See, E. Aga Rossi, *Una nazione allo sbando. L'armistizio italiano del settembre 1943,* (Bologna: Il Mulino, 1985).

6. A perspective on the collapse of 8 September from below can be found in C. Dellavalle (ed.), *8 settembre 1943: storia e memoria,* (Milan: F. Angeli, 1989).

7. See the definitive study by G. Schreiber, *Die italienischen Militär-internierten im deutschen Machtbereich,* (Munich: Oldenbourg, 1990).

8. P. Spriano, *Storia del Partito Comunista Italiano,* Vol.V, (Turin: Einaudi, 1975) p.34.

9. Ibid. p.102.

10. Ibid. p.103.

11. On the internal evolution of Communist policy during the war of liberation, see the book by one of the protagonists: P. Secchia, *Il Partito Comunista e la guerra di liberazione* (Milan: Feltrinelli, 1971).

12. See, G. Arteri (ed.), *Le Quattro Giornate. Scritti e testimonianze* (Naples: Marotta, 1963).

13. See, R. Lamb, *War in Italy 1943-1945. A Brutal Story* (London: Penguin, 1993). On the reconstructed Italian Army in the South, see L. Lollio, *Le unità ausiliarie dell'esercito italiano nella guerra di liberazione* (Rome, 1977).

14. Cited in G. Bocca, *Storia dell'Italia partigiana* (Milan: Mondadori, 1966) p.108.

15. For a general overview, see M. De Leonardis, *La Gran Bretagna e la Resistenza partigiana in Italia* (Naples: ESI, 1988). E. Aga Rossi, *L'Italia nella sconfitta. Politica interna e situazione internazionale durante la Seconda Guarra Mondiale,* (Naples: ESI, 1985).

16. H. Macmillan, *War Diaries. The Mediterranean 1943–1945* (London: 1984) p.657. Entry for 22 January 1945.

17. F. Catalano, *Storia del CLNAI* (Milan: Bompiani, 1956).

18. Cited by R. de Felice, *Mussolini l'alleato. La guerra civile,* (Turin: Einaudi, 1997) p.214.

19. G. de Luna, *Storia del Partito d'azione. La rivoluzione democratica (1942–1947)* (Milan: Feltrinelli, 1982). D. Ward, *Antifascisms.*

Cultural Politics in Italy 1943–1946 (London: Associated University Presses, 1996) pp.124–56.

20. C. Pavone, *Una guerra civile. Saggio storico sulla moralità nella Resistenza* (Turin: Bollati-Boringhieri, 1991) p.568.

21. B. Gariglio (ed.) *Cattolici e Resistenza in Italia settentrionale* (Bologna: Il Mulino, 1997) and for an overview of all major political trends and parties, see R. Ruffilli (ed.) *Cultura politica e partiti nell'età della Costituente* (Bologna: Il Mulino, 1979).

22. See, Spriano, *Storia*, V, pp.315ff. P. de Loreto, *Togliatti e la questione della 'doppiezza'* (Bologna: Il Mulino, 1991).

23. Amongst the major difficulties were the complete lack of experience, the difficulty in obtaining help from the civilian population and the lack of weapons. To give just one example, a partisan brigade in Piedmont composed of 400 men had at their disposal only two heavy and eighteen light machine guns, fourty-five rifles and about 150 hand grenades. Spriano, *Storia*, V, p.182.

24. See F.W. Deakin, *The Brutal Friendship – Mussolini, Hitler and the fall of Italian Fascism* (London: Weidenfeld and Nicholson, 1962). P.P. Poggio (ed.) *La repubblica Sociale Italiana* (Brescia: Fondazione L.Micheletti-Annali, 1986)

25. See the report from General Touissaint, dated November 1942, in: *Europa unterm Hakenkreuz VI, Südosteuropa und Italien* (Berlin: Hüthig, 1992) p.281.

26. L. Valiani, G.Bianchi, E.Ragionieri, *Azionisti, cattolici e comunisti nella Resistenza* (Milan: F.Angeli, 1988).

27. Pavone, *Una guerra civile*, pp.1255ff.

28. A. Rossi-Doria, 'Le donne sulla scena politica' in: F.Barbagallo (ed.) *Storia dell'Italia repubblicana*, Vol I (Turin: Einaudi, 1994) pp.780–848.

29. Cited in G. de Luna and M. Revelli, *Fascismo-antifascismo. Le idee, le identità* (Florence: la Nuova Italia, 1995) p.110.

30. On the background to this hostility, see Spriano, *Storia*, pp.196f.

31. On the massacre itself, see D. Francheschini, *Porzûs. La Resistenza lacerata* (Trieste: Qualestoria, 1997). A recent film about the event has aroused a general storm of debate.

32. Pavone *Una guerra civile*, p.225ff.

33. Cited in Spriano, *Storia*, V, p.109.

34. L.Canfora, *La sentenza. Concetto Marchese e Giovanni Gentile*, (Palermo: Sellerio, 1985).

35. Pavone, *Una guerra civile*, p.445.

36. See, A. Ascarelli, *Le Fosse Ardeatine* (Bologna: Cappelli, 1965).

37. Cited in Bocca, *Storia*, p.205.
38. On the strikes in Emilia, see L. Arbizzani, 'Azione operaia, contadina, di massa', in *L'Emilia-Romagna nella guerra di liberazione*, vol. II, 4 vols (Bari: De Donato, 1975–6).
39. See the exhaustive study by Roger Absolom, *A Strange Alliance. Aspects of Escape and Survival in Italy* (Florence: Olschky, 1991).
40. Bertolo, *Operai e contadini*, p.430.
41. De Felice, *Mussolini l'alleato*, pp.332ff.
42. For a general survey of the attitudes of the ecclesiastical hierarchy, see Pavone, *Una guerra civile*, pp.280ff.
43. G. Galli, *Storia della Democrazia Cristiana* (Rome: Laterza, 1978) p.47.
44. Bocca, *Storia*, p.282.
45. On German occupation policy, see E. Collotti, *L'amministrazione tedesca nell'Italia occupata 1943–1945*, (Milan: Lerici, 1963) and more recently, L.Klinkhammer, *L'occupazione tedesca in Italia 1943–1945*, (Turin: Bollati-Boringhieri, 1993).
46. Spriano, *Storia*, V, p.225ff.
47. A. Scalpelli (ed.) *Scioperi e guerriglia in Val Padana* (Urbino: Argalia, 1972).
48. Bertolo, *Operai e contadini*, p.228 and on the first wave of strikes, pp.212ff. Spriano, *Storia*, V, pp.232f.
49. Even the *New York Times* devoted a great deal of attention to this impressive strike which had no counterparts in occupied Europe. Bocca, *Storia*, p.208.
50. On the German reaction to the strikes, see the documents published in *Europa unterm Hakenkreuz*, VI, pp.299, 307.
51. R. Battaglia, *Storia della Resistenza italiana* (Turin: Einaudi, 1953) p.338.
52. Ibid. p.350.
53. The text of this brutal ordinance is published in *Europa unterm Hakenkreuz*, VI, p.333.
54. F. Andrae, *La Wehrmacht in Italia* (Rome: Editori Reuniti, 1997). G. Schreiber, *Deutsche Kriegsverbrecher in Italien. Täter-Opfer-Straf-verfolgung* (Munich: Beck, 1996). L. Klinkhammer, *La guerra contro i civili* (Rome: Donzelli, 1997) and P. Pezzino, *Anatomia di un massacro. Controversia sopra una strage tedesca* (Bologna: Il Mulino, 1997).
55. The most comprehensive study of the Free Zones is M. Legnani, *Politica e amministrazione nelle republiche partigiane*, (Milan: INSMLI, 1967).

56. E. Gorrieri, *La repubblica di Montefiorino* (Bologna, Il Mulino, 1966).
57. A. Bravo, *La repubblica partigiana dell'Alto Monferrato* (Turin: Giappichelli, 1964). A literary treatment of one of these proud republics can be found in B. Fenoglio, *I ventitrè giorni di Alba* (Turin: Einaudi, 1975).
58. Legnani, *Politica e amministrazione*, p.20.
59. Cited in De Felice, *Mussolini l'alleato*, p.326.
60. On the negative repercussions of the proclamation, see Bocca, *Storia*, pp.444f.
61. Ibid, p.445.
62. G.E. Rusconi, *Resistenza e postfascismo* (Bologna: Il Mulino, 1995).
63. But see G. Vaccarino, C. Gobetti and R. Gobbi, *L'insurrezione di Torino* (Parma: Guanda, 1968).
64. Pavone, *Una guerra civile*, p.413. De Felice, *Mussolini l'alleato*, p.162 provides different statistics on the number of losses.
65. A very important example of a rhetorical evaluation of the resistance can be found in the anthology, *Fascismo e antifascismo. Lezioni e testimonianze* (Milan: Feltrinelli, 1976).
66. See, for example the essential document editions, G. Carocci and G. Grassi (eds), *Le Brigate Garibaldi nella resistenza*, 3 vols. Milan: Feltrinelli, 1979, and G. Rochat (ed.) *Atti del Comando Generale del CVL* (Milan: F.Angeli, 1975).
67. This is the case for many of the studies on the resistance already cited, such as Battaglia, *Storia*, and Bocca, *Storia*, but also of G. Vaccarino, *Problemi della Resistenza italiana* (Modena: Stem, 1966). For a local study, see P. Secchia and C. Moscatelli, *Il Monte Rosa è sceso a Milano* (Turin: Einaudi, 1958).
68. Pathbreaking in this field were the studies in Bertolo, *Operai e contadini*.
69. See especially, G. Quazza, *Resistenza e storia d'Italia* (Milan: Feltrinelli, 1976) and P. Secchia, *La resistenza accusa 1945–1973* (Milan: Mazzotta, 1973).
70. N. Gallerano (ed.) *L'altro dopoguerra. Roma e il Sud 1943–1945* (Milan: F. Angeli, 1985).
71. A typical example of the 'neo-fascist' viewpoint of the civil war is G. Pisanò, *Storia della guerra civile in Italia*, 3 vols. (Milan: FPE, 1965–6).
72. See, for example, Pavone, *Una guerra civile* and also by the same author, *Alle origini della repubblica: scritti sul fascismo, antifascismo e continuità dello stato* (Turin: Bollati-Boringhieri, 1995).

73. For a discussion of Pavone's thesis, see M. Legnani and F. Vendramini (eds) *Guerra, guerra di liberazione e guerra civile*, (Milan: F. Angeli, 1990).

74. General critical analyses of the evolving historiography of resistance can be found in N. Tranfaglia, *Labirinto italiano: il fascismo, l'antifascismo, gli storici* (Florence: La Nuova Italia, 1989) and F. Argenteri, A. Baldassare and G. Crainz (eds) *Fascismo e antifascismo negli anni della repubblica*, a special edition of *Problemi del socialismo*, VII (1986). P. Scoppola, *25 aprile Liberazione*, (Turin: Einaudi, 1995).

75. N.Gallerano, 'Critica e crisi del paradigma antifascista', *Viaggi di Erodoto*, X (1996) pp.14–27.

76. Not without some crudely politicized polemics and debates. See especially R. De Felice's interview in *Il Rosso e il Nero*, Milan: Baldini and Castoldi, 1995, in which he severely attacked the so-called 'antifascist paradigm'.

77. Scoppola, *25 aprile*.

7

The Netherlands
Dick van Galen Last

Introduction

'Hitler provoked the resistance himself.' So said the West German President, Theodor Heuss, on the tenth anniversary of the 20 July 1944 bomb plot against Hitler. The same was undoubtedly true of the countries occupied by Germany during the Second World War. The Dutch response to Nazi rule involves many familiar elements: intelligence gathering, the creation of an illegal press, the fomenting of strikes, the organization of escape routes, and help for those evading forced labour or persecution, sabotage and paramilitary activities, but it also had its own peculiar variations, just as the German occupation regime in the Netherlands differed from those in other countries.

The German authority on comparative Nazi occupation policy, Hans Umbreit, asserts that as far as the German armed forces and civil authorities in northern and western Europe were concerned, resistance did not pose a real danger in 1940–1. The Germans reacted with increasing force against resistance activities primarily because they were seen as denting the occupier's prestige.[1] In a general survey on Nazi policy of repression in western Europe, one of the leading historians on the Nazi occupation of the Netherlands, In 't Veld adds that from 1942 onwards, the Wehrmacht's policy of repression against resistance was prompted by the fear of an Allied invasion, and the fear of partisan movements similar to those that were causing so much trouble in the Balkans and Eastern Europe.[2] Conversely, the resistance saw its role as embodying the essential irreconcilability of Dutch and German ideological interests. In between stood the vast majority of the Dutch population who tried as far as possible to reconcile these two opposing interests in the course of their everyday lives.

The absence of a *maquis* or partisan movement in the Netherlands was almost entirely due to its geographical position and topography. The country encompassed 33,000 square kilometres and contained nearly nine million people, but it had no mountains and very little forest.[3] Thanks to an excellent transport infrastructure, the garrison of three German infantry divisions and a few regiments of Ordnungspolizei could be anywhere in the country within a couple of hours. Underground activities such as sabotage, raids and executions only served to attract the unwelcome attentions of the Germans and, for that reason, local community leaders insisted on restraint. Although paramilitary activities did increase in the north after the liberation of the south in September 1944, there was hardly any question of an organized military resistance in the Netherlands.

These same geographical constraints could also be found in Belgium and Denmark, but the Netherlands were in certain respects more isolated. Unlike Norway, Denmark and France, the Netherlands had no common frontier with a neutral country, and the North Sea coast was closely guarded by the Germans. Thus only around 200 Dutchmen succeeded in making the dangerous crossing to Britain in small boats whereas some 80,000 Norwegians managed to slip across the border into neutral Sweden. Moreover, the position of the Netherlands on the direct route between Allied airfields in Britain and the industrial heartland of Germany meant that the dense concentrations of anti-aircraft artillery there hindered the dropping of secret agents or supplies to resistance groups.[4] In this small and densely populated country, Allied aircraft had no recourse to secret airfields, as in France or Norway. Largely cut off from outside help, resistance in Netherlands was essentially an isolated affair, albeit less in the countryside than in the cities. The fact that people were forced to act alone also affected the character of the resistance in the Netherlands. Thus in 1965, Henri Michel wrote that 'as a whole, the Dutch resistance was primarily a moral and intellectual resistance, and manifested itself as a movement for national solidarity'.[5] The three major strikes that took place in 1941, 1943 and 1944 were undoubtedly examples of this, but it is nonetheless the case that the spirit of the resistance was just as diverse as public opinion generally during the occupation.

In assessing the nature of resistance in the Netherlands, it is important to consider three factors; the intentions of the occupying power and its practical policies, the reaction of the Dutch population, and the course of the war itself. In relation to the first factor, it is possible to distinguish four goals set by the Germans. Firstly, to maintain the security of the military occupation through the preservation of public order and the prevention of all aid to Germany's enemies, whether through sabotage, espionage or guerrilla activity. Secondly to maximize the exploitation of the Dutch economy and manpower resources for the benefit of the German war economy. Thirdly, to expedite the nazification of the Netherlands through the conversion of the Dutch population to national socialism and the organization of Dutch society along National Socialist lines in order to facilitate its incorporation into the German Reich after the war. Finally, and associated with the above, there was the ideological imperative of dealing with the 'Jewish Question'.[6]

In line with the broad definition employed by Michel, it is important to look beyond the activities designed to thwart the first German aim and to look at resistance in its wider sense. Thus the doyen of Dutch historians on World War Two, Louis de Jong, defined resistance as 'every act that opposed any of the four German goals',[7] and while those actions direc-ted against the first German aim might best be called underground activities, the underground movement has to be seen as only one of many manifestations of resistance against the occupying power.[8] The intention here is to look at the plans and practical policies of the occupying power and the reactions to them against the background of the changing military situation of the war. This was of decisive importance for the dynamics of the relationship between occupier and resistance. This will be followed by an examination of the legacy of the resistance for postwar Dutch society and an assessment of the national historiography.

May 1940 – February 1941: The First Phase

The Netherlands was both materially and psychologically unprepared for war when the German troops crossed the border on 10 May 1940. The country was unable to cope, either with a numerically and materially superior enemy or, after the capitulation of 15 May 1940, with occupation by a foreign power. The Netherlands had not been occupied since the Napoleonic era and it had not been involved in a European war for more than a hundred years. The horrors of World War One had been avoided, thanks to the policy of strict neutrality pursued by the Dutch government of the day, but a price had to be paid for this innocence. Thus Dutch inexperience in matters of war, occupation and illegal activity soon became apparent.

During the first days of the war, it became clear that the Dutch Army would be unable to hold out for long. Queen Wilhelmina and the Dutch Cabinet left the country to form a government-in-exile in London. Further disaster was to follow when the Empire in the East Indies was overrun by the Japanese at the beginning of 1942, leaving only the Dutch West Indies to give continued support to the Allied war effort. The Dutch government in exile, just like its Norwegian counterpart, maintained the

Netherlands' formal existence as an independent state and was therefore in a position to have some influence on resistance throughout the war. However, it was not until 1943 that formal contact was established between representatives of the various resistance organizations and the government in exile in London. Thanks to her rousing addresses on Radio Oranje, broadcast over the BBC, Queen Wilhemina gradually became the central figure and inspiration for the Dutch fight for freedom, or as de Jong expressed it, 'the living symbol of the nation's will to survive'.[9]

After a short period of military governance, Hitler appointed a so-called Aufsichtsverwaltung (Supervisory Civil Administration) for the Netherlands under the leadership of an Austrian, Dr Arthur Seyss-Inquart, who was given the title of Reichskommissar (High Commissioner). Seyss-Inquart was assisted by four Generalkommissare who took charge of the various Dutch ministries that, after the Dutch Cabinet had left for London on 13 May 1940, were run by the senior permanent civil servants, the Secretaries General. Seyss-Inquart was empowered to issue decrees that had the force of law and during the first three years of occupation more than 600 rules and regulations were heaped on the conquered country, leaving the population unsure about what was and was not permitted. The Dutch civil administration was, however, left intact and Seyss-Inquart and his German-Austrian Generalkommissare limited themselves to outlining policy and supervising the administration. The execution of policy was left to the Dutch civil servants who had been instructed by the outgoing government to continue administering the country in accordance with the Laws of War set out in the Hague Conventions of 1899 and 1907. In practice, this allowed them to cooperate with the occupying power insofar as this did not conflict with the interests of the Netherlands.

One exception to this maintenance of the existing structures was in the policing of the country. SS-Brigadeführer Hanns Albin Rauter was appointed as Generalkommissar für das Sicherheitswesen as well as Hohere SS- und Polizeiführer (General Commissioner for Security and Higher SS and Police Chief). Thus he had control of the German Security Police (SiPo), Sicherheitsdienst (SD) and Ordnungspolizei (Order Police) as well as the Dutch police. In the first two years of the occupation, activities against resistance were in principle the responsibility of the SiPo, but when there were forms of mass protest such as demonstrations, Rauter could call on some battalions of Ordnungspolizei. Initially the responsibility for the day-to-day maintenance of law and order remained in the hands of the Dutch police authorities, but the role played by German police became more important in later years.

In this first phase of occupation, the attitude of the German occupiers could be characterized as outwardly correct. They did not see the Dutch as the enemy, but as a kindred Germanic race. In his inaugural address on 29 May 1940, Seyss-Inquart was at pains to point out that there was no intention of imposing National Socialist ideology on Dutch society, and indeed, he hoped to win the Dutch over to the benefits of Nazism in a friendly manner.[10] The great fear engendered by the German invasion had not materialized and at this stage; what might be termed 'opportunist accommodation' – cooperation with the enemy where necessary – seemed to offer the Dutch population the best strategy for survival.

Dutch citizens who did want to demonstrate their opposition to the regime tended to focus their attention on the leaders of Dutch National Socialist organizations such as the Nationaal Socialistische Beweging (National Socialist Movement, NSB) and the Nationaal Socialistische Nederlandse Arbeiders Partij (Dutch National Socialist Workers Party, NSNAP). Perceived as traitors, these men were more hated than the Germans themselves. The Germans tolerated the aggressive behaviour of NSB formations on the streets, although this provoked quarrels and fights with the rest of the population. As the largest collaborationist political party, the NSB did experience an increase in membership after May 1940, but this never amounted to more than 4 per cent of the Dutch population. Its leader, Anton Mussert, harboured the hope that he would eventually be allowed to form a government, but Seyss-Inquart thought him incapable of converting the people to the Nazi New Order, a view that had been reinforced by the party's poor electoral showing in 1939. In essence, it was clear to all sides that National Socialism was profoundly alien to the Dutch mentality.

This aversion to National Socialism, and the sense of outrage against curbs on personal freedom manifested themselves in all manner of small, largely symbolic, patriotic acts. The Dutch were able to show their true feelings in these deeds of 'symbolic resistance' and for some, they became the first steps on the road to underground activity. Telling anti-Nazi stories or carrying and distributing pictures of the royal family were expressions of everyday popular dissent. In theory, expressions of anti-German sentiment were illegal, but during this period of 'mutual courtesy' they went unpunished. The first serious threat to this peaceful compromise came six weeks after the start of the German occupation when there was a spontaneous demonstration of national sentiment to commemorate the birthday of the Queen's son-in-law, Prince Bernhard. This involved large numbers of people in the streets wearing carnations – the Prince's favourite flower.

In June 1940, the members of both Dutch Houses of Parliament were suspended – effectively ending any pretence of a democratic forum. On 20 July of the same year, the Dutch Communist Party (CPN) was banned and this effectively prevented the Party from adopting a policy of 'tactical collaboration', something that its leadership seems to have been prepared to undertake.[11] In September, the CPN published the first edition of its illegal newspaper, *De Waarheid* (The Truth). Other, smaller, left-wing revolutionary groups, also began to distribute their own illegal newspapers at this time. The leaders of the mainstream democratic political parties had refused to compromise on the question of the Netherlands' independence and the sovereignty of the House of Orange. These were the first expressions of resistance in this period, but they had no great consequences. However, they did form the kernels of intellectual resistance among those who felt that the enemy should be obstructed as much as possible. One such kernel formed around Koos Vorrink, the chairman of the Dutch Social Democratic Labour Party (SDAP) and its parliamentary leader, the future postwar Prime Minister, Willem Drees.

Hurt national pride manifested itself in a new feeling of national solidarity. This was evident in the massive success of the Nederlandsche Unie (Netherlands Union), which filled the political vacuum left by the German ban on political parties. Created on 24 July 1940, this new movement attracted 800,000 members in the space of six months. The leadership took as its starting point the reality of German hegemony in Europe and hoped to negotiate the best possible position for the Dutch people within this new order.[12] It was an illusion that they continued to cherish until the summer of 1941, but even after this, the policy of negotiation persisted at a non-political level. Dutch civil servants continued their working relationship with the Germans until the last chaotic months of the war although some also maintained contacts with resistance organizations throughout the occupation.[13] However, for the vast majority of members, the name Nederlandse Unie and wearing its badge were simply expressions of patriotism and therefore also a form of resistance against the enemy, however small.

The first attempts to create organized forms of resistance came mainly from members of the demobilized Dutch Army who had been frustrated by their country's embarrassingly quick defeat. Not only were the founders and members of these groups from military circles, but their aims and organizational structures also took military forms. This was the case with the oldest of the resistance groups, the Geuzen. On 15 May 1940, the day of the capitulation, a small handwritten pamphlet entitled *Geuzenaktie* was distributed from hand to hand. In uncompromising terms, it called on its readers to resist the usurper. The author of this pamphlet, Bernardus IJzerdraad, became one of the leaders of the Geuzen. Other illegal newspapers followed in the summer from many different parts of the political spectrum, but all shared the same principled stand against foreign oppression and aversion to National Socialism that had been inspired by the Geuzen.[14]

Alongside this initial development of an illegal press were other activities, which included the accumulation of weapons, spying on behalf of the Allied powers, the organization of escape lines, attempts to make contact with the Dutch government-in-exile in London, and some small-scale sabotage actions such as the cutting of military telephone cables. All of this was done by volunteers, and often hampered by severe financial difficulties. Amateurism, innocence and unfamiliarity with illegal activity meant that these first attempts at organized resistance were quickly countered by the German security apparatus. A great many of the early resisters fell victim to their own, or someone else's talkativeness.

Others came to the resistance through principled stands against specific German measures, for example the first anti-Jewish legislation. When Jews were forbidden to be air-raid wardens in the summer of 1940, the sculptor Gerrit van der Veen refused to sign the form declaring that he was not a Jew. Van der Veen later became an important leader of the artists' resistance. Similarly, resistance by doctors, academics, students and artists originated in small, and often very small, groups of individuals with exceptional moral courage and strong convictions.[15] In October 1940, all civil servants had to sign the so-called 'Aryan declaration', a form which asked for details about family history and which was designed to root out anyone with a trace of Jewish ancestry. It was characteristic of the innocence and deference to authority (*gezagsgetrouwheid*) in this first phase of the occupation that 98 per cent of the civil servants dutifully completed and signed the declaration. Six protestant churches and 229 signatories from various Dutch universities did protest against the declaration 'for making a distinction between Jewish and other Netherlanders'. A student newspaper commented that 'a cold pogrom has begun' when all the civil servants of Jewish descent were removed from office soon afterwards. On 23 November, some 3,000 students in Delft organized a strike to protest against the dismissal of Jewish academics, and unrest also occurred at the universities of Leiden and Utrecht.

The sequence of anti-Jewish legislation and the German attempt to create a ghetto in Amsterdam were the main causes of the first of three major strikes in the Netherlands, the so-called *Februaristaking* (February strike) of 25–26 February 1941.[16] This was a protest against two German raids (*razzias*) in the Jewish quarter of Amsterdam when more than 400 Jewish men and boys were arrested and maltreated in public, before being deported to Mauthausen concentration camp. Centred in Amsterdam, the strike involved thousands of workers, but was suppressed by the SS and German police after two days. The following month, three communist strikers (two of whom were Jews), together with Bernardus IJzerdraad and fourteen members of the Geuzen were executed as a reprisal for the strike. These were the first executions to take place in the Netherlands, a country marked by its parliamentary traditions and absence of extremism and violence. They brought an end to attempts at conciliation between the German authorities and the Dutch population. The façade of Seyss-Inquart's diplomatic stance towards the Dutch had been exposed in both word and deed and he moved quickly to order the enforced 'coordination' of Dutch society on 12 March 1941.

Increasing Radicalization: March 1941–April 1943

This phase was characterized by growing problems and the use of more coercive measures by the Germans. The Dutch were forced to adapt to the physical realities of the occupation, for example in coping with food shortages, and also psychologically with the continued expectation of the enforced nazification that had thus far failed to materialize. For the time being, the attitude remained one of businesslike pragmatism or, put another way, 'cooperation where it was inevitable and aloofness where it was possible', but pressure for the introduction of National Socialist structures and practices continued to increase during 1942 and 1943.[17]

Organized and structured resistance was still in its infancy, although in the cases of the underground press, Orde Dienst (Order Service, OD) and aid to people in hiding, the foundations were laid for what later became large-scale organizations. Passive resistance also undoubtedly increased, for example, with the hoarding of essential supplies, or deliberate slowing of work. Resistance on principle in both Protestant and Catholic communities manifested itself in refusals to fulfil German demands, either on conscientious grounds, or because the individual was opposed to everything German. This occurred primarily in response to conscription for compulsory labour service or provocative Nazi measures in the field of education. Listening to the radio broadcasts of Radio Oranje and the BBC from London were another form of civil disobedience, and these broadcasts were also the most important source of information for the illegal presses inside the Netherlands. Moreover, they served to maintain the morale of the Dutch and thereby stimulate their 'spirit of resistance'.[18] The increasing severity of German reactions to such activities shows that they were regarded by the occupiers as outright resistance and not just a lesser form of opposition.

In spite of this, there was still a considerable amount of grassroots unrest. In a number of Dutch towns and cities there were disturbances in the streets. These were finally suppressed in September 1941 and followed up by a German decree of 16 October 1941 (VO195/1941) that stipulated that anyone who committed public order offences or who endangered the security of the state would be treated as a saboteur and sentenced to death. There was also a growing level of criminality as shortages began to occur – a criminality that indicated a waning respect for the law and a collapse of the norms of Dutch society. Resistance could normally be distinguished from ordinary criminal behaviour by its political character, but this distinction became increasingly blurred as the occupation progressed.

The police was the only Dutch state institution to be radically restructured by the Germans – a restructuring that included the appointment of many committed Dutch Nazis to high-ranking positions. The year 1941 saw the introduction of the German Ordnungspolizei to help in the fight against terrorism, but by 1942 the Germans were still uneasy about the growth of underground movements. As a result, a decree of 21 May 1942 made the mere membership of an illegal organization a capital crime. This decree prompted an increase in the activities of both German and Dutch Gestapo spies who were paid for their information. Evidence of the harder line being taken by the Germans came in August 1942 when the first five innocent civilian hostages were executed in reprisal for a sabotage attempt on the railway lines near Rotterdam. This action undoubtedly marked a new low in the relationship between the Dutch public and the German occupiers. The escalation of terror has been attributed to Rauter's influence within the German leadership, but it was also prompted by growing fears of paramilitary actions after the invasion of the Soviet Union, primarily from the communists who already had a well-established underground network.

Rauter also played an important part in the deportation of 107,000 Jews from the Netherlands to Eastern Europe, which began in July 1942 and continued almost uninterrupted until September 1944. While official protests from both the Roman Catholic and Protestant churches were ignored by the Germans, the deportations did give rise to new forms of resistance, namely the creation of organizations to help hide Jews, and especially Jewish children. These were mainly instigated by student groups to rescue children from the hands of the Germans and then distribute them to foster families in different parts of the country. Around 4,000 children were saved in this way. The students were able to react quickly to the deportations because they had an existing organizational structure.[19] Furthermore, the fact that they were all from different parts of the country meant that they could call on contacts in their home towns and villages, those of their parents, and also others whom they could trust. Although the leadership of the Amsterdam Jewish Council stood aloof from attempts at rescue, its branch in Enschede worked with non-Jewish groups to set up an organization to help those in hiding after the first local German roundups in September 1941. This initiative also saved around 750 Jews, but actions of this nature were the exception rather than the rule.[20]

After the German attack on the Soviet Union on 22 June 1941, the remaining Dutch political parties were formally dissolved. In December that year, the Nederlandse Unie was also banned by the Germans on the grounds that it was 'untrustworthy', in other words, it had not lived up to their expectations as a collaborating organization. Many of its leaders subsequently became involved in underground activity – for example Walraven van Hall in the Nationaal Steunfonds (National Assistance Fund, NSF), Father Bleys in the Catholic resistance, and the artist Willem Arondeus in the artists' resistance. In contrast to France, the Germans did not rely on traditional conservatives but chose to favour committed Nazis, the hated NSB, which became the only permitted political party. With the demise of the Nederlandse Unie, the only way in which the public could thenceforward read uncensored opinion was through the rapidly expanding underground press.

One year later, in December 1942, Anton Mussert was proclaimed as 'leader' of the Dutch people by the Germans. This raised resistance fears that it might lead to the installation of an NSB government and prompted the killing of a number of collaborators. These killings led to fierce debates in the underground press about the legitimacy of such actions and their strategic worth, and they were roundly condemned both by the government in exile and by the Churches. The German reaction was to speed up the process of nazification. This meant that every form of organization – newspapers, churches, education, professions, associations, radio, businesses – all came under the direct influence of the National Socialist authorities. In most cases, this meant the appointment of a representative into the administration who would not only carry out German wishes but also shared their ideological outlook. The coordination of the journalists, followed by artists and doctors prompted a good deal of opposition from all these groups. The population would have nothing to do with the

National Socialist welfare organization, the Winter Help (Winterhulp). The coordinated trade unions lost their members, the Nederlandsche Landstand which all farmers, smallholders and fishermen had to join, was largely boycotted by its members, and the coordination of the liberal professions backfired badly. The Churches continued to protest against particular German ordinances, and National Socialism ostensibly made little headway in the school system. In some of these groups, the resistance did not remain passive. The artists, for example, set up their own organization, which gave rise to a whole network of illegal activities.

The extent of this passive resistance or civil disobedience is difficult to estimate but must have been substantial, given the evidence which exists for its growth. There was an explosion in the numbers of people who ignored German orders or who avoided labour conscription. This anti-German attitude was proof for the occupying power that the vast majority of the Dutch population remained loyal to the House of Orange, the government-in-exile and the Church leaders who refused to cooperate with the occupier. Whether inspired by religious, political or humanitarian principles in their rejection of National Socialism, they were all united in their opposition to the threats that the German ideology posed to the traditional nature of Dutch society.

May 1943–August 1944: Exploitation and Repression

This phase saw a growing level of Dutch hostility towards the occupying power as laws and ordinances further infringed on the people's personal liberties and everyday lives. Until the end of 1942, the Germans had been careful not to antagonize the entire population. However, the worsening military situation prompted further measures, with increasingly oppressive legislation, arbitrary arrests and imprisonments, and attacks on personal liberty, all of which served to expose the true nature of Nazi rule. The effects that the news of German defeats in North Africa and Eastern Europe had on Dutch public opinion is also difficult to gauge. The majority of Dutch men and women were convinced that the Netherlands would soon be liberated, and this optimism provided a strong incentive for people to disobey German orders and to engage in resistance activity.

The dissatisfaction and frustration engendered by these increasingly coercive German policies came to a head in the second national strike of April-May 1943. After the capitulation, the Germans had allowed the demobilized Dutch armed forces to return home. However, the Spring of 1943 brought rumours that the Allies might open a second front in Europe, and there were fears that these demobilized Dutchmen might rush to join the invading Allied forces. More importantly, the Germans were now in dire need of more industrial labour. Thus, on 29 April 1943 the Dutch were suddenly confronted with an announcement by the German military commander in the Netherlands, General Christiansen, that all former members of the Dutch Army would have to report for internment in Germany.

Immediately after the publication of this decree, a wave of spontaneous strikes broke out, which soon involved more than 500,000 people. Beginning in the industrial area of Twente, it spread with lightning speed to nearly all the other industrial centres of the country, including the coal mines in Limburg, and the Philips factories in Eindhoven. In contrast to the *Februaristaking* of 1941, this strike was also strongly supported in rural areas, and nowhere more so than in the northern province of Friesland. There and elsewhere, farmers refused to deliver their milk to the dairies for several days. Rauter, who was responsible for the maintenance of law and order, reacted swiftly and decisively. An SS regiment was moved to Twente and a form of martial law (*standrecht*) was imposed. By the time the strike had ended in the first week of May, it had claimed at least 175 victims.[21] Most of them were workers who had been sentenced to death by special courts and executed, but there were at least sixty who had been the victims of random shootings. However, the strike was ended not by German repression but by the strikers themselves. A German public opinion report of 10 May 1943 noted that '[the strikers] wanted to express their indignation, and when they felt that this had been done with sufficient bluntness, they went back to work'.[22] Soon after the strikes had ended, the Germans extended the compulsory labour service scheme and called up men between the ages of 18 and 50, with officials being instructed to target former soldiers, industrial workers and students. Faced with the prospect of leaving home and family for an uncertain future abroad, many decided to go into hiding. Their enforced idleness also acted as an incentive to join resistance organizations and become an active participant in the struggle against the Germans.

The drastic increase in the total number of people in hiding throughout the country necessitated the creation of a structured and permanent relief operation. The Landelijke Organisatie voor Hulp aan Onderduikers (LO) was established in the autumn of 1942 and although the founders, the minister Frits Slomp (Frits de Zwerver) and Riek Kuipers-Rietberg (Tante Riek) were both members of the Calvinist community, this did not mean it was restricted to protestants. In the southern province of Limburg, numerous and predominantly younger and socially committed Catholic clergymen were the most active in hiding and supporting those who went underground.[23] Moreover, although the LO became by far the largest organization, there were many other, smaller, groups in all parts of the country doing similar work.

As the LO network was built up to meet the increased demand in the summer and autumn of 1943, provision also had to be made to feed and clothe those in hiding. To that end, raids were mounted by paramilitary units known as *knokploegen* to steal identity and ration cards from government·offices. Later their operations were coordinated by a national organization Landelijke Knokploegen, (LKP) which worked closely with the leadership of the LO. Between May 1943 and September 1944, there were 233 raids on government offices, of which approximately two-thirds were successful. More sensational were the attacks on population registers (to destroy the telltale evidence about individuals that the Germans had previously used so successfully against the Jews), and those on prisons to free resistance workers captured by the authorities. Thirty-six of these so-called 'liberation actions' took place, but two in mid-1944 cost the lives of two of the most reckless resistance leaders, Gerrit van der Veen and Johannes Post. Another resistance movement involved in armed attacks on government offices was the more left-wing Raad van Verzet (RVV). Established at the end of April 1943, this developed into one of the most important sabotage organizations. At the same time, the production of false papers became a major undertaking. Often begun on the initiative of individuals such as Eduard Veterman or Van der Veen, whole groups of specialists were then formed to meet the ever increasing demand. Finance could also have been a major problem had it not been for the creation of the NSF, 'the banker of the resistance movement', which provided funds for the LO and other organizations to continue their work.[24]

No matter how severe the German measures became, the resistance effectively thwarted their attempts to deport large numbers for labour service. Thus in July 1944, only 7 per cent of the male labour force required was actually delivered. By this stage, it was undoubtedly true that Dutch men and women were increasingly unwilling to submit to German coercion. The extreme German reaction to the strikes convinced many people that illegal work was a more effective outlet for anti-German sentiments than mass public protests. More and more of them refused to obey German orders and increasingly also turned to illegal actions, thus in turn making greater demands on the resources of the underground welfare organizations. In response to this, German repression also grew. The results of the April–May strikes of 1943 provided some succour for the remaining Jews hiding in the countryside as aid organizations extended their activities and provided more help. The tragedy remains that this development came too late for the majority of the Jews in the Netherlands, who had already been arrested and deported to the death camps in Eastern Europe.

The efficacy of collecting military intelligence was hampered initially by the lack of contact with the UK. However, by 1943, there were at least a dozen large networks covering all parts of the Netherlands that were in contact with the Dutch government in exile. Another, less regular source of information about conditions in the occupied Netherlands came from the so-called *Engelandvaarders* (voyagers to England). At least two hundred made the hazardous North Sea crossing by boat, but the vast majority, around 1,600, arrived in the United Kingdom after a long and often equally dangerous journey through Belgium, France, Switzerland and Spain, or via Sweden. Nearly 200 of them subsequently returned by parachute as secret agents. The SOE operations in the Netherlands proved to be a major disaster. Having captured one of the first British agents to be dropped into the Netherlands, the Abwehr managed to convince London that its network was operating normally. Thus between March 1942 and November 1943, SOE continued to send supplies of arms, ammunition and explosives, as well as a large number of agents, all of whom fell into the hands of the Sipo. The so-called *Englandspiel* was probably one of the major Allied intelligence disasters of World War Two as it claimed the lives of at least 132 people and led to the arrest of many others. While the operation was undoubtedly a success from the German point of view, it failed to give them the one piece of information they really sought – the place and timing of the planned invasion of north-western Europe.

In the aftermath of Stalingrad, people's minds turned more and more to the future. The communist underground resister Jan Postma, who was executed in July 1944, wrote in his farewell letter, 'the First World War brought about many changes for the better in society and I am sure this one will do the same.'[25] Similar sentiments can also be found in the various organs of the underground press. These increased in number and in circulation after the 1943 strike and in response to the German confiscation of radio sets, when they became the main source of news from the free world. This growing importance was reflected in the aspirations of the clandestine press. *Het Parool*, for example, saw itself primarily as the mouthpiece for the spiritual resistance, but wanted also to represent a group that supported the political, social and cultural renewal of the country. Its circulation rose to at least 25,000 copies and often, in tandem with its fellow illegal paper, *Vrij Nederland*, it tried to encourage the coordination of diverse resistance groups. In April 1944, *Het Parool* and *Vrij Nederland* published a joint manifesto designed to bring together all those groups committed to national renewal. This appeal fell largely on deaf ears as its audience of resisters did not wish cooperation to extend beyond the field of resistance activities. Only when the government in exile explicitly expressed its desire for the coordination of illegal groups was a Grote Adviescommissie der Illegaliteit (Central Advisory Council for Underground Groups, GAC) created, with a contact committee to facilitate communications between the various groups.[26]

In general terms, this phase can be seen as important in marking the reorganization of the early resistance groups and their increasing professionalization in the wake of ever more stringent German oppression. It is also possible to speak of a second generation of resistance movements with a national rather than local character, of which the OD, LO and RVV are the best examples.[27]

August 1944–May 1945: The Collapse of Civil Society

It is difficult to overestimate the impact of the long-awaited Allied invasion of Normandy on 6 June 1944. The Allies and the government in exile in London both told the Dutch not to rise up against the Germans but to wait for further instructions. Being forced to wait quietly for liberation was especially hard for those underground. However, there were also those who, fearing a postwar purge by the government, tried to cloak their doubtful or collaborationist behaviour by joining a resistance movement; a trend that grew as the Allies marched across Belgium. On 14 September, Maastricht was the first Dutch town to be liberated and it then seemed likely that the Germans would rapidly be driven out of the whole country.

However, the attempted airborne landing at Arnhem failed and the Allied offensive ground to a halt, effectively dividing the Netherlands into two parts; the liberated south and the still-occupied north. On 17 September - the day the Allied airborne assault began – the Dutch government had ordered the Dutch railway workers to strike to prevent the Germans from bringing up reinforcements. The failure of Mont-gomery's offensive meant that the 30,000 employees who took part in the strike had to stay in hiding. The financial arm of the resistance, the NSF, nevertheless made sure that all the strikers in hiding continued to receive their wages. One unforeseen result of the strike was the German reaction. Rather than try to restore the railway system, they used it as a pretext to hamper supplies of food and fuel to the west of the country. This punishment visited on Dutch civilians led to widespread famine and at least 15,000 deaths in what became known as the *hongerwinter* (hunger winter).

A new phase of military resistance began on 5 September, just before the Allied attack on Arnhem. The Allied powers insisted on a unified resistance movement before they would consider supplying weapons and consequently the government in exile in London ordered the various armed groups to amalgamate. This created a single organization, the Nederlandse Binnenlandse Strijdkrachten (Dutch Forces of the Interior, NBS) and consisted of the LKP, RVV and the right-wing OD with Prince Bernhard as supreme commander. The main function of the NBS was to help the advancing Allies and to assume responsibility for order in the interim period between the German surrender and the return of the government from London. However, the NBS only began to function as a military unit after a great deal of internal wrangling. One major problem was its shortage of weapons and explosives. Thus from September until the liberation, the Allies made a total of 221 parachute drops of equipment for the LKP and RVV. This allowed for a major increase in the number of sabotage actions, and even of counter-sabotage actions – to prevent the Germans from destroying the transport and communication infrastructure in front of the Allied advance. Other important activities included the creation of new specialist resistance groups that set up clandestine telephone networks. Apart from facilitating contacts between resistance groups in the occupied north, they also made direct communication possible with the liberated south.

The relationship between the Dutch government in London and the majority of the resistance organizations had always been very difficult. Some refused to recognize the authority of the government-in-exile, because it represented the prewar political élites who had so comprehensively failed in 1940. In the expectation of possible rapid liberation, and after appeals from the government in London, a new spirit of cooperation became evident, both between London and the resistance organizations on the ground, and between the various resistance groups themselves. This found expression in the GAC, an institution comparable to the French CNR. At the same time, the government in exile appointed a College van Vertrouwensmannen (College of Trustees) to act as its representatives in the event of a possible power vacuum between the departure of the occupying Germans and the arrival of Allied forces.

The various resistance organizations also began to consider what their role might be after the liberation. This brought with it a heightened level of political activity and awareness. The debates on reconstruction and renewal brought demands for more information, and several underground newspapers devoted special issues to the subject, discussing whether and how the prewar political parties were to reorganize after the liberation. Other issues were also discussed in depth, most notably the future of the Dutch East Indies and the possibility of the Netherlands annexing German territory. However, this increasingly politicized debate served only to accentuate the ideological and practical divisions between the various groups.

The discussion was most marked in the liberated south of the country, but the area was left in limbo as the Dutch Cabinet remained in London until the entire country had been freed. The administration in the liberated south was delegated to the Militair Gezag (Military Authority), which operated under the aegis of SHAEF. It had extensive powers, including the right to arrest people suspected of collaboration, and these powers continued for ten months after the liberation as the returning government took time to restore order to the civil administration of the country. Inevitably, clashes took place between the Militair Gezag, representing the legitimate government in London, and the resistance organizations, which followed their own political agendas. These clashes arose primarily over the purging of alleged collaborators and the restoration of local elites. Gradually, however, resistance leaders were incorporated into the administration of the liberated south and into the government in exile. Thus the demobilization of resistance organizations began even before the final German capitulation.

In the occupied north, the civil administration began to disintegrate [28] and the Germans saw their ordinances ignored by the population . Thus, for example, the increasingly comprehensive call-ups for the construction of defence works were more-or-less sabotaged by the local civil servants. Alongside thousands of others, the civil servants either went underground or were dismissed from their posts and arrested, thus making the administrative chaos complete. A total breakdown was averted by organizations such as the Red Cross, Churches and the private initiatives of local élites working in close cooperation with the resistance who stepped in to do whatever the retreating Germans would allow.[29]

Another, no less important reason why there was no power vacuum was the increasingly hard line taken by the Germans. This manifested itself in the raids carried out to find workers. For example, a two-day raid on Rotterdam 10-11 November 1944 resulted in the arrest and deportation of over 50,000 Dutchmen. They also took a severe line on public order. Raids were not just used to seize a suitable labour force. The Germans became increasingly fearful of a fifth column behind the lines. In German eyes, all young men were potential resisters and therefore needed to be removed from areas that might become a battleground.

Probably in response to international developments, several hundred captured resisters were shot at the Vught concentration camp in July and August 1944. In the summer of 1944, it became the norm for the occupation regime to abandon juridical processes altogether; resisters and saboteurs were held as hostages and then shot after an attack on a German or a sabotage action took place. Generalkommissar Hanns Albin Rauter and the newly appointed head of the Sicherheitspolizei und SD Eberhard Schöngarth also sanctioned public executions on an increasing number of occasions.

Furthermore, after Seyss-Inquart had proclaimed a state of siege on 5 September 1944, the Wehrmacht took an increasing role in maintaining public order alongside the Sipo. The Wehrmacht had won some influence in the Netherlands during and after 1943 and it began carrying out actions against the resistance on its own initiative, often rivalling the Sipo in its brutality. Thus a resistance action near the village of Putten on 1 October 1944, to obtain German defensive plans for the crucial Veluwe region, led to the death of a German officer and the severe wounding of another. This became the excuse for making an example of the village. The Wehrmacht burnt about a hundred houses and other buildings to the ground and deported 660 men and boys from in and around the village. Barely 10 per cent of those deported returned from the camps. Fear of a repetition of what had happened in the Balkans goes some way to explaining this reaction. The attack near Putten provided a welcome pretext to show the population at large that they were still in control after the failure of Operation Market Garden and that any help given to the armed resistance would be mercilessly punished.[30] After the war there was a considerable debate on the usefulness of the original raid and the responsibility of the resistance for the consequences. Such was the official sensitivity about this that the official files remained closed for fifty years. However, there were also questions asked about the even grimmer reprisals carried out by the Germans after other resistance attacks, a prime example being the one that accidentally involved Rauter himself and led to the murder of at least 263 Dutch hostages.[31]

Approximately 1,000 Dutch citizens fell victim to German executions in the last eight months of the occupation. These undoubtedly had an intimidating effect, not least because local people were frequently required to attend the executions and the bodies were often left on the streets. This, added to the extreme cold, lack of fuel, scarcity of food, forced population movements, Allied bombing and ever-increasing levels of German repression made this last year of war harder than all the previous ones. As a result, it would be the year that would frame the collective memory of the war for the majority of the population.

The end of the war was particularly unheroic. The German capitulation on 6 May 1945 left the armed elements of the resistance with no chance to engage in combat. Their frustration was heightened when it became apparent in the last month that the College van Vertrouwensmannen had been negotiating with the Germans for a softening of repressive policies and for permission for the Allies to drop foodstuffs to the population in the west of the country. Moreover, the national resistance council was allowed to play no part in the negotiations for the surrender so that when the event for which they had prepared for so long took place, the representatives of the resistance were more-or-less ignored.

Transition, Liberation and Legacy

The military defeat and the occupation period not only shaped a stronger sense of national unity, but also strengthened Dutch democracy. The nation rebuilt itself around the inheritance of democratic traditions, which were reinforced by the experience of war and occupation, and derived its legitimacy from the struggle of the organized resistance against the enemy, and more generally from the refusal of the Dutch people to allow themselves to become nazified. This was the position taken in the editors' introduction to the first historical work on the occupation. *Onderdrukking en Verzet* (Oppression and Resistance), a collection in which every sect and every social group were given the chance to highlight their part in the struggle for national survival.[32] The resistance, which had actually been very small and ideologically diverse, was thus proclaimed as the vanguard of national resurrection and served as the legitimizing source for the restoration of the democratic state. Undoubtedly this myth of a brave and unified resistance against the oppressor dovetailed well with the strong national consensus of the early postwar years. However, unlike in some other liberated countries, the resistance did not play an important political role in reconstruction. One explanation for this is that the legitimacy of the monarchy or the government in exile was never really questioned. Nevertheless, there was a view in some resistance circles that the 'illegals' of the underground, in contrast to the 'legals' of the discredited civil servants and administrators, had the right to set the tone for the postwar Netherlands. They, and not the representatives of the old order, formed 'the conscience of the nation' and should be brought in to bridge prewar conflicts.

The Chinese saying 'withdraw when the work is complete, that is the way to heaven' was a wisdom that went unheeded by most of the former resisters. For many of them, it was difficult to reintegrate into a society once again governed by laws and where practices like theft, forgery and armed assault, which had been essential parts of their behaviour during the occupation, were no longer considered as acts of heroism or patriotism. The former resisters in the liberated zone organized themselves into the Gemeenschap Oud-Illegale Werkers Nederland (Community of Ex-Illegal Workers, GOIWN). They had aspirations to create a new political movement and sought to exercise a 'healthy popular influence' on the postwar evolution of Dutch society. The mass arrests of genuine and alleged collaborators by the former resistance workers during the power vacuum in the liberated southern Netherlands led to rising tensions with the government-in-exile. The government itself fell in February 1945 – under pressure from the Militair Gezag, the NBS leadership, the Queen and the GOIWN. The Gerbrandy Cabinet that replaced it included representatives from the liberated south and this power shift marked the beginning of a normalization and the loss of influence by the resistance. Henceforward, it was possible for the new government and the Militair Gezag to bypass the resistance and take effective control themselves. In the rest of the country, normalization took place even more quickly. The new government formed in May 1945 under the leadership of Prime Minister Schermerhorn moved quickly to demobilize the resistance and its advisory bodies, thus the GOIWN and GAC soon lost all influence.

Nevertheless, one cannot speak of a complete restoration of prewar relations. Only a few personalities from the pre-1940 regime returned to public life and many talented former resisters were employed by the organizations set up to run the Netherlands after the liberation, albeit that there were fewer than the resisters would have liked. Overall, however, it can be said that little of the 'renewal' that had been discussed in the more important underground newspapers during the occupation and that formed part of the public debate between 1944 and 1946 actually came to pass. The ideas about reconstruction were essentially a product of the crisis years of the 1930s and of the occupation period. They were difficult to encapsulate coherently and their political form remained a controversial issue. The political debate centred not only on what role the united resistance movements might adopt in postwar politics, but also on the principle of whether they should have a role at all. The left-wing resistance groups of *Het Parool* and *Vrij Nederland* were anxious not to return to the crisis years of the 1930s. They advocated a managed economy, a system of social security, decolonization and an end to the prewar policy of neutrality, together with a powerful people's party to bring these changes about. The same ideas about breaking down old conflicts and building a new unity could also be found in the Nederlandse

Volksbeweging (Dutch People's Movement, NVB) and appeared in underground newspapers such as *Je Maintiendrai* and *Christofoor*, which were both associated with the Nederlandse Unie.

Right-wing groups took the view that resistance experience conveyed no special rights to influence postwar developments. Paramilitary groups such as the OD believed that political peace was essential in the transitional period and that the resistance should not attempt to obtain any political power. Fear of a communist takeover was strong in these circles. Similarly the Trouw group, which represented much of the wartime LO organization, also set itself against postwar political activity on the grounds that it put religious conviction above unity – thereby tacitly supporting a return to political parties based on confessional divisions.

Despite all the discussions about a fundamental change from the prewar political system, the elections of 1946 merely served to demonstrate that political and social divisions in the Netherlands had remained unchanged. Thus the immediate postwar years can be characterized, not as a period of renewal but as 'years of discipline and asceticism'[33] and of a collective effort towards reconstruction. The national monument on the Dam in Amsterdam with its anonymous asceticism can be seen to represent the self-sacrificing austerity of these reconstruction years.

The lack of renewal in Dutch society was often blamed on the resistance, but the various movements had very different ideas about political, social and moral renewal during the war, and carried these into the postwar era. Many former resisters were disappointed that the ideals expressed during occupation had not been achieved and that they had not been afforded the role they considered to be their right. Worse still, they saw themselves superseded by others who had not risked their lives. One of the most intransigent old resistance fighters, Willem Nagel, expressed this disappointment in 1954. 'It was obvious that the unjust had won the war. They had preserved their status quo at the expense of the resistance workers.'

All resistance movements ceased their activities after the liberation, except for the Stichting 40–45 of the LO-LKP which looked after former resisters and their families in need, and it was officially recognized by the government in 1947 when the latter awarded special pensions for resisters. The only other group to continue its activities for resisters was the communists. Their members were expelled from other veterans and ex-political prisoners' organisations in 1948 and 1949 as a result of the Cold War. The Party therefore created a separate organization, but this was banned from parading openly and became the subject of widespread discrimination by the authorities.

On account of their collective experience of deprivation in the last months of the occupation, at the end of the war, all Dutch citizens saw themselves as victims and therefore took the view that no single group deserved any special status in this regard – a view that was also applied to the 280,000 people repatriated from Germany. This noteable lack of differentiation was further reinforced by a deliberate government policy of ignoring all pressure groups, including those associated with the resistance. Postwar governments, backed by the former leaders of the GAC and GOIWN, strove to create a consensus on the memory of resistance, but this required them to ignore the claims of individual veterans groups. Indeed, it gave rise to a form of 'anti-veteranism' which was almost a precondition for the organization of commemorations and exhibitions, and for the creation of monuments, street names, and decorations. This anti-veteranism served to rekindle the resentment of former resisters, many of whom chose to go to the East Indies in the expectation of being seen as liberators, but became ensnared in the war to regain the colonies. Returning after Indonesian independence was declared in 1949 they felt themselves left in the lurch by the government – and these feelings of a lack of appreciation for their efforts survive to this day.[34]

In the struggle for recognition, there was also competition between the resisters and the Jews. Although the persecution of the Jews was never an important concern for the resistance, it was only when the fate of the Jews took a more prominent place in collective remembrance after the 1960s that the remembrance of the resistance and that of the Holocaust were inextricably linked.[35] Thus pride in the heroic acts of the resistance was replaced by a sense that the Dutch population had failed to protect its Jewish fellow citizens. Only in the 1960s, when the period of concerted reconstruction was successfully completed did the astonishing coherence and national consensus over memory come to an end – to be replaced by a more differentiated remembrance.[36] The time was ripe for the singling out of particular groups such as the resistance, and in 1980, the government introduced a decoration, the commemorative resistance cross, which was ultimately awarded to about 15,500 people.

Historiography

'Unwilling adjustment was the rule, intentional resistance the exception.' Thus did Louis de Jong characterize life in German occupied countries during World War Two.[37] As has been shown, in the first phase, various forms of resistance developed through scattered acts of defiance in different areas. As a result of their ignorance or inexperience of illegal work (the communists excepted) or dilettantism, nearly all of these early resistance groups made up mainly of former soldiers were broken up by the Germans.

Thereafter resistance was centred on the illegal press, and after May 1943 on help to people in hiding. From that time onwards, there was clearly a reorganization and Van der Pauw speaks of a 'second generation' and professionalization, which made a growth of resistance activity possible.[38] Gradually the various resistance organizations also came to accept the need to use violence, primarily executions and sabotage actions, although this happened later and was less pronounced than in Belgium or France.[39] Although the resistance undoubtedly took on a more military character after September 1944, in the end the paramilitary contribution to the liberation was almost nil.[40]

If we return to the four objectives which the Germans set themselves, it can be seen that they succeeded by and large in exploiting the economic potential of the Netherlands, and in their main ideological task of deporting most of the Jews – proportionally many more than from any other Western European country. Their attempts at nazification, however, failed miserably, not least because of what Henri Michel called the intellectual and moral resistance of the people, a sentiment that was embodied in the illegal press, which served both to 'immunize' people from National Socialism and to mobilise them against the occupiers and their policies. De Jong summarizes the three aims of the resistance as follows: to keep up people's morale (principally through the underground press); to care for the hundreds of thousands of people who had gone into hiding; and to provide the Allies with vital military information.[41]

A characteristic of the Dutch resistance is that, in spite of all the talk about renewal, it often took organizational forms that mirrored those of prewar society. Dutch prewar society was very clearly divided into distinct Roman Catholic, orthodox Protestant, Social Democrat and Liberal groups or *zuilen* (pillars), and these remained a feature of the development of resistance organizations. These divisions could be seen in many aspects of the resistance and even the upsurge in nationalist sentiment failed to break down their influence. The illegal press mirrored perfectly all the various facets of prewar society and culture, but there were other forms of resistance in which there was cooperation between people from different *zuilen*, for example in the doctors', students' and intelligence groups.[42] However, recent regional studies such as the one by Hilbrink on the eastern region of Twente have tended to contradict de Jong's view that resistance did break down the divisions within a *verzuild* society.[43]

Only in the later part of 1943 was there a form of cooperation between the Calvinist members of the LO in the north of the country and the Roman Catholic priests and chaplains of the LO in the southern province of Limburg, and even then there was no real breakdown of confessional divisions, with those in hiding still being sheltered for preference by members of their own denomination.[44] It was not only the Communist Party that emerged strengthened from the war,[45] but also the Christian Churches and their secular organizations. They had united to protest against German measures at specific times, carefully at first but growing more vehement as time went on.

Another example of the continuity of prewar societal structures was the railway strike of 1944, which, according to the historian Rüter, not only provided links between the strikers and the general population, but also between the worlds of 1940 and 1945. As Henry Mason stated: 'The railroads' willingness to fight for survival symbolised similar feelings in the nation as a whole, and the fight was led by the traditional leaders . . . The men of 1940 were also the men of 1945'.[46] Furthermore, Hans Blom has stressed that 'in the long run it [was] not the degree of change but the measure of continuity which stands out'.[47] However, these were all observations on the immediate impact of the occupation period, and its longer term effects on the breakdown of social divisions in the 1960s and on gender relations still await further research.

As to the dynamics of repression and resistance, the historiography is dominated by the idea of a gradual increase in opposition to German rule. When placed in the wider context of the five years of occupation, this is undoubtedly true, but recent studies such as that by Meershoek on the Amsterdam police have served to modify the picture.[48] Following Sijes's study of the February strike of 1941, it was widely assumed that this event had been the catalyst for awakening a spirit of resistance and the reaction towards the plight of the Jews was from that moment the touchstone for the attitude taken towards the enemy. Meershoek comes to the opposite conclusion in relation to large parts of the Dutch population. According to him, the February strike and the rivalries between various German authorities, especially that between Seyss-Inquart and Rauter, accelerated the propensity of the Dutch bureaucrats to anticipate German wishes.

The winter of 1942–43 was a major turning point in that it marked a radical acceleration in the German attempts at nazification in the Netherlands, while their all-conquering military image was undermined by defeats at El Alamein and Stalingrad. In many sections of society there was an increased desire to break the grip of the occupying power and this acted as a catalyst for more organized illegal action. However, the April–May 1943 strikes clearly demonstrated the dangers of inadequately prepared open resistance. The deportation of students, prisoners of war and entire age cohorts of young men for compulsory labour service in Germany nonetheless stimulated the willingness to resist still further. De Jong argues that the strikes acted as a catalyst for an exponential growth of resistance, although this view has also been questioned by more recent authors such as Hilbrink and Flim.[49] According to them, this explosion of activity only took place after September 1944.

The vast majority of the Dutch population pragmatically stayed aloof from resistance activity. According to De Graaff and Marcus, the following factors made participation in some form of resistance more likely: being a member of a profession, especially the liberal professions, civil servants and teachers; a higher education; being unmarried or married without (young) children; being between the age of 20 and 30; and being a member of the Calvinist Church or an atheist.[50] Although Calvinists and Communists were undoubtedly overrepresented in the paramilitary resistance, Cammaert stresses the importance of a Catholic-humanitarian, non-violent resistance in Limburg. This took the form of the setting up of escape lines for Allied aircrew and other persecuted groups and help to people in hiding.[51]

Cammaert and Hilbrink also confirm the importance of social networks. People joined resistance groups because their friends were also involved. Hilbrink characterizes the so-called organized resistance as little more than 'a collection of . . . flimsy networks of illegal contacts'. According to him, there was no question of a strongly unified leadership or close coordination of activities. He criticizes other historians' emphasis on the importance of the discussions between the leaders of the various resistance groups. He argues that even in the last year of the occupation, these resistance leaders had no clear backing from the rank and file.[52] A definitive account of the ways in which resistance was organized in the Netherlands will require further local and regional studies, but the evidence to date suggests considerable confusion and complexity. Thus, resistance in the Netherlands bears out Mark Mazower's contention that 'resistance groups were fragmented, localized and poorly informed of one another's existence; they were drawn from very diverse political and social elements of the population; above all, they were wartime phenomena, with all the flux, uncertainty and ideological confusion which the conditions of war produced'.[53]

How important and widespread was the resistance? De Jong estimates that 25,000 men and women were active prior to September 1944. Around

10,000 of them were arrested and, of those, 6,000 did not survive the war. From September onwards, the resistance north of the great rivers was augmented by a further 10,000 volunteers.[54] There were relatively few women active in the resistance, perhaps around 3,000 in total. The majority of them were engaged in relief activities, for example by providing practical help for those in hiding or acting as couriers.[55] This became more important in the last year of occupation when men of working age found it impossible to be seen on the street for fear of arrest for forced labour in Germany, but women were still able to travel by bicycle to bring money and ration cards to railway workers in hiding and distribute copies of clandestine newspapers.

The most characteristic form of resistance in the Netherlands was undoubtedly going into hiding. This was a punishable offence as it violated German occupation decrees. The total number of men, women and children involved is estimated at around 350,000 and this could only have occurred with substantial material and public support. All those in hiding had to be cared for by networks of family members and friends. Unofficial estimates speak of at least 500,000 people being involved. Many resistance activities were set up from 1943 onwards in order to support those in hiding. Thus for example, the LO-LKP became the largest resistance organization with 15,000 members. Then there were at least 20,000 people engaged in the other characteristic form of Dutch resistance; the production and distribution of illegal newspapers. However, in trying to quantify this help, one has to take account of overlapping functions. For example, the group round the newspaper *Trouw* also provided help for those in hiding, the LO and the armed activities of the LKP.

As the occupation continued and the tide of war turned against the Third Reich, the relationships between occupier and the occupied worsened appreciably. The downward spiral of increased German demands followed by resistance and then further German repression was undoubtedly evident in the Netherlands, but not to the same extent as in Belgium or France until the last winter of the occupation. The German authorities in the Netherlands, primarily the SS and SD, but after 1943 the Wehrmacht as well, were given a good deal of latitude to deal with resistance activities by their masters in Berlin. They could define what constituted resistance and also determine the ways in which it could be countered, for example by police actions, the application of criminal law, summary justice, incarceration in labour or concentration camps, and from 1942 onwards, the regular seizure of hostages. Moreover, they were helped by the attitudes of certain Dutch authorities, which appeared to have been more than willing to assist in countering resistance among their fellow countrymen.

For example, on his own initiative Inspector Bakker of the Bureau Inlichtingendienst (Political Investigation Branch, Amsterdam Police) managed to inflict a great deal of damage by infiltrating Vrij Nederland and other left-wing resistance groups. Just as in other parts of Western Europe, partisan activities tended to provoke German reprisals, which outweighed any damage that might have been inflicted on the occupying power. The myth that the Germans did not transgress international law in their suppression of resistance has now been sufficiently debunked, thus allowing for some degree of comparison between occupation policies in the West and the war of annihilation carried out in the East. After the liberation, the rapid 'nationalization' of the resistance served to assist in the process of reconstruction in the short term. At the same time, a rose-tinted view of the resistance arose which took many years to break down.

Resistance was, by its very nature, a secret activity. This may help to explain why surveys, let alone detailed studies, took so long to appear in the Netherlands. Immediately after the liberation, historical writing on the occupation period was geared to a defence of the *verzuild* political system. Commentators sought the origins of resistance in the principles of a certain religion, religious denomination, or intellectual circle. The conclusion drawn was that the various *zuilen* had coped well with the occupation and that their resistance had had its roots in the 1930s and the struggles against the NSB.

Each *zuil* had its own heroes. For the Calvinists there were Frits de Zwerver and Tante Riek, the founders of the LO, together with Johannes Post of the LKP. For the Roman Catholics, Father Bleijs and Titus Brandsma, for the Liberals, Professor Telders, for the Socialists, Wiardi Beckman, and for the Communists, Hannie Schaft. They were all installed in the pantheon of the resistance, even before the war was over. The study on the role of the Roman Catholic bishops' resistance appeared immediately after the war, that of the Dutch Reformed Church a year later, and that of the Calvinists in 1950. The only dissenting voices to this hagiography came in novels by authors such as Vestdijk and Hermans.

The immediate postwar period also saw a stream of (sometimes fictionalized) published memoirs. Histories of specific resistance groups or resistance actions also appeared, often written by individuals involved, and these were usually anecdotal or hagiographic rather than analytical. Some groups wrote their own histories, for example the LO-LKP. As an illustration of the national patriotic vision of the period, the first edition of the book in 1951 mentioned no names, and it was only in the 1989 reprint that the names of the heroes were added. Other groups, such as the RVV, have no published histories to date.

Until the 1980s, there was little analytical study of the resistance or collaboration, the one exception being some sections of the collection published as *Onderdrukking en Verzet* between 1949 and 1954. This has to some extent been compensated for by the ongoing public debates which have taken place on the behaviour of the majority of the Dutch population which did not engage in resistance, but chose accommodation with the occupier, or even collaboration. The concept of collaboration developed over time, from a purely juridical-moral perjorative perspective to a more functional perspective that was closely related to the use of a broader definition of collaboration, which increased the numbers implicated.[56] In the later 1960s, research on resistance declined as it was seen as a legitimation of the patriotic idea of a 'nation of heroes', a concept that was increasingly challenged by a younger generation of historians.

The fourteen volumes of the work by De Jong on the history of the Netherlands in the World War Two, published between 1969 and 1988 have undoubtedly acted as a deterrent for further syntheses on this period. When published, each successive volume gave rise to much public debate, but subsequent detailed studies have served to alter or contradict many of the general conclusions drawn by De Jong. A new general history of the resistance could undoubtedly profit from the methodological approach and insights contained in the many local and regional studies, and the studies 'from below' that emerged around the anniversary years, 1985, 1990 and 1995.[57]

This leaves the question of areas that have not been properly researched to date. The Dutch historian Jan Romein attempted an evaluation of wartime public opinion less than a year after the liberation,[58] but the only scholar to follow up his work was Warmbrunn in 1963. There is no doubt that a new study, using the German *Stimmungsberichte* and weekly SD *Meldungen*, together with a detailed analysis of the legal and illegal press and the dossiers on resistance workers held by the Stichting 1940–1945, would be worthwhile and shed new light on the subject. In comparison with Italy and France, the importance of religious belief to the development of resistance, and the Christian Churches as conduits for 'alternative communication' has received little attention. This could be seen as surprising given that these were the only organizations to emerge from the occupation stronger than before. Another noticeable omission, which is apparent in the historiography of all the occupied countries, is the question of the punishments meted out by the legal system for civilian acts of political opposition and underground activities deemed to be directed against the German state. The question of whether postwar Dutch politics succeeded in providing a synthesis between the old system and the need for change, as Peter Romijn contends, remains a subject for discussion.[59] Finally, there has been little published research to date either on the political legacy left by the resistance, or on its place in the collective national memory of the postwar Netherlands.

Notes

1. Hans Umbreit, *Das Deutsche Reich und der Zweite Weltkrieg. Band 5: Erster Halbband: Kriegsverwaltung, Wirtschaft und personelle Ressourcen 1939–1941* (Stuttgart: Deutsche Verlags-Anstalt, p.91.
2. Nanno in 't Veld, 'Die Wehrmacht und die Widerstandsbekämpfung in Westeuropa' in: Johannes Houwink ten Cate and Gerhard Otto, eds., *Das organisierte Chaos. "Ämterdarwinismus" und "Gesinnungsethik". Determinanten nationalsozialistischer Besatzungsherrschaft* (Berlin: Metropol, 1999), pp.279–301.
3. This particular factor has been analysed and placed in context. See, Bob de Graaff, 'Collaboratie en Verzet: Een vergelijkend perspectief', in: J.P.B. Jonker et al., eds, *Vijftig Jaar na de Inval. Geschiedschrijving en Tweede Wereldoorlog* ('s-Gravenhage: SDU, 1990), p.100
4. M.R.D. Foot, 'What Use was Resistance' in: Jonker, *Vijftig Jaar*, p.113.
5. Henri Michel, *Les mouvements clandestins en Europe* (Paris: PUF, 1965), p.63.
6. Louis de Jong, *The Netherlands and Nazi Germany* (Cambridge MA: Harvard UP, 1990), p.33.
7. Ibid.
8. The term 'underground' has been used here, rather than the more formalistic 'illegality', which is nonetheless still common in Dutch historiography.
9. Louis de Jong, 'The Dutch Resistance Movements and the Allies, 1940–1945' in: *Proceedings of the Second International Conference on the History of Resistance Movements – Milan, 26–29 March 1961* (Oxford: Pergamon, 1964), p.10.
10. Gerhard Hirschfeld, 'Nazi propaganda in occupied Western Europe: the case of the Netherlands' in: David Welch (ed.), *Nazi Propaganda: The Power and the Limitations* (London: Croom Helm, 1983) p.144.

11. The Dutch Communist Party and the small Revolutionair-Socialist-ische Arbeiderspartij were the only two parties to go underground in the summer of 1940.

12. The term 'policy of negotiating' is taken from Ole Kristian Grimnes, 'The Beginnings of the Resistance Movement' in: Henrik S. Nissen ed., *Scandinavia during the Second World War* (Minneapolis: University of Minnesota Press, 1989), p.184. He notes that this cooperation with the Germans lasted from the beginning of the occupation until 29 August 1943. In the Dutch case, it lasted until the Nederlandse Unie was banned in December 1941 although most negotiations had ceased in the summer of that year.

13. Peter Romijn, 'Niederlande – Synthese, Säuberung und Integration' in: Ulrich Herbert and Axel Schildt eds, *Kriegsende in Europa. Vom Beginn des deutschen Machtzerfalls bis zur Stabilisierung der Nachkriegsordnung, 1944–1948* (Essen: Klartext Verlag, 1998), p.211. Bob de Graaff, 'Widerstand und Kollaboration in den Nieder-landen 1940–1945' *Zentrum für Niederlande–Studien Jahrbuch* 2 (1991), p.90.

14. Harry Paape, *De Geuzen* (Amsterdam: Sijthoff, 1965).

15. A. Kessen, 'Historiografie van het Verzet', *De Gids*, no.2 (February 1952) p.130.

16. Guus Meershoek, *Dienaren van het Gezag: De Amsterdamse Politie tijdens de Bezetting* (Amsterdam: van Gennep, 1999) p.137. See also, Guus Meershoek, 'The Amsterdam Police and the Persecution of the Jews' in: Michael Berenbaum and Abraham J.Peck (eds) *The Holo-caust and History: The Known, the Unknown, the Disputed and the Reexamined* (Bloomington: Indiana University Press, 1998) p.298.

17. Warmbrunn, *The Dutch*, p.47.

18. De Jong, 'The Dutch Resistance Movement', p.358.

19. Bert Jan Flim, *Omdat Hun Hart Sprak* (Kampen: Kok, 1996), p.427.

20. For local variations, see Henk Flap, Kathy Geurts and Wout Ultee, 'De Jodenvervolging in lokaal perspectief' in Henk Flap and Wil Arts, eds, *De Organisatie van de Bezetting* (Amsterdam: Amsterdam UP, 1997), pp.31–45.

21. Liesbeth van der Horst, *April–Mei '43. De Stakingen als Keerpunt* (Amsterdam: Verzetsmuseum Amsterdam, 1998), p.30.

22. P.J. Bouman, *De April–Mei Stakingen van 1943* ('s-Gravenhage, 1950), p.423.

23. A.P.M. Cammaert, *Het verborgen front. Geschiedenis van de georganiseerde illegaliteit in de provincie Limburg tijdens de Tweede Wereldoorlog* (Leeuwarden: Eisma, 1994), p.1185.

24. P. Sanders, *Het Nationaal Steunfonds. Bijdrage tot de Geschiedenis van de Financiering van het Verzet, 1941–1945* (The Hague, 1960).

25. 'Four farewell letters', *Delta: A Review of Arts Life and Thought in the Netherlands* VIII/1, pp.7–18, see p.17.

26. Madelon de Keizer, *Het Parool 1940–1945. Verzetsblad in Oorlogstijd* (Amsterdam: Otto Cramwinckel, 1991) p.651.

27. J.L. van der Pauw, *Guerrilla in Rotterdam. De paramilitaire verzetsgroepen 1940–1945* ('s-Gravenhage: SDU, 1995) p.12.

28. Romijn, 'Niederlande', pp.207–24.

29. Ibid. p.213.

30. Madelon de Keizer, *Putten. De razzia en de herinnering* (Amsterdam: Prometheus, 1998) p.231.

31. Henk Berends, *Woeste Hoeve* (Kampen, 1995) p.18. Louis de Jong, *Het Koninkrijk der Nederlanden in de Tweede Oorlog*, 14 vols ('s-Gravenhage: Staatsuitgeverij, 1969–1988), vol.Xb, p.442.

32. C.D.J. Brandt in the introduction to J.J. Bolhuis et al. eds, *Onderdrukking en Verzet*, 4 vols, (Arnhem: Van Loghum Slaterus, 1949–55).

33. J.C.H. Blom, *Crisis, Bezetting en Herstel. Tien Studies over Nederland, 1930–1950* ('s-Gravenhage: Nijgh and van Ditmar, 1989) p.213.

34. There are a number of books written by those involved in the Indonesian campaign with emotive titles, for example, Ant. P.de Graaff, *De heren worden bedankt: met het vergeten leger in Indië, 1949–1958* (The Gentlemen are Dismissed: with the Forgotten Army in the Netherlands East Indies) (Franeker: Wever, 1986).

35. Ido de Haan, *Na de Ondergang. De herinnering aan de jodenvervolging in Nederland, 1945–1955* ('s-Gravenhage: SDU, 1997). See also, Pieter Lagrou, 'Victims of genocide and national memory: Belgium, France and the Netherlands, 1945–1965', *Past and Present*, CLIV (1997), pp.181–222.

36. Lagrou, 'Victims', p.205.

37. Preface by Louis de Jong to Warmbrunn, *The Dutch*, p.v.

38. Van der Pauw, *Guerrilla in Rotterdam*, p.381

39. De Graaff, 'Collaboratie en Verzet', p.96. The low figures given by de Graaff have been challenged, for example, by van der Pauw who notes that many more sabotage actions and liquidations took place than were actually recorded.

40. Christ.Klep and Bert Schoenmaker eds, *De bevrijding van Nederland 1944–1945. Oorlog op de flank* ('s-Gravenhage: SDU, 1995) pp.151–2.

41. De Jong, *The Netherlands and Nazi Germany*, p.49.

42. Kessen, 'Historiografie', p.132.
43. De Jong, *Het Koninkrijk*, VII, p.1089.
44. Coen Hilbrink, *De Illegalen. Illegaliteit in Twente en het aangrenzende Salland, 1940–1945* ('s-Gravenhage: SDU, 1989) p.62.
45. In the parliamentary elections of 1946, they captured ten seats, having held only three before the war.
46. A.J.C. Rüter, *Rijden en Staken. De Nederlandse Spoorwegen in Oorlogstijd* (The Hague, 1960). Henry Mason, *Mass Demonstrations against Foreign Regimes. A Study of Five Crises* (New Orleans, 1966) p.94.
47. J.C.H. Blom, 'The Second World war and Dutch Society: Continuity and Change' in A.C. Duke and C.A. Tamse eds, *Britain and the Netherlands, Vol. VI: War and Society* ('s-Gravenhage, 1977), p.248.
48. Guus Meershoek, *Dienaren ven het gezag. De Amsterdamse politie tijdens de bezetting* (Amsterdam: van Gennep, 1999).
49. See, for example, Hilbrink, *De Illegalen* and Flim, *Omdat Hun Hart Sprak.*
50. Lidwien and Bob de Graaff, 'Vrouwen in het Nederlands Verzet' *Intermediar* (16 May 1980) pp.69–73.
51. See, for example, Cammaert, *Het verborgen front.*
52. Hilbrink, *De Illegalen*, pp.391–2.
53. Mark Mazower, *Dark Continent: Europe's Twentieth Century* (London, Penguin, 1998) pp.192–3.
54. De Jong, *The Netherlands and Nazi Germany,* pp.47–8.
55. See, for example, Bob de Graaff and Lidwien Marcus, *Kingerwagens en Korsetten. Een Onderzoek naar de sociale achtergrond en de rol van vrouwen in het verzet, 1940–1945* (Amsterdam: Bert Bakker, 1980).
56. Konrad Kwiet, *Reichskommissariat Niederlande. Versuch und Scheitern nationalsozialistischer Neuordnung* (Stuttgart: Deutsche Verlags-Anstalt, 1968).
57. Kees Ribbens, *Bewogen jaren: Zwolle in de Tweede Wereldoorlog* (Zwolle: Waanders, 1995) J. van Miert ed. *Een gewone stad in een bijzondered tijd: Utrecht 1940–1945* (Utrecht: Spectrum, 1995). P. Wijbenga, *Bezettingstijd in Friesland* (Leeuwarden: De Tille, 1995) G. van der Ham, Zeeland, 1940–1945, Vol. 2 (Zwolle: Waanders, 1990). Bart van der Boom, *Den Haag in de Tweede Wereldoorlog* ('s-Gravenhage: Sea Press, 1995). Friso Roest and Jos Scheren, *Oorlog in de stad. Amsterdam 1939–1941* (Amsterdam: van Gennep, 1998). J.W.M. Schulten, *De geschiedenis van de Ordedienst. Mythe*

en werkelijkheid van een verzetsorganisatie ('s-Gravenhage: SDU, 1998).

58. Jan Romein 'The Spirit of the Dutch People during the Occupation' *The Annals of the American Academy of Political and Social Science* (May 1946) pp.169ff.

59. Peter Romijn, 'The Synthesis of the Political Order and the Resistance Movement in the Netherlands in 1945' in Gill Bennett (ed.) *The End of War in Europe 1945* (London, 1996) pp.139–47, see p.146.

60. Geraldine von Frijtag Drabbe Künzel, *Het Recht van de Sterkste. Duitse Strafrechtspleging in bezet Nederland* (Amsterdam: Bert Bakker, 1999). Pieter Lagrou, *The Legacy of Nazi-occupation in Western Europe. Patriotic Memory and National Recovery* (Cambridge: Cambridge University Press, 1999).

8

Norway
Arnfinn Moland

Resistance Activities – A Brief Outline

When the Germans invaded Norway on 9 April 1940, they allegedly came as 'friends'. Hostilities were triggered off in the early hours of that morning when the Norwegian King and government unanimously decided to turn down the German conditions for surrender. On 7 June, after almost 60 days of fighting, at a last Cabinet meeting on Norwegian soil, it was resolved that King Haakon and the Labour government headed by Prime Minister Johan Nygaardsvold, should continue to function abroad, and fighting in Norway cease. Thus, in spite of the Norwegian military capitulation on 10 June, the war against Germany and the fight to liberate Norway was to be continued from Britain.

The summer of 1940 was a difficult time for Norway, as it was for all parts of Europe occupied by German forces. The main aim of Norwegian policy was to keep 'the wheels of the nation' turning and to prevent a total disruption. During this period of trial and error, through a mixture of promises and threats and aided by the impression given by their victories in Europe, the Germans came very close to succeeding in their aims. It was a period of defeatism and a time of negotiations. This led to the formation of an Administrative Council and a search for a more permanent 'Council of the Realm'. It also prompted an appeal from the Presidium of the Norwegian Storting (Parliament) to the King to abdicate. The King's reply was a resolute 'no'. Parallel to this, public anger and frustration with the self-appointed 'Prime Minister' Vidkun Quisling, grew stronger and stronger. Quisling was the leader of the Norwegian Nazi Party, Nasjonal Samling (NS), who had attempted a *coup d'état* on 9 April, announcing in a nationwide broadcast that he had taken over the reins of government and declared resistance to German troops to be a crime.[1] This Quisling initiative and the subsequent activities of the Norwegian NS became one of the main stimulants for Norwegian civilian resistance. 'No Norwegian for sale' became a popular slogan, first coined by a newspaper editor, who was quickly thrown into jail for his pains and his newspaper prohibited. As a result of this, those sections of the press that wanted to write without constraints and censorship went underground. The first underground newspapers appeared as early as the summer of 1940. By the autumn of 1943, there were some sixty in circulation, with about 5,000 people involved in their production and distribution.[2]

In a proclamation entitled 'The Road Ahead' issued on 25 September 1940, the German Reichskommissar in Norway, Josef Terboven, introduced the 'New Order' and clarified the nature of Nazi rule: 'There is only one road ahead and that leads via NS'. It was now evident what role the NS would play in the future governance of Norway, and also where resistance activities should be directed. New laws were introduced that impinged on both private and public life. These laws, often dictated by Quisling, a man who later gave his name to the concept of collaboration, aroused great uproar and protest within a wide range of diverse Norwegian organizations. Voluntary movements, professional organizations, and the whole network of formalized social groups, all committed to the cause of democracy in Norway, mobilized for political purposes in defence of what they felt was an integral part of their heritage. Norwegian athletes and athletic clubs protested against the 'Department of Labour and Sport', by refusing to take part in Nazi-arranged competitions, and the public were also conspicuous by their absence. In November 1940 an attack was made on the independence of the law courts, and the Supreme Court reacted the following month with a wholesale resignation of its judges. Forty-three organizations, representing about 750,000 members of Norway's business and cultural bodies, delivered a united written protest against the NS and rampant lawlessness to the Reichskommissar Terboven. He reacted by arresting and removing from office people in positions of trust. As a result, the embryonic resistance movement was able to bring these leaders together and out of this co-operation a *Koordinasjons-komitèen* (Co-ordinating Committee, KK) was created in the autumn of 1941, which later directed civilian resistance against the Germans and NS. At this point Norwegian civilian resistance went underground. The period of openly writing letters to the occupiers was over.

The response from the embryonic military resistance was less pronounced, with no head-on collisions or direct confrontations. Having recovered from the shock of the German attack, different groups of people in Norway began to plan for some sort of resistance. Some youths on the western coast even found life in an occupied country so unbearable that initiated the most common but also the most dangerous way of escaping Norway: in a boat, usually a fishing smack, to the Shetlands or Great Britain. Officers returning from captivity and soldiers having experienced battlefields or frustrating surrenders without fighting were intent on carrying on the struggle. Combined with the recruiting of athletes, marksmen and students, the largely symbolic acts of hiding away weapons and preparing for more auspicious times gradually became the starting point of a later clandestine army called Milorg (Military Organization). Parallel to this development, some people started to observe German military operations, and find ways of reporting them to British or exiled Norwegian authorities, thus forming the basis of what later became an effective clandestine intelligence service, comprising more than 5,000 agents and assistant agents.[3]

By the end of 1940, it is fair to say that Milorg had been firmly established. It was founded, inspired, and directed by Norwegians in Norway, and was recognized as part of the Norwegian Armed Forces under the command of the Norwegian Government and the Army High Command in London on 20 November 1941. During this initial phase, an unknown number of men, probably some thousands, joined Milorg. The aim of the early leadership was to build up a secret army carefully, avoiding actions and even weapons, and to prepare for the day of liberation. Milorg wanted to 'lie low, go slow'[4] in order not to attract the Germans' attention and thereby jeopardize the lives of civilians and have the fragile organization nipped in the bud.

What, then, was the German power base that the emerging resistance movement confronted in Norway? Firstly, there was the Wehrmacht, which at the end of the war numbered over 350,000. Secondly, there was the Reichskommissariat, which formed the political administrative body, subject only to Hitler, and was authorized to create a new legal code in Norway to supersede the existing system. Thirdly, the Gestapo was assigned the task of crushing Norwegian resistance to the occupying power and the New Order, in close co-operation – though often competing with – the Sicherheitsdienst. If one adds the Abwehr, the German intelligence organization, the picture of the German iron grip is fairly complete. Yet one important factor has to be added when it comes to describing the most dangerous enemies of the resistance. The Norwegian Nazi Party, and especially the informers, constituted a real threat, and in the five years of occupation the resistance undertook the execution of nearly a hundred persons to try and counter this problem. During 1941, the Germans tightened their grip, effecting the first executions of resistance fighters, introducing a state of emergency and carrying out mass civilian executions, at least by Norwegian standards. They also meted out a collective punishment on an individual community, arresting all the male inhabitants and sending them to concentration camps in Germany. The silk glove was replaced by the iron fist. In London, the Norwegian government organized its contribution to Allied warfare, which consisted primarily of Norway's Merchant Navy, the fourth largest in the world. In the meantime, the internal resistance movement went through a period of organization and policy formation.

1942 has been labelled the 'great year' of Norwegian resistance. It was the year when the President of America, Franklin D. Roosevelt, in a speech, used Norway as an example of the spirit that was needed to defeat Nazism. Besides the role played by the Norwegian Crown Princess Märtha, who never failed to keep Norway on the President's agenda, Roosevelt was impressed and encouraged, in a time of defeat and evil omen, by the news of what had been going on in Norway. 'Look to Norway' was his repeated slogan, highlighting the role of Norwegian parents, teachers and priests and their stubborn fight against new Nazi-inspired laws.[5] After Quisling's *Machtübernahme* (take-over of power) in February 1942, when he was installed as Ministerpräsident in a pompous ceremony at the old fortress Akershus in Oslo, he had set out to indoctrinate the country's youth, to dominate the schools and churches, and to force the professional organizations to form a corporative Riksting. In all these fields the NS met with fierce resistance. This has become known in the history of Norwegian resistance as *holdningskamp*, a Norwegian word meaning something like 'a battle of the minds'. Having had their territory conquered, the Norwegians fought a battle to prevent the conquest of Norwegian minds and mentality as well, against a Nazi administration trying to force upon them its ideology by penetrating their homes, schools and churches with *die neue Zeit*.

The first NS endeavour was to 'organize' all teachers. A decree of 5 February 1942 aimed to enforce national service for all young people. In silence, and especially inspired by women, a strategy was worked out for a mass protest from the parents. More than 200,000 letters, with the same wording, were posted on the same day (6 March) to the Ministry of Church and Education: 'I do not wish my child to participate in the service of the youth association of the NS, as the lines laid down for this activity run counter to my conscience.' That was quiet a convincing 'no' from Norwegian parents. The teachers refused to sign a declaration of loyalty to the Nazi authorities, in which they were to promise to instruct their pupils 'in the new spirit'. On 20 March over a thousand of them were arrested and half were then transported from Trondheim to Kirkenes – a journey of more than a thousand miles – crammed into the hold of a ship. For a while all the schools were closed, but ultimately the regime, which had been the driving force behind this attack on the very soul of Norway, had to give way. Stunned by this defeat, Quisling said in a speech some months later, 'You teachers have ruined everything'.[6]

As early as February 1941, the Church had published a pastoral letter on the nature of the Church and the Constitution, and in the spring of 1942 the struggle came to a head. On 24 February, the bishops resigned their offices, in protest at attempts by the regime to control the Church. Soon afterwards, the pastoral letter, 'The Church's Foundation', was read from the pulpit in practically every church in the country. Of a total of 858 incumbent clergy, 797 resigned their livings. All the bishops and fifty-five clergy were interned and a further 127 were banished from their parishes, ninety-two of them being imprisoned for some time. The churches were empty wherever a priest loyal to the Nazi government preached. In this field, too, the Quisling regime had to yield.[7]

For the military resistance, 1942 provided a good many setbacks. Milorg had to learn 'the hard lesson of security' and they had to learn it 'in the bitter school of experience', as the British put it.[8] It took time to master the techniques of resistance and to get used to the mentality of illegality that was crucial for survival. In all fields of clandestine activity, improvements were made that resulted in a greater degree of professionalism and security. The activities involved included intelligence gathering, spreading information, moving people in danger, organizing relief to people already in prison, helping families with members in hiding or abroad, providing food and equipment to the resistance, and producing false passports and identity papers. The Central Leadership (Sentralledelsen, SL) of Milorg had to choose either to be a poorly trained resistance group, built on the organizational principles of the prewar army and not armed until the very day of an Allied invasion, or a decentralized, fully trained and armed guerrilla organization. In the spring of 1942, through the 'Directive Nr.1 to the District Leaders', the SL chose the latter alternative. This did not mean, however, that resistance policy in Norway was settled once and for all. The decisive debate on the issue took place from the autumn of 1942 until the spring of 1943 between the leadership of Milorg and its civilian equivalent, Sivorg. In January 1943, the SL gave an unequivocal answer to the Norwegian High Command (Forsvarets Overkommando, FO) in London: Milorg wanted weapons – indeed their whole existence depended on it. Sivorg protested strongly, but its leaders became reconciled to the inevitability of this decision soon afterwards.[9]

Although the German and NS ideological offensive was somewhat reduced in 1943, the occupying power intensified its policy and reactions towards all kinds of resistance. There were mass arrests of students and officers, as well as terror and executions. In 1943 and 1944, besides consolidating its strength and agreeing upon certain questions of strategy, the most important issue for the resistance was the Quisling regime's attempt to mobilize Norwegian youth for war service on the Eastern Front against Russia. Ever since Quisling had issued his first unsuccessful appeal in January 1941, attempts had been made to recruit young Norwegians for German front line service. The Labour Service (AT) went through a metamorphosis, changing it from a more-or-less harmless organization for community work established in 1940 to an instrument for the Nazi government. Slowly but steadily, this fact was recognized by the resistance. The Oslo Labour Registration Board was blown up by saboteurs in March 1943, but the resistance did not realize the full gravity of the situation until the content of a memorandum issued by the Nazi Minister of Justice in January 1944 was revealed. He suggested that 75,000 men should be conscripted for German war service. The plan was to remain a secret, but its content became known to the resistance thanks to the vigilance of a typist who smuggled a copy out of the office. The resistance leaders feared that the AT might be used as camouflage for the planned conscription. The authorities in London were immediately informed, and the following instruction was transmitted by the BBC: 'No one must obey the call-up to report for Labour Service.'[10]

When mobilization of the AT was finally announced in May 1944, London issued a fresh appeal: 'No one reports for registration.' In order to support this appeal, the resistance carried out several acts of sabotage against punch-card machines and registration offices. Instructions from London, spread by the underground press, were loyally obeyed. Thousands of young people left home to avoid registration, and 'the boys in the forest' became a byword. As a countermove, the Nazi authorities decided to issue ration cards only to those who applied in person. The resistance solved this by seizing 80,000 ration cards *en route* from the printing works. As a result, the Nazi Government was forced to give up its campaign. That was the first and last time that food was used as a means of exerting pressure on the resistance.

From the beginning of 1944, the Supreme Headquarters of the Allied European Forces (SHAEF) dictated the broad outline of policy to be followed in Norway. In other words, the joint British/Norwegian resistance had to adjust itself to the framework of SHAEF. Because of the primacy of SHAEF plans for the invasion of the Continent, Milorg was strongly warned that it should not encourage any rising in Norway. Ironically, the old Milorg slogan 'lie low, go slow' now underwent a renaissance. The object was to grow in strength and wait for the day to come. Any untimely rising, like that of the French *maquis* in the Vercors in France, would not be supported. Nevertheless, the 30,000 or more men in Milorg were eager to do something more than mere training, and after the Allied invasion on the Continent, they were allowed to attack and sabotage German shipping, petrol and oil supplies, and various industrial targets. This became ever more important as the restlessness amongst the rank and file increased. The attacks on labour conscription offices in the spring of 1944 had provided one opportunity for letting off steam. However, when the directive came in June, the opportunities for action increased, although direct clashes with the Germans were still to be avoided. Meanwhile, Milorg grew in strength and numbers. Supplies, equipment, instruction and training were provided by the British Special Operations Executive (SOE) and FO in London. This was no easy task considering Norway's topography and climate. 'Of all the countries in Europe to which men, weapons and stores were delivered by air during the war, Norway undoubtedly presented the greatest difficulties to the Air Forces concerned', Colonel J.S. Wilson, head of SOE's Norwegian Sector, said in his report after the war. All in all, Allied aircraft carried out 717 successful sorties (from a total of 1,241) dropped 208 agents, 9,662 containers and 2,762 packages with arms, munitions, explosives, radio equipment, uniforms, medicine etc. In addition, supplies were shipped in 194 voyages from the Shetland Islands: 190 agents and 385 tons of arms and other supplies were landed in Norway and 345 agents were brought back to England. Instructors were sent to train personnel, together with wireless operators, and this gradually increased Milorg's potential striking power.

The SHAEF directive of June 1944 was based on the assumption that it would be easier to let the Germans retreat from Norway and defeat them in Central Europe. However, as the situation in this part of Europe altered towards the end of 1944, SHAEF changed its strategy. In a directive of 5 December 1944, Milorg was told to attack the railways in Norway on a large scale to prevent the Germans from withdrawing their fresh troops from Norway as reinforcements for the Central European theatre of war against the Allies. Milorg was more than pleased to get this opportunity. After the surrender in Finland, an enormous number of German troops were withdrawn into Finnmark in Northern Norway and southwards. In close co-operation with SOE and with careful advance planning, Milorg attacked railways and bridges on a large scale. So well did Milorg carry out its task, according to the head of SOE, Major General

Sir Colin Gubbins that, 'from Norway, there was a reduction in rate of movement from four divisions to less than on division a month'.11 However, German documents such as the relevant *Kriegstagebuch* (war diary), do not support his assertion. It records that eleven divisions were withdrawn from June 1944 until the end of the war, seven of which were moved in the first four months of 1945.[12]

In the last year of the war, the main Milorg objective was transformed from sabotage to its exact opposite, namely to prevent the German destruction of communications, transport, industries, port facilities and the like, lest they attempted a withdrawal accompanied by the scorched earth policy as practised in Finnmark in the autumn of 1944. Detailed plans were made in London and a total of 110 officers were sent in from Great Britain to lead this work. In addition, a considerable number of Norwegian SOE agents (the so-called Linge-Company) already in Norway on various other missions, were directed to similar tasks in the last phase of the war. Milorg also established a few bases – groups of specially handpicked men placed in camps deep in the forests or up in the mountains, ready to strike if the signal was given. The leaders and instructors were SOE personnel. At this stage, in the spring of 1945, approximately 40,000 Milorg personnel, equipped, trained and well disciplined, were prepared for the worst possible outcome, a German last stand in Norway. Milorg obeyed the SHAEF orders not to provoke the Germans, but could not avoid a few clashes when the Germans attacked. On these occasions, Milorg demonstrated its capability to defend itself and even strike back. Its losses were small compared to German casualties.

The German Commander in Norway, General Boehme, signed the German surrender in Norway on 8 May 1945.[13] Milorg did not have to fight at all. Their role in this rather risky period of transition was to stand guard, protect buildings, arrest traitors and so forth. They were finally demobilized in July 1945. As for the Linge Company, it was officially inspected by Colonel Wilson on 30 June and demobilized.

The Main Types of Resistance and their Organizational Forms

As we have seen by the previous sections, the main types of resistance were the military-based Milorg with its Rådet (Council) and Central Leadership, and the civilian-based Sivorg, including the Co-ordination Committee. During 1944, these two main streams of resistance merged in one leadership called the Hjemmefrontens Ledelse (Resistance Leadership, HL). Milorg's organizational form changed from being based on the prewar military divisions based on five areas to an *ad hoc* structure adapted to the new situation, the country being divided into 14 districts. Each district was subdivided into regions, and these, in turn, into areas consisting of groups, platoons and finally sections of eight to ten men.

Civilian resistance in Norway has often been mistakenly portrayed as having a pacifist ideology. This is not the case. It was just a matter of circumstances. To engage in armed resistance in a country occupied by hundreds of thousands of German soldiers, was just not sensible. Using the power of words in slogans, appeals and clandestine newspapers, in an occupied country where the German did not treat the population as *Untermenschen* but as 'Aryans', proved to be both sensible and successful. However, if an illegal press 'office' was raided by the Gestapo, the civilians fighting with their pens would most probably use pistols lying ready on the desk. The crux of the matter was 'how can one achieve the most without heavy German reprisals against the civilian population?' Towards the end of the war, the resistance prepared for the possibility of a general strike, dependent on certain conditions being met. Firstly, the strike had to be fully supported by the population, as a result of a 'spontaneous and real desire' with a 'general urge to strike a blow against the enemy'.[14] Two possible scenarios could be foreseen: 'a protest against an act of terror from the occupying force or the NS' or 'to stop an action which had already been started by the occupiers'. This general strike never came about. Two incidents almost triggered it off. The first was the German scorched earth policy in the autumn of 1944 in the Finnmark region. The fact that news of these atrocities did not reach the public in the south of Norway quickly enough, or with sufficient impact, meant that it never created the necessary outrage and uproar. The second was the executions in February 1945, after the resistance had executed the head of the Norwegian State Police. This time opinion was not considered to be 'mature' enough.

The Norwegian *holdningskamp*, the civilian resistance, can be seen as having five phases.[15] Firstly, there was *the phase of spontaneity*. The label speaks for itself and consisted primarily of unorganized outbursts of anger and frustration by ordinary people, protesting against their new status of being occupied and unfree. The second, overlapping the first, can be labelled as *the phase of legality*. It was characterized by a political struggle against the NS that relied on legal arguments expressed in open letters addressed to the dictatorship. It lasted until 1942, before slipping into the third phase, that of *values*. The dominating values were (a) the right to give your children an education free of an unwanted ideology, (b) the right to keep the said ideology out of the education system and

(c) the right to religious freedom without interference from the Nazi state. As we have already seen, the year 1942 was the great period of the *holdningskamp* and it coincided with the fight for these values. A distinctive religious resistance, with an existence separated from other forms of opposition, never came into existence in Norway. It was an integrated part of the common struggle against the oppressor's aggressive will to impose new Nazi laws on the Norwegian people.

The year 1943 constitutes *the phase of consolidation*. The great 'battle of the minds' was over, its success was complete, but it had taken its toll. However, the extent of this success so influenced the leadership of the KK and other groups that they voted down all other kinds of resistance. A sort of fatigue was evident amongst the leaders, and no effective measures were mounted to prevent or protest against mass arrests of students and officers. Some internal struggles and disagreement also led to a waste of energy. Conflict with the communists and their resistance policy was an added problem. Characteristically and consequently, no measures were taken against the mounting threat of forced conscription disguised as labour service. As we have already seen, this very threat finally brought the civil and military leadership together in a united struggle that included the use of sabotage and the threat of a general strike against the Nazi authorities. This period from the spring of 1944 to the end of the war is *the phase of revitalisation*. The civilian resistance was back on the offensive. German sources show that the leadership of the Wehrmacht was opposed to Reichskommissar Terboven's plan of severe reprisals in the spring of 1945 to counter increasing resistance activity because it might serve to provoke the resistance's 'secret weapon', namely a general strike.[16] Although referred to as secret by the resistance, the efficacy of the strike weapon was that the Germans knew of it and limited their behaviour accordingly.

In parallel, and often competing with the so-called 'official' resistance, the communists advocated their own left-wing version. When the Germans attacked, the Norwegian Communist Party, NKP, took a definite stand against the Norwegian Government's military resistance and its alliance with Great Britain. The Party in Norway, as well as communist parties in other countries, looked upon the war as 'imperialistic' until 22 June 1941, when Germany attacked the Soviet Union. Armed struggle against the German occupation was not part of their policy. In practice, however, their activity did not differ much from the official Norwegian policy after the capitulation in June 1940. Even Milorg did not organize itself for military resistance before there was some chance of a British or Allied invasion, and the emphasis of Norwegian resistance until 1944 was, as we have already seen, on non-violent resistance against the Nazi government's attempts to nazify different elements of Norwegian society.

Although the Communist Party as a whole initially refused to engage in armed resistance to the German occupation, rank-and-file members did participate in the fighting. Prominent communists backed the resistance, and some were involved on the Soviet side in military intelligence activity against Germany as early as the summer and autumn of 1940.[17] The NKP was banned in August 1940, and both the Party itself and its members took a definite stand against Quisling, the NS, and the attempts to nazify Norway. However, when the German attack on the Soviet Union made resistance indisputable for both the party and its members, the communists developed a policy of resistance characterized by an activism that often ran counter to the official resistance policy. This often created severe problems for the main resistance leadership. For example, on the western coast of Norway, one group attempted to install a so-called Frihetsråd (Freedom Council) led by communists and in direct competition with the resistance bodies backed by the Norwegian government in London.

In addition, disputes occurred within the party and different groups and alliances arose. During the whole wartime period, the party work continued, unlike all other political parties in Norway. The leadership went into permanent hiding in the woods, working for an uncompromising armed struggle against the Germans. Especially in the early years of resistance, this caused problems for the Milorg leadership as well as for the Norwegian government. This coincided, as we shall see later, with the activism of SOE and a growing wish among the rank and file of the Milorg members to move on from training and directives ('the paper war') to more warlike activities. However, the opportunity to engage in acts of sabotage in the last couple of years of the occupation functioned as a kind of safety valve. Consequently, the attraction the communists had exerted partly by their rhetorical emphasis on 'crushing' Nazism and partly by their activities, more-or-less vanished. A kind of understanding, a 'ceasefire', between the communist and the resistance leadership was established towards the end of the war. Both sides wanted to cooperate, but the arrangement was clearly on the terms of the official leadership.

The five years of occupation that engendered the formation of resistance organizations also served to forge some new links between persons and movements engaged in a common struggle. For the first time, labour leaders and conservatives came together in a joint effort towards a common goal. Two political cultures totally unfamiliar to each other met and co-operated, both in leadership and in imprisonment, resulting in personal friendships and mutual understanding in a way unheard of before the occupation. In the same way, the two different sports federations, one associated with the labour movement and the other independent, united in a common effort to boycott Nazi sports meetings. This union became a lasting phenomenon, introduced as an *ad hoc* solution to an external threat, but preserved after the war as the best solution for the Norwegian athletic federation. Finally, the two most noted religious leaders in Norway, one representing the conservative and pietistic dogmas in Christianity, the other being a spokesman for a more liberal tradition, came together to unite against the common threat of constraints in religious matters. Nevertheless, parallel to unity and new alliances, Norway also saw conflicts and failures to cooperate. We have already touched on this, and we will return to it later. The different views held by Milorg and Sivorg on resistance policy in the years 1942–3, the skirmishes between the official resistance backed by the government in exile and the communists, internal problems linked to some radical sections inside the resistance movement, and last, but not least, the problems connected with the links and relationship between internal resistance organizations and external espionage and sabotage organizations.

Three external espionage and sabotage organizations operated in Norway. Two were British and played an important role, namely SOE and the Secret Intelligence Service (SIS). Some of the Norwegian SOE agents were also in contact with the American Office of Strategic Services (OSS), but this organization played only a minor role in Norway. Their only major operation came very late in the war, in March 1945, and was intended to sabotage railways in the Trondheim area. The participants were all Americans of Norwegian origin.

As mentioned earlier, some Norwegians escaped their occupied country in order to come back as trained soldiers, resistance fighters or intelligence agents. In the military intelligence area, a good relationship and close co-operation developed early with SIS. Those who came to Great Britain were often recruited to SIS and returned to Norway as SIS agents, frequently serving as radio operators. It was vitally important for the Allies to keep track of German fleet movements along the coast of Norway, and for this purpose a chain of radio stations was set up close to the shipping lanes, entrusted with the task of reporting on all seaborn traffic. One of the greatest achievements was the reports and pictures of the German battleship *Tirpitz*, from the moment she was identified off the coast of south Norway in January 1942 until she went to the bottom after having been bombed in north Norway in November 1944. Apart from minor disputes and conflicts of interest with the local Milorg and SOE agents, often caused by overlapping activities that threatened to expose the operators and jeopardize both the operation and the lives of the agents, SIS maintained as few links as possible with internal and other external resistance organizations.

However, the majority of Norwegians recruited for clandestine activities by British organizations joined SOE. It was the dominant external organization in Norway, and the links and relationships between SOE and internal resistance counterparts, that is to say Milorg, need to be examined in some detail. The wartime period can be divided into three phases. The first might be regarded as *the phase of non-collaboration.* This attitude, which was mutual, lasted from the summer of 1940 throughout the year 1941 and into the latter part of 1942, at least as far as the rank-and-file of the two organizations were concerned. At the top level, however, there were attempts at conciliation, and consequently a period of coexistence and even co-operation began to developed from the autumn of 1941 onwards. It was, however, the last two years of the war that constituted the period of maximum co-operation at all levels.

As for the British, their Military Intelligence had jumped the gun and dispatched a few men to Norway a few days before the German attack. One of these officers was Major Malcolm Munthe. In addition, the man who later became the Head of SOE, Major-General Gubbins, participated in the military campaign in Norway in the spring of 1940. Between them, these men established contacts with quite a few Norwegians, and when SOE was established in July 1940, they became the core of the Norwegian component in the British effort to hamper the German exploitation of Norway.

The SOE Scandinavian section began its development under the direction of Charles Hambro. Norwegian refugees were happy to be asked to go to special training courses with the purpose of becoming British agents in Norway. Gradually, this resulted in the formation of the Norwegian Independent Company No. 1, later called the Linge Company, named after the leader Captain Martin Linge. In December 1940 an important base was established on the Shetland Islands as a joint base for SOE and SIS. Norwegian refugees, who had crossed the sea in their fishing-boats, were hired as agents. These agents joined the Linge Company and Shetland Base, and adopted the British view of active resistance policy in occupied countries, which corresponded roughly with their own. However, this meant that they were bound to clash with their Milorg colleagues – in spite of having the same goal, a free Norway – as their methods of achieving this objective differed so much.

While the Milorg leadership attempted to build up a centralized, secret army, slowly and carefully over a long period, avoiding activities that might endanger the work of the organization, the British SOE leadership was in a hurry to promote activity that would produce results to present to the Ministry of Economic Warfare. The SOE had Churchill on its side as he favoured any offensive strategy, especially in Norway, his favourite preoccupation during the war. The SOE's solution was raids and sabotage, contrary to the policy of Milorg. Inside the SOE Norwegian Section, both in London and Stockholm, there were several Britons who were adamant that SOE should conduct its work without interference from Milorg. Colonel Wilson put it like this: 'There was still amongst its staff the inherent British attitude of kindly – but none the less galling – superiority to the foreigners. There existed . . . a distrust of Milorg's ability to take ordinary security precautions. The arrests in the autumn of 1941 gave apparent reason for this distrust.' Wilson concluded that 'the tendency of the British officers concerned was to demand that all SOE organisation should be independent of Milorg.'[18]

As a result, the SOE leadership decided to carry out its resistance activities in Norway independent of Milorg, the Norwegian government or other Norwegian authorities in London. The crucial decision on this appears in a report dated 11 December 1940.[19] Headed 'Norwegian Policy', it demonstrated the importance that the British attributed to Norway and also gave directives to those Norwegians who worked for SOE in Norway. Although the document stated that the liberation of Norway most probably would come as a result of an Allied invasion, it was seen as important that SOE boost Norwegian morale by means of propaganda and sabotage. Norway was to become 'a thorn in the German side'. As an ultimate aim, SOE foresaw a general rising. This could only be achieved by having a separate SOE organization in each district in Norway. Finally, the document stated that SOE had a 'long-term pro-gramme' and a 'short-term programme'. The former aimed at building up a Secret Army, trained in guerrilla and sabotage, and assisting an Allied invasion. The 'short-term programme' aimed at raids and sabotage, so-called 'tip-and-run landings and air raids', to be carried out in association with the Directorate of Combined Operations (DCO). One such raid was the 'Claymore' operation against the Lofoten Island on 4 March 1941. The British evaluated this raid as a great success, 'a classic example of a perfectly executed commando-raid'.[20] This laudatory British attitude was not shared in Norway. The Germans took heavy reprisals: homes were burned, people arrested. Besides, the targets destroyed were regarded in Norway as Norwegian property, and not seen as a blow against Germany's capacity to wage war. It even struck a jarring note among the participating Norwegian soldiers who began to doubt whether it was right to operate under British orders and carry out British plans, especially if this was done without consulting the Norwegian government. The SOE, however, was thrilled by the success of the 'Claymore' operation. It resulted in another document, entitled 'Scandinavian Policy' of 16 April 1941, where the leadership stressed its desire to pursue its own policy and get things going in Norway's fight for freedom. By doing this, however, they undoubtedly overestimated the Norwegian willingness to fight the German occupation regardless of the consequences.

Why then this concern for the consequences? The Norwegian resistance leaders felt the heavy burden of responsibility. Norway had lived in peace for 126 years and its population had not been mentally prepared for war. When the Norwegian government recognized Milorg in November 1941, SOE responded quickly with the memorandum called 'Anglo-Norwegian Collaboration regarding the Military Organisation in Norway', expressing a wish to co-operate with the Norwegian government and other Norwegian authorities.[21] However, Milorg was required to work along the same lines that SOE had drawn up for resistance in other German-occupied countries, based on mutual confidence and harmonious cooperation between British and Norwegian resistance leaders in England. The invitation was accepted by the Norwegian Defence Minister who confirmed that 'not only was he in favour of continuing the arrangements that existed between the Norwegian authorities and SOE, but that he wanted to facilitate them.' In return he personally expected to be taken into SOE's confidence 'absolutely'. In the meantime, a report on 'Operation Anklet', the raid against Måløy on the western coast of Norway in December 1941, noted that the year had 'ended on a sad note', with Captain Linge himself being among those killed. At the beginning of 1942, the raids ceased, and from then on, SOE concentrated on its long-term programme. On 1 January 1942, a special Norwegian section, headed by Wilson, was established within the SOE to direct its work in Norway. In addition, the talks between SOE and the Norwegian Defence Minister resulted in the instituting of the important Anglo-Norwegian Collaboration Committee (ANCC).

A month later, on 6 February, the Norwegian High Command (FO) was established, and on 16 February, the first meeting of the ANCC was held, with representatives of SOE and FO. It could be said that the two organizations now entered a phase of co-operation, and it might consequently be concluded that this applied to the relationship between SOE and Milorg as well. However, although these organizational improvements at the top marked a great step forward, the problems in the field were far from being solved. The gap between word and deed was in fact at its greatest in the year of 1942, as the policy of non-collaboration continued amongst the rank and file. Agents were still sent to Norway with strict orders to avoid contact with members of Milorg. Throughout the year, the main debate in SOE–Milorg relations remained the question of their respective roles in the reconquest of Norway. As for Milorg, a Norwegian committee in Great Britain had drawn up a list of its main tasks, and their view was then evaluated by SOE. Finally SOE delivered its report in April on 'The Reconquest of Norway. SOE's Role'. Here they summed up their activity and their will to co-operate. However, it would still be necessary to maintain separate SOE organizations in the districts in Norway, with no contact to their Milorg colleagues. The report talked of 'certain lines of parallel action'. SOE and Milorg should, however, in due time let these lines fuse 'when the proper time for amalgamation comes'. SOE considered the establishment of radio communications between Norway and Great Britain, between Sweden and Norway, and inside Norway, to be SOE's main role in the future, together with supplying Norway with weapons and explosives, and training and transporting Norwegian agents. Finally SOE would do the utmost to help with 'long-term planning with a view to the reconquest of Norway'.

During 1942, the policy of 'parallel action' often had grave conse-quences, the details will not be given here. As this tragic year in the history of military resistance in Norway progressed, the Milorg leaders were on the verge of giving up their work, and top level meetings were held. To solve the crisis of confidence, SOE issued a new document on 21 September. Written by Wilson himself, this amounted to nothing less than a new programme called 'SOE Long-term Policy in Norway' in which SOE finally gave up its independent course.[22] The SOE admitted that mistakes had been made on both sides, including the 'lines of parallel action' and declared that a 'drastic revision' was necessary. Wilson's attitude played a major role in this process of mutual understanding: 'in time all realized that it was impossible to run two independent paramilitary underground movements side by side. Inevitably it would lead to crossing of lines and to the two cutting each others' throats'. One of the leading Norwegian resistance pioneers who was then in London and a member of the ANCC expressed it this way: 'We have experienced that it is impossible to maintain two separated military organizations without intermixing and creating complications which may trigger off the worst consequences. We must therefore go for *one* effective organization with *a strong united* leadership.'[23]

Directives were issued by both SOE and FO aimed at securing a good relationship at all levels. SOE and FO agreed on what were to be their respective responsibilities and duties. Initiative, planning, education of agents and instructors, transport and supplies were all to be taken care of by SOE, in cooperation with FO. Milorg would, generally speaking, provide the rank and file. Resistance policy was be a matter for the ANCC, whereas the day-to-day running of events in Norway would be handled by the Milorg leadership. Although some sources suggest that, 'especially from December 1943 . . . the co-operation has had an intimate character',[24] it is fair to say that the period of non-collaboration in the field and coexistence at the top level transformed itself into full cooperation at all levels from the beginning of 1943 onwards. An important factor in this ongoing process was Milorg's own decision concerning the future character of its organization. The acceptance of the reality of war, and of the need for military resistance, inevitably made it easier to adjust to British policies and to fall into line with SOE's new policy of co-operation *in the field*.

During this period, SOE intensified its sabotage activities and Milorg and its personnel were gradually integrated. The usual pattern was for Linge-soldiers to be dropped in the vicinity of the target, or even sometimes in Sweden. They would then launch the attack, often helped by local Milorg men. Three groups of targets were hit: ships, industry, and railways. The most famous, 'Operation Gunnerside', against the heavy water plant at Vemork in February 1943 provides a good example of thorough Anglo-Norwegian planning, the use of Norwegian agents who knew the area like the back of their hand, and, in the sinking of the Hydro ferry carrying semi-finished heavy water, the co-operation with a local Milorg group. It is also an example of the effectiveness of *coup-de-main* operations when compared to heavy bombing in terms of accuracy and minimizing casualties. This comparison was often on the agenda in Anglo-Norwegian meetings and SOE, FO and Milorg took a unanimous view in favour of the former. Attacks were usually planned and launched by combined groups of Milorg and SOE personnel. Milorg's role in these joint British-Norwegian operations had been steadily increasing. The last British operation planned outside Norway was in April 1944. Henceforward, decision-making was transferred to the Milorg central leadership inside the country.

In this rough survey of the links and relationships between the two main internal and external resistance organisations Milorg and SOE, I have tried to show how two *ad hoc* organizations, with basically the same goal, but that nonetheless began virtually as antagonists with an attitude of non-collaboration, gradually managed to establish a level of co-operation and, in the last years of the war, achieved such a high degree of co-operation that the SOE characterization of an 'amalgamation' seemed appropriate. Although it may be said that both sides shared 'basically the same goal', the inherent contradiction in the SOE programme of the building up of a secret army *combined* with offensive actions made the first two or three years difficult. The former required an attitude that did not attract the attention of the Germans and thus dovetailed perfectly with Milorg's policy. On the other hand, the consequences of offensive actions produced precisely the opposite effect, and this was Milorg's constant worry. For reasons already described, SOE had to concentrate on offensive strategies early in the war. However, as the conflict developed, SOE toned down this aspect of its activity. At the same time, Milorg adjusted its policy to the harsh reality of war. In this way the two lines met and converged.

Individual Acts of Resistance – their Extent and Impact

In Norway, individual acts of resistance were initially restricted to silent demonstrations of a kind that very soon became very popular and widespread. For example: people using symbols like paper clips on cuffs and collars ('we stick together') and flowers in a buttonhole (on the King's birthday), painting King Haakon's initials (H 7) on exterior walls inside the V for Victory, refusing to sit next to Germans and Norwegian Nazis on trams and buses, and wearing red woollen caps (headgear ultimately banned by the occupying power). This happened in a period when there was a rather naive but natural urge to 'do something'. Spontaneous reactions and symbols of unity created a so-called 'icefront' against NS members – all representing a body of opinion looking for a new organizational framework. Hundreds were arrested and put in jail for such deeds, and all-in-all these symbolic acts played an important role in boosting morale for those living in occupied Norway. Firstly, these individual acts of resistance signalled to those who planned and led the active resistance that they had the support of the people. Secondly, they served as a kind of warning to the collaborators and to the members of the NS. Thirdly, they soured the atmosphere for the occupying power, their troops and civilian apparatus. Finally, as this activity had to be dealt with, it served to undermine the somewhat problem-free existence that the Germans enjoyed from time to time in Norway, particularly compared to Eastern Europe.

The Resistance in the Post-War World

In terms of national liberation, the final victory over the Axis came through the massive military effort of the major Allied powers – an effort in which Norway and its Home Forces (the official term from the autumn of 1944), could only play a minor part. The only contribution crucial to the Allied warfare was Norway's merchant fleet. However, together with Norway-in-exile, the Resistance enabled Norway to play its limited part effectively. In the transition from war to peace, through its unity, discipline and strength, the resistance contributed to establishing a transitional period that corresponded to the very principles it had fought for. However, the fact that Norway had built up an *armed* military force and had also successfully fought against Nazi indoctrination gave the people a feeling of having participated and contributed to the liberation. The rationale for choosing to arm Milorg, was given in a letter to FO in January, 1943 by the organization's council. 'Those who in the end shall settle the profit and loss account of the military contribution by the Resistance during an Allied invasion, must [. . .] not neglect or underestimate the national value of a rising, in addition to its military value as such.'[25] In other words, a *rebuilding* of 'national honour' was never on the agenda in Norway: it was simply unnecessary given how the nation had dealt with the occupation. The 'Look to Norway' effect completely overshadowed the fact that Germany had kept the economic wheels turning in Norway more or less undisturbed for five years. If Germany had settled for the military and economic advantage of an occupied Norway, the need for a rebuilding of national honour after the war might have been an issue of greater interest. This is, however, one of the 'ifs' of history and should not be dealt with too closely by historians. Nevertheless, it is fair to say that more than anything else it was on the one hand the people's contempt for the Quisling regime and on the other the inherent urge of the Nazis to impose their ideology on their subject peoples that caused Norwegians by the thousands to engage in a struggle from which they acquitted themselves sufficiently heroically to enter the postwar period carrying their heads high.

In terms of postwar reconstruction the picture is somewhat similar. The formation of a coalition government across the old party lines was a direct result of the mutual understanding between old political enemies that had sprung up in the wake of resistance. The feeling that the old party quarrels had to be put aside was strong in the aftermath of the occupation. It did not, however, last long. Conversely, the tendency to underline the important role of the resistance, in the broadest sense of the word, in uniting the nation across party lines and in bridging class gaps, lingered on and was even strengthened as the decades passed. In that respect resistance contributed to and strengthened the so-called 'national honour'. To some extent it may even be said that the official rhetoric on the phenomenon of resistance has at times tended to slide into the world of mythology, evoking an image of the Norwegian people, with its fists clenched and the 'boys in the forest' armed as guerrilla soldiers awaiting the next striking blow to the occupying force. This picture is true for some of the people some of the time, but not as an adequate description of Norwegian resistance as such.

The Debates on Resistance Since 1945

The general impression of the national debates on resistance and the most striking feature of the historiography is the degree of consensus. The fundamental interpretations and conclusions established in the early 1950s and 1960s, by historians who themselves had participated in the resistance movement, have never been seriously challenged. New aspects and new subjects have, of course, been added to the list of research areas, but none of the results have altered the established structure of the history of Norwegian resistance. Nevertheless, some aspects have been debated on a more-or-less national level. Firstly, the postwar judicial proceedings, in which thousands of members of the NS were charged with high treason, created a dispute on whether Norway had been at war with Germany after the capitulation on 10 June 1940. For some years after the war, it was assumed to be the case as a matter of course. In addition, during the war, the state of war between the two nations was never disputed either by the Germans or the NS. However, in 1948 defence counsel for NS members attempted to argue that assistance to the enemy could not be considered as constituting an offence unless Norway was at war with Germany during the occupation and it took a Supreme Court decision in March of that year to confirm the existence of a state of war as an indisputable fact.[26] Magne Skodvin has written extensively on the year 1940 and its implications for the rest of the war-time history.[27] His conclusions are shared by the great majority of Norwegian historians: (a) The Government based its resistance on an authority (the 'Elverum Authorization') given by the Storting; (b) The Capitulation Agreement was a military agreement relating to the surrender of the remaining Norwegian forces in northern Norway and did not include those who had already left for Great Britain to continue the struggle for a free Norway. That is why an *ad hoc* formulation acceptable for the Norwegian negotiator was used in this case instead of the internationally recognized legal text for surrender; (c) as there is no doubt about the existence of a state of war, the Norwegian resistance as such did not operate in violation of international law; and (d) the government in exile was the only legal government, entitled to pass laws that would be applied after the liberation to people who had assisted the enemy. Nevertheless, themes along these lines have repeatedly popped up, thanks to former NS-members, centred around their periodical *Folk og Land* and journalists and authors hunting sensations.

Another theme that has been made the subject of debate is the relationship between the communists and the so-called official resistance. This has bearing on another subject, namely resistance policy itself and the use or non-use of violence, weapons and sabotage. After the German attack on the Soviet Union, the communists had advocated supporting the 'giant force' of the people, a rhetoric quite alien to the more 'bourgeois' resistance leadership, and this became part of their post-war political platform. Together with some left-wing historians, they argued that Milorg and the government-based Norwegian resistance as a whole had been too reserved and cautious. Fear of German reprisals had been allowed to play too important a role and had overshadowed the necessity of an unprincipled struggle against the evil of Nazism. The answer given by the resistance leaders has been that the 'lie low, go slow' policy was rational, considering the lack of experience, the complexity of the situation and German military superiority. To concentrate on a building up of forces with a view to a contribution in the liberation of Norway, parallel to vigorous protest against the Nazi propaganda thrusts against the soul of the nation, seemed to be the most reasonable behaviour. Most historians have continued to champion this latter view.

The liquidation of informers carried out to protect the work of the resistance organizations and their members, has been challenged now and then in the postwar years. The Public Prosecutor decided in 1945 that if and when it was established, after an investigation, that a homicide case was a liquidation and the responsibility had been taken by the resistance, no further action would be taken. This practice was accepted by a vast majority, but some have queried the decision. In the 1980s and 1990s, there has been a new wave of unfounded rumours containing all sorts of allegations against the resistance. A new book published in 1996 by a journalist aroused extensive discussion in the press and a corresponding uproar among the veterans. Because of numerous faults and its overall imperfection, the book was subsequently withdrawn from the market.[28]

Another recurring theme has been the fate of the Jews. To what extent were the Norwegian police a contributing factor to their arrest, and how well did the resistance respond to the challenge of getting the refugees over the border to Sweden? For this subject as well as for the others, the pendulum has been swinging to and fro. The Norwegian police were ordered to participate in the final mass arrests of the Jews in October 1942. Several policemen had, however, done their best to warn Jews in their districts during the preceding days. As for the resistance, they managed to evacuate more than half, or approximately 1,000 people. This happened at a time when the escape lines of the resistance organizations had been badly affected by betrayals and arrests. This achievement has traditionally not been recognized by Jewish organizations, and the different Holocaust Memorial Museums usually stress the Danish example, without considering the completely different conditions pertaining in Norway. The resistance was also seriously embarrassed when it was revealed in 1947 that two of the so-called 'refugee pilots' (people who acted as couriers for those on the run), had killed a Jewish couple in 1942 on their way to Sweden. They were found not guilty of murder, but were sentenced for theft. The case created quite a stir in the early postwar years.

Apart from the themes closely connected with the resistance, related issues have, at intervals, also been the subject of national debates. For example, the role of the Labour Party's traditional antipathy towards military expenditure and its effects on the building up of defence in the 1930s; the prelude to the German attack and the 'forewarnings' allegedly neglected by the Labour government; the postwar use of retrospective Acts to prosecute NS members and the mass inquiries introduced after the war to punish those who had assisted the enemy in various ways. It is fair to say that the resistance heritage, or rather the wartime heritage, has played a vigorous part in the lives of Norwegians in the postwar period and continues to do so, even today.

New Directions

In the 1990s there has been a growing interest in the so-called 'wrong side'– those who joined the NS and the different aspects of the occupying power. Although veteran historians like Skodvin have been dealing continuously with related topics in the last few decades, the point has been made that the smallest details related to resistance have been scrutinized at the expense of other aspects of the history of occupation. Part of this criticism was raised by a group of younger historians at the University of Oslo, who constituted themselves as a kind of 'school' opposed to what they characterized as the 'Skodvin-school'. This has led to the publication of some books about the NS and certain famous

German and NS leaders. Even a Norwegian wartime dictionary was published in connection with the fifty-year anniversary in 1995 with a clear tendency in this same direction.[29]

In 1996, the main figure in this revisionist group, Professor Hans Fredrik Dahl, wrote articles in the newspaper *Dagbladet* that, to a certain extent, supported the revisionist historian David Irving. In addition, Dahl turned out to be the author's consultant for the withdrawn book about the liquidation of informers. The meeting of minds between a representative of what had been seen as a mild cry for revision of certain aspects of war time history with the blunt and sometimes neo Nazi-inspired writings of certain freelancers came as something of a shock. The historian Odd Bjørn Fure called Dahl to account in the pamphlet *Kampen mot glemselen* (The Fight against Oblivion).[30] In some ways, this was a turning point but there are some signs of an evolution away from the resistance perspective to one more concerned with the occupiers, the NS Party and its members, the postwar proceedings against enemy collaborators, and the effect on those who were sentenced, their children, and the children born as a result of German–Norwegian love affairs.[31]

Apart from the group associated with Dahl, the main feature has been consensus, as mentioned above. Some fields have been dealt with thoroughly only in the recent years. Of those, the work done by Ragnar Ulstein on the secret intelligence community deserves to be mentioned. In three comprehensive volumes he describes the different intelligence groups and their activities. Just as important, and impressive, are the six volumes on the vast subject of imprisonment, in concentration camps and in prisons, in Norway and abroad, including one on the faith of the Jews, all of them written by Kristian Ottosen. Characteristically, both men are World War Two veterans, besides being self-educated historians. After decades of pressure from wartime merchant mariners, a five-volume work on the Norwegian merchant fleet during the war was completed in 1997. A comprehensive work on the Norwegian Air Force, including a wartime volume already released, written by Vera Henriksen, is also about to be completed.

Though most aspects of the history of resistance have been dealt with, there are areas that still require more detailed studies. Important work on the Communist Party and the communist resistance activity is in progress, as well as a pioneer study of the liquidations carried out by the Resistance. The role of women in resistance was put on the agenda by women's organizations in the 1980s. Some books and pamphlets related to the subject have now been published, and hundreds of valuable tape recordings related to women's resistance activity have been collected and placed in the archives.[32] However, the overall analysis of their contribution to resistance, especially the military part, has yet to be thoroughly analysed by historians. The same goes for several other areas related to occupied Norway, aside from resistance history as such. Economic collaboration and compulsory labour service are two such areas, and the fate of foreign prisoners of war worked to death in Norway, as well as certain aspects of the Jewish deportation also demand further attention. Similarly, a thorough study of the NS regime's participation in the German war on the Eastern Front is lacking. Certain aspects related to the postwar effects of the war may also be mentioned here. For example, how did the postwar proceedings against enemy collaborators become so extensive – more than 90,000 were charged – and how did this affect the thousands of families with members stigmatized as traitors? I think it is fair to say that although the national consensus has been deservedly strong, based on sound judgement and good research by many prominent historians, this consensus syndrome based on a tradition of positive interpretation may nonetheless have overshadowed some of the more difficult and traumatic aspects of the occupation.

Notes

1. See Oddvar Høidal, *A Study in Treason* (Oslo: Universitetsforlaget, 1988).
2. Tore Gjelsvik, *Norwegian Reistance* (London: Hurst, 1979).
3. Ragnar Ulstein, *Etterretningstenesta i Norge 1940–1945*, 3 vols., (Oslo: Det Norske Samlaget, 1989-92).
4. Sverre Kjeldstadli, *Hjemmestyrkene* (Oslo: Aschehoug, 1959) p.9.
5. Speech by Franklin D.Roosevelt in Washington, September 1942, at a ceremony for the handing over of the subchaser, 'King Haakon VII'. Mage Skodvin (ed.), *Norge i Krig*, 8 vols., Volume 7, Olav Riste, *Utefront* (Oslo: Aschehoug, 1988), p.127.
6. Magne Skodvin (ed.), *Norge i Krig*, 8 vols., Volume 4, Berit Nøkelby, *Holdningskamp* (Oslo: Aschehoug, 1987) p.121.
7. Ibid.
8. J.S. Wilson, *SOE Norwegian Section History* (Unpublished Mss.) Norway's Resistance Museum (NRM) cited in Kjeldstadli, *Hjemmestyrkene*, p.89.
9. Magne Skodvin (ed.), *Norge i Krig*, 8 vols, volume 6, Ivar Kraglund and Arnfinn Moland, *Hjemmefront* (Oslo: Aschehoug, 1987).

10. See, Gjelsvik, *Norwegian Resistance* for a more detailed account.
11. Kjeldstadli, *Hjemmestyrkene*, p.226.
12. *Kriegstagebuch* IV-2 p.1332, NRM.
13. See Jens Chr.Hauge, *The Liberation of Norway* (Oslo: Gyldendal Norsk Forlag, 1995).
14. Kraglund and Moland, *Hjemmefront*, pp.269–72.
15. Arnfinn Moland, 'Den sivile motstand i Norge under okkupasjonen', in: John Kristen Skogan (ed.) *I frigjøringens spor* (Oslo, 1995) pp.95–112.
16. Taken from *Meldungen aus Norwegen*, fairly objective German reports about the general mood and public opinion in Norway during the occupation (NRM).
17. Terje Halvorsen, *Mellom Moskva og Berlin. Norges Kommunistiske Parti under ikke-angrepspakten mellom Sovjet-Unionen og Tyskland 1939–1941* (Oslo: Universitetsforlaget, 1996).
18. Wilson, *SOE Norwegian Section History* (unpublished MSS) p.23, (NRM).
19. See the SOE Collection, (NRM).
20. Ibid.
21. Olav Riste, *'London-Regjeringa': Norge i krigsalliansen 1940–1945* (Vol.1: 1940–1942), (Oslo: Det Norske Samlaget, 1973).
22. Wilson, *SOE Norwegian Section History*, cited in Kjeldstadli, *Hjemmestyrkene*, p.184.
23. The archives of the Norwegian High Command (Forsvarets Overkommando, FO) Archive, File 32, (NRM).
24. FO Rapport Del.1, p.16. Part one of several official reports from the Norwegian High Command released in 1945 (NRM).
25. Kraglund and Moland, *Hjemmefront*, p.128.
26. *Rettstidende*, (Court Reports), October 1948, p.164.
27. See, for example, Magne Skodvin, *Samtid og historie: utvalde artiklar og avhandlingar* (Oslo: Det Norske Samlaget, 1975) and *Som Seilene Fylles Av Stormen* (Oslo: Det Norske Samlaget, 1982). See also the articles written by Skodvin in Helge Paulsen (ed.) *Norge og den 2.verdenskrig: mellom nøytrale og allierte* (Oslo: Det Norske Samlaget, 1968) and Helge Paulsen (ed.) *Norge og den 2.verdenskrig: 1940: fra nøytral til okkupert* (Oslo: Det Norske Samlaget, 1969).
28. Egil Ulateig, *Med rett til å drepe* (Oslo: Tiden Norsk Forlag, 1996).
29. Hans Frederik Dahl, Guri Hjeltnes, Berit Nøkelby, Nils Johan Ringdal and Øystein Sørensen (eds.) *Norsk Krigsleksikon 1940–1945* (Oslo: Cappelen, 1995).

30. Odd Bjørn Fure, 'Kampen mot glemselen' (Oslo: Universitetsforlaget, 1997).
31. See, Kåre Olsen, *Krigens barn. De norske krigsbarna og deres mødre* (Oslo: Forum – Aschehoug, 1999).
32. Most of the interviews were conducted in the 1960s and 1970s. The tapes are located in the NRM.

–9–

Comparing Resistance and Resistance Movements

Bob Moore

It is tempting to assume that the countries of Western Europe were sufficiently alike in 1940 to allow for a straightforward comparison of the development of resistance organizations and activities. Certainly there were some superficial similarities, but as the preceding chapters have shown, the societies involved were far from identical, and their differing political, economic and social structures on the eve of war undoubtedly had an effect on the forms taken by resistance in the following four or five years of occupation. Moreover, it is important to remember that the structures of German rule also varied from one territory to another. Thus at a political level, the burden of German rule was probably felt more immediately in countries like Belgium, the Netherlands and Norway, than in Denmark or Vichy France, which were left with a greater degree of self government. This distinction may well have been tempered to an extent by the Nazis' perception of the conquered, where so-called 'Aryans' were treated with more circumspection than other nationalities. In this context, the Norwegians, Danes, Dutch and Flemings may have been better placed initially than other conquered peoples. Only over time, as the war turned against Nazi Germany, did these distinctions become blurred. In the later years of occupation, Nazi rule became increasingly onerous for all concerned and was extended to include territories and peoples previously left alone. The previously unoccupied parts of Vichy France were taken over in November 1942, the Danes were similarly treated when their government ended its collaboration in the summer of 1943, and northern Italians suddenly found themselves overrun with German soldiery as the Badoglio regime, which had replaced Mussolini, sued for peace with the Allies.

Differences in the nature and objectives of Nazi rule are only one factor in qualifying any comparative study of resistance. The circumstances in each country also have to be taken into account. One example is the topography, both of specific regions and of entire countries. Mountainous and sparsely populated areas undoubtedly provided scope for activities that would have been impossible in an urban environment or in country-side that provided little or no natural cover. Thus the rural landscape of southern France could give sanctuary to an underground *maquisard* movement, and the provinces of northern Italy had similar advantages for the partisan movement after 1943, but going into hiding in Denmark the Channel Islands or the Netherlands presented very different problems and served to limit the scope of both organizational and practical activities. Political boundaries were also influential. Access to a neutral frontier, as in the case of Norway with Sweden, or France with Spain and Switzerland seems to have some effect on the scope and potential for resistance, for example in the creation of escape lines for Allied airmen and others pursued by the Nazis. While these elements have always formed part of the analysis, there are others that also bear some examination. For example, the differences between rural and urban-industrial environments for the participation in, and attitudes towards resistance. In this context, the peasantry in both France and Italy were undoubtedly ambivalent.[1] For as long as the Vichy authorities continued to favour rural life and target the urban working class, the French peasantry saw little reason to mount opposition to Pétain's regime or the Germans, especially while STO held out some hope of the prisoners-of-war being repatriated. In common with their Italian counterparts, they also equated resistance with communism, a prejudice that was reinforced by adherence to traditional Catholicism. This therefore highlights another factor, namely the role played by religious belief and church affiliation within particular societies or communities, and the influence of both Catholic and Protestant Church leaders in advocating or deprecating opposition to the occupying power.

While these are important qualifications, there are clearly many elements common to all or most of the case studies presented here. The relative mildness of German policy towards the countries defeated in the spring and summer of 1940 seems to have been a major feature in the initial phase of occupation. Most populations seem to have expected something far more onerous and were thus surprised to find enemy soldiery being polite and even courteous. Even the Belgians, who had more reason for fear than most, having experienced a German occupation less than a generation before, were taken aback by the 'correctness' of the occupiers' behaviour. This gap between expectation and reality undoubtedly served to calm popular unease and removed justification for immediate protests. The German desire to minimize manpower costs and not to alienate the conquered nations was undoubtedly initially a success. It appears that the vast majority of the populations in north-western Europe were content to resume their normal, everyday lives, and accept what they saw as the reality of occupation.

This seems to have remained the case for as long as the Germans continued their 'hands-off' approach. Thus bureaucracies in Belgium, Norway and the Netherlands were left in place, as were entire governmental structures in Denmark and the unoccupied parts of France. Many prisoners-of-war were released from captivity or just demobilized as an act of good faith, with only the French and some Belgian soldiers being held as permanent 'hostages'.[2] In most countries, this period of acclimatization continued into 1941. Inevitably, frictions did occur as populations had to learn what was permitted and what was no longer permitted. Many early protests were engendered, not by the Germans, but by the behaviour of indigenous fascists or National Socialists and the fear that these formerly marginal political extremists might be favoured by the occupying power. For the most part, such fears remained unfounded as Berlin quickly realized that these small groups would never achieve any substantial support, and their leaders were more of a liability than an asset. Thus National Socialist leaders like Anton Mussert in the Netherlands or the Rexist, Léon Degrelle were never given the roles they coveted. Only in Norway did Vidkun Quisling, the leader of the indigenous National Socialists, achieve a degree of power as Prime Minister from February 1942 onwards, but even he clashed regularly with the German plenipotentiary, Reichskommissar Josef Terboven.

There is no doubt that in 1940 and even 1941, rational minds in the occupied countries could see little, if any, chance of German rule being overthrown in the foreseeable future. Axis armies were apparently driving all before them. Only when the Germans' all-conquering image began to be dented by the first failures against Soviet forces on the Eastern Front, and the US entered the war at the end of 1941 could people begin to believe that an alternative future was a possibility. Apart from convincing many that the Germans had finally taken on a task that was beyond them, the attack on the Soviet Union also served to simplify matters for communist parties in Western Europe. Although horribly compromised by Comintern directives after the Nazi–Soviet non-aggression treaty was signed in August 1939, it is clear that many communists refused to remain passive in response to persecution, either from the Nazis or from indigenous police forces. The party organizations tried to uphold the Comintern line, but the realities of life at grassroots level forced the membership to rely on their clandestine cell networks for their own protection, and from this mode of self-defence (a form of resistance in itself) it was only a short step to the establishment of more proactive organizations. The precise timing and nature of shifts in policy in each occupied country may have varied slightly, but the general pattern was very similar across all of Western Europe.

Despite Moscow's attempts to control them, some individual communists were among the earlier resisters against Nazi rule in Western Europe. However, their counterparts in this early period came from the other end of the ideological spectrum. These were the right-wing nationalist groups that emerged in the first weeks and months after the capitulation. Often based on military connections and disaffected members of the officer corps who refused to accept surrender and wanted to go on fighting, these early organizations had similar advantages to the communists. Although unused to clandestine activity, they could rely on personal links through the institutions of the armed forces to extend networks within a trusted circle. Many, as in Norway, Belgium and the Netherlands, also had strong royalist elements, and individuals from these groups often provided the first contacts between indigenous resistance and the governments in exile in London.

These first attempts at resistance organization by both left and right generally proved ill equipped to meet the challenge of an increasingly ruthless enemy. Even the communists, who were far more used to clandestine activity and cell organization, found it difficult to maintain security when faced with the attentions of the police, the Gestapo and their informers. It soon became apparent that errors could have fatal consequences, and many of these early networks were 'rolled up' by the Germans within months or even weeks of their inception. While these early efforts may now be viewed as naïve amateurism, there is no doubt that they did lead to important lessons being learned, as would-be resisters became aware of what was required to maintain successful networks and began to understand more clearly the nature of the enemy they faced. This increasing professionalization seems common to resistance in all occupied countries, with specialization of function and personnel becoming more prevalent, and better security systems being implemented to counter the threat from informers. Although many of these changes were instituted as a result of hard-won and often costly experience 'on the ground', increasing contacts with the Allied military and espionage services also undoubtedly helped this process. However, these agencies were also still learning – as the disaster of the *Englandspiel* makes abundantly clear.

This raises another issue, namely the relationship between resistance organizations inside occupied Europe, and the various Allied agencies that attempted to work with them or harness them to further Allied war aims. The competition and often outright hostility between the likes of SOE, SIS and the military planners on the one hand, and the multitude of different organizations in each of the occupied countries on the other, made contacts and any form of coordination very difficult in the early period. It could be argued that all parties had the same basic objective – to drive out the German invader – but this was probably the only point on which all were agreed. The story of relationships between London and the indigenous resistance organizations shows that there were disagreements on targets, methods and objectives. Allied military impera-tives were often at variance with the desires and political agendas of individual networks. The Norwegian case provides a good example of London wanting some specific resistance operations for military reasons when those inside the country counselled caution. Conversely, the build up to the Allied invasion of north-west Europe in the summer of 1944 saw London doing its best to keep enthusiasm for direct action in France and the Low Countries in check.

There was a further element in this already complex set of relationships, namely the governments in exile in London. Although they were the official representatives of their countries and could negotiate directly with the major powers, this position was more nominal than real. There is no doubt that the exiled Heads of State, Wilhelmina of the Netherlands and Haakon of Norway did act as important figureheads for resisters in their respective realms, and were keen to receive any men or women who had managed to escape to England. However, the influence of the governments in exile on resistance organizations was extremely limited and many networks ignored their countrymen and dealt instead primarily or exclus-ively with British or American agencies. Exceptional in this was the Free French administration led by de Gaulle. While never a government in exile, there is no doubt that the General had more frequent, if seldom cordial, contacts with the British and American leaderships than the other governments in exile, and his organization also played a pivotal role in the unification of the major resistance groups inside occupied France during 1943 and 1944.

As was suggested in the introduction, there has been a tendency for English-language publications to focus on the European resistance primarily as a facet of the Allied war effort against the Axis, and to judge it in relation to the success of that war effort. This approach has yielded a great deal of information about both the Allied agencies and their partners inside occupied Europe, but it has tended to marginalize or ignore features of resistance unconnected with the outside. While this balance has been redressed since the 1980s, with greater attention being paid to indigenous movements and networks with the Allies, there remains the discussion of how the populations at large reacted to occupation. Active resisters were never more than a small proportion of the total population in any occupied country, and narrow definitions of resistance would exclude others from consideration. Yet, as the foregoing chapters show, there were also many aspects of 'popular' opposition and resistance to Nazi occupation.

A detailed examination of the 'muddled majority', those who were neither active resisters nor active collaborators, has taken a long time to emerge, and to some extent had its methodological origins in research carried out on public opinion in Germany. In attempting to assess the reactions of populations at large to the occupation, a number of general patterns emerge. While many thousands engaged in forms of passive protests against specific measures, or against the Germans in general in the early years of occupation, these were merely tokens and seldom if ever hindered Nazi objectives. The growing or wearing of significant flowers, or the use of particular symbols, was more of an embarrassment to the ruling Germans than a real threat to their dominance. To some extent, the level of these protests depended on the degree of ideological imposition placed on indigenous populations. This varied according to the Nazis' view of the people concerned and their freedom to act. Thus in countries like Norway and the Netherlands, where control was more-or-less complete and the people were considered as 'fellow-Aryans', attempts were made to introduce national socialist ideology, for example into the education system. Elsewhere, there were constraints. In Belgium for example, the military government resisted SS and NSDAP attempts at nazification and thereby prevented such complete interference

The overriding factor in the development of popular resistance against Nazi rule was undoubtedly the changing war situation. Initial intentional resistance from the political extremes of left and right was supplemented by a much more widespread functional opposition to German rule as new regulations began to infringe on patterns of everyday life and the accepted norms of society. These ranged from the apparently trivial to the funda-mental and provoked a range of responses from avoidance, through individual and collective protests to permanent and organized resistance. For example, the German attempt to confiscate radio sets to prevent owners listening to BBC broadcasts led to many receivers being hidden. Other ordinances were also ignored or avoided. This change in the nature of Nazi rule produced a situation in which normally law-abiding citizens would find themselves becoming criminalized merely for adhering to previously permitted modes of behaviour. As the situation for the Nazis became more desperate, both at home and in the occupied territories, so their legislation became more and more draconian and the attendant punishments more severe. One has only to look at the number of offences carrying the death penalty in Germany by 1944–5 and the number of sentences carried to out to see the scale of this escalation. Yet this took place at a time when, for example, large numbers of men and women found it necessary to flout laws on black marketeering just in order to feed their families.[3] Thus in the final stages of the war and occupation, opposition and resistance could be characterized more as an imperative for survival than a choice born of ideological or ethical principles.

There is no doubt that large numbers of people in all the occupied countries did ultimately disobey laws and ordinances imposed by the Germans. Insofar as this behaviour hindered German objectives, then it has to be considered as a form of resistance. Carried out by large enough numbers, it ceased to be just an irritant and could develop into a major problem for the occupiers, and for the Nazi regime as a whole. The best example of this, again common to all the occupied territories, including Italy, was the Germans' economic demands, and specifically their demand for labour from occupied Western Europe that acted as the catalyst for a mass movement towards illegality. In almost every country, the desire to avoid being drafted or deported for labour in Germany sent many hundreds of thousands of men and women underground. Whether they fled to the hills, or merely moved from one district to another to avoid detection depended on the circumstances. In addition to these *réfractaires*, there were also the many people who sheltered them, or helped in other ways. They, too, effectively became implicated in the illegality and added immeasurably to the numbers involved, especially in rural areas. At one level, all these people were engaging in resistance – by attempting to frustrate German policies, but it is important to bear in mind the qualification that the graduation from avoiding the labour draft to active resistance was not an automatic one. Probably the majority of people who went into hiding to avoid being drafted in this way did nothing more. Their resistance was limited to protecting their own interests and depriving the Germans of their services, but no more than that. Nonetheless, as the search for labour became more and more ruthless in the final year of the war, so the numbers of people available to be drawn into other forms of resistance grew enormously and inflated beyond all recognition those who could then claim to be resisters.

While these people may have arrived late on the scene, they did possess some credibility as part of the resistance, but there were many others who attempted to jump on the bandwagon at an even later stage – as the

Allied armies were at the door. These 'resisters of the thirteenth hour' were essentially opportunists who had seen which way the wind was blowing. Moreover there were others whose pasts were less than unsullied who attempted to cover their tracks by claiming to be resisters. Given the clandestine nature of the enterprise, these claims were initially hard to disprove. One interesting example is that of the Paris police. Having been agents of the Vichy regime from the beginning of the occupation, they found themselves involved in securing the city during and immediately after the German withdrawal. As a result, they were hailed as part of the French resistance that had liberated the capital. Only when the police resumed their normal functions and those whom they had helped deport started to return from Germany did the honeymoon period come to an end.[4]

The importance of self or community interest in motivating opposition to German measures among populations at large may go some way to explaining the relative failure across Western Europe to subvert another Nazi ideological objective, namely the deportation of the Jews. Only in Denmark can one speak of a major contribution from resistance organizations in the saving of the Jewish population, but even here, the specific circumstances and relative lateness of the German actions undoubtedly facilitated matters. While the persecution itself did lead to the establishment of some Jewish resistance groups, these often had to operate independently. Moreover, the relative isolation of the Jews from mainstream society in many countries created barriers to help from individual gentiles, and the beginnings of the mass deportations in July 1942 came before major organized resistance groups had been established. Thus only later were the groups and individuals dedicated to helping Jews absorbed into these larger organizations, or at least provided with greater material help. Thus, the rescue of Jews from Nazi persecution has tended to be studied as an element within the history of the holocaust and divorced from mainstream analyses of national resistance to Nazi occupation. As a result, it has developed a distinct and separate historiography with important contributions from sociologists as well as historians.[5]

One element that comes across clearly in many of the chapters is the importance of the clandestine press during the occupation period. Often overshadowed by more direct forms of action, there is little doubt that illegal newspapers, broadsheets, and pamphlets played a crucial role in many areas, and in a number of respects. Their sheer numbers in each country are surprising – although issues were often sporadic and circulations difficult to estimate. In addition, some early examples were little more than typed sheets passed from hand to hand, and often produced by small groups, families, or even individuals. Their most obvious function was as a conduit for information – a function that increased in importance as the Germans restricted access to news. In this way, resistance newspapers could pass on local information as well as details of the war in general gleaned from BBC broadcasts and elsewhere. However, it could be argued that this was only one facet of their importance. The mere existence of such newspapers demonstrated to the population at large, at a time when normal social contacts were restricted, that there were other people determined to speak out against the Germans. Thus they could become forces for cohesion within particular communities or provide linkage between like-minded people in different areas – providing a 'voice' for the resistance. Some were attached to overtly political organizations, most notably the communist party, but others began as forms of protest in their own right which later gave rise to movements engaging in a whole range of activities. Another crucial element was their function as a forum for discussion, both about the conduct of resistance and about the future in the post-liberation period. The clandestine press became the intellectual battlefield on which ideas about political, social and economic reconstruction were championed or denigrated and thus provided a yardstick of opinion for those on the outside, including the governments-in-exile.

Another factor that emerges specifically from the French case, but which may have resonances elsewhere is that of resistance as a long-standing tradition. In most countries of Western Europe, one could point to communist and radical left-wing parties organizing against the (bourgeois) state in the 1920s and 1930s. While such parties did have an 'official' existence and could generally organize and campaign openly, they were the subject of close surveillance by the police and security forces and thus developed a clandestine existence as well – something that was to stand them in good stead when the occupation began. However, one can also identify traditions of resistance to state authority that stretch back much further. In the case of France, back to the revolution of 1789 and the French Constitution of 1793,[6] or even back to the Cathar heretics of the thirteenth century.[7] These were traditional responses to attempted extensions of state power, or the impositions of what were seen as unreasonable demands on the people. In effect, offences against the norms of the society. Thus while the fact of occupation may not have encouraged any specific forms of resistance as it did not bring any real changes to the day-to-day existences of most people, the increasing German ideological and economic impositions on societies did provoke a response.

It is also important to recognise that much resistance in occupied countries was directed, not at the occupiers themselves, but at the

indigenous national socialist or fascist fellow travellers. This conceptuali-
zation of resistance as civil war rather than as a war of liberation has
been prominent in Italian historiography where there is plenty of evidence
presented of partisan warfare after September 1943 being directed
primarily against the residual fascists of Mussolini's Salò Republic rather
than the Germans. Explanations for this include the possibility that the
fascists were an easier target or that they were primarily responsible for
the attempted suppression of resistance activities among fellow Italians
while the Germans concentrated on warfare against the advancing Allies.
However, another explanation may be that this form of civil war had more
to do with resistance groups jockeying for position in anticipation of an
Allied victory and the reconstruction of an Italian state. Similar patterns
can be found in France during the latter stages of the war, culminating
with armed resisters openly taking on the Milice in the streets.[8] Yet, both
there and in other occupied countries such as Norway and the Netherlands,
attacks on perceived or actual collaborators had been a facet of the
resistance struggle from the very beginning of the occupation. This
included intimidation or even assassination of over-zealous civil servants
and direct actions against collaborationist organizations and indigenous
Nazi parties.

In Germany, any acts deemed detrimental to the state could be
interpreted as treasonable and thus subject to the harshest penalties. This
moral or ethical issue may well have influenced many inside the Nazi
state before desperation set in during the final year of the war. However,
many of the occupied countries also retained the semblance of a functioning state, and this meant that attacks on bureaucracies or functionaries
could similarly be interpreted as treasonable activities. The greater the
degree of indigenous autonomy, the more of an issue it was likely to
become. Certainly, the *Pétainiste* Vichy governments attempted to equate
loyalty to *la patrie* with loyalty to the collaborationist regime – thus
implying that any acts directed against it were acts detrimental to the
interests of France. While the use of patriotic and nationalist sentiment
to encourage conformity lost its effectiveness as Vichy and other collaborating regimes continually acquiesced to ever greater German demands,
it undoubtedly created doubts in some minds about the legitimacy of
resistance.

Another general trend was the gradual unification or at least coordination of resistance groups from different regions or with different political,
organizational or ideological backgrounds. In some cases, this unification
was driven by external influences. Governments-in-exile saw the need to
co-ordinate the internal resistance organizations, both to streamline their

activities and make them more efficient, and to bring them under control. Similarly, Allied military planners and the various British espionage and counterespionage organizations were keen on centralized control and often made this a condition of help in the form of weapons, food and other supplies. Underlying the pressure from London was the fear that without some form of unity the resistance would be less effective, prone to fragmentation and internecine strife, and likely to become dominated by the communists. All these outcomes were seen as undesirable, the latter especially so. Thus, driven by governments-in-exile in London or by the British authorities, some form of co-operation and unity was established, even in France where the work of Jean Moulin brought together disparate groups and established the CNR in March 1943.[9]

In France, the gradual collapse of Vichyite authority and, in Italy, the discrediting of the Fascist regime as the Germans arrived from the north gave the various resistance organizations some chance to participate in direct action to secure the liberation of their respective countries. They could never have succeeded unaided and they knew that the end of the war rested on the ultimate victory of the Allied armies, but this did not prevent them engaging in some military activity, often at great cost. Thus the *maquis* was sufficiently strong to try and establish a 'national redoubt' in southern France in the days following the Normandy landings and expectation of the Allied advance from the Mediterranean coast. Their establishment of an enclave in the Vercors flying the French *tricolore* within sight of the German garrison at Grenoble was partly an act of defiance but also a political statement about the French playing a role in the liberation. This proved to be a suicidal enterprise as, although the *maquisards* were able to hold their own against German patrols, they were soon faced with a full-scale German assault, and in the absence of expected Allied reinforcements, were routed. Elsewhere the FFI waged an unofficial war against the Germans, carrying out sabotage actions and even taking enemy prisoners. A similar pattern emerged in northern Italy where the partisans were able to drive both the Germans and the Fascists out of certain valleys and establish self-governing enclaves. These may have been the result of military activity, but there is no doubt that, unlike the French examples, they also had an ideological basis – important as much for the system of government they had established as for the fact that they were free of Axis control.

With the exception of the Italian and French networks and organizations, the resistance generally played little or no role in the military liberation of Western Europe. Having reluctantly been held back from precipitate action by the planners in London in the expectation of a role when the Allied armies drew near, the resisters were nonetheless to be disappointed. The German withdrawal from northern France and almost the whole of Belgium meant that the resisters there had little to do except welcome Allied soldiery on their way northwards. Similarly, the Norwegians and Danes found their countries liberated, not by military action, but by the stroke of a pen when General Jodl surrendered all German forces on behalf of the German government at Reims on 7 May 1945. It could be argued that the Dutch resistance north of the great rivers was asked to contribute to its own liberation, but paid a heavy price for so doing. The limited sabotage actions and the railway strike demanded by Allied planners in tandem with Operation Market Garden in September 1944 were delivered, but the failure to establish a bridgehead at Arnhem left the country in German hands for a further eight months and with resisters, strikers and the general population at the mercy of an increasingly vindictive occupation regime.

One final question that cannot be ignored because of its importance to the overall perception of popular responses to the occupation is the question of numbers. Few would now doubt the characterization of responses across Western Europe as consisting of a minority of active resisters and outright collaborators with the vast majority of the population as being neither one nor the other. However, even if one accepts this pattern, it does not address the proportion of people in each category. Perhaps in response to the charge that latecomers had inflated numbers, estimates of the numbers of active resisters by historians of the occupation have tended to take a narrow view of what constituted resistance and have consequently arrived at very low participation rates. For France, Paxton puts the total at 2 per cent while de Jong's estimate for the Netherlands is a mere 0.6 per cent.[10] Both accept that the number of passive resisters and sympathizers was much larger, perhaps tenfold or even more. However, attempts to verify such claims are fraught with difficulty and, if Sweets is to be believed, we will never have a statistical description of the French (or any other) resistance 'short of a roll call in the hereafter'.[11]

If numbers remain a puzzle for the historians, so too does the role of women in the resistance. Every movement could boast a few heroines who were recognized and honoured in the postwar period, but their numbers were extremely small as the French case indicates. The highest award for resisters was the *compagnon de la libération* where of 1,059 awards, only six went to women.[12] This understating of women's contribution to resistance and the liberation may owe much to the perception of resistance as essentially a male activity and the rewarding of specific types of activity. However, if one takes a wider view of resistance infrastructures, then the involvement of women increases exponentially. There is no doubt that women played crucial roles in hiding, feeding and clothing both resisters, Jews and others on the run from the Germans.[13] Moreover, they were essential to many forms of direct action. Later in the war, when men could not be seen in public or make journeys without arousing the suspicion that they were avoiding labour service, women could move around much more easily; carrying messages and clandestine newspapers, acting as couriers or escorts for those in hiding, or moving supplies and equipment. Inevitably, quantifying these, and many other roles fulfilled by women throughout occupied Western Europe remains problematic, and in most countries, these lesser known and unsung heroines of the resistance still await their historians.[14] A rather different approach to this same question has been taken by Schwarz, who has examined the role played by women in the French resistance in breaching the gender stereotypes of the pre-war era and their engagement in activities which had previously been thought of as male preserves.[15]

Perhaps it should come as no surprise that the resistance as a separate political organization played little role in the reconstruction process in Western Europe. In the immediate post liberation period, resisters at local level, and even some national organisations did provide structures to maintain order and replacements for compromised or absent government functionaries, but these were never perceived as anything more than interim measures. The unity created in order to defeat the common enemy could not be maintained once the threat disappeared, and the inevitable fissures between groups with widely differing political and social agendas re-emerged. This was compounded by the suspicion with which the British, Americans and especially the governments-in-exile viewed the resistance. Fears of the communists and their front organisations were, if anything, heightened by the increasing frostiness in relations between the western powers and the Soviet Union. Right-wing organisations were seen as having anti-democratic tendencies were also regarded as a threat in some quarters. While the communist and social democratic parties did well in the first postwar elections, there was no question of resistance alliances being maintained. Moreover, although some of the leaders became important figures in postwar politics, those that did were diffused across the ideological spectrum, and many others felt themselves excluded and their achievements ignored. While changes in party structures and groupings were inevitable, especially on the right, it could be argued that the pattern of politics after 1945 owed more to its inheritances from 1939 than from the experiences of occupation. This apparent lack of real change has served to reinforce the idea that the reconstruction process in western Europe was more about continuities, and that the effects of war and the occupation period had few long term effects.

If it can be argued that the role of the resistance was limited in terms of effecting liberation, and in terms of the political reconstruction, there is no doubt that it did have one important function - that of providing a focus for the reconstruction of postwar social cohesion. As the war came to an end, so societies attempted to develop the myth of nations of resisters in order to gloss over the less edifying aspects of their behaviour during the occupation. This was true across Europe, and even in Germany where the occupying Allied powers were keen to rehabilitate some sections of the population to act as the basis for co-operation in the future. The identification of 'good' Germans extended to those who had been martyred after the attempt to assassinate Hitler in July 1944 and ultimately created the unlikely linkage of many right-wing military and aristocratic figures with the restoration of democracy in West Germany.

One element that comes across clearly in all the case studies is the recognition that resistance in all its forms can no longer be seen or analysed in isolation. The participants, motivating forces, forms, structures and objectives can only be fully understood in relation to the society from which they emerged. To that extent, recent scholarship has tried to place resistance in a wider social context. Thus, for example, the emergence of resistance and collaboration during the period of Nazi occupation and oppression are now seen as two sides of the same coin rather than as two entirely separate phenomena. Moreover, the analysis of a society as a whole, rather than just the actions of a minority, allows questions to be asked about the 'muddled majority', the overwhelming mass of people in all the occupied countries, and perhaps in Germany as well, who were neither resisters nor collaborators. The foregoing chapters make abundantly clear what work has already been done in analysing resistance in the different countries of occupied Western Europe, but they also demonstrate that there are still many aspects of the subject that have been under-researched or ignored altogether. While work already in progress will answer some of the questions posed, there is undoubtedly a need for historians to take up the challenge posed by Semelin and others, to place the phenomenon known as 'resistance' into the wider framework of the national and perhaps even the international social histories of World War Two. This will never supersede the regional, local and communal peculiarities which serve to confound detailed comparison but form the bedrock of resistance narratives, however it may serve to cast new light and suggest new perspectives on the behaviour patterns and motivations of those involved.

Notes

1. José Gotovitch and Pieter Lagrou, 'La Résistance française dans le paysage européen' *Les Cahiers De L'Institut D'Histoire de Temps Présent* XXXVII (1997) pp.147–79 esp. pp.148–9. For the Netherlands, see also Coen Hilbrink, *De Illegalen. Illegaliteit in Twente en het aangrenzende Salland 1940–5* (Oldenzaal, 1989) and for Italy, Roger Absolom, 'Escaping into History: Italian Peasants and Allied Prisoners of War in the *Resistenza*, 1943–44 in Jean-Marie Guillon and Robert Menchinni, *La Résistance et les Europé du sud* (Paris: L'Harmattan, 1999).

2. Warmbrunn, *The German Occupation of Belgium 1940–1944* (New York: Peter Lang, 1993) pp.188–9.

3. See, for example, Jeremy Noakes, *Nazism 1919–1945 A Documentary Reader, Vol.4. The German Home Front in World War II* (Exeter: Exeter University Press, 1998) pp.572–6.

4. Simon Kitson, 'The Police in the Liberation of Paris' in H.R.Kedward and Nancy Wood (eds.) *The Liberation of France: Image and Event* (Oxford: Berg, 1995) pp.43–56.

5. It is only possible to list a few of the major academic studies of rescue here. Sam and Pearl Oliner, *The Altruistic Personality: Rescuers of Jews in Nazi Europe* (New York: Free Press, 1988); Nechama Tec, *When Light Pierced the Darkness: Christian Rescue of Jews in Nazi-Occupied Poland* (New York/Oxford: Oxford University Press, 1986); Eva Fogelmann, *The Courage to Care: Rescuers of Jews during the Holocaust* (London: Victor Gollancz, 1995); Modechai Paldiel, *The Path of the Righteous: Gentile Rescuers of the Jews during the Holocaust* (Hoboken NJ: Ktav, 1993) Yisrael Gutman and Efraim Zuroff (eds) *Rescue Attempts during the Holocaust: Proceedings of the Second Yad Vashem International Historical Conference* (Jerusalem: Yad Vashem, 1977)

6. Semelin, *Sans armes face à Hitler*, p.vii.

7. Kedward, *In Search of the Maquis*, pp.150–1, 236, 270.

8. Bertram M. Gordon, *Collaborationism in France during the Second World War* (Ithaca: Cornell University Press, 1980), pp.326–7. John M. Sweets, *Choices in Vichy France: The French under German Occupation* (New York/Oxford: Oxford University Press, 1986) pp.224–5.

9. Foot, *SOE in France*, p.82.

10. Robert O. Paxton, *Vichy France* (New York: Alfred A. Knopf, 1972) pp.294–5. Louis de Jong, *The Netherlands and Nazi Germany*

(Cambridge MS: Harvard University Press, 1990) pp.47–8. See also, Bob de Graaff, 'Collaboratie en Verzet' in: J.P.B. Jonker et al.. *Vijftig jaar na de inval* (Amsterdam: SDU, 1985) p.95 H.Balthazar, 'België onder Duitse bezetting' 10 mei 1940–8 september 1944' in D.P. Blok et al. (eds) *Algemene Geschiedenis der Nederlanden* XV (Haarlem: Fibula–Van Dishoeck, 1982) pp.29–54, esp. p.47. W. Meyers and F. Selleslagh, *De vijand te lijf: de Belgen in het verzet* (Antwerpen, 1984) p.13. L .de Jong, *Het Koninkrijk der Nederlanden in de Tweede Wereldoorlog* VII ('s-Gravenhage: Staatsuitgeverij, 1976) p.1047.

11. Sweets, *Choices*, p.228.
12. Claire Gorrara, 'Reviewing Gender and the Resistance: the Case of Lucie Aubrac' in: Kedward and Wood, *The Liberation*, p.52 fn.7.
13. As evidence of this, one might cite the number of women awarded the title 'Righteous among the Nations' by Yad Vashem for their work in helping Jews during the Nazi era.
14. There are some exceptions. See for example, Jane Slaughter, *Women and the Italian Resistance 1943–1945* (Denver CO: Arden, 1997) and Margaret Collins Weitz, *Sisters in the Resistance: How Women Fought to Free France, 1940–1945* (New York: John Wiley, 1995).
15. Paula Schwarz, 'Redefining Resistance – Women's Activism in Wartime France' in: Margaret T.Higonnet et al. (eds) *Behnid the Lines – Gender and the Two World Wars* (New Haven: Yale University Press, 1987) pp.141–53. Paula Schwarz, '*Partisanes* and Gender Politics in Vichy France' *French Historical Studies* XVI/1 (1989) pp.126–51.

Glossary

AA	Auswärtiges Amt. The German Foreign Ministry.
Abwehr	The foreign and counterintelligence organization of the German High Command, headed by Admiral Wilhelm Canaris.
ANCC	Anglo-Norwegian Collaboration Committee founded in 1942.
Armée Secrète (Bel.)	Secret Army, the military resistance formation originating in Belgian royalist military circles and recognized by the government in exile at the end of 1943.
Armée Secrète (Fra.)	The military wing of the MUR (q.v.) led from the winter of 1942–43 by General Delestraint. Although theoretically separate from the maquis, in practice this was widely ignored.
ARP	British Air Raid Protection service.
AT	Arbeidstjenesten. Norwegian Labour Organization ultimately used by the Germans to recruit men for work in Germany.
Attentisme	Literally the policy of 'wait and see'. Also rendered in Italian as attendismo.
BBC	British Broadcasting Corporation.
Befehlshaber	(German) commander.
BOPA	Danish communist sabotage organization.
Caviar	French escape network created by industrialist Paul Joly.
CDJ	Comité de Défense des Juifs. Belgian Jewish resistance organization.
CDLL	Ceux de la Libération. A resistance movement in the occupied northern zone of France.
CDLR	Ceux de la Résistance. A resistance movement in the occupied zone of France.
CFLN	Comité Français de Libération Nationale. The governing body of the Free French,

	established under the leadership of Generals Giraud and de Gaulle.
CGE	Comité Générale d'Etudes. Committee created by General Charles de Gaulle to consider France's political future after the liberation.
CLN	Comitato di Liberazione Nazionale. (Italian National Liberation Committee.) A body formed by delegates from the principal anti-Fascist parties to co-ordinate their political strategy as the war came to an end.
CLNAI	Comitato di Liberazione Nazionale Alta Italia (Italian National Liberation Committee – Northern Italy) Organisation based in Milan created by representatives of anti-Fascist parties to coordinate the armed resistance inside German occupied territory. Although linked to the CLN, the CLNAI enjoyed a good deal of autonomy.
CNR	Conseil National de la Résistance. French National Council of Resistance formed in May 1943 to unite all elements of the resistance. Its main role was to give shape to resistance aims for a liberated France.
College van Vertrouwensmannen	College of Trustees. The representatives of the Dutch government in exile inside the Netherlands during the last months of occupation.
Combat	French clandestine newspaper in the unoccupied zone founded by Captain Henri Frenay, which gave rise to a resistance movement bearing the same name. Ultimately incorporated into the CNR.
Comète	French escape network.
Confrérie-Notre-Dame	One of the largest Gaullist information networks in occupied France.
CPN	Communistische Partij in Nederland. The Dutch Communist Party.
CVL	Corpo Volontari per la Libertà (Volunteer Corps for Freedom). A body created in 1944 to co-ordinate the actions of the various branches of armed resistance in occupied Italy.

CVR	Combattant volontaire de la Résistance. Award made to French resisters after the war.
DF	Défence de la France. French clandestine newspaper.
DKP	Danish Communist Party.
(Ver)Dinaso	Verbond van Dietsche Nationaal-Solidaristen. Explicitly fascist movement founded by Joris van Severen in Belgium in 1931.
Engelandvaarders	Name given to Dutch men and women who escaped to England during the war.
Englandspiel	Codename given to the Abwehr operation that persuaded the British SOE that its network in the Netherlands had not been penetrated. It led to loss of fifty-four agents, fifty RAF personnel and a number of Dutch civilians.
Feldgendarmerie	German military police.
FFI	Forces Françaises de l'Intérieur. The official organization formed at the end of 1943 and charged with merging all armed resistance movements. Initially commanded by General Koenig, the FFI never achieved its aim of subordinating all the various groups under a single leadership and local groups retained much of their autonomy.
FN	Front National de lutte pour l'independence de la France. Umbrella organization for resistance movements created by the French communists.
FO	British Foreign Office.
FO	Forsvarets Overkommando. The Norwegian High Command in London.
FTPF	Francs-Tireurs et Partisans Français. The military wing of the FN in France, which was identified with the Communist Party, but recruited widely and consequently local groups often manifested a broader political spectrum.
Front de l'Independence	Broad-based Belgian resistance organisation founded by the communists in summer 1941 but including rank-and-file socialists and Catholics. (Onafhankelijksfront).

GAC	Grote Adviescommissie der Illegaliteit. Dutch Central Advisory Committee for Underground Groups created in 1944 at the behest of the government in exile.
GAP	Gruppi d'Azione Patriottica (Patriotic Action Groups) Groups of armed Italian partisans active in the principal Italian towns.
Geheime Feldpolizei	German secret military police.
GOIWN	Gemeenschap Oud-Illegale Werkers Nederland. The association of former illegal workers in the Netherlands.
GPRF	Gouvernement provisoir de la République Française. An organization which grew out of the CFLN and, led by General de Gaulle, became the de facto government of France at the liberation.
Grossgermanischen Reich	The greater German Reich.
Groupe G	Belgian sabotage team headed by scientists and engineers from the University of Brussels.
GUNS	Guernsey Underground News Service
HL	Hjemmefrontens Ledelse. The united leadership of the Norwegian resistance created in 1944.
Hoherer SS-und Polizeiführer	Higher SS and police leader.
Holdningskamp	Norwegian term meaning the battle for hearts and minds.
ISK	Internationaler Sozialistischer Kampfbund. German international socialist action group.
JCP	Jersey Communist Party.
JDM	Jersey Democratic Movement.
KK	Koordinasjonskomitèen. The co-ordinating committee of the Norwegian civilian resistance.
Komintern	The Communist (Third) International.
KPD	Kommunistische Partei Deutschlands. The German Communist Party.
Légion Belge	Precursor of the Belgian Armée Secrète and formed in early 1941 from different groups of right-wing career soldiers.

Libération-nord	Resistance organization in the occupied zone of France, which included representatives of the socialist and trade union movements.
Libération-sud	Resistance organization in the unoccupied zone of France, which included representatives of the socialist and trade union movements.
LKP	Landelijke Knokploegen. National action groups formed in the Netherlands in 1943 primarily to attack rationing offices and population registries to secure ration books and identity cards for resisters and those in hiding.
LO	Landelijke Organisatie voor Hulp aan Onderduikers. Dutch National organization for assistance to those underground. Founded at the end of 1942, it had 15, 000 members by the summer of 1944 and helped shelter between 250, 000 and 300, 000 people.
Maquis	Name given to Frenchmen and women who took refuge in the countryside to avoid compulsory labour service, and who were converted into armed bands of resisters.
MI9	A branch of the British War Office's military intelligence directorate and charged with helping Allied military personnel escape from enemy hands.
Militair Gezag	The Dutch Military Authorities attached to SHAEF.
Milorg	Militærorganisasjonen. The military organization of resistance in Norway.
MLN	Mouvement de Libération Nationale. Democratic French resistance movement founded by Captain Henri Frenay.
MRP	Mouvement Républicain Populaire. French political party founded after the liberation espousing Christian Democrat ideas.
MOI	Main d'Oeuvre Immigrée. A branch of the Belgian communist partisans composed of immigrants, mainly Jews, who were involved in actions against the deportation of Jews and

	the execution of collaborators in 1942 and 1943.
Mouvement National Belge	Belgian resistance movement created by Camille Joset, a hero of the resistance in World War One.
MUR	Mouvements Unis de la Résistance. The organization created by Jean Moulin that unified the three main resistance organizations in the southern zone of France, Combat, Libération-sud and Franc-Tireur.
NBS	Nederlandse Binnenlandse Strijdkrachten. Dutch forces of the interior, a name given to the unification of the Dutch resistance movements in 1944.
Nederlandse Unie	Broad based political grouping created in the Netherlands during 1940, but finally banned by the Germans in 1942.
NKP	Norges Kommunistiske Parti. The Norwegian Communist Party.
NS	Nasjonal Samling, The Norwegian Nazi Party.
NSF	Nationaal Steunfonds. The National Assistance Fund set up to finance resistance activities in the Netherlands.
OCM	Organisation Civile et Militaire. French resistance organization in the occupied zone made up from former army officers and right-wing intellectuals.
Operation Barbarossa	The German plan for the attack on the Soviet Union, implemented on 22 June 1941.
Operation Overlord	The Allied Plan for the amphibious assault on North West Europe, 6 June 1944.
Operation Weserübung	The German Plan for the Invasion of Denmark.
ORA	Organisation de Résistance de l'Armee. The French Army Resistance Organization which supported General Giraud in North Africa and subsequently joined the Gaullists in the CNR.
Ordedienst	The Order Service, a Dutch quasi-military organization set up by the resistance towards the end of the occupation.

Orpo	German Ordnungspolizei (Order Police) also referred to as Grüne Polizei.
OSS	Office of Strategic Services. The principal United States intelligence organization.
OT	Organisation Todt. A German semi-military unit created in 1938 to construct military installations.
Pd'A	Partito D'Azione (Action Party) One of the most active Italian political parties after the fall of the fascist regime in 1943. With a socialist-radical programme, it recruited mainly intellectuals and members of the upper classes.
PCF	Parti Communiste Français. The French Communist Party.
PCI	Partito Communista Italiano. Italian Communist Party. Principal anti-Fascist organization both before and after 1943, controlling the largest number of armed partisans in the German occupied regions of central and northern Italy.
Phalange Blanche	Small and isolated resistance group in the Belgian province of Hainault, responsible for the first attacks against collaborationists in August and September 1941.
Réfractaires	French men and women who went into hiding to avoid compulsory labour service (STO).
Reichsbevollmächtiger	(German) Reich Plenipotentiary.
Reichskommissar	Reich Commissioner. Title given to Arthur Seyss-Inquart as head of the German administration in the Netherlands.
Reichswehr	Name given to the German Army until 1935 when it was changed to Wehrmacht (the German Armed Forces) and included the newly refounded Navy and Air Force.
Rex	Catholic fascist movement created in 1936 by Léon Degrelle.
RSI	Repubblica Sociale Italiana. Italian Social Republic. created under the German aegis in the occupied north. Also known as the Salò Republic, the RSI engaged in a war against

	the partisans and attempted to establish some degree of autonomy from the Germans.
RVV	Raad van Verzet. Council of Resistance, the largest Dutch left-wing resistance organization.
SD	Sicherheitsdienst. The Nazi Party security service, which operated in tandem with the Gestapo.
SDAP	Sociaal-Democratisch Arbeiders Partij, the Dutch Social Democratic Party.
SFIO	Section Français de l'International Ouvrière. The French Socialist Party.
SHAEF	Supreme Headquarters Allied Expeditionary Force, which controlled the Allied Forces fighting in north-west Europe.
Sipo	Sicherheitspolizei – German security police.
SIS	The Secret Intelligence Service, also known as MI6, and responsible for the gathering of foreign intelligence relating to national security.
Sivorg	Sivilorganisasjonen. The Norwegian civilian resistance movement.
SL	Sentralledelsen. The central leadership of the Norwegian Milorg.
Société Générale (de Belgique)	Major business enterprise that controlled large sections of the Belgian economy and had great influence on government policy.
Socrates	Scheme set up by the Belgian government in exile to distribute financial aid to workers in hiding.
SOE	Special Operations Executive – a British secret service organization intended to promote subversive warfare in enemy-occupied territory.
SPD	Sozialdemokratische Partei Deutschlands. German Social Democratic Party.
STO	Service du Travail Obligatoire. Compulsory Labour Service for Frenchmen in Germany.
Storting	The Norwegian Parliament.
Témoignage Chrétien	French, Lyon-based, Catholic resistance group led by Father Chaillet.

ULTRA	Name given to the Allied decryptions or German messages sent using the ENIGMA coding machine.
VNV	Vlaamsch Nationaal Verbond. The Flemish National Union, founded in Belgium in 1933 to federate right-wing Flemish nationalist organisations.
Waffen-SS	The armed or military wing of the Nazi SS.
Wehrmacht	Collective term used to describe the German Armed Forces (army, navy and air force) from 1935 until the end of the Third Reich.

Bibliography
English Language Publications

General

Améry, J., et al. (eds) *Great Britain and European Resistance 1939–45 Proceedings of a Conference at St Antony's College, Oxford 10–16 December 1962* (Oxford: n.p., 1964).

European Resistance Movements 1939–1945: First International Conference on the History of the Resistance Movements held at Liege–Bruxelles–Breendonk 14–17 September 1958 (London: Pergamon, 1960).

European Resistance Movements 1939–1945: Second International Conference on the History of the Resistance Movements, Milan 1960 (London: Pergamon, 1964).

Foot, M.R.D. *Resistance: An Analysis of European Resistance to Nazism* (London: Eyre Methuen, 1976).

Foot, M.R.D. and Langley, J.M. *MI9: Escape and Evasion* (London: Bodley Head, 1970).

Hæstrup, J. *Europe Ablaze. An Analysis of the History of the European Resistance Movement* (Odense: Odense University Press, 1979).

Hawes, S and White, R. *Resistance in Europe, 1939–1945* (London: Allen Lane, 1975).

Kedward, H.R., 'Resistance: the discourse of personality' in K.G. Robertson (ed.) *War, Resistance and Intelligence: Essays in Honour of M.R.D. Foot (Barnsley: Leo Cooper, 1999)* pp.135–50.

Lagrou, P. *The Legacy of Nazi Occupation: Patriotic Memory and National Recovery in Western Europe 1945–1965* (Cambridge: Cambridge University Press, 1999).

Macksey, K. *The Partisans of Europe in World War II* (London: Hart-Davis, MacGibbon, 1975).

Michel, H. *The Shadow War: Resistance in Europe 1939–1945* (London: André Deutsch, 1972).

Michel, H. 'The Allies and the Resistance, *Yad Vashem Studies* V (1963) pp.317–32.

Michel, H. 'Jewish Resistance and the European Resistance Movement' *Yad Vashem Studies* VII (1968) pp.7–16.

Milward, A. 'The Economic and Strategic Effectiveness of Resistance' in Hawes and White, *Resistance in Europe* pp.186–203.

Rings, W. *Life with the Enemy: Collaboration and Resistance in Hitler's Europe, 1939–1945* (London: Wiedenfeld and Nicholson, 1982).

Rossiter, M. *Women in the Resistance* (New York: Praeger, 1986).

Seaman, M. 'Good Thrillers, But Bad History: A review of published works on the Special Operations Executive's work in France during the Second World War' in K.G. Robertson (ed.) *War, Resistance and Intelligence: Essays in Honour of M.R.D. Foot* (Barnsley: Leo Cooper, 1999) pp.119–34.

Seth, R.R. *The Undaunted: The Story of the Resistance in Western Europe* (London: F. Muller, 1956).

Semelin, J. *Unarmed Against Hitler: Civilian Resistance in Europe, 1939–1943* (New York: Praeger, 1993).

Siefken, H. 'What is Resistance' in: Siefken, H. and Vieregg, H. (eds) *Resistance to National Socialism: Arbeiter, Christen, Jugendliche, Eliten* (Nottingham: Nottingham University Press, 1993).

Stafford, D. *Britain and the European Resistance 1940–1945: A Survey of the Special Operations Executive* (London: Macmillan, 1983).

Stafford, D. 'The Detonator Concept: British Strategy, SOE and European Resistance after the Fall of France' *Journal of Contemporary History* II (1975) pp.185–217.

White, R. 'Teaching the Free Man how to Praise. Michael Foot on SOE and Resistance in Europe' in K.G. Robertson (ed.) *War, Resistance and Intelligence: Essays in Honour of M.R.D. Foot* (Barnsley: Leo Cooper, 1999) pp.105–18.

White, R. 'The Unity and Diversity of European Resistance' in Hawes and White, *Resistance in Europe*, pp.7–23.

Belgium

Bles, M. *Child at War : The True Story of a Young Belgian Resistance Fighter* (Mercury House, 1991).

Bodson, H. *Agent for the Resistance: A Belgian Saboteur in World War II* (Texas A&M University Press, 1994).

De Ridder, Y. *The Quest for Freedom: The Life of a Belgian Resistance Fighter in World War II* (Fithina Press, 1991).

Goris, J-A. *Belgium in Bondage* (Antwerp, 1946).

Goris, J-A. *Belgium under Occupation* (New York, 1947).

Michman, D. *Belgium and the Holocaust: Jews, Belgians, Germans* (Jerusalem, Yad Vashem, 1998).

Somerhausen, A. *Written in Darkness. A Belgian Woman's Record of the Occupation 1940–1945* (New York: Knopf, 1946).

Channel Islands

Aufsess, Baron von *The von Aufsess Occupation Diary* (Chichester: Phillimore, 1985).

Bihet, M. *A Child's War* (Guernsey: Guernsey Press, 1985).

Briggs, A. *The Channel Islands. Occupation and Liberation 1940–1945*. Published in association with the Imperial War Museum (London: Batsford, 1995).

Bunting, M. *The Model Occupation: the Channel Islands Under German Rule 1940–1945* (London: HarperCollins, 1995).

Cohen, F.E. 'The Jews in the Islands of Jersey, Guernsey and Sark during the German Occupation 1940–1945', *Journal of Holocaust Education*, vol. 6 (1997) pp. 27–81.

Cortvriend, V.V *Isolated Island* (Guernsey: Guernsey Star and Gazette, 1947).

Cruikshank, C. *The German Occupation of the Channel Islands. The Official History of the Occupation Years* (Guernsey: Guernsey, Press 1975) by arrangement with the trustees of the Imperial War Museum.

Durand, R. *Guernsey Under German Rule* (London: Hamish Hamilton, 1946).

Falla, F.W. *The Silent War* (London: Leslie Frewin, 1967).

Harris, R.E. (1980) *Islanders Deported*, 2 vols (Channel Islands Specialists Society: Picton, 1980).

Heaume, R. Marie Ozanne, *Channel Islands Occupation Review* 23 (1995) pp. 79–82.

King, P. *The Channel Islands War 1940–1945* (London: Robert Hale, 1991).

Le Ruez, N. *Jersey Occupation Diary* (St Helier: Seaflower Books, 1994).

Le Sueur, F. *Shadow of the Swastika. Could It All Happen Again?* (Guernsey: Guernsey Press, 1990).

Lewis, J. *A Doctor's Occupation* (Guernsey: Guernsey Press, 1982).

Maugham, R.C.F. *Jersey Under the Jackboot* (London: W.H.Allen, 1946).

Mollet, R. *Jersey Under the Swastika* (London: Hyperion Press, 1945).

Sinel, L.P. *The German Occupation of Jersey* (London: Howard Baker, 1969).

Stroobant, F. *One Man's War* (Guernsey: Guernsey Press, 1967).

Denmark

Bennett, J. *British Broadcasting and the Danish Resistance Movement 1940–1945* (Cambridge: Cambridge University Press, 1966).

Goldberger, L. *The Rescue of Danish Jews: Moral Courage under Stress* (New York: New York University Press, 1987).

Grimnes, O.K. 'The Beginnings of the Resistance Movement' in H.S. Nissen (ed.) Scandinavia during the Second World War (Minneapolis: Minnesota University Press, 1983) pp.182–220.

Hæstrup, J. *Secret Alliance: A Study of the Danish Resistance Movement 1940–1945,* 3 Vols. (Odense: Odense University Press, 1976–77).

Hæstrup, J. 'Denmark's Connection with the Allied Powers during the Occupation' in: *European Resistance Movements 1939–1945: Second International Conference,* pp.282–97.

Hillingso, K. 'The Danish Resistance Movement and its Relations with Great Britain' *Revue Internationale d'Histoire Militare* LIII (1982), pp.105–12.

Lund, E. *A Girdle of Truth. The Underground News Service Information, 1943–1945* (Copenhagen, 1970).

Schreiber Pedersen, B. and Holm, A. 'Restraining Excesses: Resistance and Counter-Resistance in Nazi occupied Denmark 1940–45' *Terrorism and Political Violence, X/1 (1998) pp.60–89.*

Trommer, A. 'Scandinavia and the Turn of the Tide' in: H.S. Nissen (ed.) *Scandinavia during the Second World War* (Minneapolis: Minnesota University Press, 1983) pp.221–77.

Yahil, L. *The Rescue of the Danish Jews: Test of a Democracy* (Philadephia PA: Jewish Publication Society, 1969).

France

Adler, J *The Jews of Paris and the Final Solution: Communal Responses and Internal Conflicts, 1940–1944* (New York/Oxford: Oxford University Press, 1985).

Ariel, J. 'Jewish Self-Defence and Resistance in France during World War II' *Yad Vashem Studies* VI (1967) pp.221–50.

Aubrac, L., *Outwitting the Gestapo* (Lincoln NE: University of Nebraska Press, 1993).

Azéma, J-P. *From Munich to the Liberation, 1938–1944* (Cambridge, Cambridge University Press, 1984).

Blumenson, M. *The Vildé Affair: Beginnings of the French Resistance* (Boston: Houghton Mifflin, 1977).

Dank, M. *The French Against the French*: *Collaboration and Resistance* (Philadephia: Lippincott, 1974).

Diamond, H., *Women and the Second World War in France, 1939–1948* (London: Longman, 1999).

Farmer, S. 'The Communist Resistance in the Haute-Vienne' *French Historical Studies* XIV/1 (1989) pp.89–116.

Foot, M.R.D. *SOE in France* (London: HMSO, 1966).

Funk, A.L. *Hidden Ally: The French Resistance, Special Operations, and the Landings in Southern France* (Westport CT: Greenwood, 1992).

Funk, A.L. 'The Debate over the Jewish Communist Resistance in France' *Contemporary French Civilisation* XV/1 (1991) pp.1–17.

Gordon, B.M. *Historical Dictionary of World War II: The Occupation, Vichy and the Resistance, 1938–1946* (Westport CT: Greenwood, 1998).

Kedward, H.R. 'Behind the Polemics: French Communists and Resistance 1939–1941' in Hawes and White *Resistance in Europe*, pp.94–116.

Kedward, H.R. *In Search of the Maquis: Rural Resistance in Southern France, 1942–44* (Oxford: Clarendon, 1993).

Kedward, H.R. *Resistance in Vichy France* (Oxford: Oxford University Press, 1978).

Kedward, H.R. 'Resiting French Resistance' *Transactions of the Royal Historical Society*, Sixth Series, IX (1999) pp.271–82.

Kedward, H.R. *Occupied France. Collaboration and Resistance, 1940–1944* (London: Blackwells, 1985).

Kedward, H.R. 'Resistance: The Discourse of Personality' in: Roberston, K.G. (ed.) *War, Resistance and Intelligence. Essays in Honour of M.R.D. Foot* (London: Leo Cooper, 1999).

Kedward, H.R. 'Rural France and Resistance' in S. Fishman et al. (eds) *France at War: Vichy and the Historians* (Oxford: Berg, 2000) pp.125–44.

Kedward, H.R. and Austin, R. (eds) *Vichy France and the Resistance: Culture and Ideology* (London: Croom Helm, 1985).

Knight, F. *The French Resistance 1940–1944* (London: Lawrence & Wishart, 1975).

Latour, A. *The Jewish Resistance in France (1940–1944)* (New York: Holocaust Library/Schocken, 1981).

Lazare, L. *Rescue as Resistance: How Jewish Organisations Fought the Holocaust in France* (New York: Columbia University Press, 1986).

Novick, P. *The Resistance versus Vichy* (New York: Columbia University Press, 1968).

Paxton, R. *Vichy France* (New York: Alfred A. Knopf, 1972).

Pike, D.W. 'Between the Junes: The French Communists from the Collapse of France to the Invasion of Russia' *Journal of Contemporary History* XXVIII (1993) pp.465–85.

Poznanski, R. 'A Methodological Approach to Study of Jewish Resistance in France' *Yad Vashem Studies* XVIII (1987) pp.1–39.

Rossiter, M. 'Ordinary Acts and Resistance: Women in Street Demonstrations and Food Riots in Vichy France' *Proceedings of the Annual Meeting of the Western Society for French History* XVI (1989) pp.400–7.

Schoenbrun, D. *Maquis. Soldiers of the Night: The Story of the French Resistance* (London: Robert Hale, 1990).

Simmonds, J.C. 'The French Communist Party and the Beginnings of Resistance' *European Studies Review* (1981) pp.517–42.

Sweets, J.F. *The Politics of Resistance In France (1940–1944): A History of the Mouvements Unis de la Résistance* (De Kalb: Northern Illinois University Press, 1976).

Sweets, J.F. *Choices in Vichy France: The French under Nazi Occupation* (New York/Oxford: Oxford University Press, 1986).

Sweets, J.F. 'Hold that Pendulum! Redefining Fascism, Collaboration and Resistance in France' *French Historical Studies* XV (1988) pp.731–58.

Taylor, L. 'Collective Action in Northern France, 1940–1944' *French History* XI/2 (1997) pp.190–214.

Veillon, D., 'The Resistance and Vichy' in S. Fishman et al. (eds) *France at War: Vichy and the Historians* (Oxford: Berg, 2000) pp.161–80.

Weinberg, H.M. 'The Debate over the Jewish Communist Resistance in France' *Contemporary French Civilisation* XV/1 (1991) pp.1–17.

Weitz, M.C. *Sisters in the Resistance: How Women Fought to Free France, 1940–1945* (New York: John Wiley, 1995).

Weitz, M.C. (ed.) *Mémoire et Oubli: Women of the French Resistance.* Special Issue of *Contemporary French Civilisation* XVIII/1 (1994).

Weitz, M.C. 'As I Was Then. Women in the French Resistance', *Contemporary French Civilisation* XV/1 (1991).

Wright, G. 'Reflections on the French Resistance' *Political Science Quarterly* LXXVII/3 (1962) .

Italy

Absalom, R. '"Hiding History": The Allies, the Resistance and the Others in Occupied Italy 1943–1945' *Historical Journal* XXXVIII (1995) pp.111–31.

Absalom, R. 'Escaping into History: Italian Peasants and Allied Prisoners of War in the *Resistenza* 1943–1944' in Guillon, J-M and Mencherini, R. (eds) *La Résistance et les Européens du Sud.* (Paris: L'Harmattan, 1999).

Absalom, R. 'Peasant Memory and Italian Resistance' in: Bosworth, R.J.B and Dogliani, P. (eds) *Italian Fascism. History Memory and Representation* (London: Macmillan, 1999).

Battaglia, R. *The Story of the Italian Resistance* (London: Odhams, 1957).

Blasio Wilhelm, M. de *The Other Italy. Italian Resistance in World War II* (New York: W.W.Norton, 1988).

Delzell, C. *Mussolini's Enemies. The Italian Anti-Fascist Resistance* (Princeton: Princeton University Press, 1961).

Ellwood, D. *Italy 1943–1945* (Leicester: Leicester University Press, 1985).

Lewis, L. *Echoes of Resistance. British Involvement with the Italian Partisans* (Tunbridge Wells: Costello, 1985).

Neri Serini, S. 'A Past to be Thrown Away? Politics and History in the Italian Resistance' *Contemporary European History* IV/3 (1995) pp.367–81.

Parri, F. and Venturi, F. 'The Italian Resistance and the Allies' in: *European Resistance Movements 1939–1945: Second International Conference.*

Puzzo, D.A. *The Partisans and the War in Italy* (New York: Peter Lang, 1993).

Rosengarten, F. *The Italian Anti-Fascist Press* (Cleveland OH: Press of the Case Western Reserve University, 1968).

Slaughter, J. *Women and the Italian Resistance* (Denver CO: Arden, 1995).

Wilson, P.R. 'Saints and Heroines: Rewriting the History of Italian Women in the Resistance' in: Kirk, T. and McElligott, A. (eds) *Opposing Fascism. Community, Authority and Resistance in Europe* (Cambridge, Cambridge University Press, 1999).

Woolf, S. *The Rebirth of Italy* (London: Longman, 1972).

The Netherlands

Avni, H. 'Zionist Underground in Holland and France and the Escape to Spain' in: Y. Gutman and E. Zuroff, *Rescue Attempts during the Holocaust* (Jerusalem: Yad Vashem, 1997) pp.555–90.

Barnouw, D. 'The Image of Occupation' in: *Holland Film Promotion. Occupation, Collaboration and Resistance in Dutch Film* (Utrecht, 1986) pp.17–30.

Boas, J.H. *Religious Resistance in Holland* (London: Allen & Unwin, 1945).

Boas, J.H. *Resistance of the Churches in the Netherlands* (New York: Netherlands Information Bureau, 1944).

Bruins Slot, J 'Resistance' *Annals of the American Academy of Political and Social Sciences* CCXLV (1946) pp.144–8.

Cookridge, E. 'Dutch Tragedy' In: E.H. Cookridge, *Inside SOE. The First Full Story of Special Operations Executive in Western Europe 1940–1945* (London: Tinking, 1966).

Foot, M.R.D. (ed.) *Holland at War Against Hitler. Anglo Dutch Relations 1940–1945. Proceedings of a Conference held at University College London 3–5 April 1989* (London: Frank Cass, 1990).

Foot, M.R.D. 'What Use was Resistance?' in J.B.P. Jonker et al. (eds) *Vijftig Jaar na de inval. Geschiedschrijving en Tweede Wereldoorlog* (The Hague: SDU, 1990).

Groeneveld, E. 'The Resistance in the Netherlands' in G. van Roon, *Europäischer Widerstand im Vergleich. Die Internationalen Konferenzen Amsterdam* (Berlin: Siedler Verlag, 1985).

Hers, J.F.Ph. 'The Rise of the Dutch Resistance: A Memoir' *Intelligence and National Security* VII/4 (1992) pp.454–72.

Jong, L.de *The Netherlands and Nazi Germany* (Cambridge MS: Harvard University Press, 1990).

Jong, L.de 'Anti-nazi resistance in the Netherlands' in: *European Resistance Movements 1939–1945: First International Conference*, pp. 137–49.

Jong, L.de 'The Dutch Resistance Movement and the Allies 1940–1945' in: *European Resistance Movements 1939–1945: Second International Conference*, pp.340–65.

Jong, L.de 'Britain and Dutch Resistance 1940–1945' in: J.Améry et al. (eds) *Great Britain and European Resistance 1939–1945 Proceedings of a conference held at St.Antony's College, Oxford, 10–16 December 1962* (Oxford: n.p., 1964).

Jong, L.de 'Help to People in Hiding' *Delta. A Review of Arts, Life and Thought in the Netherlands* VIII/1 (1965) pp.37–79.

Jong, L.de and Stoppelman, J *The Lion Rampant. The Story of Holland's Resistance to the Nazis* (New York: Querido, 1943)

Maass, W.B.*The Netherlands a War* (London: Abelard-Schuman, 1970).

Moore, B. 'Occupation, Collaboration and Resistance: Some Recent Publications on the Netherlands during the Second World War' *European History Quarterly* XXI (1991) pp.109–118.

Mountfield, D. 'Netherlands' in: D. Mountfield, *The Partisans. Secret Armies of World War II* (London: Hamlyn, 1979).

Smith, M.L. 'Neither Resistance nor Collaboration: Historians and the Problem of the *Nederlandse Unie*' *History* LXXII (1987) pp.251–78.

Touw, H. 'The Resistance of the Netherlands Churches' *Annals of the American Academy of Political and Social Sciences* CCXLV (1946) pp.149–61.

Warmbrunn, W. *The Dutch under German Occupation 1940–1945* (Stanford CA: Stanford University Press, 1963).

Norway

Cohen, M.M. *A Stand Against Tyranny: Norway's Physicians and the Nazis* (Detroit: Wayne State University Press, 1997).

Eriksen, A. 'The Paper Clip War, The Mythology of the Norwegian Resistance' in: Frank, R. and Gotovitch, J (eds) *La Résistance et les Européens du Nord* (Bruxelles: CRHSGM/IHTP, 1994) vol. 1, pp.393–405.

Grimnes, O.K. 'The Resistance and the Northern Europeans: The Case of Norway' in: Frank, R. and Gotovitch, J (eds) *La Résistance et les Européens du Nord* (Bruxelles: CRHSGM/IHTP, 1994) vol.1, pp.52–68.

Grimnes, O.K. 'The Beginnings of the Resistance Movement' in N.S. Nissen (ed.) *Scandinavia during the Second World War* (Minneapolis: Minnesota University Press, 1983) pp.182–220.

Gvelsvik, T. *Norwegian Resistance* (London: Hurst, 1979).

Høidal, O., *Quisling: A Study in Treason* (Oslo: Universitetsforlaget, 1988).

Kjelstadli, S. 'The Resistance Movement in Norway and the Allies' in: *European Resistance Movements 1939–1945: Second International Conference*, pp.324–39.

Riste, O and Nökleby, B. *Norway 1940–1945: The Resistance Movement* (Oslo: Tanum-Norli, 1984).

Skodvin, M. 'Norwegian Resistance' in: Van Roon, G. (ed.) *Europäischer Widerstand im Vergleich* (Berlin: Siedler, 1985).

Sonsteby, G. *Report from No.24* (Carol Publishing, 1964).

Trommer, A. 'Scandinavia and the Turn of the Tide' in: N.S.Nissen (ed.) *Scandinavia during the Second World War* (Minneapolis: Minnesota University Press, 1983) pp.221–77.

Wehr, P. 'Nonviolent Resistance to Nazism: Norway, 1940–1945' *Peace and Change* X (1984) pp.77–95.

Index

Index